# Hammond

## UNIVERSAL

# WORLD ATLAS

# C. S. Hammond and Company

Maplewood, N. J.

New York, N. Y.             Chicago, Ill.             Los Angeles, Calif.

# Contents

# List of Modern Maps

# Hammond
# WORLD ATLAS AND GAZETTEER

## GAZETTEER-INDEX OF THE WORLD

This alphabetical list of grand divisions, countries, states, colonial possessions, etc., gives area, population, capital, seat of government or chief town, and index references and numbers of plates on which they are shown on the largest scale. The index reference shows the square on the respective map in which the name of the country, state or colonial possession is located.

| Country | Area (Sq. Miles) | Population | Capital or Chief Town | Index Ref. | Plate No. |
|---|---|---|---|---|---|
| **A** | | | | | |
| *Afghanistan | 250,000 | 14,700,000 | Kabul | J 3 | 26 |
| Africa | 11,850,000 | 272,000,000 | | | 34, 35 |
| Alabama, U.S.A. | 51,060 | 3,266,740 | Montgomery | M 6 | 43 |
| Alaska, U.S.A. | 586,400 | 266,167 | Juneau | F 8 | 42 |
| *Albania | 11,096 | 1,625,378 | Tiranë | E 5 | 21 |
| Alberta, Canada | 248,800 | 1,331,944 | Edmonton | G 4 | 40 |
| *Algeria | 919,353 | 12,000 000 | Algiers | G 5 | 34 |
| American Samoa | 76 | 20,051 | Pago Pago | J 7 | 37 |
| Andaman and Nicobar Is., India | 3,215 | 63,438 | Port Blair | F 6 | 29 |
| Andorra | 175 | 10,000 | Andorra la Vella | G 1 | 17 |
| Angola | 481,351 | 4,840,719 | Luanda | K14 | 35 |
| Antarctica | 5,500,000 | | | | 8 |
| Antigua & Dependencies | 171 | 63,000 | St. Johns | G 3 | 45 |
| *Argentina | 1,078,266 | 20,005,691 | Buenos Aires | H10 | 47 |
| Arizona, U.S.A. | 113,575 | 1,302,161 | Phoenix | E 6 | 42 |
| Arkansas, U.S.A. | 52,499 | 1,786,272 | Little Rock | K 6 | 43 |
| Armenian S.S.R., U.S.S.R. | 11,500 | 1,763,048 | Erivan | F 5 | 22 |
| Ascension Island | 34 | 382 | Georgetown | D13 | 35 |
| Ashmore & Cartier Is., Australia | | | | C 2 | 36 |
| Asia | 16,500,000 | 1,789,000,000 | | | 25 |
| *Australia | 2,974,581 | 10,508,186 | Canberra | | 36 |
| Australian Antarctic Terr. | 2,472,000 | | | C 3-8 | 8 |
| Australian Capital Territory | 939 | 58,828 | Canberra | J 7 | 36 |
| *Austria | 32,369 | 7,073,807 | Vienna | B-C 3 | 20 |
| Azerbaidzhan S.S.R., U.S.S.R. | 33,100 | 3,697,717 | Baku | F 5 | 22 |
| Azores Islands, Port. | 890 | 327,480 | Ponta Delgada, Angra do Heroísmo, Horta | B 4 | 34 |
| **B** | | | | | |
| Bahama Islands | 4,404 | 111,000 | Nassau | C 1 | 45 |
| Bahrein | 231 | 143,135 | Manama | F 4 | 26 |
| Balearic Islands, Spain | 1,936 | 443,327 | Palma | H 3 | 17 |
| Barbados | 166 | 232,333 | Bridgetown | G 4 | 45 |
| Basutoland | 11,716 | 708,000 | Maseru | M17 | 35 |
| Bechuanaland Protectorate | 222,000 | 350,000 | Lobatsi | L16 | 35 |
| *Belgium | 11,775 | 9,189,741 | Brussels | E 7 | 15 |
| Bermuda | 21 | 42,640 | Hamilton | G 2 | 45 |
| Bismarck Archipelago, Terr. of New Guinea | 19,660 | 155,173 | Rabaul | E 6 | 37 |
| *Bolivia | 412,777 | 3,549,000 | La Paz, Sucre | G 7 | 46 |
| Bonin-Volcano Islands | 105 | 210 | Yankee Town | E 3 | 37 |
| *Brazil | 3,286,170 | 70,967,185 | Brasília | K 6 | 46 |
| British Columbia, Canada | 359,279 | 1,629,082 | Victoria | F 4 | 40 |
| British Guiana | 89,480 | 560,406 | Georgetown | J 2 | 46 |
| British Honduras | 8,867 | 90.019 | Belize | C 2 | 39 |
| British Solomon Is. Prot. | 14,600 | 130,000 | Honiara | F 6 | 37 |
| Brunei | 2,226 | 83,877 | Brunei | E 5 | 31 |
| *Bulgaria | 42,796 | 8,013,000 | Sofia | G 4 | 21 |

* Members of the United Nations.

| Country | Area (Sq. Miles) | Population | Capital or Chief Town | Index Ref. | Plate No. |
|---|---|---|---|---|---|
| *Burma | 261,610 | 22,342,000 | Rangoon | G 2 | 30 |
| *Burundi | 10,747 | 2,600,000 | Bujumbura | N12 | 34 |
| *Byelorussian S.S.R. (White Russian S.S.R.), U.S.S.R. | 80,100 | 8,054,648 | Minsk | D 4 | 22 |
| **C** | | | | | |
| California, U.S.A. | 156,573 | 15,717,204 | Sacramento | C 5 | 42 |
| *Cambodia | 69,884 | 5,748,842 | Phnom Penh | E 4 | 30 |
| *Cameroon | 178,368 | 4,097,000 | Yaoundé | J10 | 34 |
| *Canada | 3,621,616 | 19,102,000 | Ottawa | | 40, 41 |
| Canal Zone | 362 | 42,122 | Balboa Heights | G 6 | 39 |
| Canary Islands, Spain | 2,894 | 944,448 | Las Palmas, Santa Cruz | B 4 | 17 |
| Cape of Good Hope, South Africa | 262,875 | 3,905,618 | Cape Town | M18 | 35 |
| Cape Verde Islands | 1,557 | 201,549 | Praia | N 5 | 6 |
| Caroline Is., Terr. Pac. Is. | 525 | 45,719 | | E 5 | 37 |
| Cayman Islands | 104 | 7,622 | Georgetown | B 3 | 45 |
| Celebes, Indonesia | 72,986 | 7,079,349 | Makassar | G 6 | 31 |
| *Central African Republic | 239,382 | 1,227,400 | Bangui | K10 | 34 |
| Central America | 217,813 | 10,311,128 | | | 39 |
| *Ceylon | 25,332 | 10,644,809 | Colombo | D 7 | 29 |
| *Chad | 455,598 | 2,797,521 | Fort-Lamy | K 9 | 34 |
| Channel Islands, Gt. Brit. | 75 | 110,543 | St. Helier | E 8 | 10 |
| Chatham Islands, N. Z. | 372 | 487 | Waitangi | J10 | 37 |
| *Chile | 286,396 | 8,200,000 | Santiago | F10 | 47 |
| China (mainland) | 3,745,296 | 730,800,000 | Peking | | 32 |
| *China (Taiwan) | 22,440 | 11,031,341 | Taipei | | 32 |
| Christmas I., Australia | 64 | 3,099 | Edinburgh | O11 | 25 |
| Cocos (Keeling) Is., Australia | 5 | 606 | Home I. | N11 | 25 |
| *Colombia | 439,828 | 15,098,000 | Bogotá | F 3 | 46 |
| Colorado, U.S.A. | 103,884 | 1,753,947 | Denver | G 5 | 42 |
| Comoro Is. | 849 | 183,133 | Dzaoudzi | P14 | 35 |
| *Congo, Rep. of | 175,676 | 900,000 | Brazzaville | J12 | 35 |
| *Congo, Rep. of the | 902,274 | 15,200,000 | Léopoldville | L12 | 35 |
| Connecticut, U.S.A. | 4,899 | 2,535,234 | Hartford | P 4 | 43 |
| Cook Islands | 99 | 18,378 | Avarua | K 7 | 37 |
| Corsica, France | 3,367 | 275,465 | Ajaccio | G 6 | 16 |
| *Costa Rica | 19,238 | 1,325,755 | San José | E 5 | 39 |
| Crete, Greece | 3,232 | 483,075 | Candia | G 8 | 21 |
| *Cuba | 42,857 | 7,203,000 | Havana | | 48 |
| Curaçao, Neth. Antilles | 173 | 125,181 | Willemstad | E 4 | 45 |
| *Cyprus | 3,572 | 577,615 | Nicosia | E 5 | 28 |
| *Czechoslovakia | 49,356 | 13,745,577 | Prague | D 2 | 20 |
| **D** | | | | | |
| *Dahomey | 42,471 | 2,200,000 | Porto-Novo | G10 | 34 |
| Daito Is., Ryukyu Is. | 18 | 4,396 | | M 6 | 32 |
| Delaware, U.S.A. | 1,978 | 446,292 | Dover | P 5 | 43 |
| *Denmark | 16,556 | 4,585,256 | Copenhagen | E 9 | 13 |
| District of Columbia, U.S.A. | 61 | 763,956 | Washington | O 5 | 43 |
| Dominica | 305 | 59,916 | Roseau | G 4 | 45 |
| *Dominican Republic | 19,129 | 3,013,525 | Santo Domingo | D 6 | 48 |

## ABBREVIATIONS

| | | | | | | | |
|---|---|---|---|---|---|---|---|
| Aust. | = Australian. | Gt. Brit. | = Great Britain. | Pak. | = Pakistan. | S. S. R. | = Soviet Socialist Republic. |
| Belg. | = Belgian or Belgium. | I. | = Island. | pen. | = peninsula. | Trust. | = Trust Territory. |
| Br. | = British Commonwealth of Nations. | Is. | = Islands. | Port. | = Portugal or Portuguese. | U. S. A. | = United States of America. |
| | | It. | = Italian or Italy. | Rep. | = Republic. | | |
| Den. | = Danish or Denmark. | Jap. | = Japan or Japanese. | S. Afr. | = South Africa. | U. S. Adm. | = U.S. Administration. |
| E. | = East. | N. | = North. | So. | = South. | U. S. S. R. | = Union of Soviet Socialist Republics. |
| Fr. | = France or French. | Neth. | = Netherlands. | Sp. | = Spain or Spanish. | | |
| Gr. | = Greece or Greek. | N. Z. | = New Zealand. | sq. mi. | = square miles. | W. | = West. |

# GAZETTEER-INDEX OF THE WORLD

| Country | Area (Sq. Miles) | Population | Capital or Chief Town | Index Ref. | Plate No. |
|---|---|---|---|---|---|
| **E** | | | | | |
| *Ecuador ..........approx. | 115,000 | 4,581,477 | Quito | E 4 | 46 |
| Egypt (U.A.R.) | 386,000 | 26,085,326 | Cairo | M 6 | 34 |
| England and Wales, Gt. Brit. | 58,344 | 46,104,527 | London | ..... | 10 |
| Estonian S.S.R., U.S.S.R. | 17,400 | 1,196,791 | Tallinn | D 4 | 22 |
| *Ethiopia | 365,754 | 20,000,000 | Addis Ababa | O 9 | 34 |
| Europe | 4,129,908 | 602,873,000 | ..... | ..... | 9 |
| **F** | | | | | |
| Faeröe Islands, Den. | 540 | 34,596 | Tórshavn | D 2 | 9 |
| Falkland Islands | 4,618 | 2,172 | Stanley | H14 | 47 |
| Fernando Po, Spain | 785 | 62,612 | Santa Isabel | H11 | 34 |
| Fiji Islands | 7,036 | 428,000 | Suva | H 7 | 37 |
| *Finland | 130,500 | 4,446,222 | Helsinki | P 4 | 13 |
| Florida, U.S.A. | 54,252 | 4,951,560 | Tallahassee | N 7 | 43 |
| *France | 212,736 | 46,520,271 | Paris | ..... | 16 |
| French Guiana | 35,135 | 35,000 | Cayenne | K 3 | 46 |
| French Polynesia | 1,544 | 76,327 | Papeete | L 8 | 37 |
| French Somaliland | 8,492 | 67,300 | Djibouti | P 9 | 34 |
| **G** | | | | | |
| *Gabon | 90,733 | 447,880 | Libreville | J12 | 35 |
| Gambia | 4,033 | 315,999 | Bathurst | C 9 | 34 |
| Georgia, U.S.A. | 58,274 | 3,943,116 | Atlanta | N 6 | 43 |
| Georgian S.S.R., U.S.S.R. | 29,400 | 4,044,045 | Tbilisi | F 5 | 22 |
| Germany, East (German Democratic Republic) | 41,535 | 17,079,000 | Berlin | ..... | 14 |
| Germany, West (Federal Republic of) | 95,914 | 56,174,826 | Bonn | ..... | 14 |
| *Ghana | 91,844 | 7,244,000 | Accra | F10 | 34 |
| Gibraltar | 2 | 24,502 | Gibraltar | D 4 | 17 |
| Gilbert and Ellice Is. | 196 | 46,186 | Bairiki | H 6 | 37 |
| *Great Britain and Northern Ireland | 94,214 | 52,709,333 | London | E 3 | 9 |
| *Greece | 51,182 | 8,387,201 | Athens | F 6 | 21 |
| Greenland | 839,999 | 33,113 | Godthaab | B12 | 8 |
| Grenada | 133 | 88,677 | St. George's | G 4 | 45 |
| Guadeloupe and Dependencies | 688 | 289,000 | Basse-Terre | F 3 | 45 |
| Guam | 209 | 67,044 | Agaña | E 4 | 37 |
| *Guatemala | 45,452 | 4,095,000 | Guatemala | B 3 | 39 |
| Guiana, British | 89,480 | 560,406 | Georgetown | J 2 | 46 |
| Guiana, French | 35,135 | 35,000 | Cayenne | K 3 | 46 |
| Guiana, Netherlands (Surinam) | 54,300 | 307,000 | Paramaribo | J 3 | 46 |
| *Guinea | 96,525 | 3,357,000 | Conakry | D 9 | 34 |
| Guinea, Portuguese | 13,948 | 544,184 | Bissau | C 9 | 34 |
| **H** | | | | | |
| *Haiti | 10,714 | 4,346,000 | Port-au-Prince | C 5 | 48 |
| Hawaii, U.S.A. | 6,415 | 632,772 | Honolulu | L 3 | 37 |
| Heard & McDonald Is., Australia | ..... | ..... | ..... | T 8 | 6 |
| *Holland (Netherlands) | 12,883 | 11,967,000 | The Hague, Amsterdam | F 4 | 15 |
| *Honduras | 45,000 | 2,100,000 | Tegucigalpa | D 3 | 39 |
| Honduras, British | 8,867 | 90,019 | Belize | C 2 | 39 |
| Hong Kong | 391 | 3,133,131 | Victoria | J 7 | 32 |
| *Hungary | 35,875 | 10,050,000 | Budapest | E 3 | 20 |
| **I** | | | | | |
| *Iceland | 39,709 | 180,058 | Reykjavík | C 2 | 9 |
| Idaho, U.S.A. | 82,708 | 667,191 | Boise | E 3 | 42 |
| Ifni, Spain | 676 | 49,889 | Sidi Ifni | D 6 | 34 |
| Illinois, U.S.A. | 55,930 | 10,081,158 | Springfield | L 4 | 43 |
| *India | 1,196,995 | 439,635,082 | New Delhi | ..... | 29 |
| Indiana, U.S.A. | 36,185 | 4,662,498 | Indianapolis | M 5 | 43 |
| *Indonesia | 735,268 | 97,085,348 | Djakarta | F 7 | 31 |
| Iowa, U.S.A. | 56,032 | 2,757,537 | Des Moines | K 4 | 43 |
| *Iran | 628,000 | 22,007,000 | Tehran | H 4 | 27 |
| *Iraq | 116,000 | 7,263,000 | Baghdad | C 4 | 27 |
| *Ireland (Eire) | 26,601 | 2,818,341 | Dublin | ..... | 12 |
| Ireland, Northern | 5,459 | 1,425,462 | Belfast | H 2 | 12 |
| Isle of Man, Gt. Brit. | 227 | 48,150 | Douglas | C 3 | 10 |
| *Israel | 7,978 | 2,183,332 | Jerusalem | ..... | 24 |
| *Italy | 116,286 | 50,623,569 | Rome | ..... | 18 |
| *Ivory Coast | 183,397 | 3,300,000 | Abidjan | E10 | 34 |
| **J** | | | | | |
| *Jamaica | 4,411 | 1,613,880 | Kingston | C 3 | 45 |
| *Japan | 142,743 | 95,900,000 | Tokyo | ..... | 33 |
| Java, Indonesia | 48,842 | 60,909,381 | Djakarta | K 2 | 31 |
| *Jordan | 34,750 | 1,752,095 | Amman | D 4 | 24 |
| **K** | | | | | |
| Kansas, U.S.A. | 82,048 | 2,178,611 | Topeka | J 5 | 42 |
| Kazakh S.S.R., U.S.S.R. | 1,061,600 | 9,309,847 | Alma-Ata | H 5 | 22 |
| Kentucky, U.S.A. | 39,863 | 3,038,156 | Frankfort | M 5 | 43 |
| *Kenya | 219,730 | 8,800,000 | Nairobi | O11 | 35 |
| Kirghiz S.S.R., U.S.S.R. | 76,100 | 2,065,837 | Frunze | J 5 | 22 |
| Korea, North | 49,096 | 8,900,000 | P'yŏngyang | C 4 | 33 |
| Korea, South | 36,152 | 27,152,000 | Seoul | C 5 | 33 |
| *Kuwait | 8,000 | 321,621 | Al Kuwait | E 4 | 26 |
| **L** | | | | | |
| *Laos | 89,343 | 2,000,000 | Vientiane | E 3 | 30 |
| Latvian S.S.R., U.S.S.R. | 24,600 | 2,093,458 | Riga | D 4 | 22 |
| *Lebanon | 3,475 | 1,646,000 | Beirut | F 6 | 28 |
| *Liberia | 43,000 | 1,290,000 | Monrovia | E10 | 34 |
| *Libya | 679,358 | 1,216,000 | Tripoli, Benghazi | K 6 | 34 |
| Liechtenstein | 65 | 16,628 | Vaduz | J 2 | 19 |
| Lithuanian S.S.R., U.S.S.R. | 25,200 | 2,711,445 | Vilna | D 4 | 22 |
| Louisiana, U.S.A. | 45,106 | 3,257,022 | Baton Rouge | K 7 | 43 |
| *Luxembourg | 999 | 314,889 | Luxembourg | J 9 | 15 |
| **M** | | | | | |
| Macao | 6 | 169,299 | Macao | H 7 | 32 |
| Madeira Islands, Port. | 308 | 268,937 | Funchal | A 2 | 17 |
| Maine, U.S.A. | 31,012 | 969,265 | Augusta | R 3 | 43 |
| *Malagasy Republic | 241,094 | 5,486,713 | Tananarive | R15 | 35 |
| *Malawi | 36,829 | 2,920,000 | Zomba | N14 | 35 |
| Malaya, Malaysia | 50,690 | 7,137,000 | Kuala Lumpur | E 6 | 30 |
| Malaysia, Fed. of | 129,594 | 10,132,827 | Kuala Lumpur | D 5 | 31 |
| Maldive Islands | 115 | 89,000 | Malé | L 9 | 25 |
| *Mali | 584,942 | 4,307,113 | Bamako | E 9 | 34 |
| Malta | 122 | 329,000 | Valletta | E 7 | 18 |
| Man, Isle of, Gt. Brit. | 227 | 48,150 | Douglas | C 3 | 10 |
| Manitoba, Canada | 219,723 | 921,686 | Winnipeg | L 3 | 40 |
| Mariana Islands, Terr. Pacific Is. | 142 | 9,586 | Garapan | E 4 | 37 |
| Marquesas Is., Fr. Polynesia | 480 | 4,170 | Atuona | N 6 | 37 |
| Marshall Islands, Terr. Pacific Is. | 61 | 15,710 | Majuro | H 4 | 37 |
| Martinique | 425 | 297,000 | Fort-de-France | G 4 | 45 |
| Maryland, U.S.A. | 9,874 | 3,100,689 | Annapolis | O 5 | 43 |
| Massachusetts, U.S.A. | 7,867 | 5,148,578 | Boston | P 4 | 43 |
| *Mauritania | 328,185 | 791,000 | Nouakchott | D 8 | 34 |
| Mauritius | 720 | 692,000 | Port Louis | S19 | 35 |
| *Mexico | 760,373 | 34,923,129 | Mexico City | ..... | 44 |
| Michigan, U.S.A. | 57,019 | 7,823,194 | Lansing | M 3 | 43 |
| Midway Islands | 2 | 2,356 | ..... | J 3 | 37 |
| Minnesota, U.S.A. | 80,009 | 3,413,864 | St. Paul | K 3 | 43 |
| Mississippi, U.S.A. | 47,223 | 2,178,141 | Jackson | L 6 | 43 |
| Missouri, U.S.A. | 69,138 | 4,319,813 | Jefferson City | K 5 | 43 |
| Moldavian S.S.R., U.S.S.R. | 13,100 | 2,884,477 | Kishinev | D 5 | 22 |
| Monaco | 370 Acres | 22,297 | Monaco | G 6 | 16 |
| *Mongolia | 625,946 | 998,000 | Ulan Bator | F 2 | 32 |
| Montana, U.S.A. | 145,736 | 674,767 | Helena | F 3 | 42 |
| Montserrat | 32 | 12,108 | Plymouth | G 3 | 45 |
| *Morocco | 171,583 | 12,600,000 | Rabat | E 5 | 34 |
| Mozambique | 297,731 | 6,592,994 | Lourenço Marques | O15 | 35 |
| Muscat and Oman | 82,000 | 565,000 | Muscat | J 5 | 26 |
| **N** | | | | | |
| Natal, South Africa | 33,578 | 2,933,447 | Pietermaritzburg | N17 | 35 |
| Nauru (Aust.-N.Z.-U.K. Trust.) | 8 | 4,849 | ..... | G 6 | 37 |
| Nebraska, U.S.A. | 76,612 | 1,411,330 | Lincoln | H 4 | 42 |
| *Nepal | 54,000 | 9,387,661 | Katmandu | D 3 | 29 |
| *Netherlands | 12,883 | 11,967,000 | Amsterdam, The Hague | F 4 | 15 |
| Netherlands Antilles | 383 | 194,000 | Willemstad | E 4 | 45 |
| Nevada, U.S.A. | 109,788 | 285,278 | Carson City | D 5 | 42 |
| New Britain, Terr. of New Guinea | 14,600 | 100,873 | Rabaul | F 6 | 37 |
| New Brunswick, Canada | 27,473 | 597,936 | Fredericton | G 4 | 41 |
| New Caledonia | 7,201 | 77,000 | Nouméa | G 8 | 37 |
| Newfoundland, Canada | 42,734 | 457,853 | St. John's | J 4 | 41 |
| New Guinea, Terr. of (Aust. Trust.) | 93,000 | 1,484,873 | Port Moresby | B 7 | 31 |
| New Guinea, West (West Irian) | 161,514 | 758,396 | Kotabaru (Hollandia) | K 6 | 31 |
| New Hampshire, U.S.A. | 9,014 | 606,921 | Concord | R 3 | 43 |
| New Hebrides | 5,700 | 65,000 | Vila | G 7 | 37 |
| New Jersey, U.S.A. | 7,521 | 6,066,782 | Trenton | P 5 | 43 |
| New Mexico, U.S.A. | 121,510 | 951,023 | Santa Fe | G 6 | 42 |
| New South Wales, Australia | 309,432 | 3,917,013 | Sydney | H 6 | 36 |
| New York, U.S.A. | 47,939 | 16,782,304 | Albany | P 4 | 43 |
| *New Zealand | 103,934 | 2,414,984 | Wellington | M 7 | 36 |
| *Nicaragua | 57,143 | 1,883,000 | Managua | E 4 | 39 |
| *Niger | 501,930 | 3,112,000 | Niamey | H 8 | 34 |
| *Nigeria | 356,093 | 36,473,000 | Lagos | H10 | 34 |
| Niue | 100 | 4,864 | Alofi | K 7 | 37 |
| Norfolk I., Australia | 13.5 | 942 | Kingston | M 5 | 36 |
| North America | 9,124,000 | 284,000,000 | ..... | ..... | 38 |
| North Borneo (Sabah), Malaysia | 29,387 | 454,421 | Jesselton | F 5 | 31 |
| North Carolina, U.S.A. | 49,067 | 4,556,155 | Raleigh | O 6 | 43 |
| North Dakota, U.S.A. | 69,457 | 632,446 | Bismarck | J 3 | 42 |
| Northern Ireland, Gt. Brit. | 5,459 | 1,425,462 | Belfast | H 2 | 12 |
| Northern Territory, Australia | 523,620 | 27,095 | Darwin | E 3 | 36 |
| Northwest Territories, Canada | 1,258,217 | 22,998 | Fort Smith | F 1 | 40 |

| Country | Area (Sq. Miles) | Population | Capital or Chief Town | Index Ref. | Plate No. |
|---|---|---|---|---|---|
| *Norway | 124,560 | 3,596,211 | Oslo | F 6 | 13 |
| Nova Scotia, Canada | 20,743 | 737,007 | Halifax | H 4 | 41 |

### O

| Country | Area (Sq. Miles) | Population | Capital or Chief Town | Index Ref. | Plate No. |
|---|---|---|---|---|---|
| Oceania | | 18,000,000 | | | 37 |
| Ohio, U.S.A. | 40,972 | 9,706,397 | Columbus | N 4 | 43 |
| Oklahoma, U.S.A. | 69,283 | 2,328,284 | Oklahoma City | J 6 | 42 |
| Oman, Muscat and | 82,000 | 565,000 | Muscat | J 5 | 26 |
| Ontario, Canada | 363,282 | 6,236,092 | Toronto | C 3 | 41 |
| Orange Free State, South Africa | 49,866 | 1,373,790 | Bloemfontein | M17 | 35 |
| Oregon, U.S.A. | 96,248 | 1,768,687 | Salem | C 4 | 42 |
| Orkney Islands, Scotland | 376 | 18,743 | Kirkwall | J 1 | 11 |

### P

| Country | Area (Sq. Miles) | Population | Capital or Chief Town | Index Ref. | Plate No. |
|---|---|---|---|---|---|
| Pacific Islands, U.S. Trust Terr. of the | 680 | 80,980 | Garapan | E-F 5 | 37 |
| *Pakistan | 364,218 | 98,612,000 | Rawalpindi | A 3,F 4 | 29 |
| Palau Islands, Terr. Pacific Is. | 189 | 9,965 | Koror | D 5 | 37 |
| *Panama | 28,575 | 1,075,541 | Panamá | G 6 | 39 |
| Papua Territory, Australia | 90,600 | 536,962 | Port Moresby | B 7 | 31 |
| *Paraguay | 150,518 | 1,816,890 | Asunción | J 8 | 47 |
| Pennsylvania, U.S.A. | 45,007 | 11,319,366 | Harrisburg | O 4 | 43 |
| *Persia (Iran) | 628,000 | 22,007,000 | Tehran | H 4 | 27 |
| *Peru | 513,000 | 11,511,000 | Lima | E 5 | 46 |
| *Philippines, Republic of the | 115,600 | 30,600,000 | Quezon City | H 4 | 31 |
| Phoenix Is. | 16 | 1,223 | Canton I. | J 6 | 37 |
| Pitcairn Island | 2 | 126 | Adamstown | O 8 | 37 |
| *Poland | 119,734 | 30,800,000 | Warsaw | | 24 |
| *Portugal | 35,413 | 9,130,410 | Lisbon | B 3 | 17 |
| Portuguese Guinea | 13,948 | 544,184 | Bissau | C 9 | 34 |
| Portuguese Timor | 7,332 | 517,079 | Dili | H 7 | 31 |
| Prince Edward Island, Canada | 2,184 | 104,629 | Charlottetown | H 4 | 41 |
| Puerto Rico | 3,421 | 2,349,544 | San Juan | G 2 | 45 |

### Q

| Country | Area (Sq. Miles) | Population | Capital or Chief Town | Index Ref. | Plate No. |
|---|---|---|---|---|---|
| Qatar | 5,000 | 55,000 | Doha | F 4 | 26 |
| Québec, Canada | 523,860 | 5,259,211 | Québec | G 3 | 41 |
| Queensland, Australia | 670,500 | 1,518,828 | Brisbane | G 4 | 36 |

### R

| Country | Area (Sq. Miles) | Population | Capital or Chief Town | Index Ref. | Plate No. |
|---|---|---|---|---|---|
| Réunion | 970 | 360,155 | St-Denis | R20 | 35 |
| Rhode Island, U.S.A. | 1,058 | 859,488 | Providence | R 4 | 43 |
| Río Muni, Spain | 10,045 | 183,377 | Bata | J11 | 35 |
| *Rumania | 91,671 | 18,567,000 | Bucharest | G 3 | 21 |
| Russian S.F.S.R., U.S.S.R. | 6,501,500 | 117,534,315 | Moscow | E 4 | 22 |
| *Rwanda | 10,169 | 2,900,000 | Kigali | N12 | 35 |
| Ryukyu Islands | 921 | 883,122 | Naha | L 7 | 33 |

### S

| Country | Area (Sq. Miles) | Population | Capital or Chief Town | Index Ref. | Plate No. |
|---|---|---|---|---|---|
| Sabah, Malaysia | 29,387 | 454,421 | Jesselton | F 5 | 31 |
| St. Christopher-Nevis-Anguilla | 138 | 56,591 | Basseterre | F 3 | 45 |
| St. Helena | 47 | 5,000 | Jamestown | E15 | 35 |
| St. Lucia | 233 | 86,108 | Castries | G 4 | 45 |
| St-Pierre and Miquelon | 93 | 4,990 | St-Pierre | J 4 | 41 |
| St. Vincent | 150 | 79,948 | Kingstown | G 4 | 45 |
| Sakhalin, U.S.S.R. | 35,400 | 632,000 | Yuzhno-Sakhalinsk | R 5 | 23 |
| *Salvador, El | 8,060 | 2,510,984 | San Salvador | C 4 | 39 |
| San Marino | 38 | 17,000 | San Marino | D 2 | 18 |
| São Tomé e Príncipe | 372 | 63,676 | São Tomé | H11 | 35 |
| Sarawak, Malaysia | 47,071 | 744,529 | Kuching | E 5 | 31 |
| Sardinia, Italy | 9,301 | 1,413,289 | Cagliari | B 4 | 18 |
| Saskatchewan, Canada | 237,975 | 925,181 | Regina | J 4 | 40 |
| *Saudi Arabia | 350,000 | 7,000,000 | Riyadh, Mecca | D 4 | 26 |
| Scotland, Gt. Brit. | 30,411 | 5,179,344 | Edinburgh | | 11 |
| *Senegal | 77,401 | 3,280,000 | Dakar | D 9 | 34 |
| Seychelles | 157 | 41,425 | Victoria | T 6 | 6 |
| Shetland Islands, Scotland | 550 | 17,809 | Lerwick | L 3 | 11 |
| *Siam (Thailand) | 200,148 | 26,257,916 | Bangkok | D 3 | 30 |
| Sicily, Italy | 9,926 | 4,711,783 | Palermo | D 6 | 18 |
| *Sierra Leone | 27,925 | 2,600,000 | Freetown | D10 | 34 |
| Singapore, Malaysia | 220 | 1,713,000 | Singapore | F 6 | 30 |
| Society Islands, Fr. Polynesia | 650 | 59,674 | Papeete | L 7 | 37 |
| Solomon Islands, Terr. N. G. | 4,070 | 51,928 | Sohano | F 6 | 37 |
| Solomon Islands Prot., Br. | 14,600 | 130,000 | Honiara | F 6 | 37 |
| *Somali Republic | 262,000 | 2,030,000 | Mogadishu | R10 | 34 |
| Somaliland, French | 8,492 | 67,300 | Djibouti | P 9 | 34 |
| *South Africa | 472,733 | 16,015,365 | Cape Town, Pretoria | L18 | 35 |
| South America | 6,894,000 | 157,000,000 | | | 46, 47 |
| South Arabia | 110,000 | 1,000,000 | Aden | E 7 | 26 |

| Country | Area (Sq. Miles) | Population | Capital or Chief Town | Index Ref. | Plate No. |
|---|---|---|---|---|---|
| South Australia, Australia | 380,070 | 969,340 | Adelaide | E 5 | 36 |
| South Carolina, U.S.A. | 30,272 | 2,382,594 | Columbia | N 6 | 43 |
| South Dakota, U.S.A. | 76,378 | 680,514 | Pierre | J 3 | 42 |
| South-West Africa | 317,725 | 512,496 | Windhoek | K16 | 35 |
| Southern Rhodesia | 150,333 | 3,857,470 | Salisbury | M15 | 35 |
| *Spain | 195,258 | 30,430,698 | Madrid | | 17 |
| Spanish Sahara, Spain | 103,243 | 23,793 | El Aaiúm | D 6 | 34 |
| *Sudan | 967,500 | 12,800,000 | Khartoum | M 9 | 34 |
| Sumatra, Indonesia | 164,148 | 14,982,910 | Medan | C 6 | 31 |
| Surinam (Neth. Guiana) | 54,300 | 307,000 | Paramaribo | J 3 | 46 |
| Svalbard, Norway | 24,294 | 3,769 | Longyearbyen | C 2 | 13 |
| Swaziland | 6,704 | 275,000 | Mbabane | N17 | 35 |
| *Sweden | 173,394 | 7,495,129 | Stockholm | J 6 | 13 |
| Switzerland | 15,944 | 5,429,061 | Bern | | 19 |
| *Syria | 72,587 | 4,555,267 | Damascus | H 5 | 28 |

### T

| Country | Area (Sq. Miles) | Population | Capital or Chief Town | Index Ref. | Plate No. |
|---|---|---|---|---|---|
| Tadzhik S.S.R., U.S.S.R. | 54,900 | 1,979,897 | Dushanbe | J 6 | 22 |
| Tahiti, Fr. Polynesia | 600 | 44,247 | Papeete | M 7 | 37 |
| *Tanganyika and Zanzibar | 343,726 | 10,046,000 | Dar es Salaam | N13 | 35 |
| Tasmania, Australia | 26,215 | 350,340 | Hobart | J 8 | 36 |
| Tennessee, U.S.A. | 41,762 | 3,567,089 | Nashville | M 6 | 43 |
| Texas, U.S.A. | 262,840 | 9,579,677 | Austin | J 7 | 42 |
| *Thailand | 200,148 | 26,257,916 | Bangkok | D 3 | 30 |
| Tibet, China | 469,413 | 2,000,000 | Lhasa | C 5 | 32 |
| Timor, Indonesia | 24,450 | 702,638 | Kupang | G 8 | 31 |
| Timor, Port. | 7,332 | 517,079 | Dili | H 7 | 31 |
| *Togo | 20,733 | 1,439,772 | Lomé | G10 | 34 |
| Tokelau Islands | 4 | 1,870 | Fakaofo | J 6 | 37 |
| Tonga | 269 | 63,874 | Nuku'alofa | J 7 | 37 |
| Transkei, South Africa | 15,590 | 1,415,789 | Umtata | M18 | 35 |
| Transvaal, So. Africa | 110,450 | 6,225,052 | Pretoria | N17 | 35 |
| *Trinidad and Tobago | 1,864 | 827,957 | Port of Spain | G 5 | 45 |
| Tristan da Cunha | 38 | 264 | Edinburgh | N 7 | 6 |
| Trucial Oman | 12,000 | 111,000 | Dubai | F 5 | 26 |
| Tuamotu Arch., Fr. Polynesia | 332 | 8,940 | Apataki | M 7 | 37 |
| *Tunisia | 48,300 | 4,254,000 | Tunis | H 5 | 34 |
| *Turkey | 296,185 | 29,418,000 | Ankara | | 21 |
| Turkmen S.S.R., U.S.S.R. | 187,200 | 1,516,375 | Ashkhabad | G 6 | 22 |
| Turks and Caicos Is. | 202 | 5,716 | Grand Turk | D 2 | 45 |

### U

| Country | Area (Sq. Miles) | Population | Capital or Chief Town | Index Ref. | Plate No. |
|---|---|---|---|---|---|
| *Uganda | 80,301 | 7,200,000 | Kampala | N11 | 35 |
| *Ukrainian S.S.R., U.S.S.R. | 220,600 | 41,869,046 | Kiev | E 5 | 22 |
| *Union of Soviet Socialist Republics | 8,570,600 | 224,700,000 | Moscow | | 22, 23 |
| *United Arab Republic (Egypt) | 386,000 | 26,085,326 | Cairo | M 6 | 34 |
| *United Kingdom | 94,214 | 52,834,249 | London | D 3 | 9 |
| *United States of America, land land and water | 3,554,609 / 3,615,221 | 189,042,000 | Washington, D.C. | | 42, 43 |
| *Upper Volta | 105,841 | 4,400,000 | Ouagadougou | F 9 | 34 |
| *Uruguay | 72,172 | 2,846,000 | Montevideo | J10 | 47 |
| Utah, U.S.A. | 82,339 | 890,627 | Salt Lake City | F 5 | 42 |
| Uzbek S.S.R., U.S.S.R. | 157,400 | 8,105,704 | Tashkent | H 5 | 22 |

### V

| Country | Area (Sq. Miles) | Population | Capital or Chief Town | Index Ref. | Plate No. |
|---|---|---|---|---|---|
| Vatican City | 109 Acres | 1,010 | | B 6 | 18 |
| *Venezuela | 352,143 | 8,144,000 | Caracas | G 2 | 46 |
| Vermont, U.S.A. | 9,276 | 389,881 | Montpelier | P 4 | 43 |
| Victoria, Australia | 87,884 | 2,930,113 | Melbourne | G 7 | 36 |
| Vietnam, North | 63,370 | 15,916,955 | Hanoi | E 3 | 30 |
| Vietnam, South | 65,726 | 15,500,000 | Saigon | F 4 | 30 |
| Virgin Islands, British | 58 | 7,340 | Road Town | H 1 | 45 |
| Virgin Islands, U.S.A. | 132 | 32,099 | Charlotte Amalie | H 1 | 45 |
| Virginia, U.S.A. | 39,838 | 3,966,949 | Richmond | O 5 | 43 |

### W

| Country | Area (Sq. Miles) | Population | Capital or Chief Town | Index Ref. | Plate No. |
|---|---|---|---|---|---|
| Wake Island, U.S.A. | 3 | 349 | | G 4 | 37 |
| Wales (incl. Monmouthshire), Gt. Brit. | 8,017 | 2,644,002 | Cardiff | D 5 | 10 |
| Walvis Bay, C. of Good Hope | 374 | 12,568 | Walvis Bay | J16 | 35 |
| Washington, U.S.A. | 66,709 | 2,853,214 | Olympia | C 3 | 42 |
| West Irian (Indon. Adm.) | 161,514 | 758,396 | Kotabaru (Hollandia) | K 6 | 31 |
| West Virginia, U.S.A. | 24,079 | 1,860,421 | Charleston | N 5 | 43 |
| Western Australia, Australia | 975,920 | 736,629 | Perth | C 4 | 36 |
| Western Samoa | 1,133 | 114,427 | Apia | J 7 | 37 |
| *White Russian S.S.R. (Byelorussian S.S.R.), U.S.S.R. | 80,100 | 8,054,648 | Minsk | D 4 | 22 |
| Wisconsin, U.S.A. | 54,705 | 3,951,777 | Madison | L 3 | 43 |
| World | 57,500,000 | 3,180,000,000 | | | 6, 7 |
| Wyoming, U.S.A. | 97,411 | 330,066 | Cheyenne | G 4 | 42 |

### X Y Z

| Country | Area (Sq. Miles) | Population | Capital or Chief Town | Index Ref. | Plate No. |
|---|---|---|---|---|---|
| Yap, Terr. Pacific Is. | 87 | 5,686 | Yap | D 5 | 37 |
| *Yemen | 75,000 | 5,000,000 | San'a, Ta'izz | D 7 | 26 |
| *Yugoslavia | 99,079 | 19,097,000 | Belgrade | C 3 | 21 |
| Yukon Territory, Canada | 205,346 | 14,628 | Whitehorse | C 1 | 40 |
| *Zambia | 290,320 | 3,494,380 | Lusaka | M14 | 35 |

* Members of the United Nations.

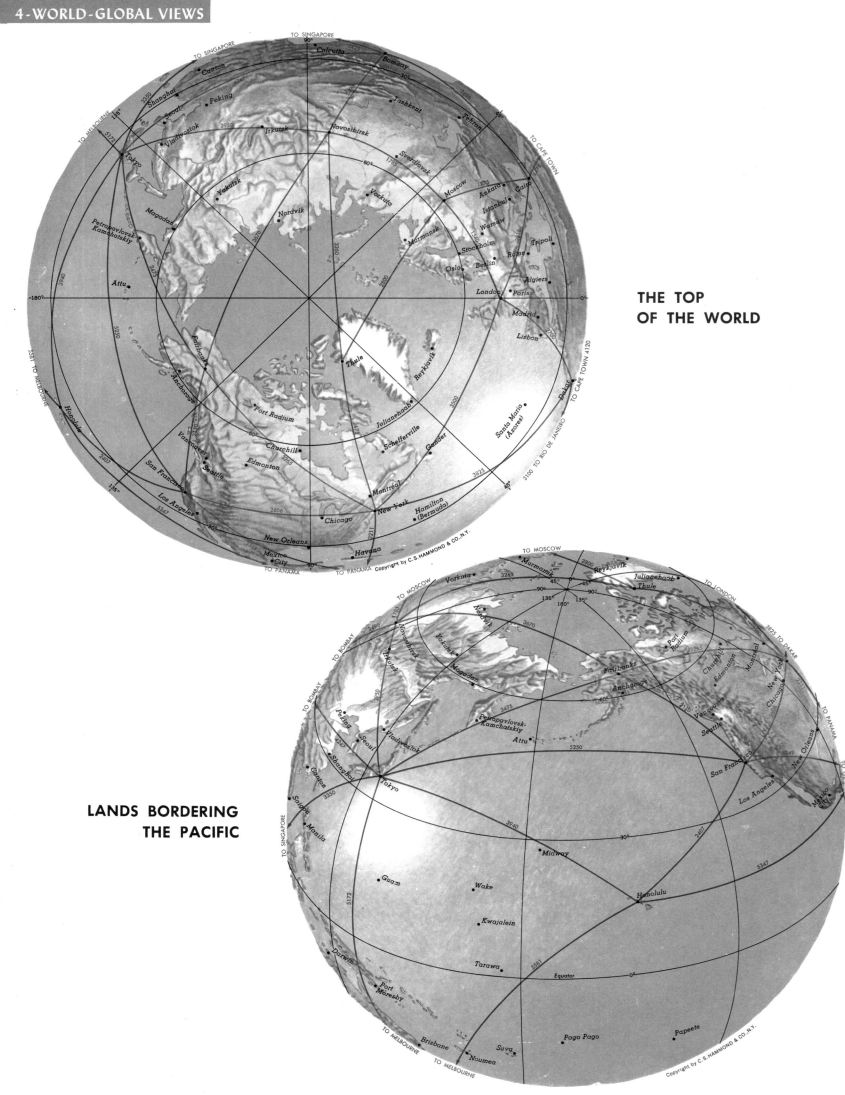

THE TOP
OF THE WORLD

LANDS BORDERING
THE PACIFIC

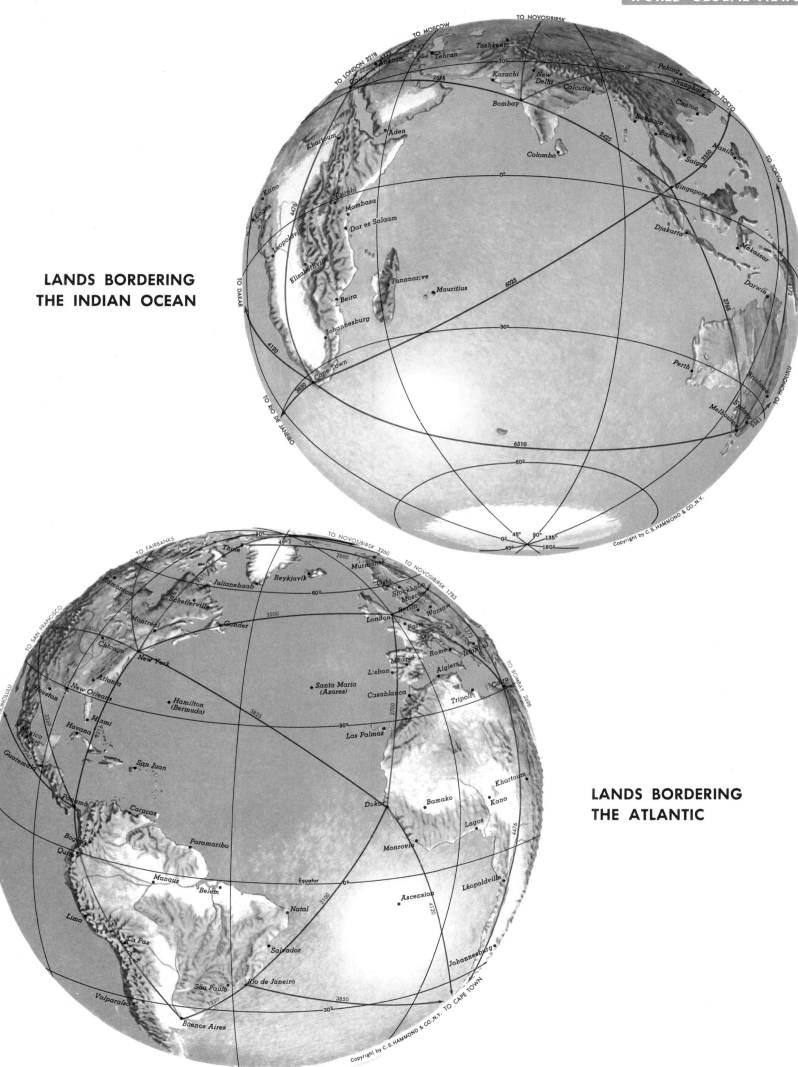

TO MOSCOW
TO NOVOSIBIRSK
TO LONDON 2218
Ankara
Tashkent
Tehran
Cairo
Karachi
New Delhi
Peking
Shanghai
Calcutta
TO TOKYO
Bombay
Canton
Khartoum
Rangoon
Aden
Bangkok
Colombo
Manila
Saigon
TO DAKAR
Kano
TO TOKYO
Lagos
Nairobi
Mombasa
Singapore
Léopoldville
Dar es Salaam
Djakarta

**LANDS BORDERING
THE INDIAN OCEAN**

Makassar
Elisabethville
Tananarive
Darwin
Mauritius
Beira
Johannesburg
Perth
Brisbane
TO RIO DE JANEIRO
Cape Town
Sydney
Melbourne
TO HONOLULU

Copyright by C.S. HAMMOND & CO., N.Y.

TO FAIRBANKS
TO NOVOSIBIRSK 3260
Thule
Murmansk
Edmonton
Julianehaab
Reykjavík
Oslo
Stockholm
Moscow
TO NOVOSIBIRSK 1785
Schefferville
Berlin
Warsaw
TO SAN FRANCISCO
Montréal
Gander
London
Paris
Chicago
New York
Madrid
Rome
Istanbul
Atlanta
Lisbon
Algiers
TO BOMBAY 2698
Houston
New Orleans
Santa Maria
(Azores)
Casablanca
Cairo
TO HONOLULU
Miami
Havana
Hamilton
(Bermuda)
Tripoli
Mexico City
Las Palmas
San Juan
Guatemala
Khartoum
Panamá
Caracas
Bamako
Kano
Bogotá
**LANDS BORDERING
THE ATLANTIC**
Paramaribo
Quito
Lagos
Dakar
Manaus
Monrovia
Léopoldville
Belém
Lima
Equator
Ascension
Natal
La Paz
Salvador
São Paulo
Rio de Janeiro
Johannesburg
Valparaíso
Buenos Aires
TO CAPE TOWN

Copyright by C.S. HAMMOND & CO., N.Y.

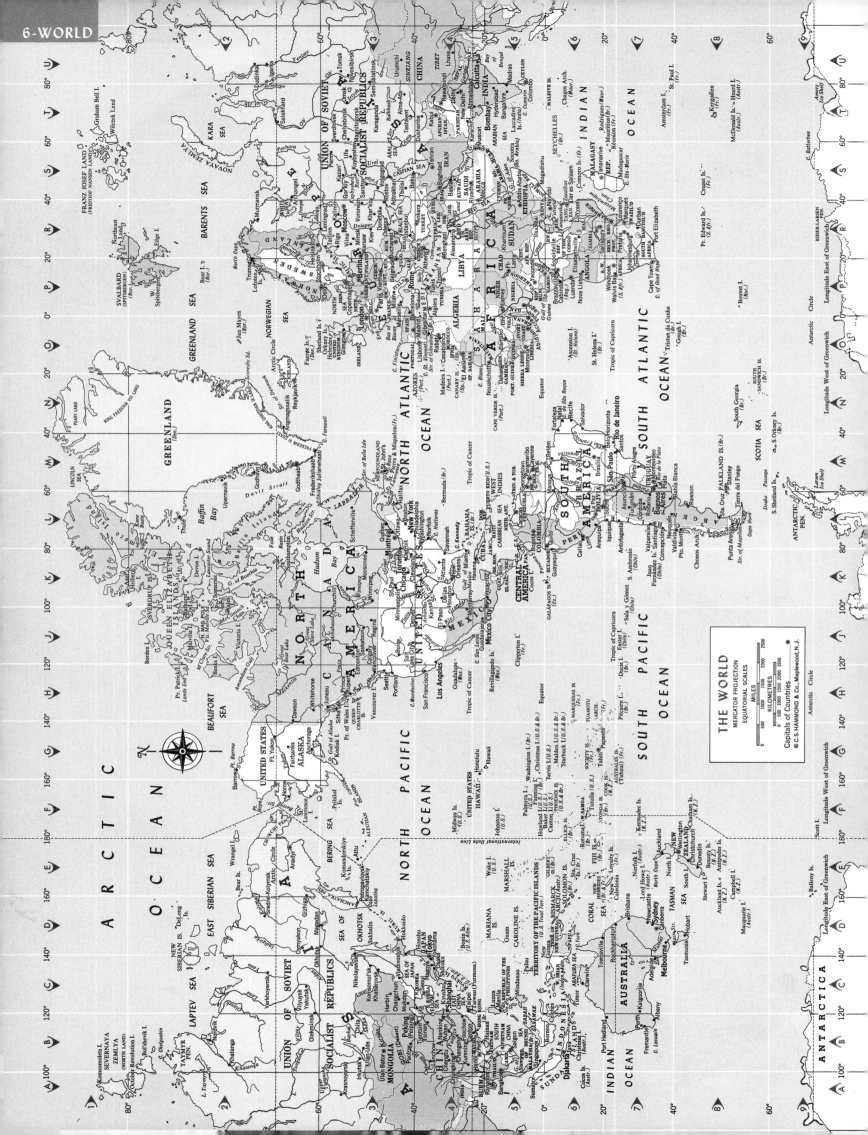

THE WORLD

MERCATOR PROJECTION
EQUATORIAL SCALES

MILES
0   500   1000   1500   2000   2500

KILOMETRES
0   500  1000  1500  2000  2500

● Capitals of Countries

© C.S. HAMMOND & Co., Maplewood, N.J.

This map has been prepared with the North Pole as the mathematical center. From it, distances to any part of the world may be measured. On Mercator's map of the world, the polar regions are so scattered that their relatively small area and availability for flight routes are disregarded. Today, with airplanes following great circle courses, often within the Arctic Circle, polar projection maps are indispensable to the people of this air-minded age.

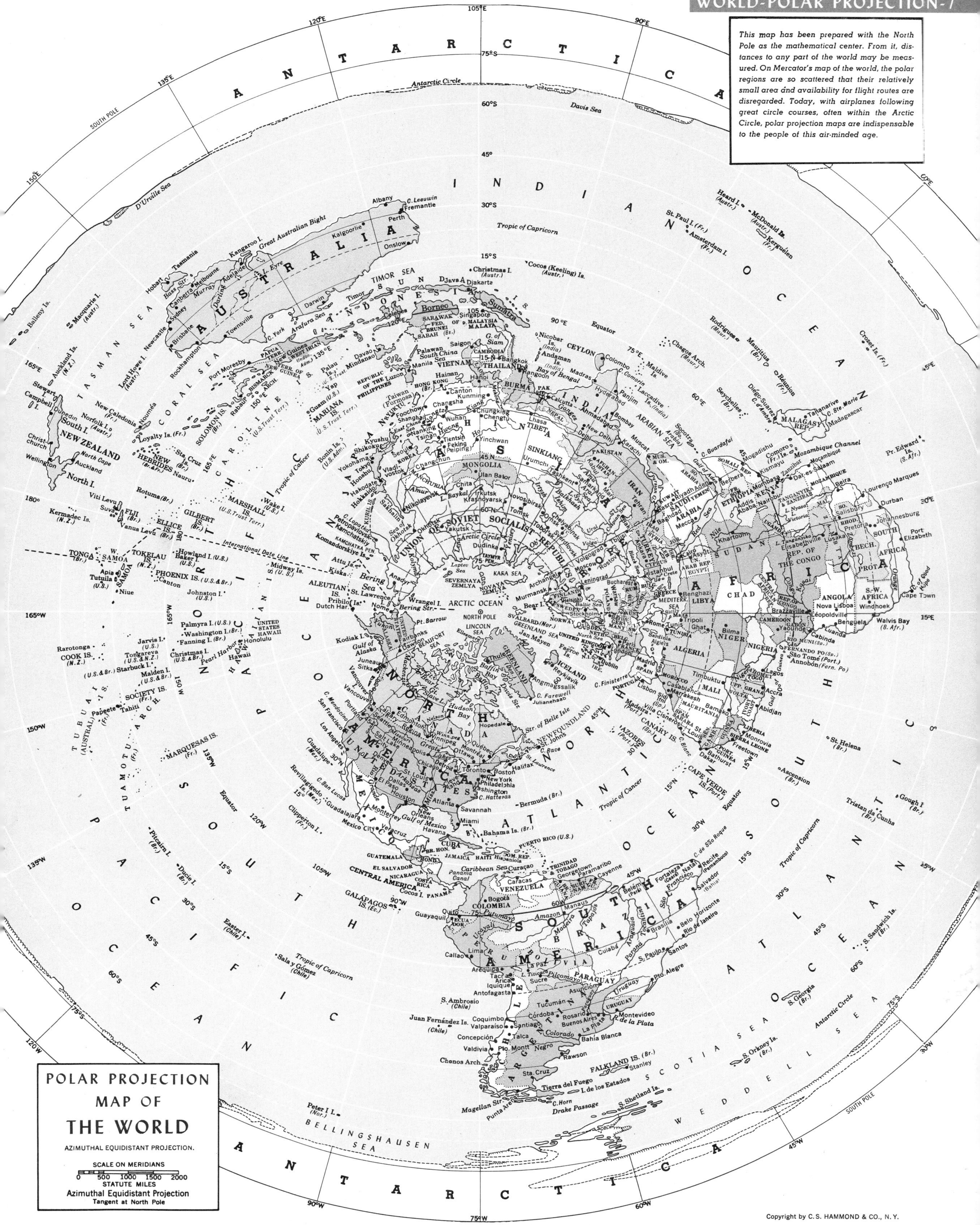

POLAR PROJECTION
MAP OF
THE WORLD

AZIMUTHAL EQUIDISTANT PROJECTION.

SCALE ON MERIDIANS

0   500  1000  1500  2000
STATUTE MILES

Azimuthal Equidistant Projection
Tangent at North Pole

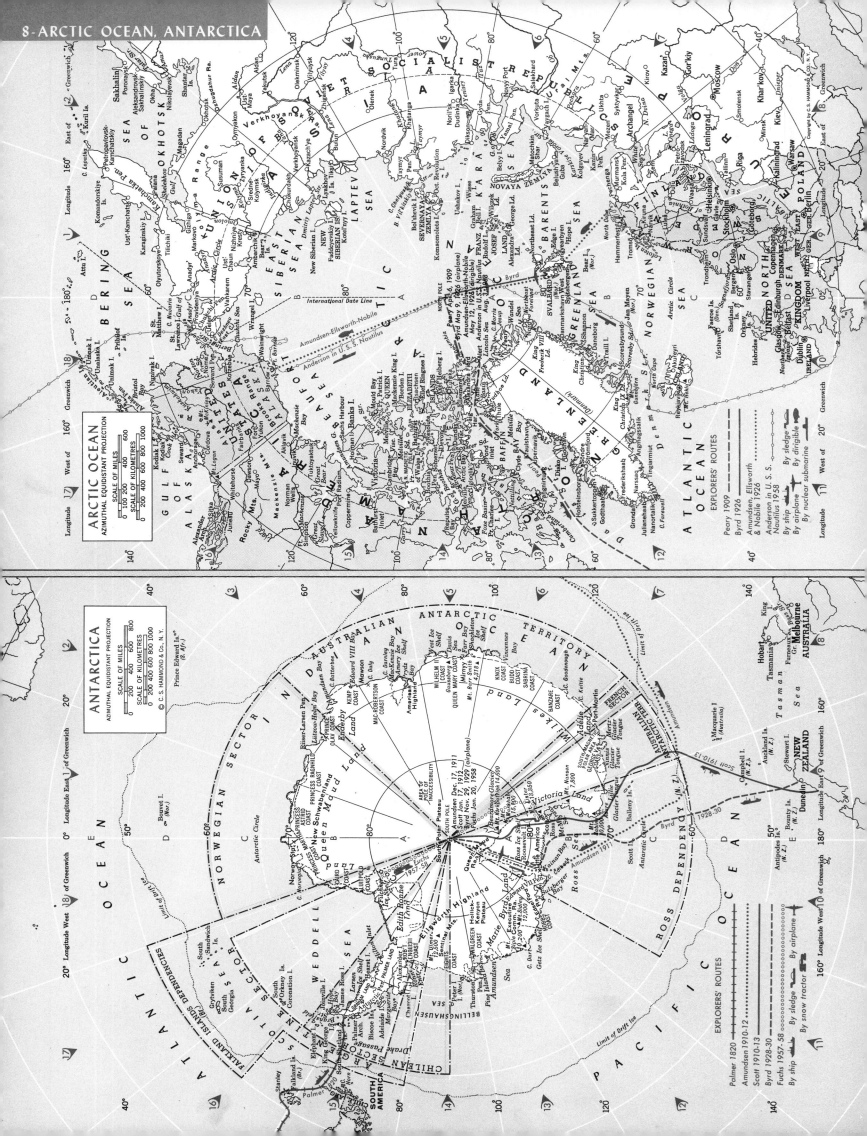

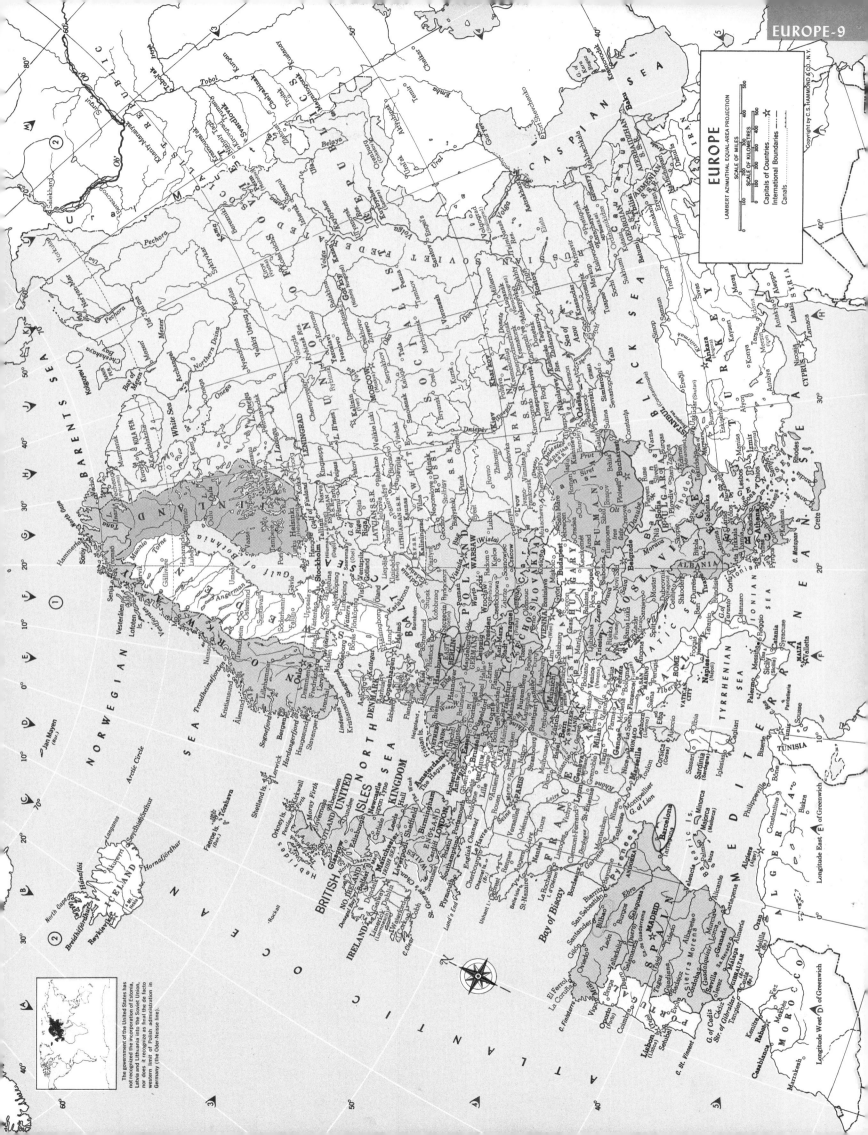

## EUROPE

LAMBERT AZIMUTHAL EQUAL-AREA PROJECTION

SCALE OF MILES

SCALE OF KILOMETRES

Capitals of Countries............☆
International Boundaries.........――――
Canals..................................

Copyright by C.S. HAMMOND & CO. N.Y.

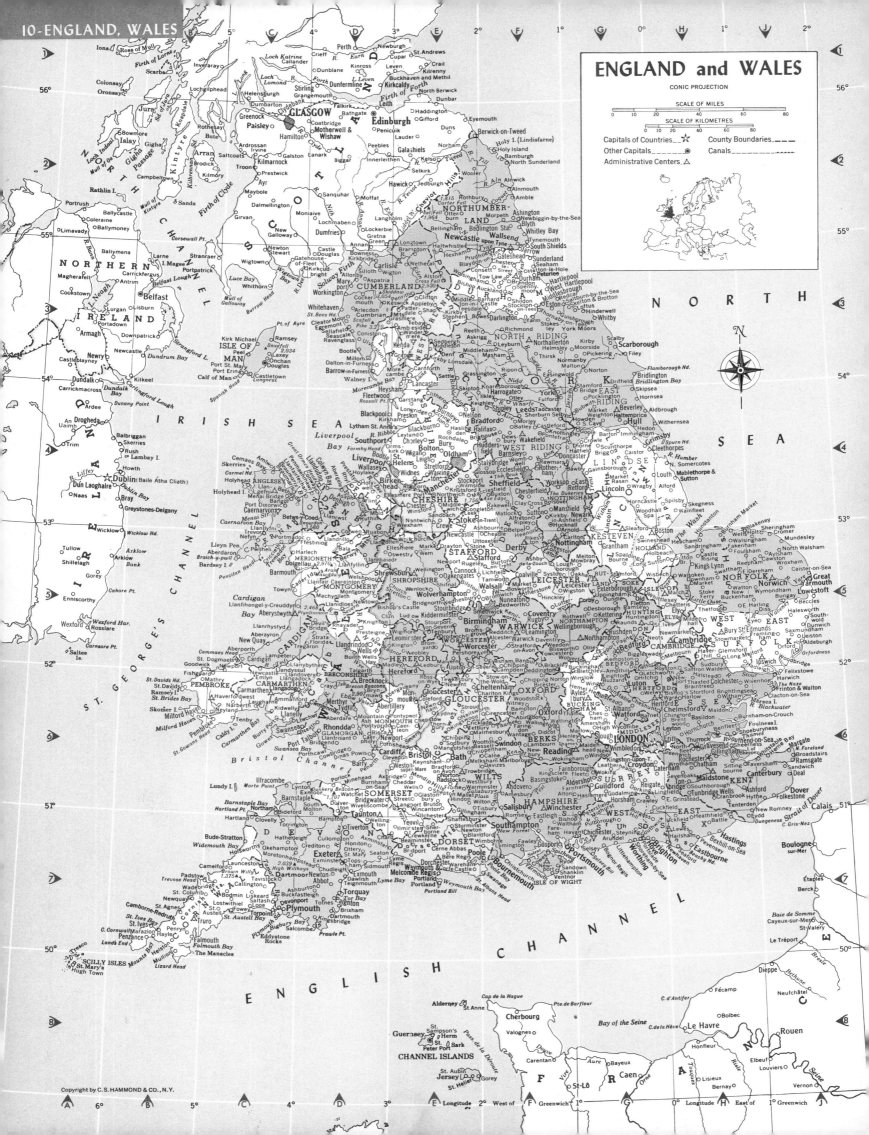

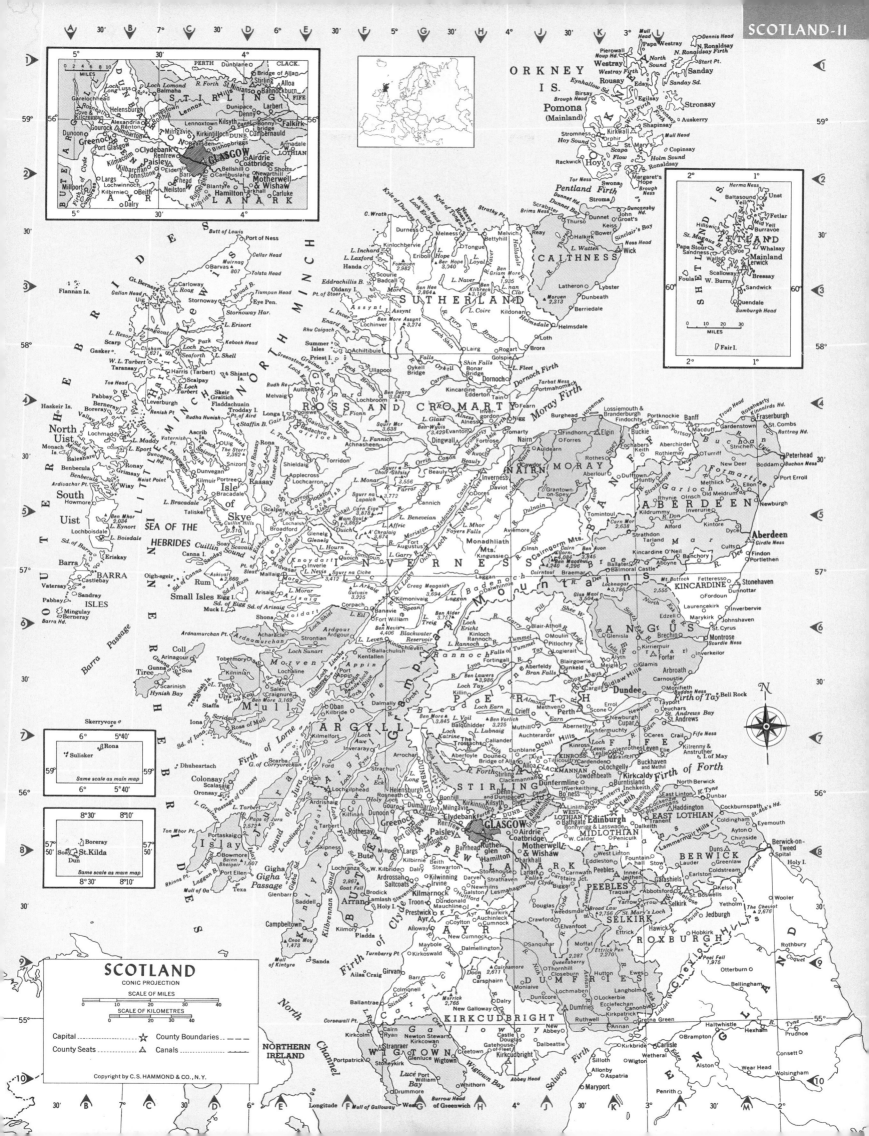

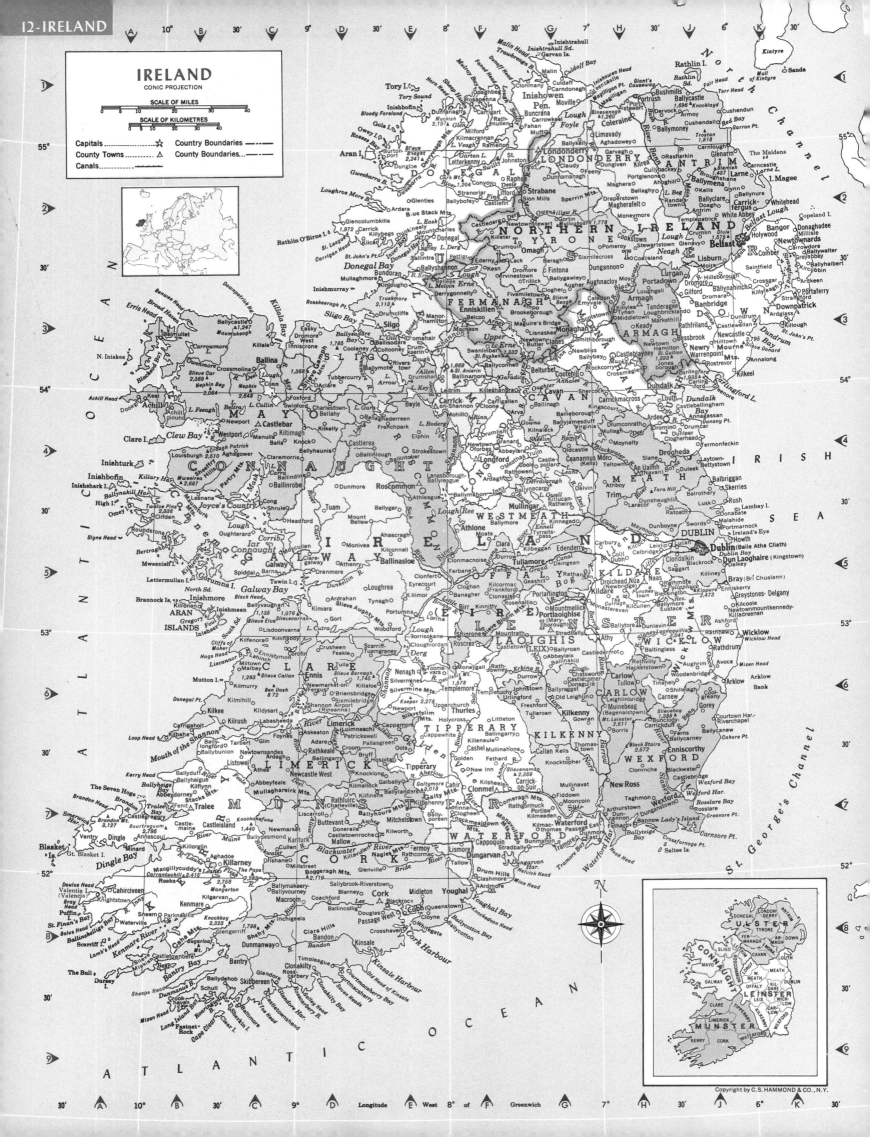

## IRELAND
### CONIC PROJECTION

SCALE OF MILES

SCALE OF KILOMETRES

Capitals ............ ☆  Country Boundaries — · · —
County Towns ...... △  County Boundaries — · — ·
Canals ............

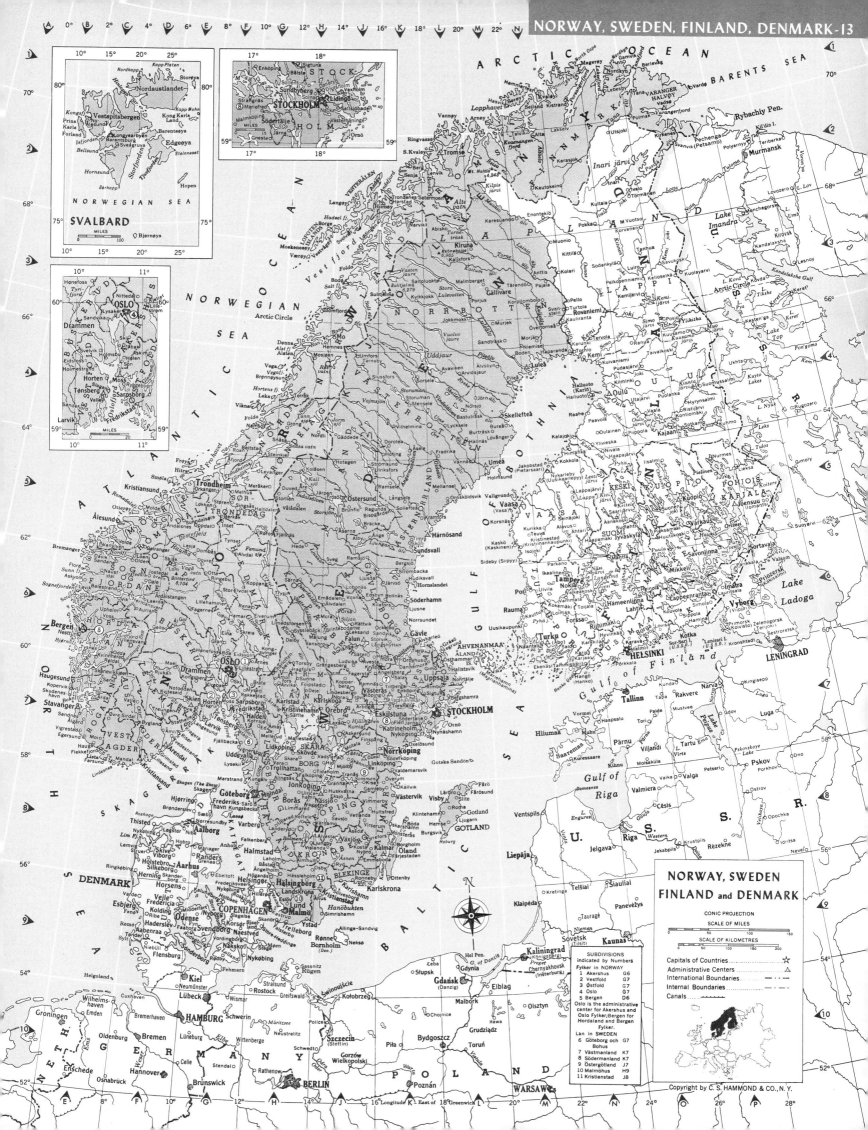

## SVALBARD

## OSLO

## STOCKHOLM

### NORWAY, SWEDEN FINLAND and DENMARK

CONIC PROJECTION

SCALE OF MILES

SCALE OF KILOMETRES

Capitals of Countries ............ ☆
Administrative Centers ............ △
International Boundaries ..........
Internal Boundaries ..............
Canals ..........................

SUBDIVISIONS
indicated by Numbers
Fylker in NORWAY
1 Akershus            G6
2 Vestfold            G7
3 Østfold             G7
4 Oslo                G7
5 Bergen              D6
Oslo is the administrative
center for Akershus and
Oslo Fylker; Bergen for
Hordaland and Bergen
Fylker.
Län in SWEDEN
6 Göteborg och        G7
  Bohus
7 Västmanland         K7
8 Södermanland        K7
9 Östergötland        J7
10 Malmöhus           K9
11 Kristianstad       J8

Copyright by C. S. HAMMOND & CO., N.Y.

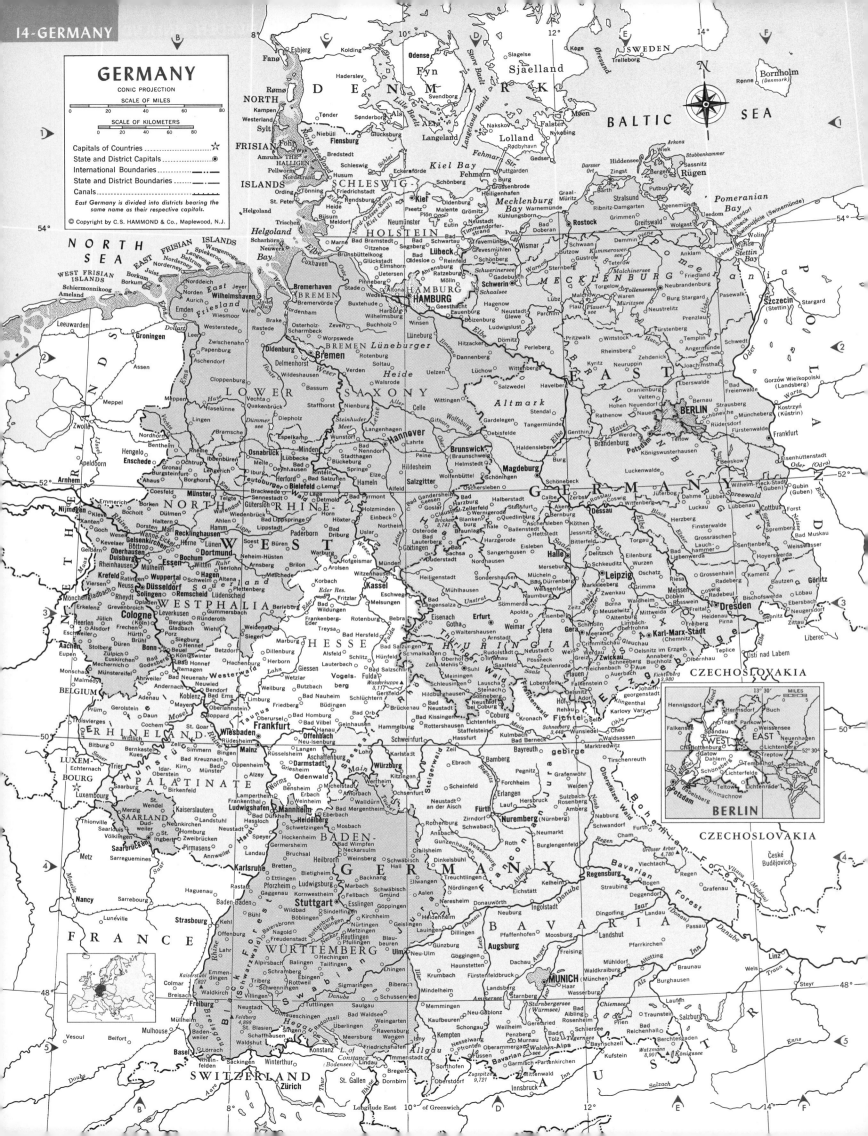

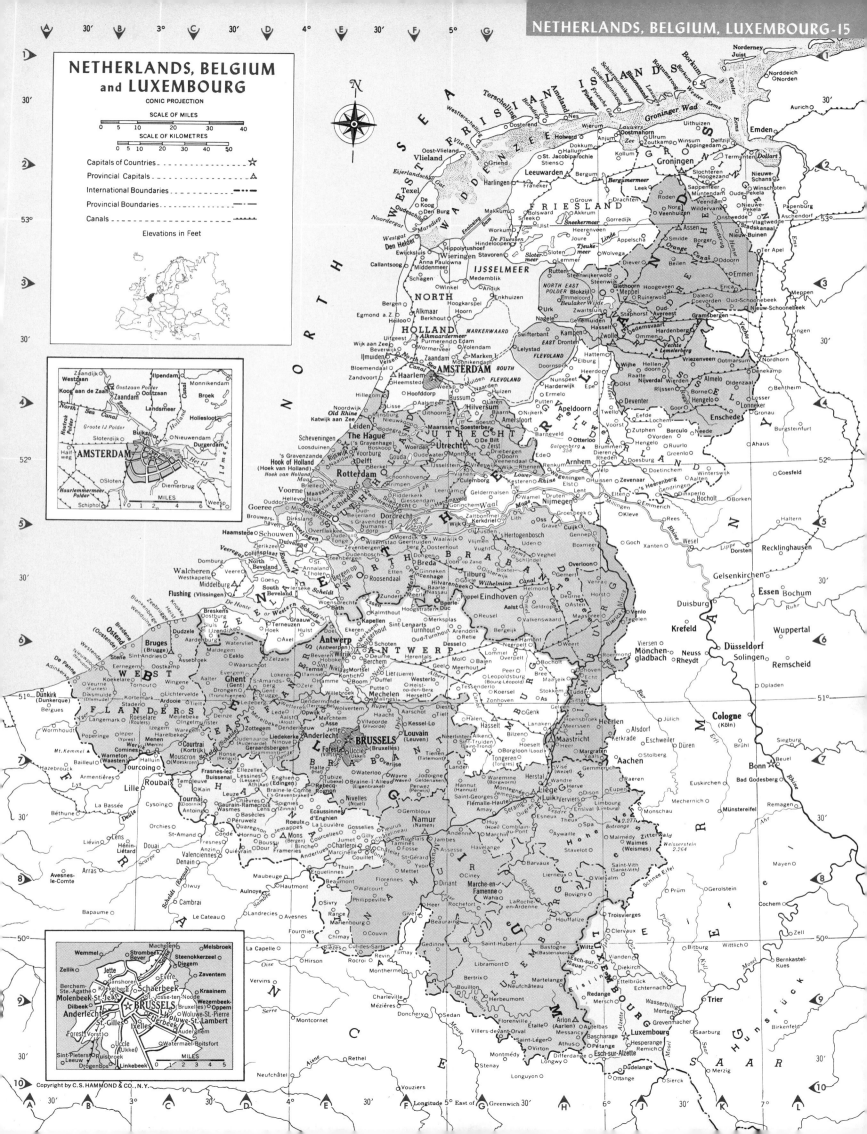

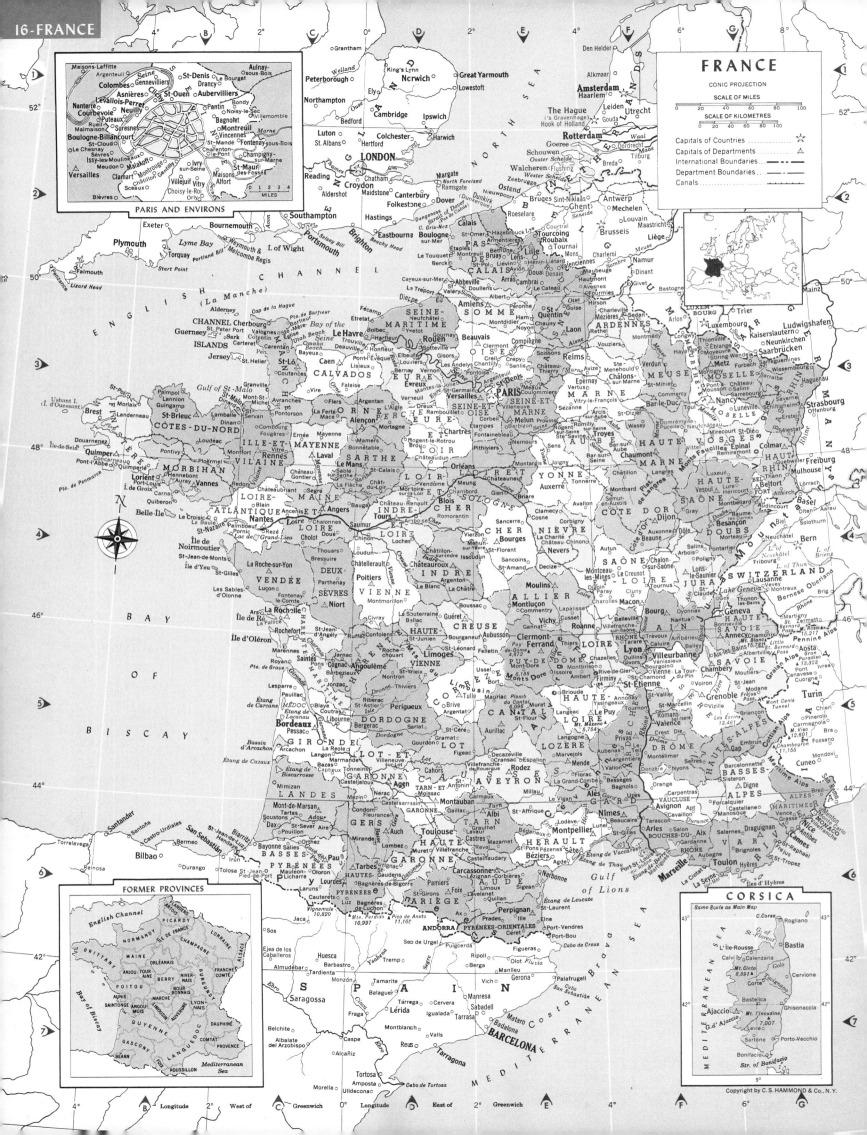
16-FRANCE

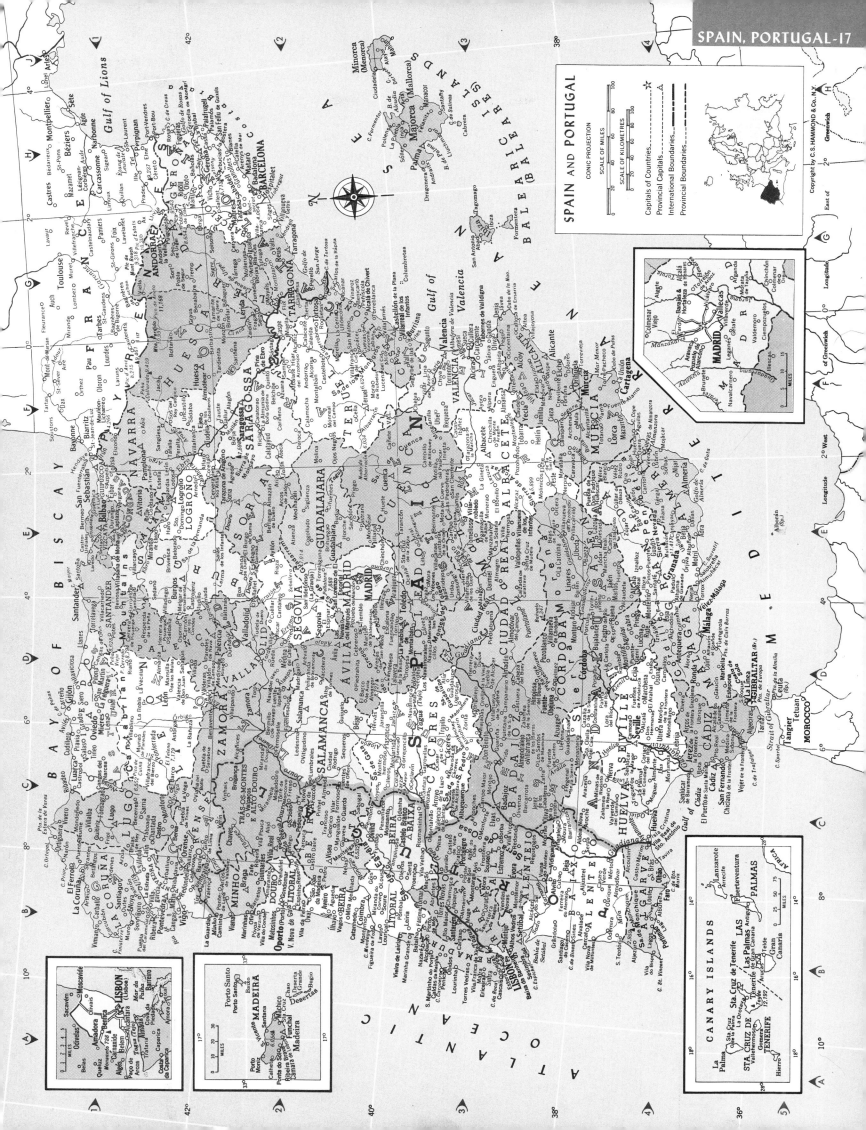

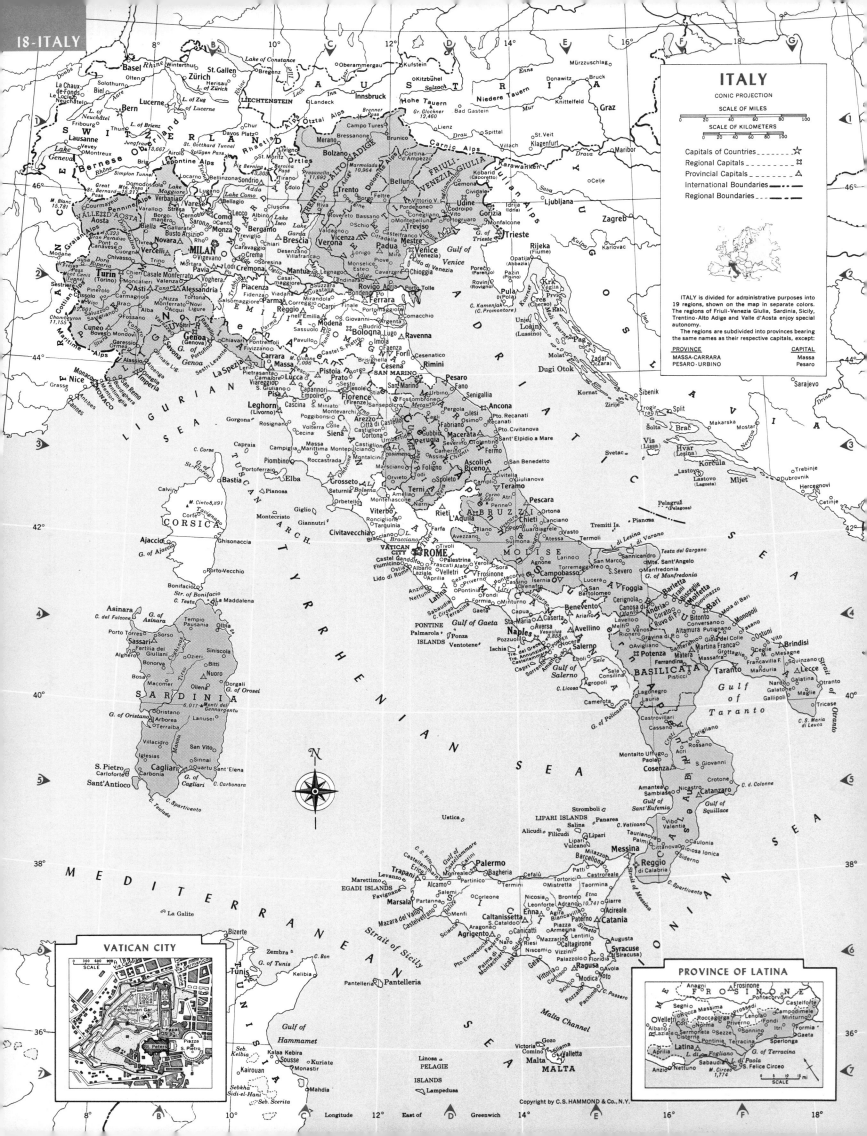

**ITALY**

CONIC PROJECTION

SCALE OF MILES

SCALE OF KILOMETERS

Capitals of Countries ......... ☆
Regional Capitals ......... ⌂
Provincial Capitals ......... △
International Boundaries ... —·—·—
Regional Boundaries ... —··—··—

ITALY is divided for administrative purposes into 19 regions, shown on the map in separate colors. The regions of Friuli-Venezia Giulia, Sardinia, Sicily, Trentino-Alto Adige and Valle d'Aosta enjoy special autonomy.

The regions are subdivided into provinces bearing the same names as their respective capitals, except:

| PROVINCE | CAPITAL |
|---|---|
| MASSA-CARRARA | Massa |
| PESARO-URBINO | Pesaro |

**VATICAN CITY**

**PROVINCE OF LATINA**

Copyright by C.S. HAMMOND & Co., N.Y.

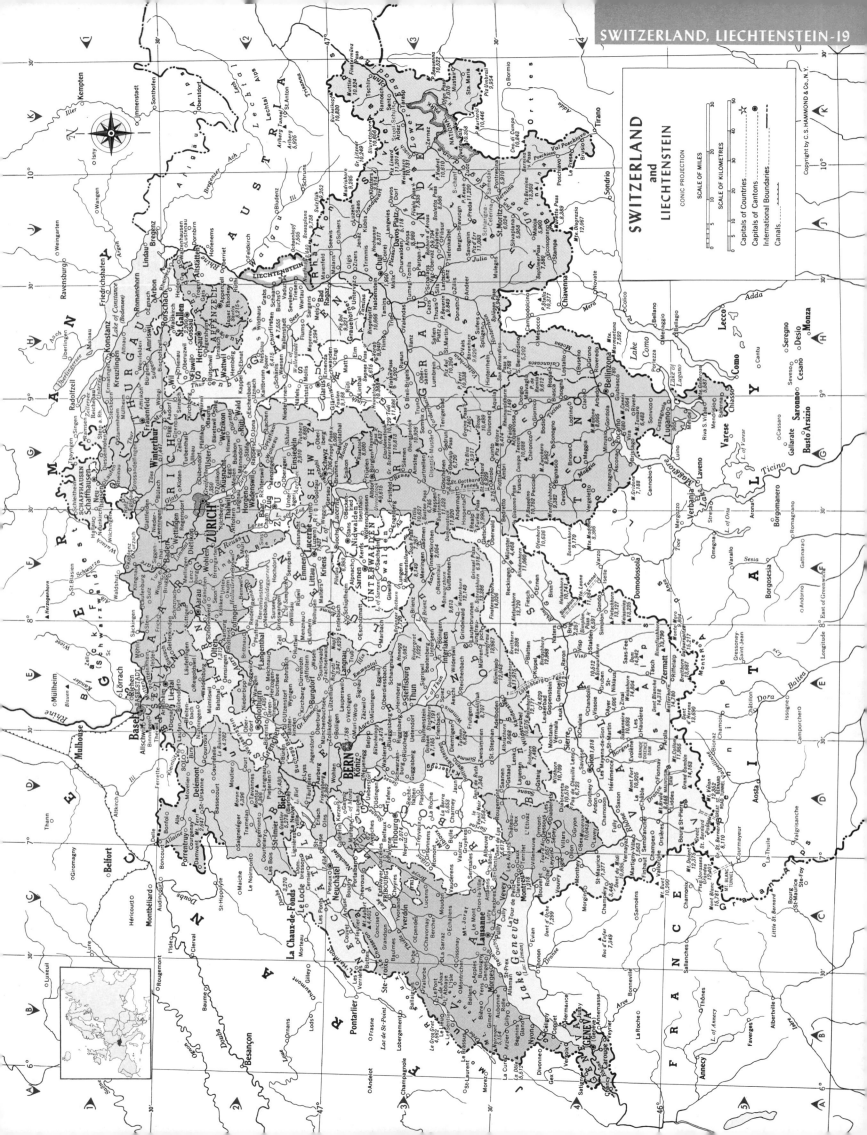

SWITZERLAND
and
LIECHTENSTEIN

CONIC PROJECTION

SCALE OF MILES

SCALE OF KILOMETRES

Capitals of Countries
Capitals of Cantons
International Boundaries
Canals

Copyright by C.S. HAMMOND & Co., N.Y.

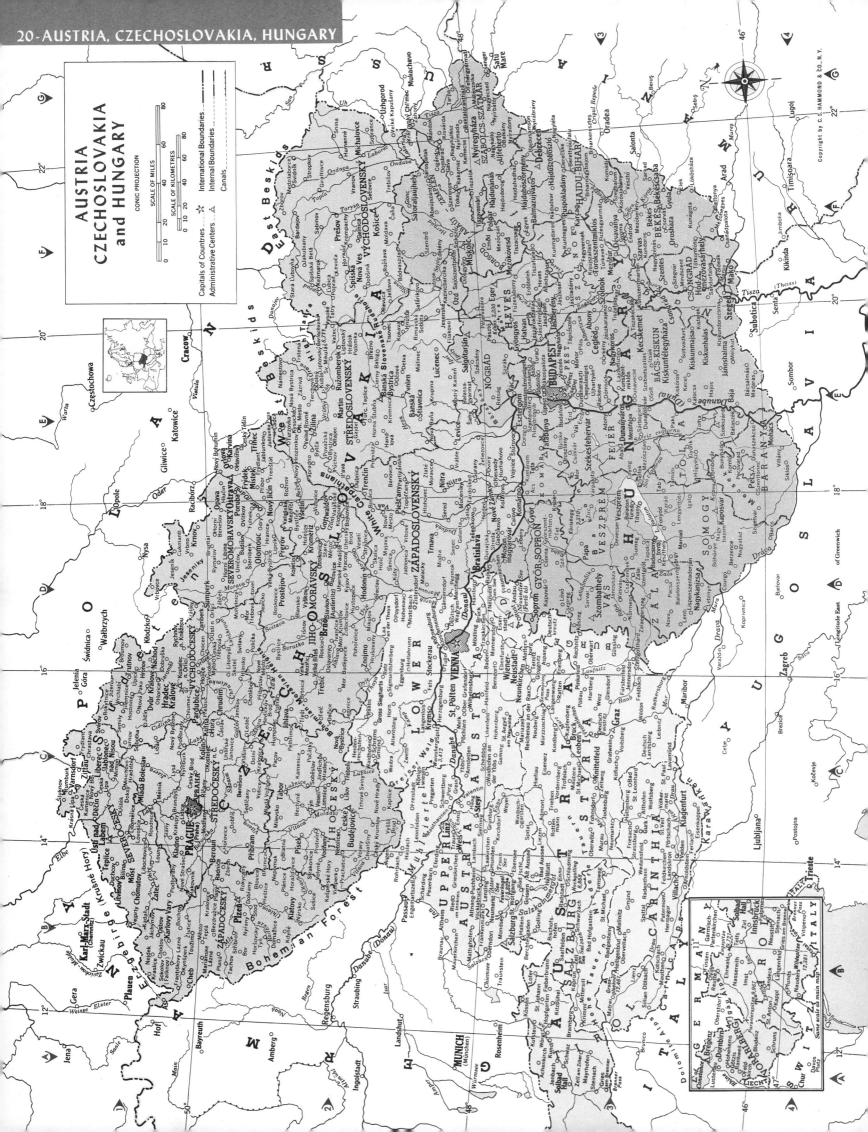

## AUSTRIA CZECHOSLOVAKIA and HUNGARY

CONIC PROJECTION

SCALE OF MILES

SCALE OF KILOMETRES

International Boundaries
Internal Boundaries
Canals

Capitals of Countries ★
Administrative Centers ▲

Copyright by C.S. HAMMOND & Co., N.Y.

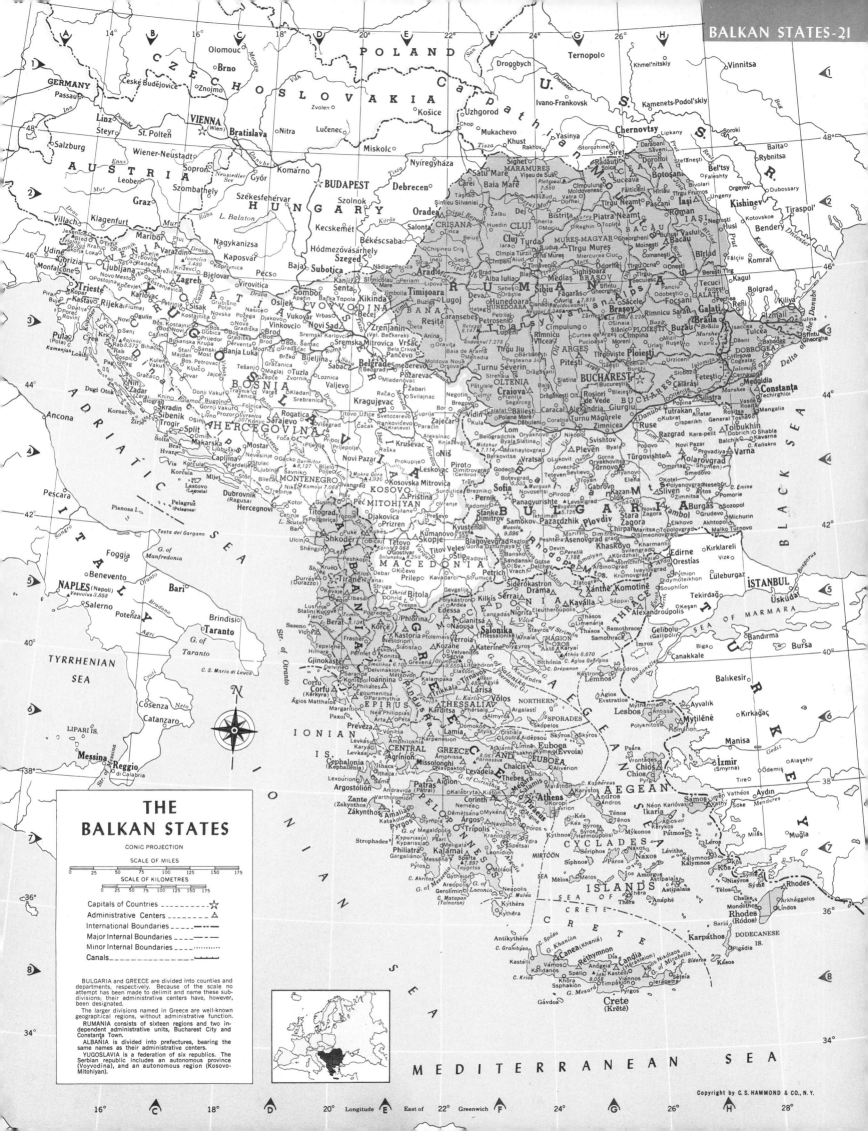

# THE
# BALKAN STATES

CONIC PROJECTION

SCALE OF MILES

0   25   50   75   100   125   150   175

SCALE OF KILOMETRES

0   25   50   75   100   125   150   175

Capitals of Countries ‒ ‒ ‒ ‒ ‒ ‒ ☆
Administrative Centers ‒ ‒ ‒ ‒ △
International Boundaries ‒‒‒‒‒
Major Internal Boundaries ‒ ‒ ‒
Minor Internal Boundaries ‒ ‒ ‒
Canals ‒ ‒ ‒ ‒ ‒ ‒ ‒ ‒

BULGARIA and GREECE are divided into counties and
departments, respectively. Because of the scale no
attempt has been made to delimit and name these subdivisions; their administrative centers have, however,
been designated.
    The larger divisions named in Greece are well-known
geographical regions, without administrative function.
    RUMANIA consists of sixteen regions and two in-
dependent administrative units, Bucharest City and
Constanta Town.
    ALBANIA is divided into prefectures, bearing the
same names as their administrative centers.
    YUGOSLAVIA is a federation of six republics. The
Serbian republic includes an autonomous province
(Voyvodina), and an autonomous region (Kosovo-
Mitohiyan).

MEDITERRANEAN SEA

Copyright by C.S. HAMMOND & CO., N.Y.

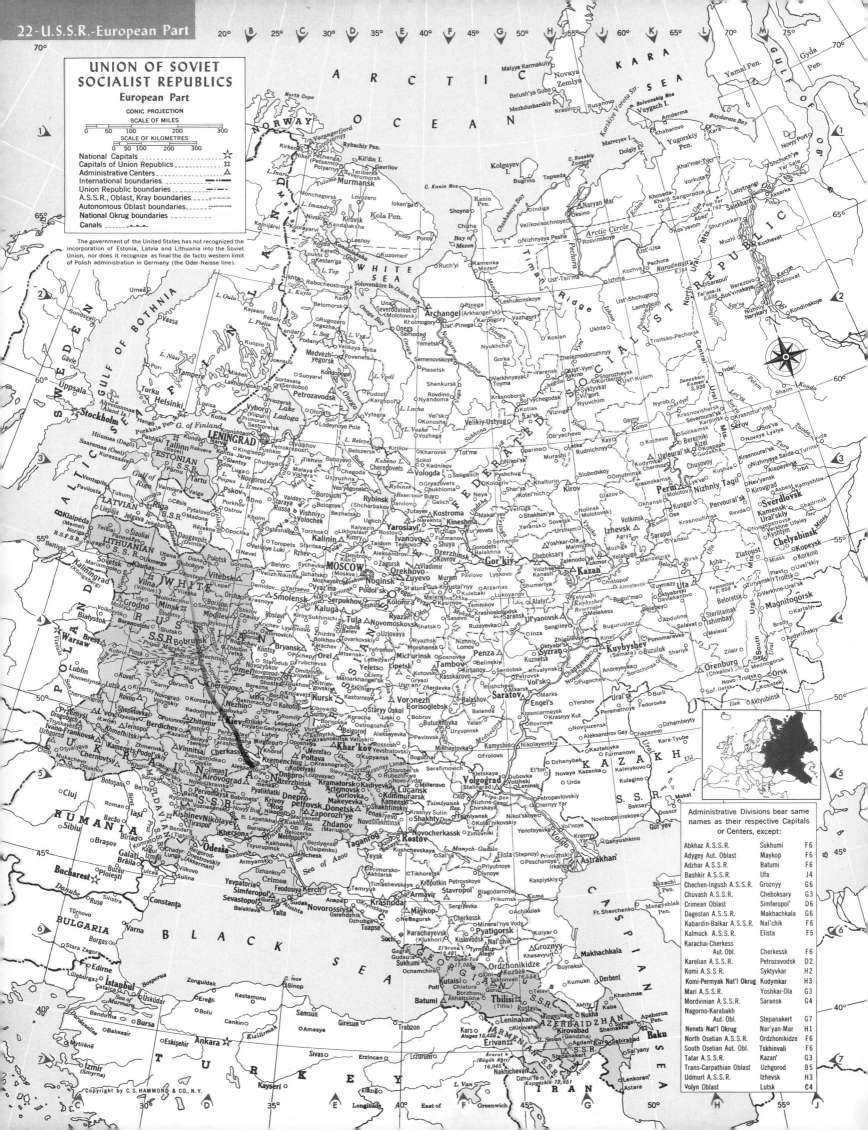

## UNION OF SOVIET SOCIALIST REPUBLICS
### European Part
CONIC PROJECTION
SCALE OF MILES
0  50  100    200    300
SCALE OF KILOMETRES
0  50  100    200    300

National Capitals ........................... ☆
Capitals of Union Republics ........... △
Administrative Centers ..................
International boundaries ................
Union Republic boundaries .............
A.S.S.R., Oblast, Kray boundaries ....
Autonomous Oblast boundaries ........
National Okrug boundaries ..............
Canals .......................................

The government of the United States has not recognized the
incorporation of Estonia, Latvia and Lithuania into the Soviet
Union, nor does it recognize as final the de facto western limit
of Polish administration in Germany (the Oder-Neisse line).

Copyright by C. S. HAMMOND & CO., N.Y.

Administrative Divisions bear same
names as their respective Capitals
or Centers, except:

| | | |
|---|---|---|
| Abkhaz A.S.S.R. | Sukhumi | F6 |
| Adygey Aut. Oblast | Maykop | F6 |
| Adzhar A.S.S.R. | Batumi | F6 |
| Bashkir A.S.S.R. | Ufa | J4 |
| Chechen-Ingush A.S.S.R. | Groznyy | G6 |
| Chuvash A.S.S.R. | Cheboksary | G3 |
| Crimean Oblast | Simferopol' | D6 |
| Dagestan A.S.S.R. | Makhachkala | G6 |
| Kabardin-Balkar A.S.S.R. | Nal'chik | F6 |
| Kalmuck A.S.S.R. | Elista | F5 |
| Karachai-Cherkess Aut. Obl. | Cherkessk | F6 |
| Karelian A.S.S.R. | Petrozavodsk | D2 |
| Komi A.S.S.R. | Syktyvkar | H2 |
| Komi-Permyak Nat'l Okrug | Kudymkar | H3 |
| Mari A.S.S.R. | Yoshkar-Ola | G3 |
| Mordvinian A.S.S.R. | Saransk | G4 |
| Nagorno-Karabakh Aut. Obl. | Stepanakert | G7 |
| Nenets Nat'l Okrug | Nar'yan-Mar | H1 |
| North Osetian A.S.S.R. | Ordzhonikidze | F6 |
| South Osetian Aut. Obl. | Tskhinvali | F6 |
| Tatar A.S.S.R. | Kazan' | G3 |
| Trans-Carpathian Oblast | Uzhgorod | B5 |
| Udmurt A.S.S.R. | Izhevsk | H3 |
| Volyn Oblast | Lutsk | C4 |

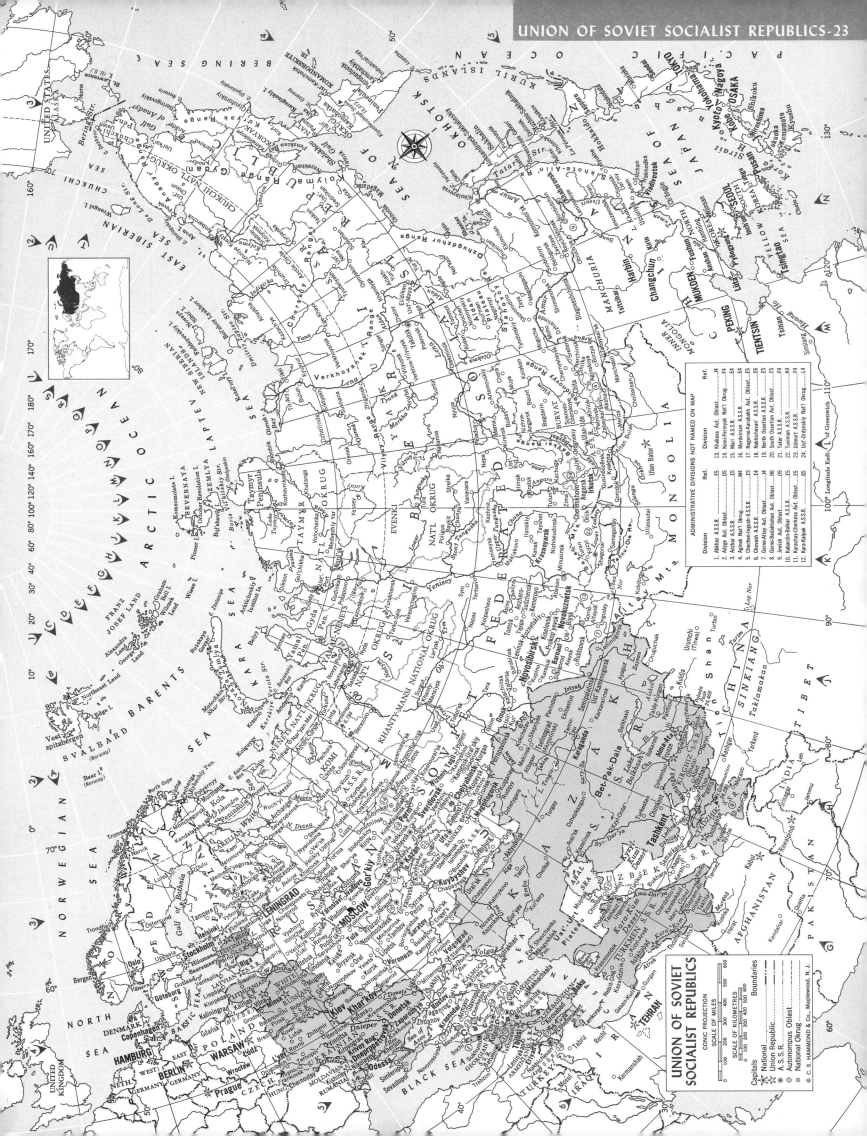

**UNION OF SOVIET SOCIALIST REPUBLICS**

CONIC PROJECTION

SCALE OF MILES
0   100   200   300   400   500   600

SCALE OF KILOMETRES
0   100   200   300   400   500   600

| Capitals | Boundaries |
|---|---|
| ★ National | National --------- |
| ⊛ Union Republic | Union Republic --------- |
| ⊙ A.S.S.R. | A.S.S.R. --------- |
| ⊚ Autonomous Oblast | Autonomous Oblast --------- |
| ⊕ National Okrug | National Okrug --------- |

© C. S. HAMMOND & CO., Maplewood, N.J.

**ADMINISTRATIVE DIVISIONS NOT NAMED ON MAP**

| Division | Ref. | Division | Ref. |
|---|---|---|---|
| 1. Abkhaz A.S.S.R. | E5 | 13. Khakass Aut. Oblast. | J4 |
| 2. Adyge Aut. Oblast. | D5 | 14. Komi-Permyak Nat'l Okrug. | F4 |
| 3. Adzhar A.S.S.R. | E5 | 15. Mari A.S.S.R. | E4 |
| 4. Aginsk Nat'l Okrug. | M4 | 16. Mordovian A.S.S.R. | E4 |
| 5. Chechen-Ingush A.S.S.R. | E5 | 17. Nagorno-Karabakh Aut. Oblast. | E5 |
| 6. Chuvash A.S.S.R. | E4 | 18. Nakhichevan A.S.S.R. | E5 |
| 7. Gorno-Altay Aut. Oblast. | J4 | 19. North Ossetian A.S.S.R. | E5 |
| 8. Gorno-Badakhshan Aut. Oblast. | H6 | 20. South Ossetian Aut. Oblast. | E5 |
| 9. Jewish Aut. Oblast. | O5 | 21. Tatar A.S.S.R. | F4 |
| 10. Kabardin-Balkar A.S.S.R. | E5 | 22. Tuvinian A.S.S.R. | K4 |
| 11. Karachai-Cherkess Aut. Oblast | E5 | 23. Udmurt A.S.S.R. | F4 |
| 12. Kara-Kalpak A.S.S.R. | F5 | 24. Ust-Ordynskiy Nat'l Okrug. | L4 |

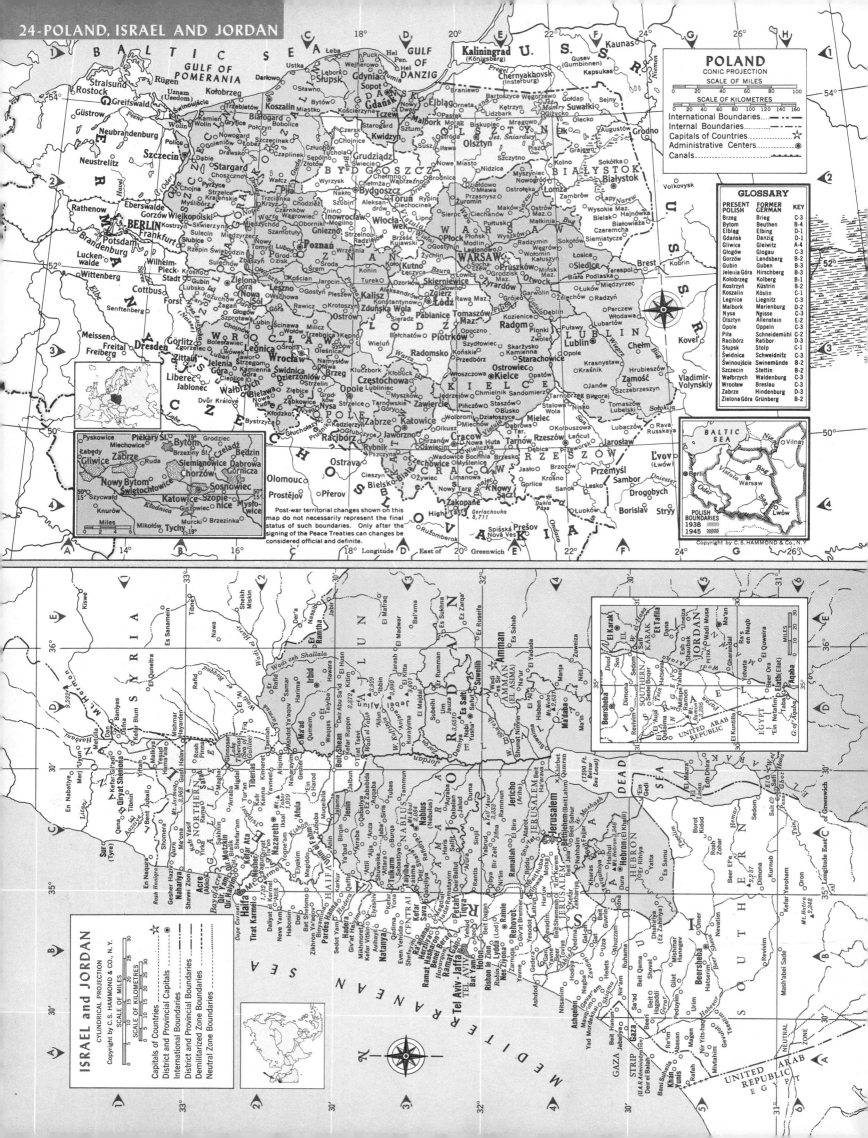

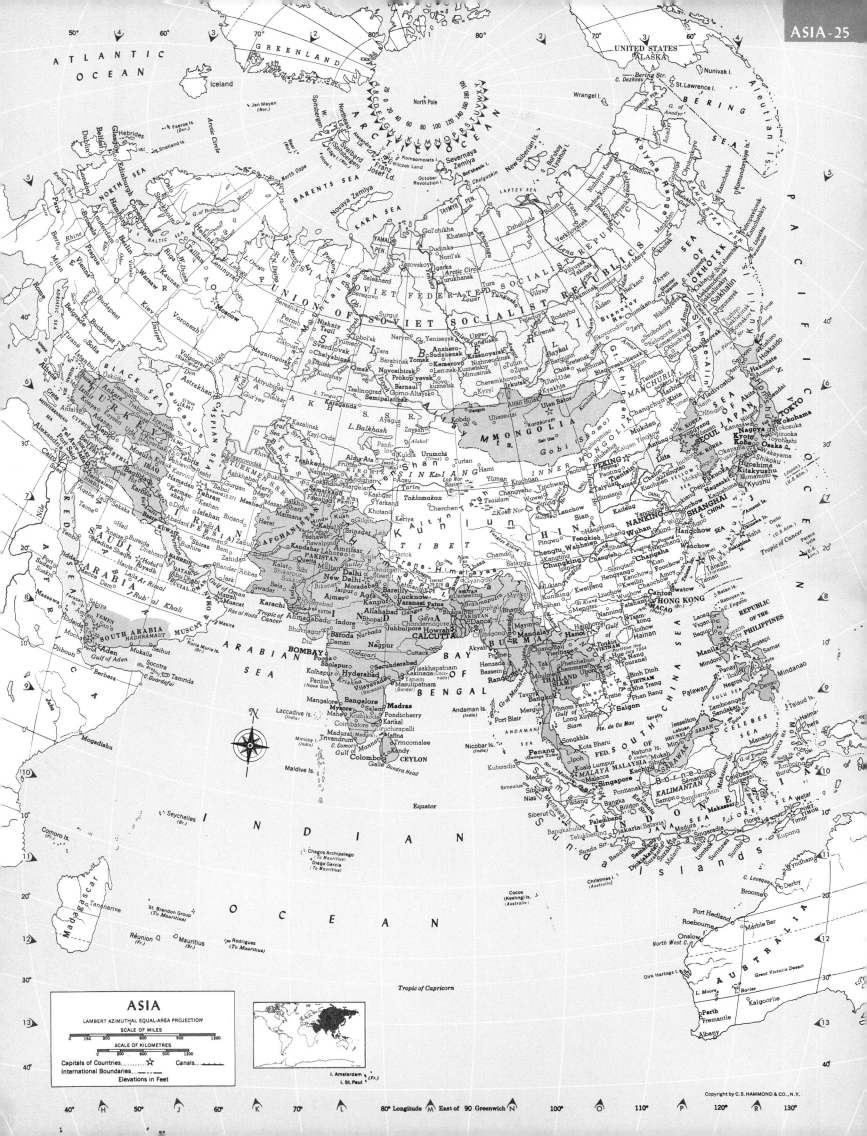

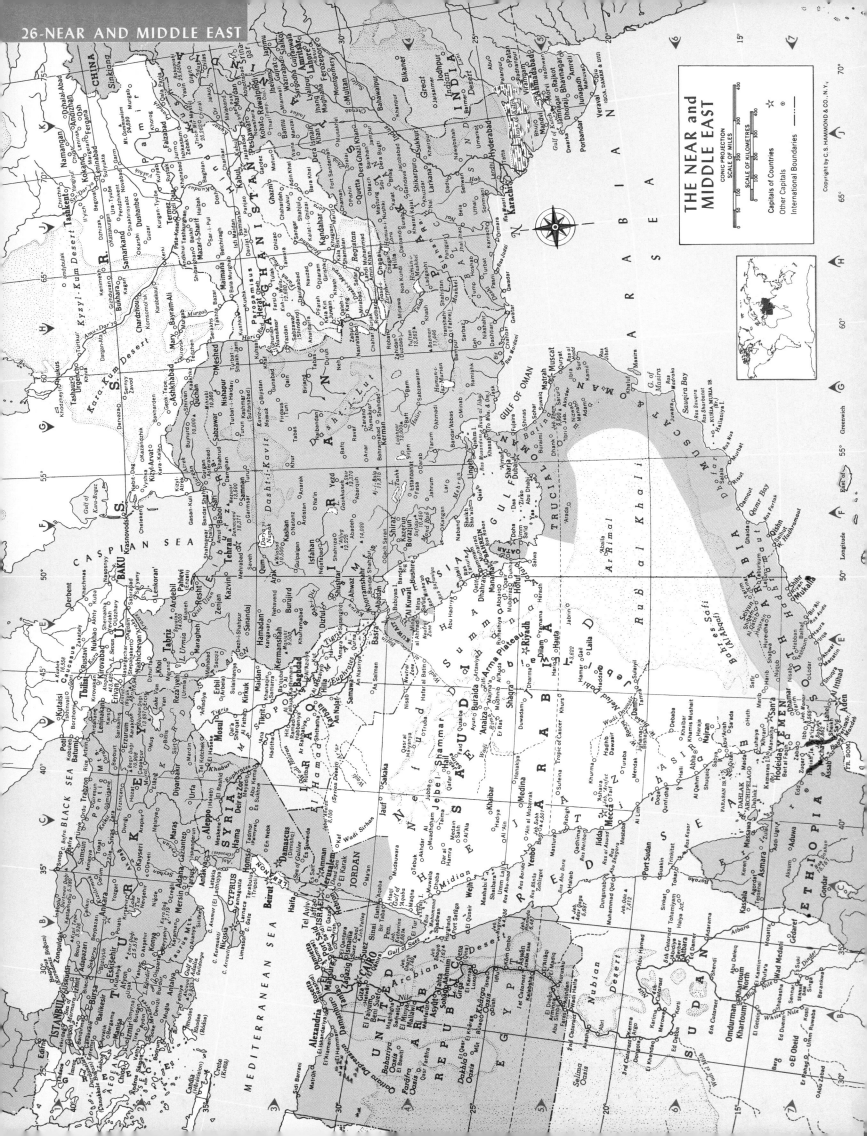

THE NEAR and
MIDDLE EAST

CONIC PROJECTION
SCALE OF MILES

SCALE OF KILOMETRES

Capitals of Countries ☆
Other Capitals ◉
International Boundaries ------

Copyright by C.S. HAMMOND & CO., N.Y.

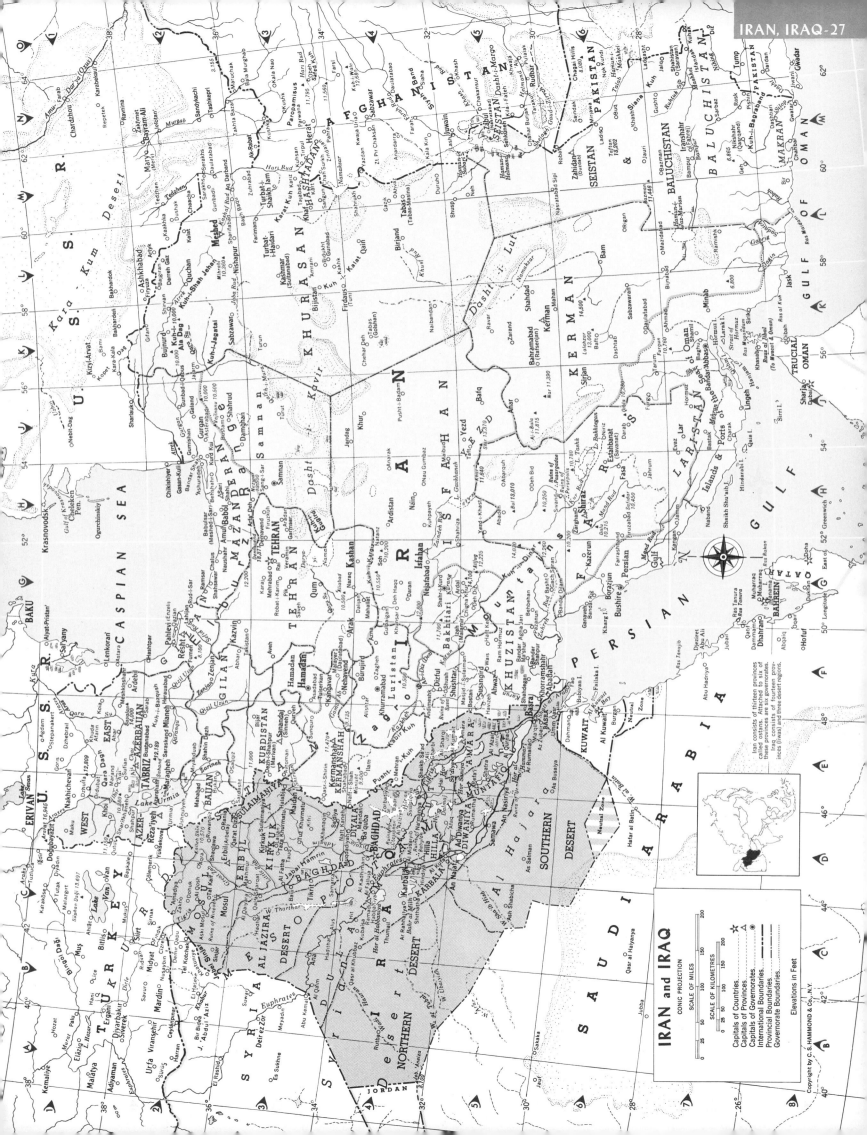

## IRAN and IRAQ
CONIC PROJECTION

SCALE OF MILES

SCALE OF KILOMETRES

Capitals of Countries............☆
Capitals of Provinces............△
Capitals of Governorates........◉
International Boundaries.........
Provincial Boundaries...........
Governorate Boundaries........

Elevations in Feet

Copyright by C. S. HAMMOND & Co., N.Y.

Iran consists of thirteen provinces called ostans. Attached to six of these provinces are six governorates. The rest consist of fourteen provinces (iran) and three desert regions.

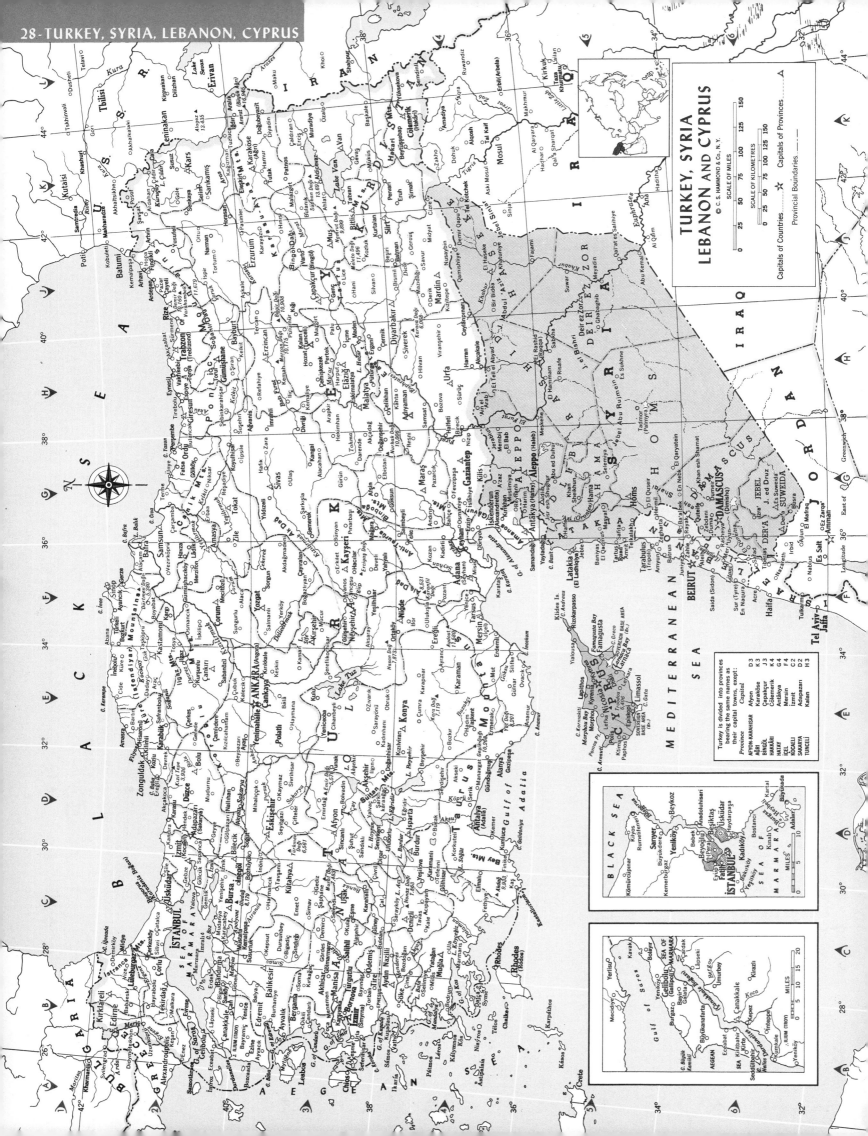

### TURKEY, SYRIA LEBANON AND CYPRUS

© C. S. HAMMOND & Co., N.Y.

SCALE OF MILES
0   25   50   75   100   125   150

SCALE OF KILOMETRES
0   25   50   75   100   125   150

Capitals of Countries ........ ★
Capitals of Provinces ........ ☆
Provincial Boundaries ........

Turkey is divided into provinces bearing the same names as their capital towns, except:

| Province | Capital | |
|---|---|---|
| AFYON-KARAHISAR | Afyon | D 3 |
| AĞRI | Karaköse | K 3 |
| BINGÖL | Çapakçur | J 3 |
| HAKKÂRI | Çölemerik | K 4 |
| HATAY | Antâkya | G 4 |
| İÇEL | Mersin | F 4 |
| KOCAELİ | İzmit | C 2 |
| SAKARYA | Adapazarı | D 2 |
| TUNCELİ | Kalan | H 3 |

BURMA, THAILAND,
INDOCHINA
and
MALAYA

CONIC PROJECTION

SCALE OF MILES

0    50    100    150    200

SCALE OF KILOMETRES

0   50  100    200    300

International Boundaries .......
Capitals of Countries ........... ☆
Capitals of States ............... ◉

Copyright by C. S. HAMMOND & CO., N.Y.

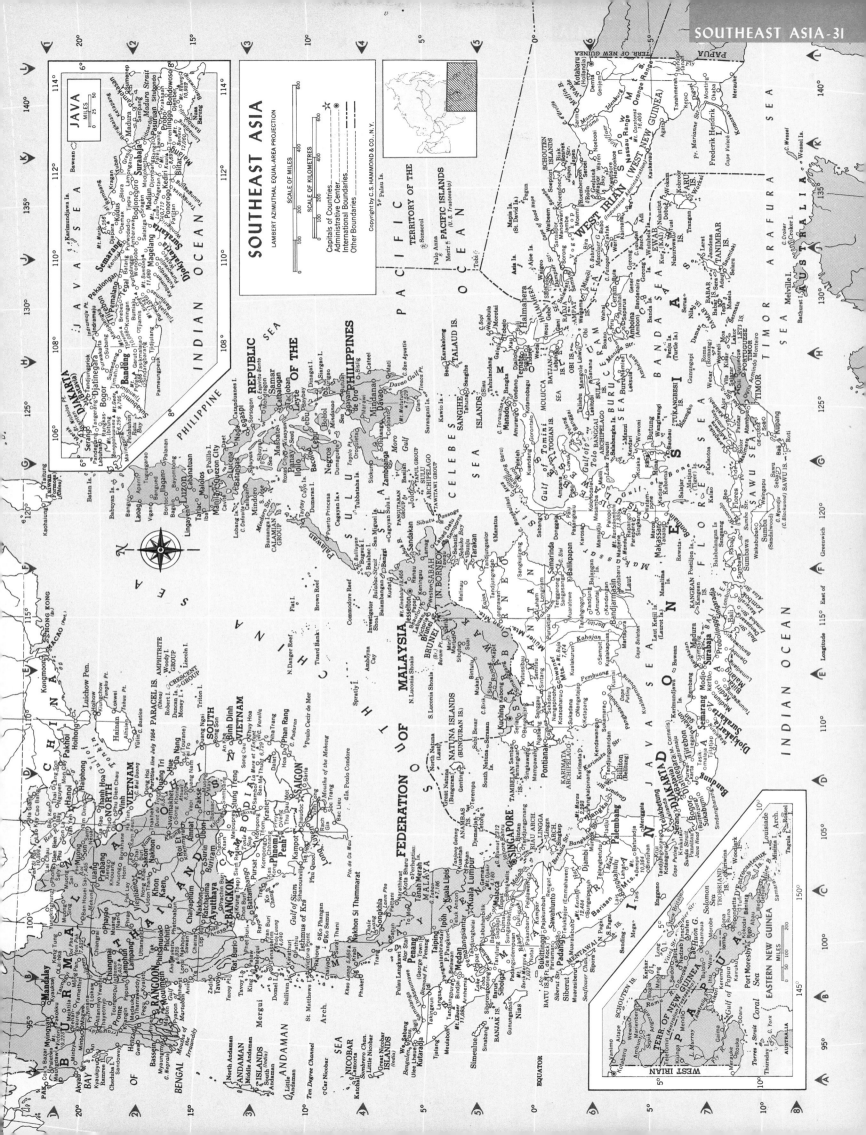

## SOUTHEAST ASIA

LAMBERT AZIMUTHAL EQUAL-AREA PROJECTION

SCALE OF MILES

SCALE OF KILOMETRES

Capitals of Countries ........................ ☆
Administrative Center ........................ ◉
International Boundaries ................... ――――
Other Boundaries ............................. ――――

Copyright by C.S. HAMMOND & CO., N.Y.

### JAVA

MILES
0  25  50

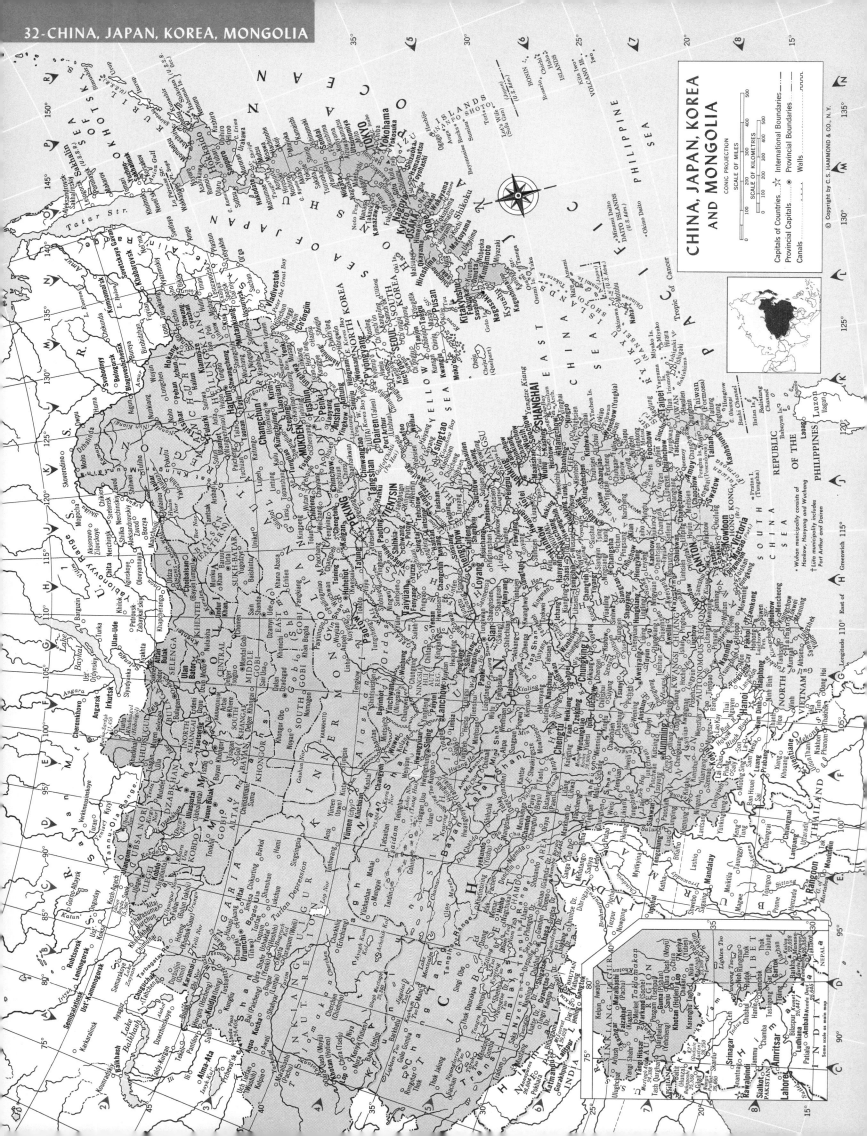

CHINA, JAPAN, KOREA
AND MONGOLIA

CONIC PROJECTION

SCALE OF MILES

SCALE OF KILOMETRES

Capitals of Countries........ ✪
Provincial Capitals........... ◉
Canals

International Boundaries........
Provincial Boundaries.........
Walls

© Copyright by C. S. HAMMOND & CO., N.Y.

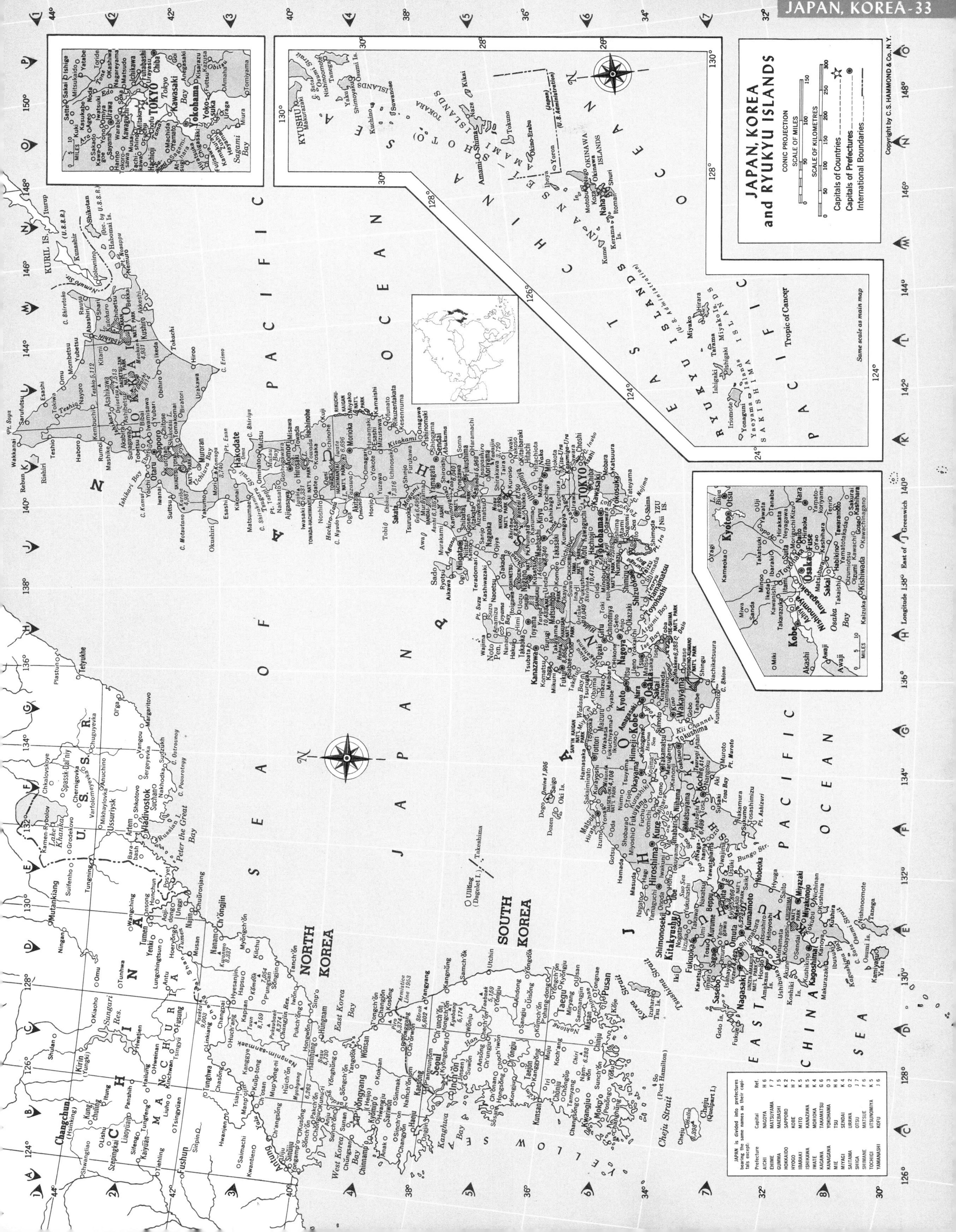

JAPAN, KOREA and RYUKYU ISLANDS
CONIC PROJECTION
SCALE OF MILES
0 50 100 150
SCALE OF KILOMETRES
0 50 100 150 200 250 300
Capitals of Countries
Capitals of Prefectures
International Boundaries
Copyright by C.S. HAMMOND & Co., N.Y.
Same scale as main map
Tropic of Cancer
SEA OF JAPAN
PACIFIC OCEAN
EAST CHINA SEA
YELLOW SEA
NORTH KOREA
SOUTH KOREA
U.S.S.R.
MANCHURIA
CHINA
HOKKAIDO
HONSHU
SHIKOKU
KYUSHU
RYUKYU ISLANDS
SAKISHIMA ISLANDS
NANSEI SHOTO
AMAMI ISLANDS
TOKARA ISLANDS
OKINAWA ISLANDS
KURIL IS. (U.S.S.R.)
Longitude 138° East of Greenwich 140°
JAPAN is divided into prefectures bearing the same names as their capitals except:

| Prefecture | Capital | Ref. |
|---|---|---|
| AICHI | NAGOYA | H 6 |
| EHIME | MATSUYAMA | F 7 |
| GUMMA | MAEBASHI | J 5 |
| HOKKAIDO | SAPPORO | K 2 |
| HYOGO | KOBE | H 7 |
| IBARAKI | MITO | K 5 |
| ISHIKAWA | KANAZAWA | H 5 |
| IWATE | MORIOKA | K 4 |
| KAGAWA | TAKAMATSU | G 6 |
| KANAGAWA | YOKOHAMA | O 3 |
| MIE | TSU | H 6 |
| MIYAGI | SENDAI | K 4 |
| SAITAMA | URAWA | O 2 |
| SHIGA | OTSU | J 7 |
| SHIMANE | MATSUE | F 6 |
| TOCHIGI | UTSUNOMIYA | K 5 |
| YAMANASHI | KOFU | J 6 |

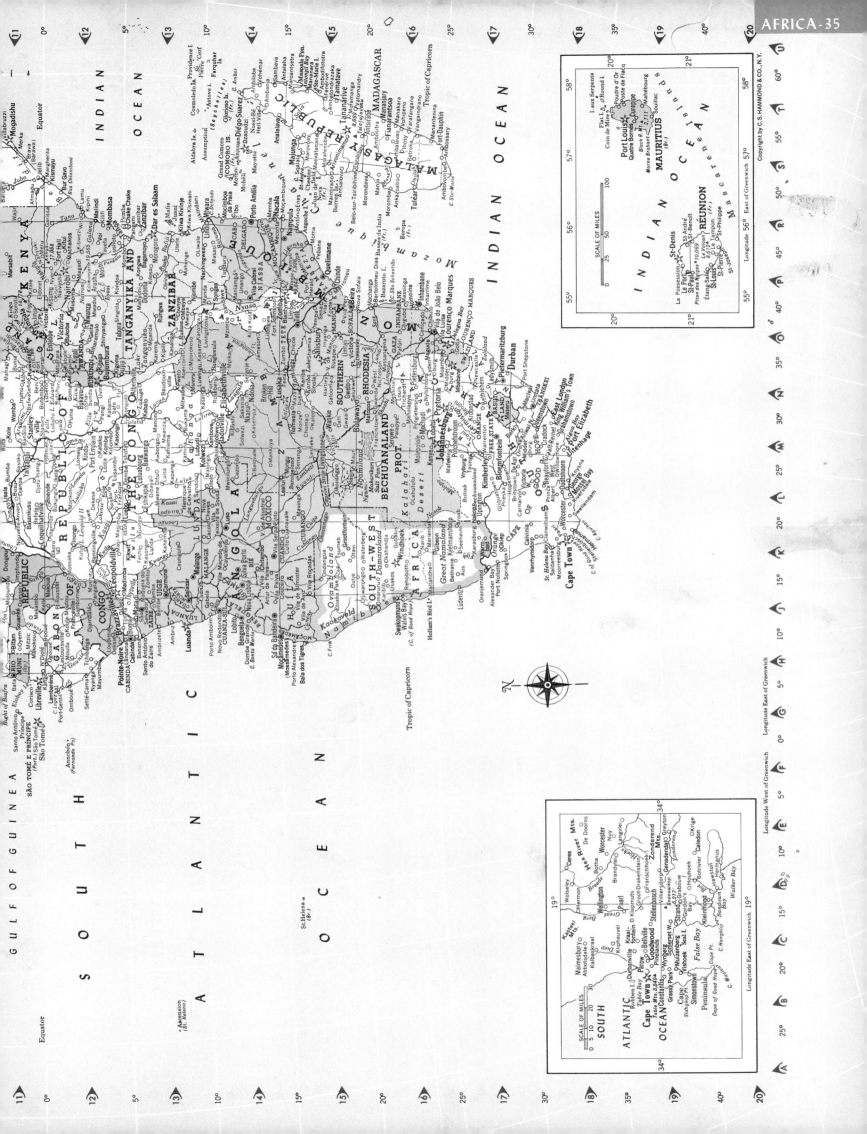

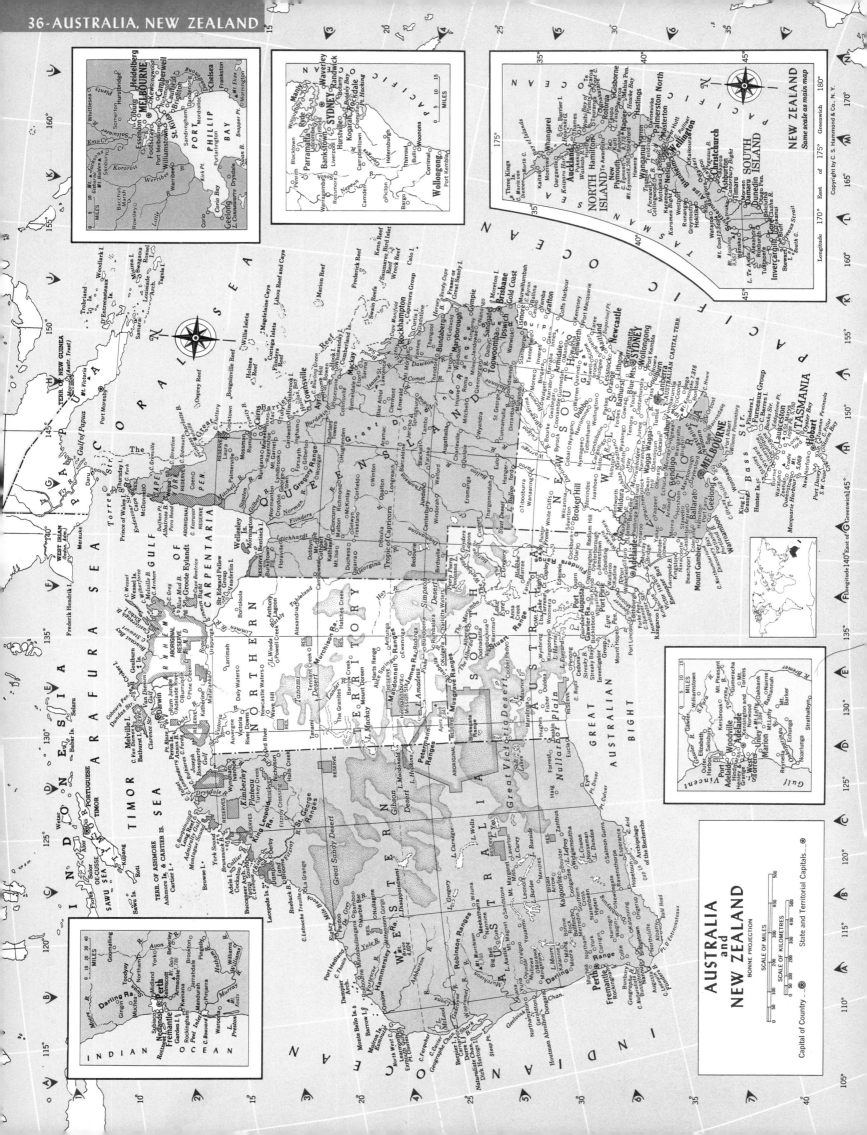

AUSTRALIA
and
NEW ZEALAND
BONNE PROJECTION

SCALE OF MILES
SCALE OF KILOMETRES

Capital of Country — ⊛    State and Territorial Capitals — ⊛

NEW ZEALAND
Same scale as main map

Copyright by C. S. Hammond & Co., N.Y.

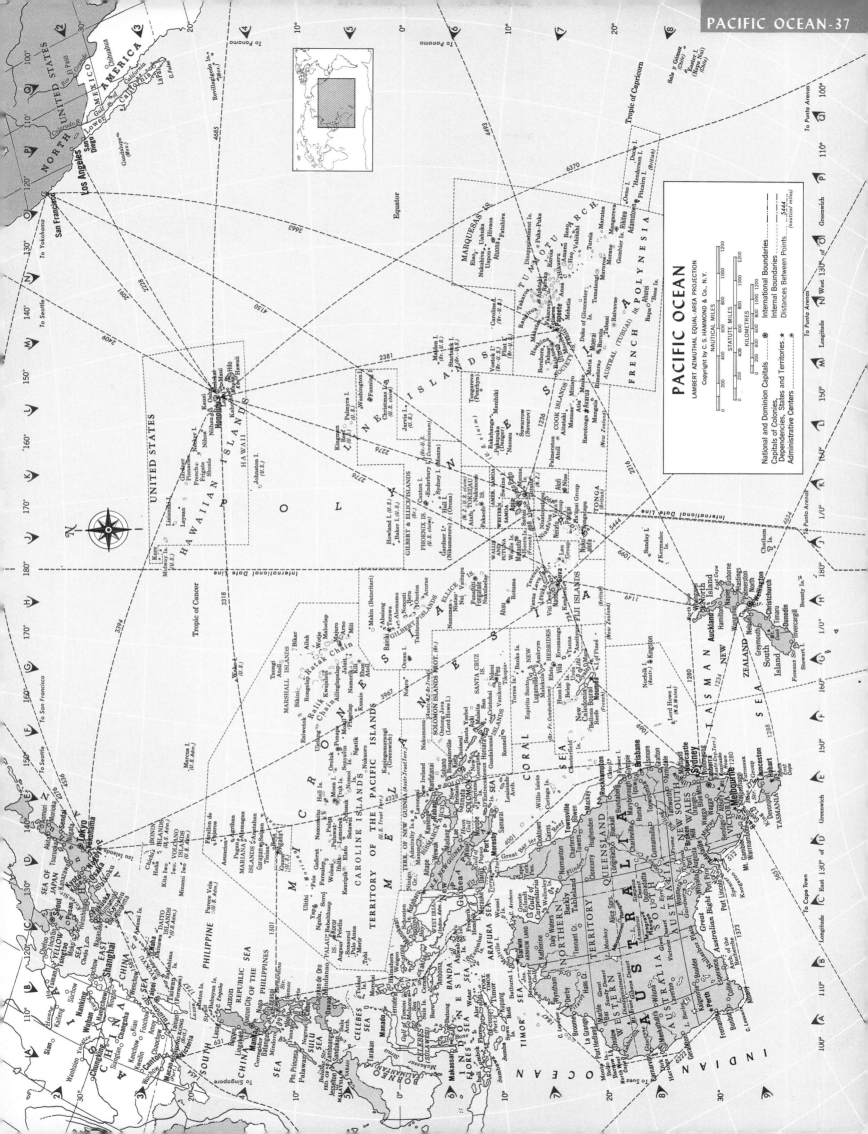

### PACIFIC OCEAN

LAMBERT AZIMUTHAL EQUAL-AREA PROJECTION
Copyright by C. S. HAMMOND & Co., N.Y.

NAUTICAL MILES

STATUTE MILES

KILOMETRES

National and Dominion Capitals ⊛
Capitals of Colonies,
  Dependencies, States and Territories ★
Administrative Centers ⊛

International Boundaries ————
Internal Boundaries ————
Distances Between Points ★ —— 5444 (nautical miles)

## NORTH AMERICA

LAMBERT AZIMUTHAL EQUAL-AREA PROJECTION

SCALE OF MILES

0  100  200  400  600  800

SCALE OF KILOMETRES

0  200  400  600  800

Capitals of Countries ............ ☆
International Boundaries ........ _ _ _ _
Other Boundaries ................ _____
Canals ............................ ┼┼┼┼┼

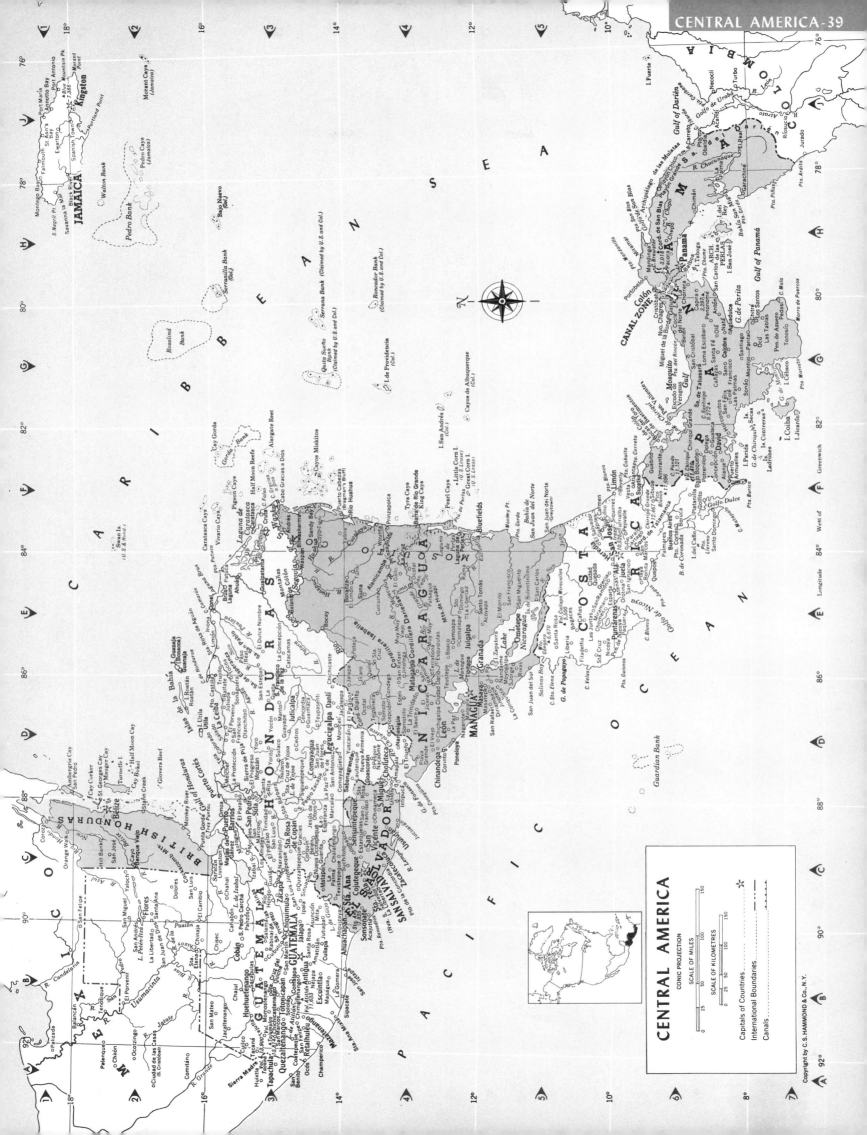

# CENTRAL AMERICA

CONIC PROJECTION

SCALE OF MILES

0   25   50        100        150

SCALE OF KILOMETRES

0   25   50        100        150

Capitals of Countries..............★

International Boundaries............

Canals.............................

Copyright by C.S. HAMMOND & CO., N.Y.

WESTERN
CANADA

Copyright by C. S. HAMMOND & Co., N.Y.

SCALE OF MILES

SCALE OF KILOMETRES

Provincial and
Territorial Capitals ......... ●
International Boundaries ........ ----
Boundaries of Provinces ....... ----

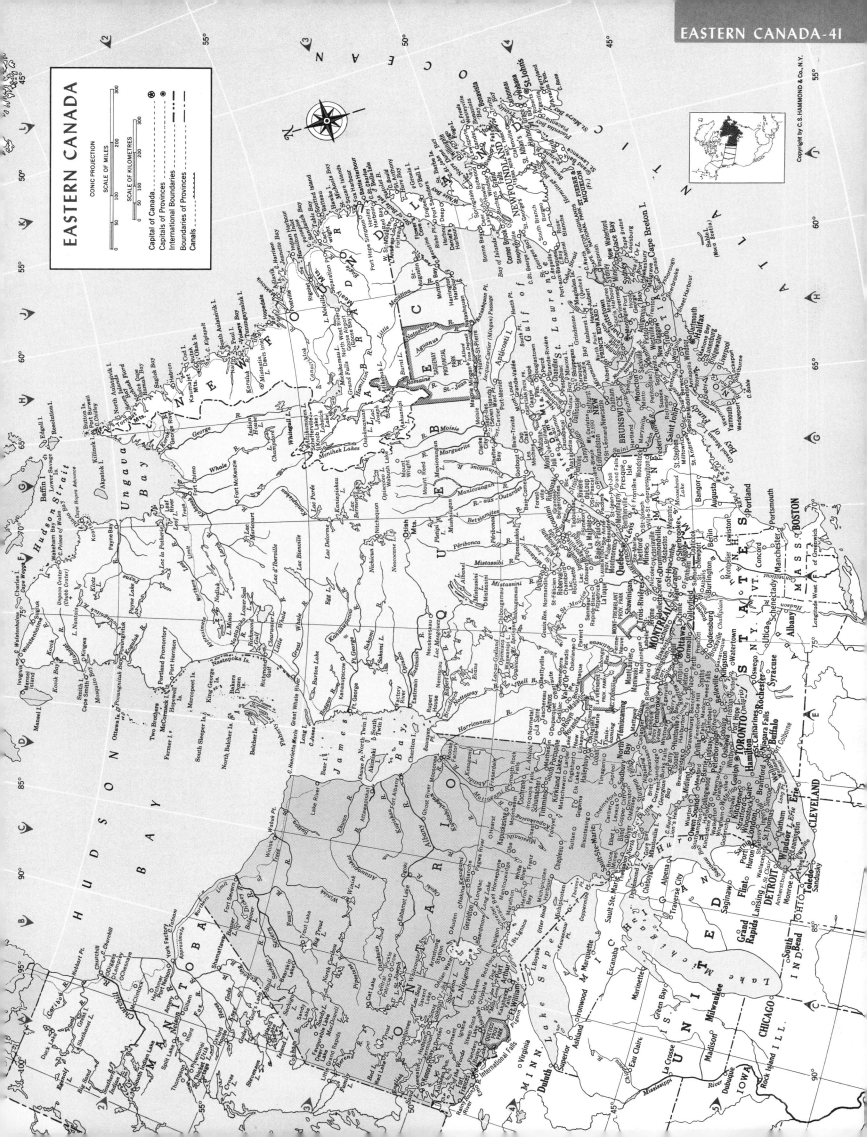

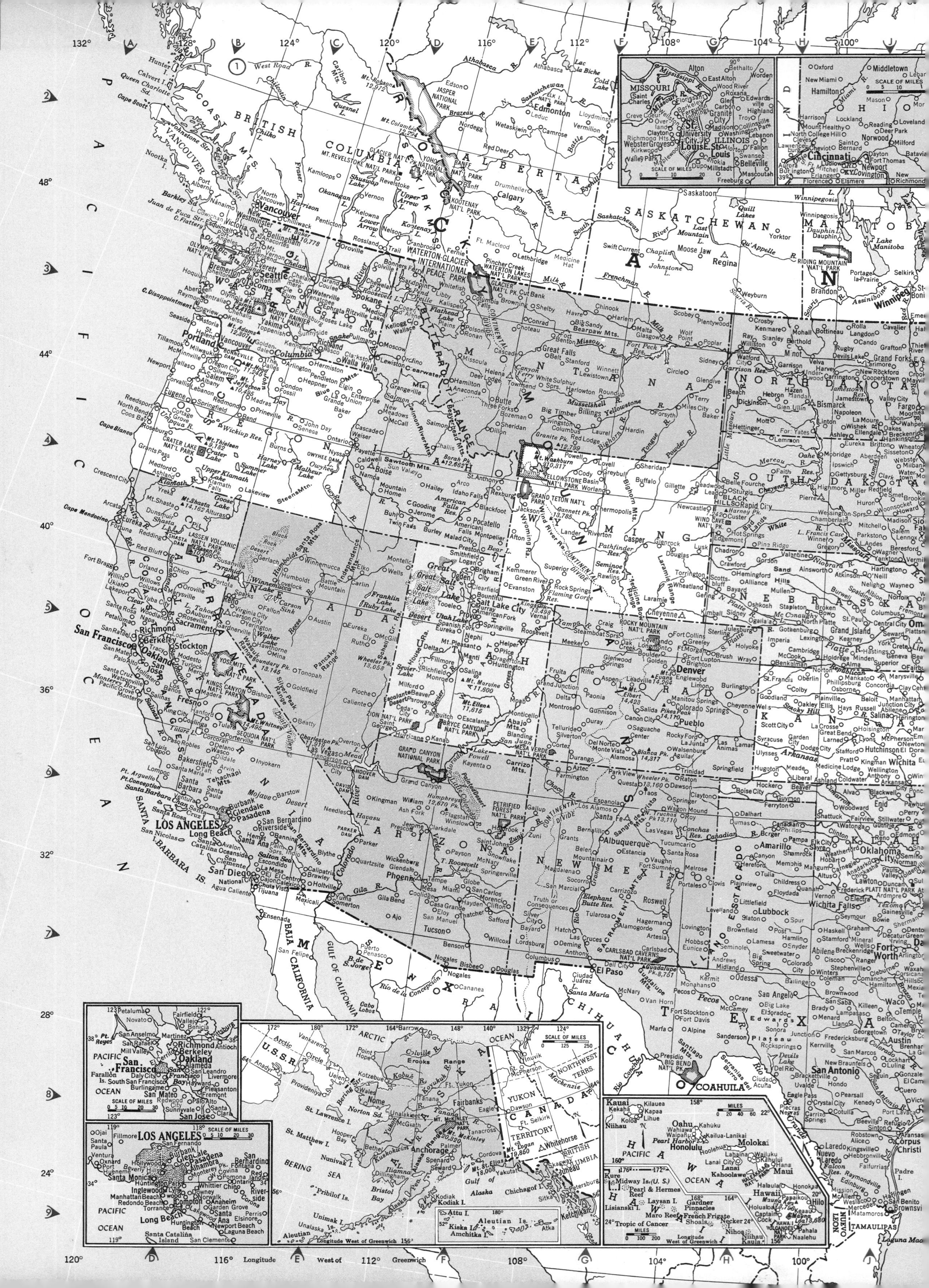

PACIFIC OCEAN

BRITISH COLUMBIA
ALBERTA
SASKATCHEWAN
MANITOBA

WASHINGTON
OREGON
IDAHO
MONTANA
NORTH DAKOTA
SOUTH DAKOTA
WYOMING
NEBRASKA
NEVADA
UTAH
COLORADO
KANSAS
CALIFORNIA
ARIZONA
NEW MEXICO
OKLAHOMA
TEXAS

BAJA CALIFORNIA
GULF OF CALIFORNIA
SONORA
CHIHUAHUA
COAHUILA
TAMAULIPAS
MEXICO

Vancouver
Victoria
Seattle
Tacoma
Spokane
Portland
Salem
Eugene
San Francisco
Oakland
Sacramento
Stockton
Fresno
LOS ANGELES
Long Beach
San Diego
Las Vegas
Phoenix
Tucson
Albuquerque
Santa Fe
El Paso
Denver
Pueblo
Salt Lake City
Boise
Great Falls
Helena
Billings
Bismarck
Winnipeg
Regina
Edmonton
Calgary
Oklahoma City
Wichita
Amarillo
Lubbock
Fort Worth
San Antonio
Austin
Corpus Christi

Crater Lake Nat'l Park
Yellowstone Nat'l Park
Grand Teton Nat'l Park
Rocky Mountain Nat'l Park
Yosemite Nat'l Park
Sequoia Nat'l Park
Kings Canyon Nat'l Park
Zion Nat'l Park
Bryce Canyon Nat'l Park
Grand Canyon National Park
Mesa Verde Nat'l Park
Petrified Forest Nat'l Park
Carlsbad Caverns Nat'l Park
Big Bend Nat'l Pk.
Glacier Nat'l Park
Waterton-Glacier International Peace Park

ST. LOUIS (inset)
MISSOURI
ILLINOIS
OHIO
Cincinnati

SAN FRANCISCO (inset)
LOS ANGELES (inset)
ALASKA (inset)
U.S.S.R.
ARCTIC OCEAN
BERING SEA
Anchorage
Fairbanks
Juneau
Aleutian Is.
HAWAII (inset)
Honolulu
Oahu
Maui
Hawaii
PACIFIC OCEAN
Tropic of Cancer

Longitude West of Greenwich

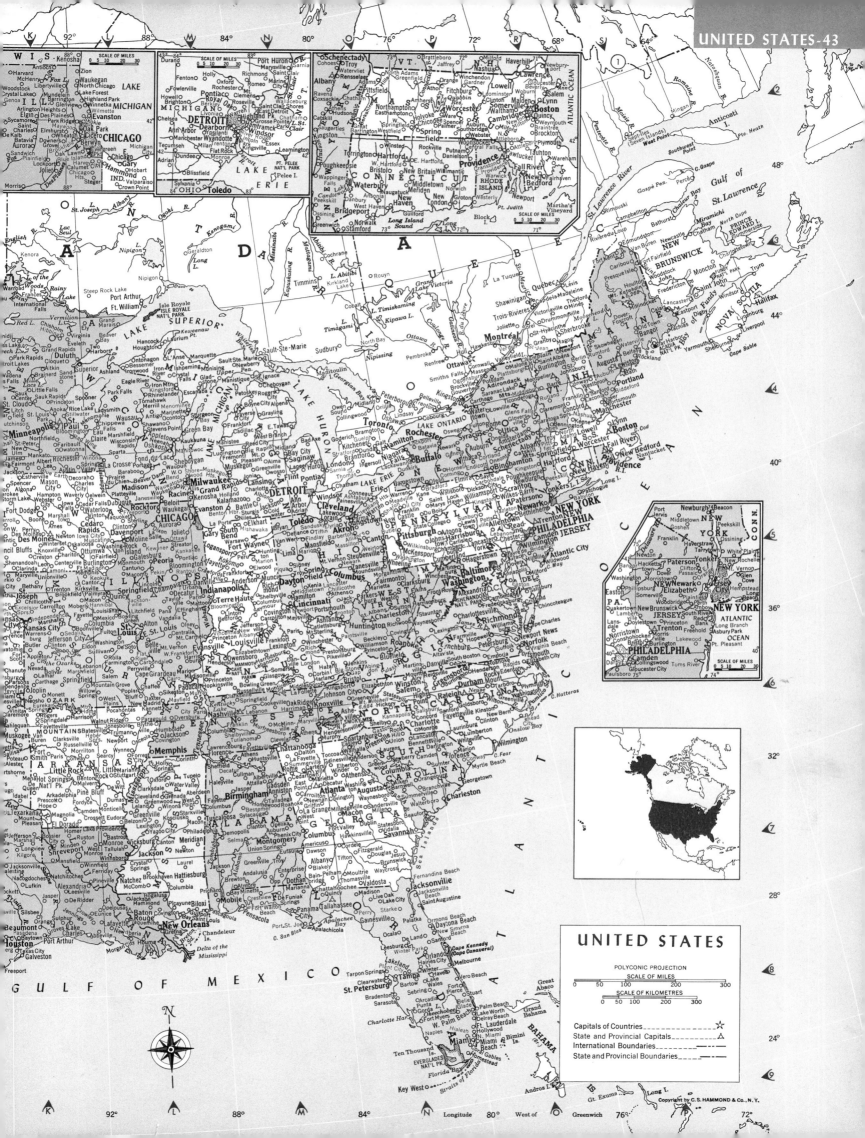

# UNITED STATES

POLYCONIC PROJECTION

SCALE OF MILES

SCALE OF KILOMETRES

Capitals of Countries _____ ☆
State and Provincial Capitals _____ △
International Boundaries _____
State and Provincial Boundaries _____

Copyright by C. S. HAMMOND & Co., N.Y.

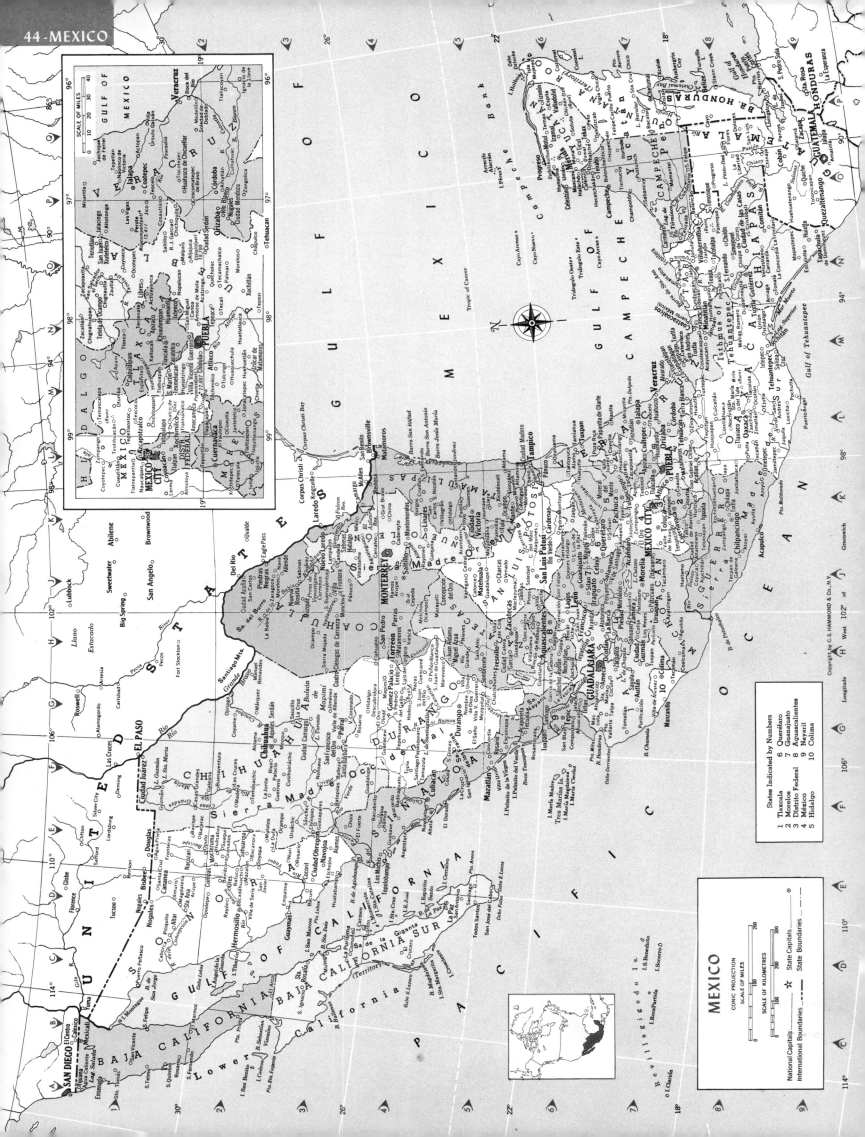

MEXICO

CONIC PROJECTION

SCALE OF MILES

SCALE OF KILOMETRES

National Capitals .......... ⊛    State Capitals .......... ☆
International Boundaries .......... -----    State Boundaries .......... -----

States Indicated by Numbers

| 1 | Tlaxcala | 6 | Querétaro |
|---|---|---|---|
| 2 | Morelos | 7 | Guanajuato |
| 3 | Distrito Federal | 8 | Aguascalientes |
| 4 | México | 9 | Nayarit |
| 5 | Hidalgo | 10 | Colima |

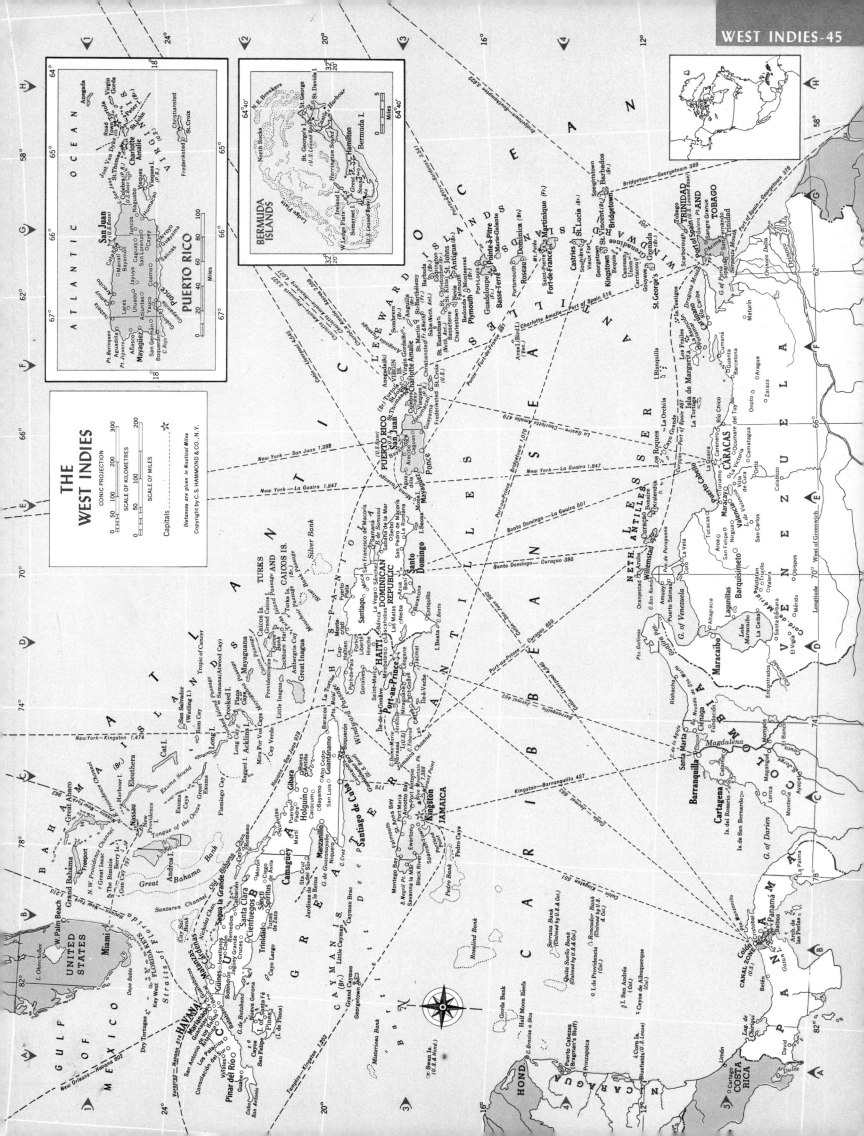

## THE WEST INDIES

CONIC PROJECTION

SCALE OF KILOMETRES
0   50   100   200   300

SCALE OF MILES
0   50   100   200

★ Capitals

*Distances are given in Nautical Miles*

Copyright by C.S. HAMMOND & CO., N.Y.

PUERTO RICO

BERMUDA ISLANDS

ATLANTIC OCEAN

CARIBBEAN SEA

GULF OF MEXICO

UNITED STATES

MEXICO

BAHAMA ISLANDS

CUBA

HAVANA

JAMAICA

HAITI

DOMINICAN REPUBLIC

TURKS AND CAICOS IS.

GREATER ANTILLES

LESSER ANTILLES

WINDWARD ISLANDS

LEEWARD ISLANDS

VIRGIN IS.

TRINIDAD

TOBAGO

VENEZUELA

COLOMBIA

PANAMA

CANAL ZONE

COSTA RICA

HOND.

NICARAGUA

NETH. ANTILLES

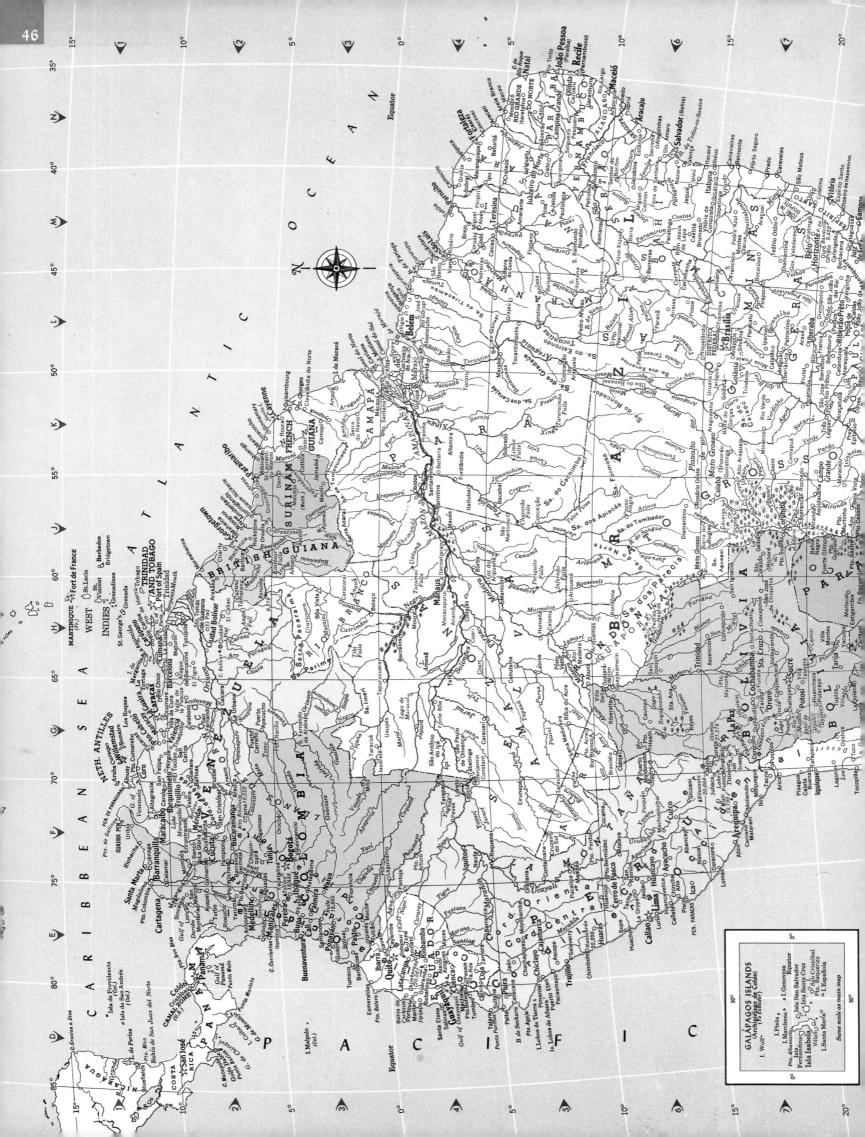

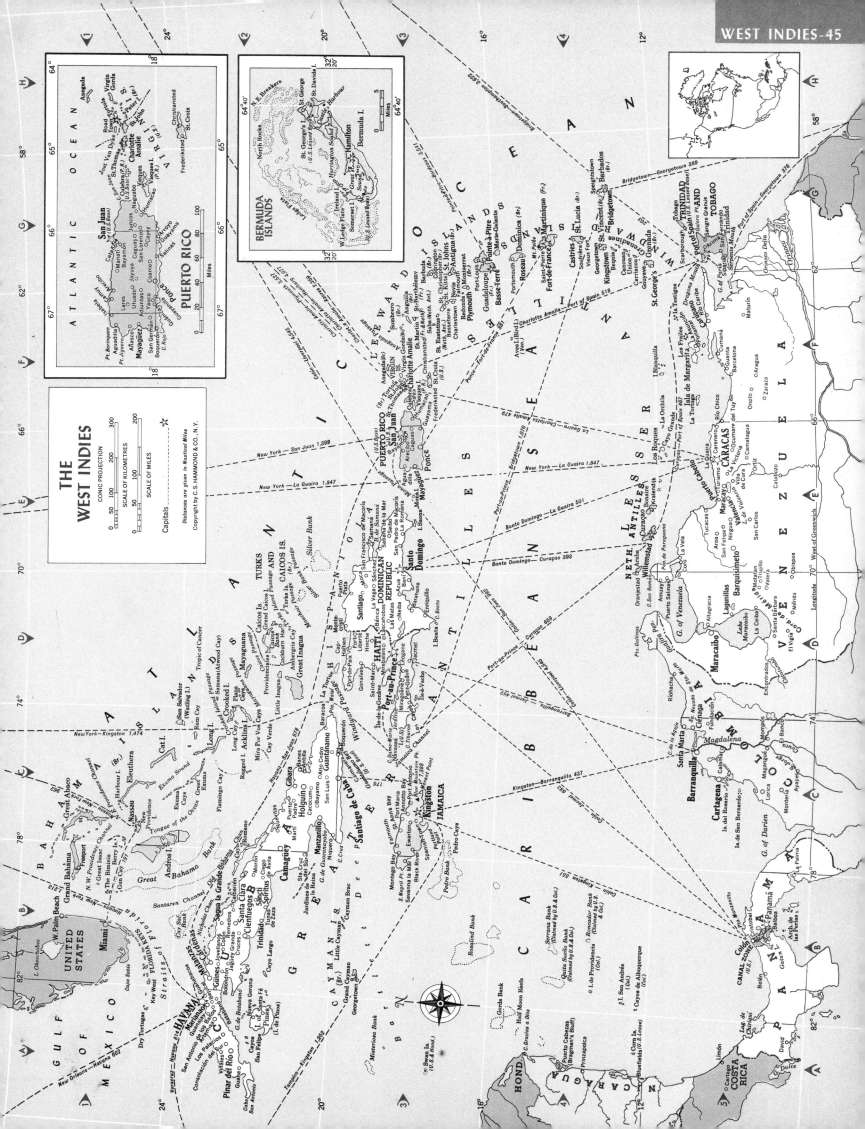

THE
WEST INDIES
CONIC PROJECTION

SCALE OF KILOMETRES
0 50 100 200 300

SCALE OF MILES
0 50 100 200

Capitals ............ ☆

Distances are given in Nautical Miles
Copyright by C.S. HAMMOND & CO., N.Y.

PUERTO RICO

BERMUDA ISLANDS

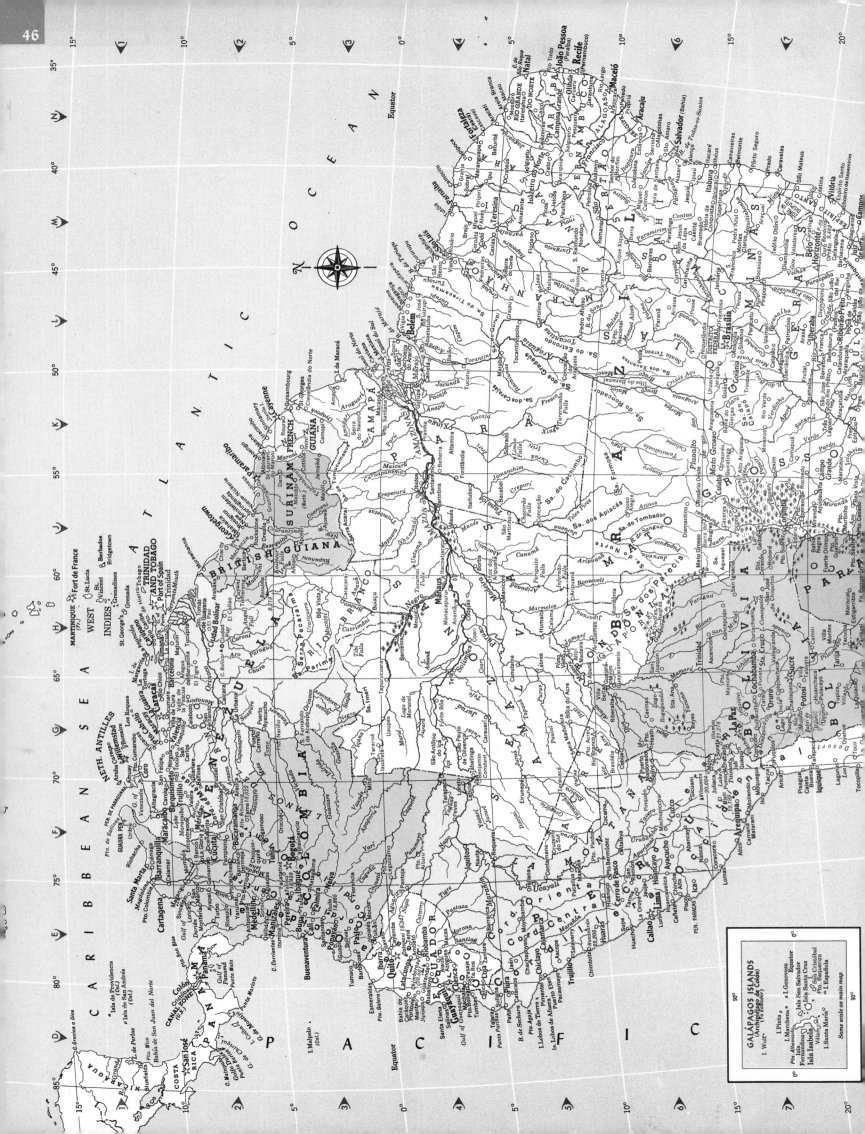

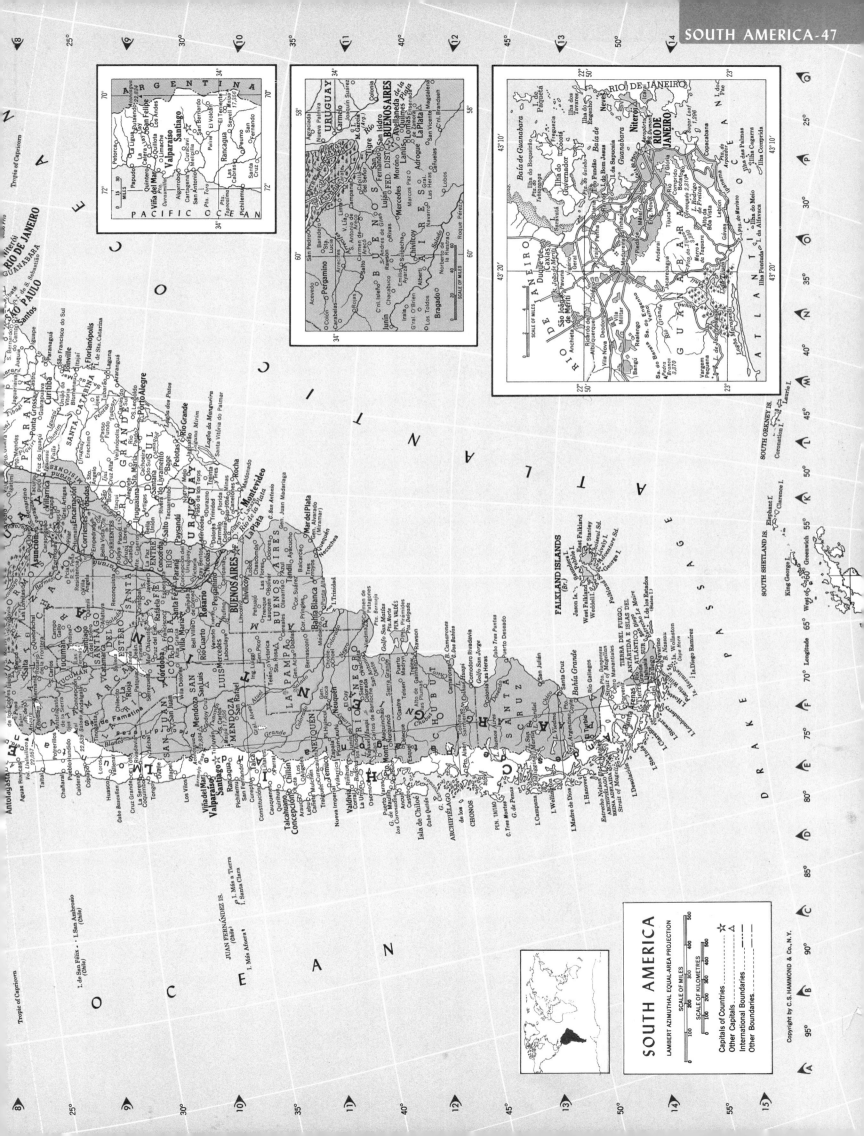

SOUTH AMERICA

LAMBERT AZIMUTHAL EQUAL-AREA PROJECTION

SCALE OF MILES

SCALE OF KILOMETRES

Capitals of Countries
Other Capitals
International Boundaries
Other Boundaries

Copyright by C.S. HAMMOND & Co., N.Y.

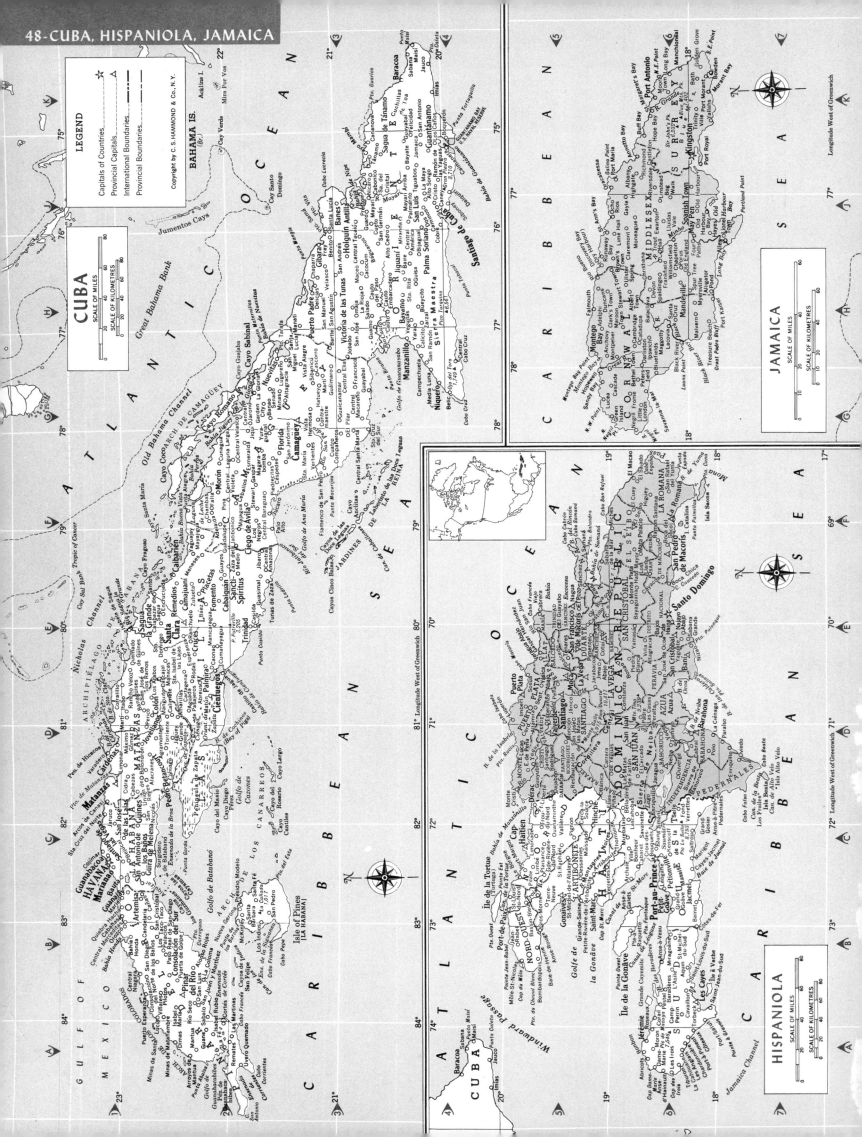

**LEGEND**

Capitals of Countries........... ⋆
Provincial Capitals.............. ◎
International Boundaries......... ▬▬▬▬
Provincial Boundaries........... ▬ ▪ ▬ ▪ ▬

Copyright by C. S. HAMMOND & Co., N.Y.

**CUBA**
SCALE OF MILES
SCALE OF KILOMETRES

**JAMAICA**
SCALE OF MILES
SCALE OF KILOMETRES

**HISPANIOLA**
SCALE OF MILES
SCALE OF KILOMETRES

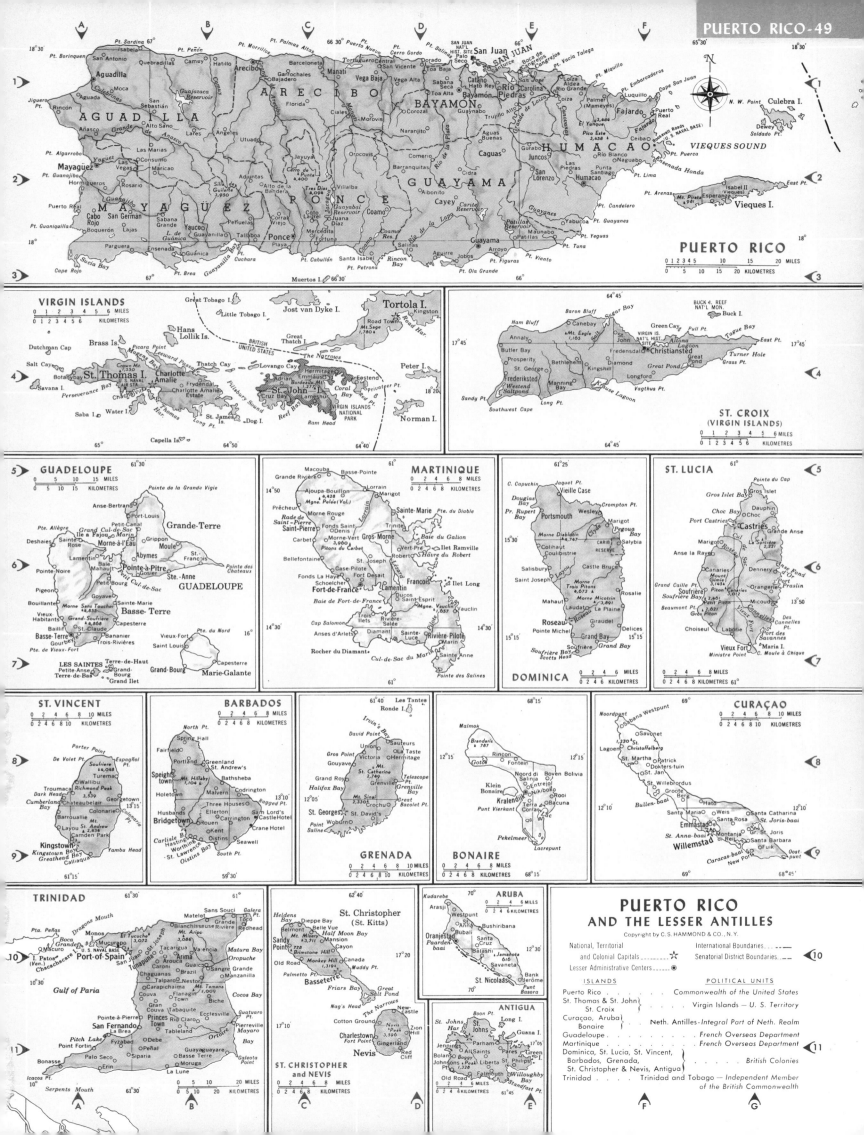

PUERTO RICO

### PUERTO RICO
### AND THE LESSER ANTILLES
Copyright by C.S. HAMMOND & CO., N.Y.

National, Territorial
and Colonial Capitals ........ ☆    International Boundaries ........ ---
Lesser Administrative Centers ........ ◉    Senatorial District Boundaries ........ -·-

| ISLANDS | POLITICAL UNITS |
|---|---|
| Puerto Rico . . . . . . . . | Commonwealth of the United States |
| St. Thomas & St. John | Virgin Islands – U. S. Territory |
| St. Croix | |
| Curaçao, Aruba | Neth. Antilles-Integral Part of Neth. Realm |
| Bonaire | |
| Guadeloupe . . . . . . . . . | French Overseas Department |
| Martinique . . . . . . . . . | French Overseas Department |
| Dominica, St. Lucia, St. Vincent, | |
| Barbados, Grenada, | British Colonies |
| St. Christopher & Nevis, Antigua | |
| Trinidad . . . . . | Trinidad and Tobago — Independent Member of the British Commonwealth |

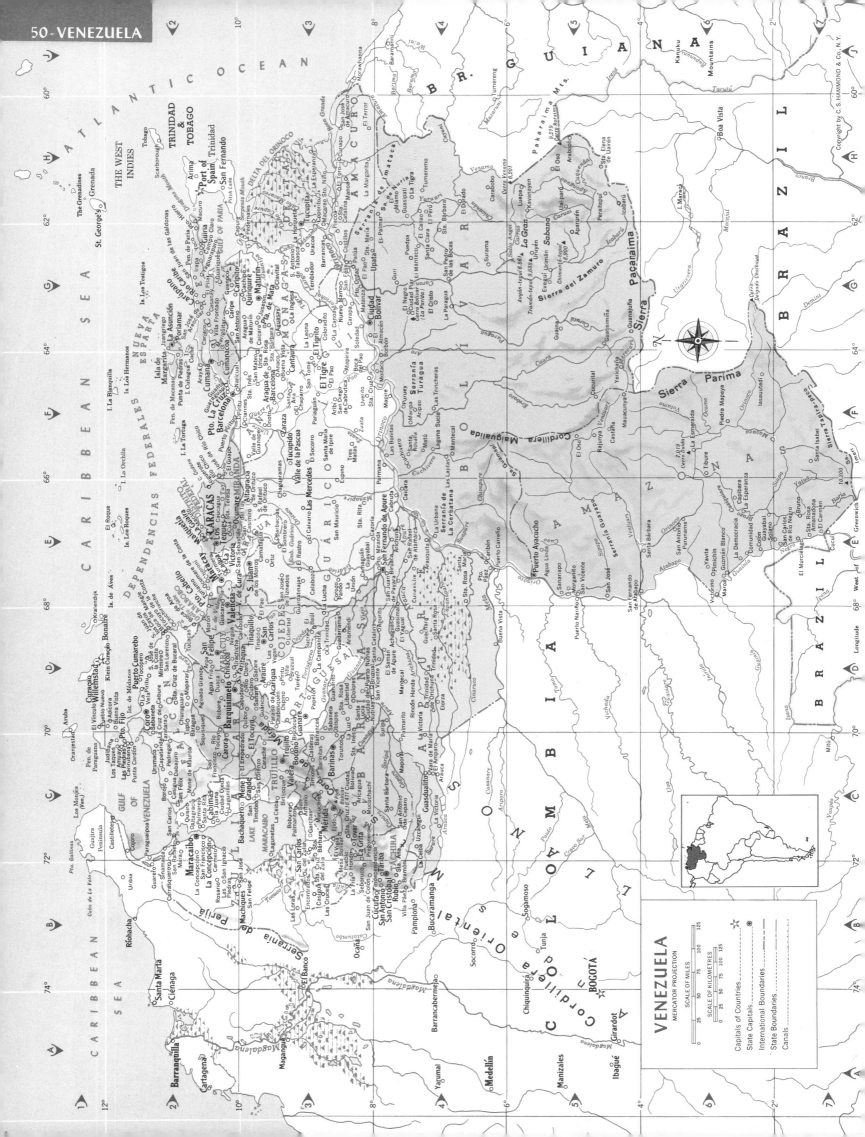

## VENEZUELA

MERCATOR PROJECTION

SCALE OF MILES
0   25   50   75   100   125

SCALE OF KILOMETRES
0   25   50   75   100   125

Capitals of Countries..........★
State Capitals....................◉
International Boundaries.......
State Boundaries.................
Canals.............................

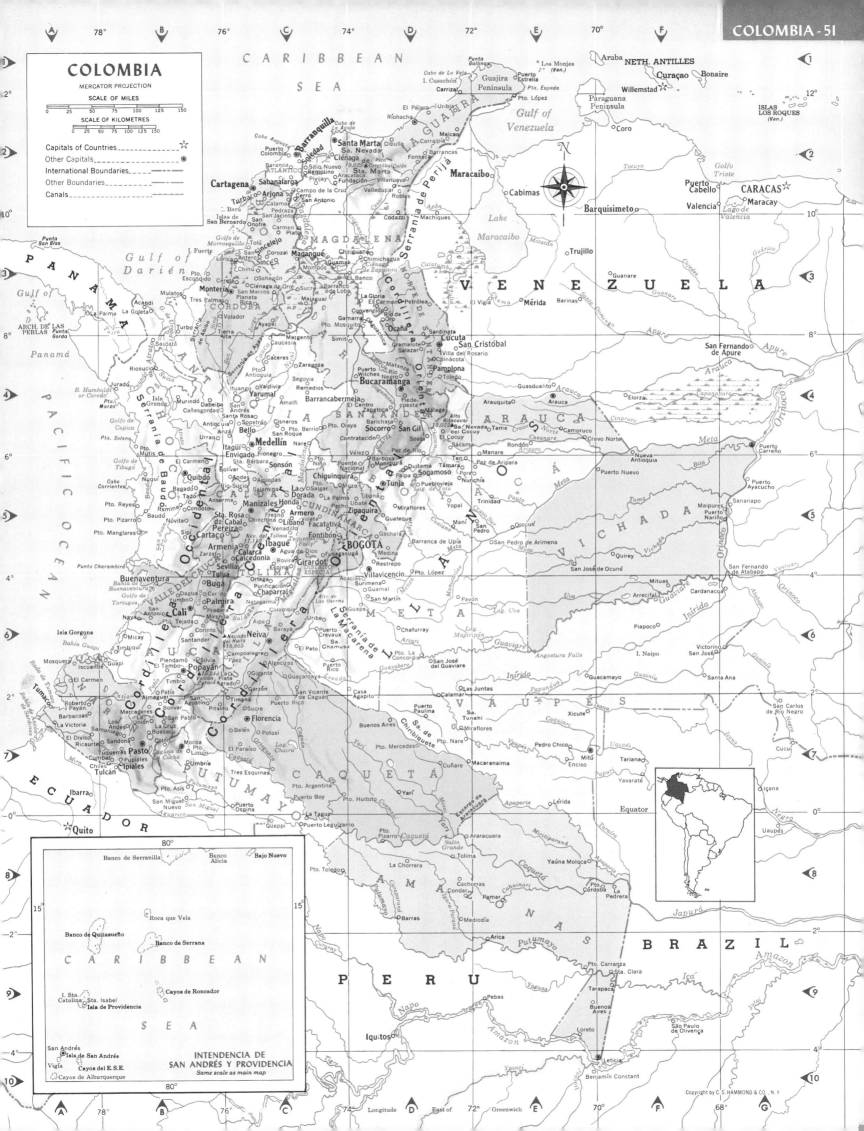

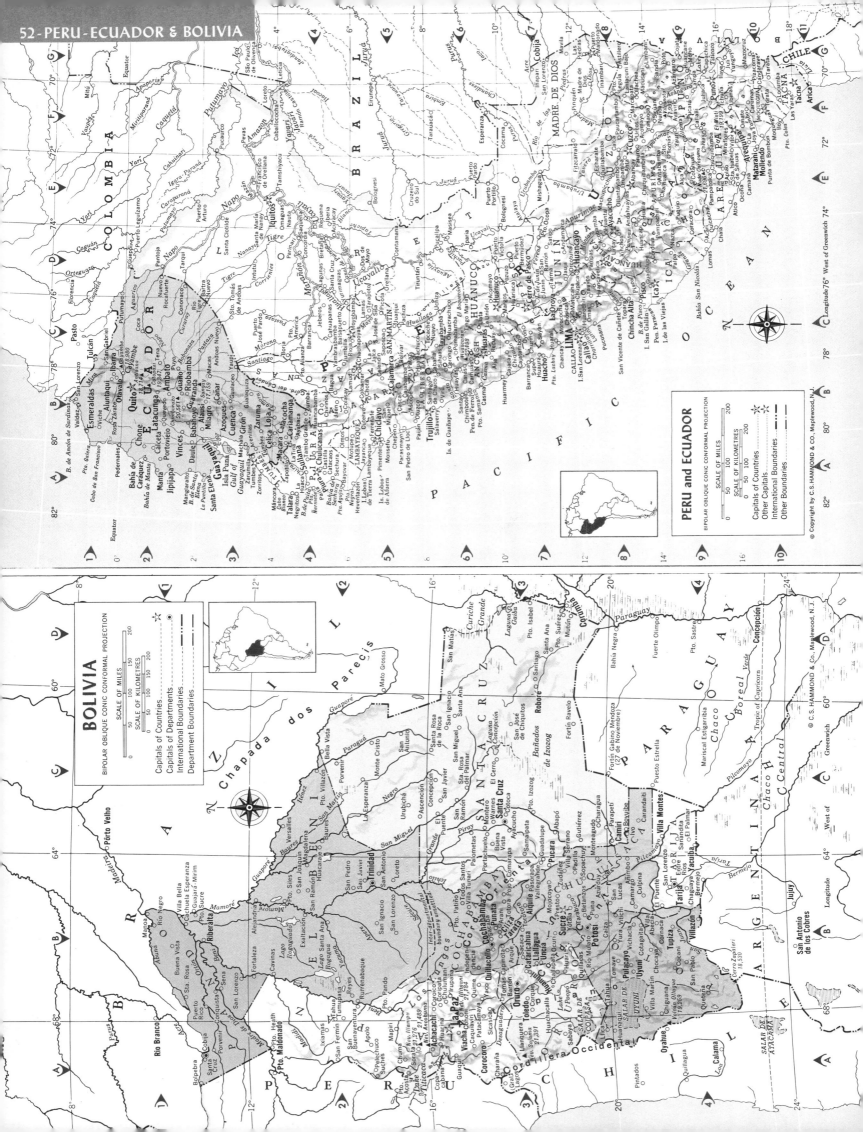

## PERU and ECUADOR

BIPOLAR OBLIQUE CONIC CONFORMAL PROJECTION

SCALE OF MILES
0    50   100   200

SCALE OF KILOMETRES
0   50  100   200

Capitals of Countries ............ ☆
Other Capitals ....................... ☆
International Boundaries .......... —·—
Other Boundaries .................... ——

© Copyright by C.S. HAMMOND & CO., Maplewood, N.J.

## BOLIVIA

BIPOLAR OBLIQUE CONIC CONFORMAL PROJECTION

SCALE OF MILES
0    50   100   150   200

SCALE OF KILOMETRES
0   50  100  150   200

Capitals of Countries .............. ☆ ⊙
Capitals of Departments .......... ○
International Boundaries ........... —·—
Department Boundaries ............ ——

© C.S. HAMMOND & Co., Maplewood, N.J.

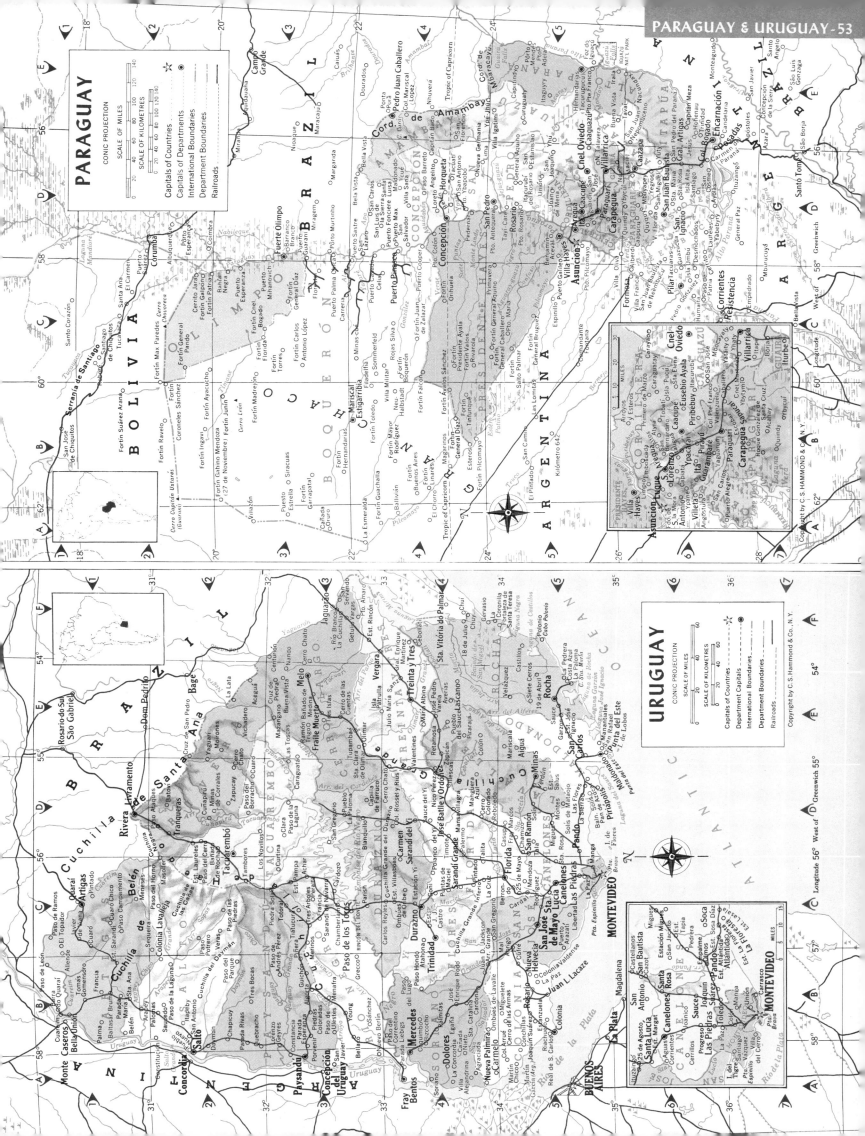

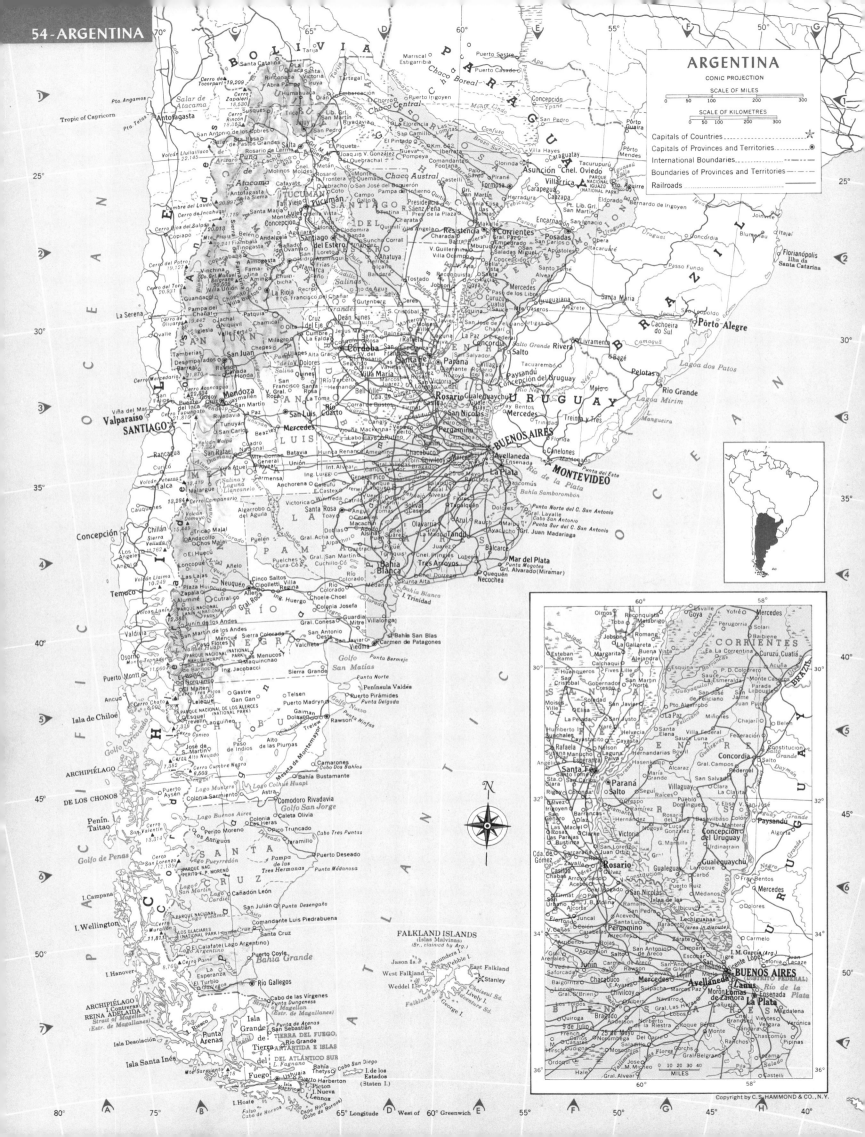

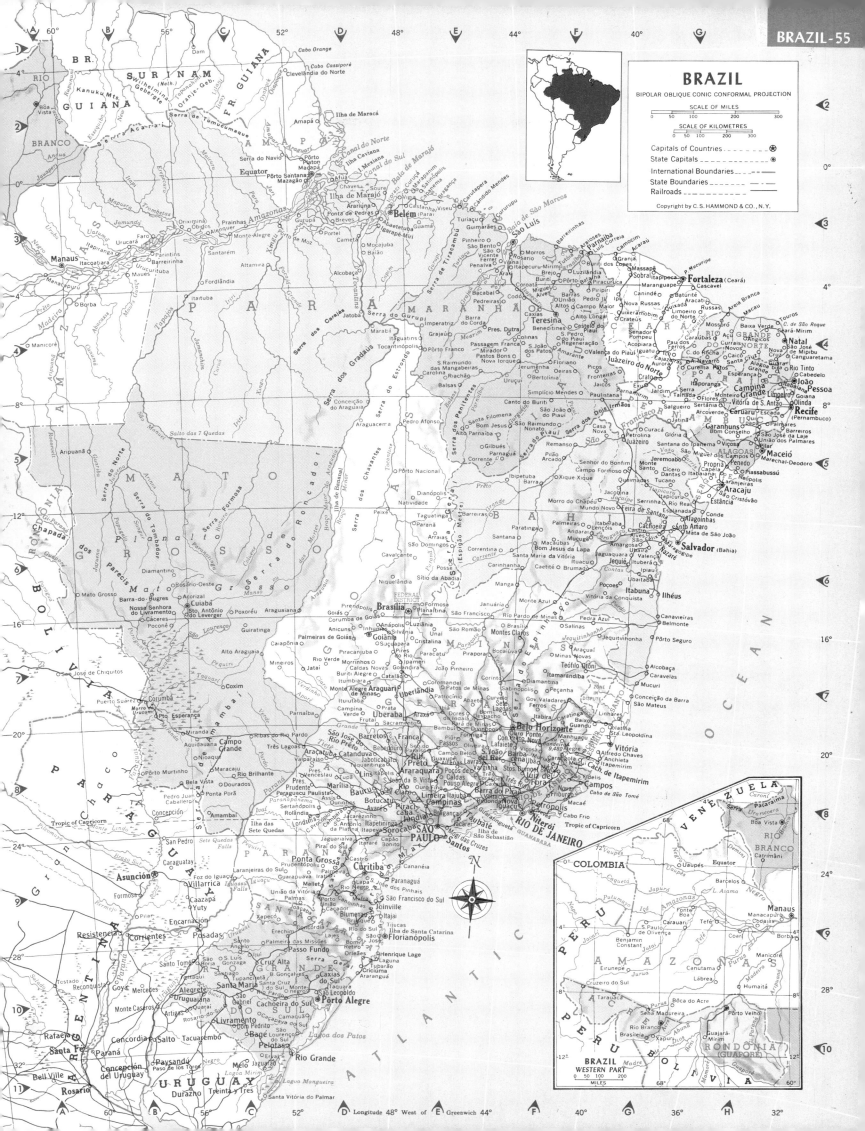

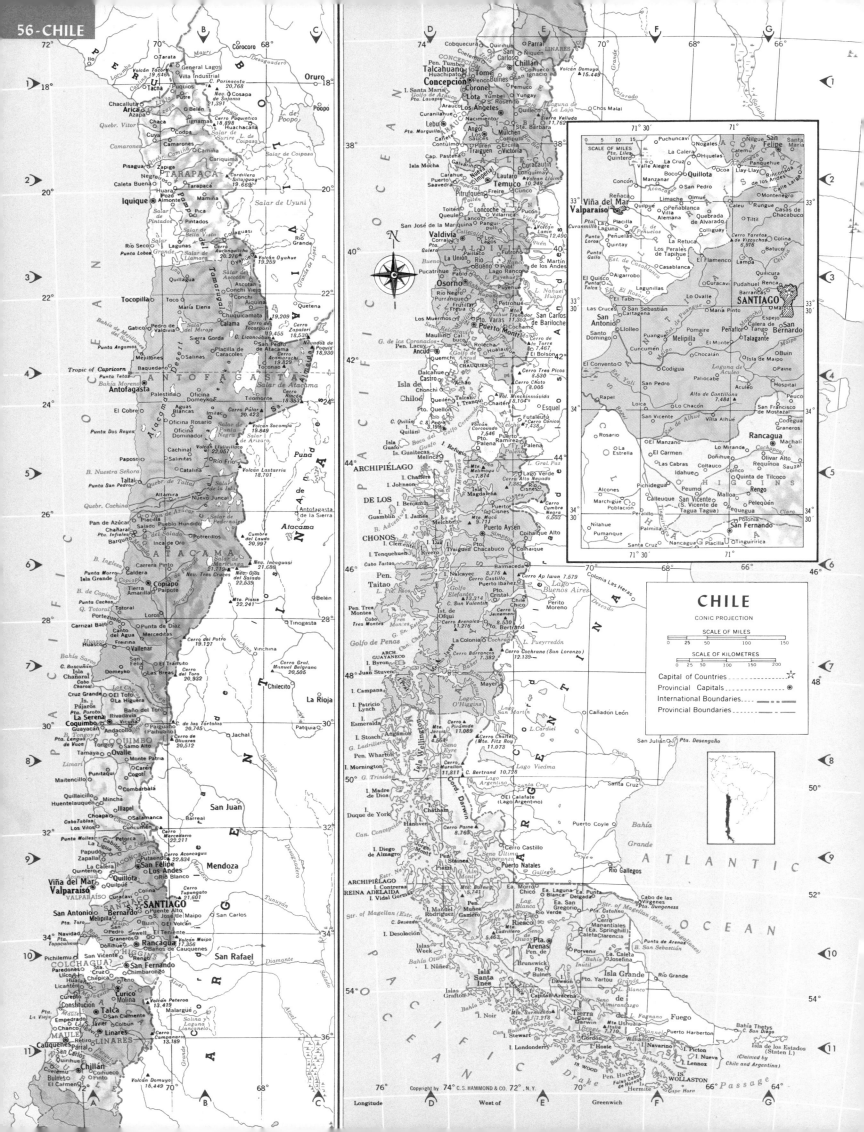

CHILE

CONIC PROJECTION

SCALE OF MILES

0  25  50        100        150

SCALE OF KILOMETRES

0  25  50  100  150  200

Capital of Countries ............... ★
Provincial Capitals ............... ◉
International Boundaries _____
Provincial Boundaries _____

Copyright by C.S. HAMMOND & CO., N.Y.

Longitude     West of     Greenwich

# Index of
# THE WORLD

## *Introduction*

THE INDEX OF THE WORLD gives the principal cities, towns and geographical features (such as mountains, rivers, bays and islands) of the world.

Each entry gives the index reference and the plate number on which the name is found. The name is found within the square formed by the two lines of latitude or longitude which enclose each of the co-ordinates — i.e. the marginal letters and numbers. In the case of maps consisting entirely of insets, the name is found near the intersecting point of the imaginary lines connecting the co-ordinates.

Where space on the map has not permitted giving the complete form of a name, the extended form is shown in the index. Where a place may be known under different names or by various spellings of the name, the different forms have been included to a large extent in the index.

The population figures given are the latest census figures or the latest official estimates.

In the belief that a geographical index should primarily serve to enable the reader to locate names quickly and accurately, we have employed the system of indexing followed in all government publications and telephone directories. All indexes sorted by mechanical means, such as the I.B.M. method, employ this system. Therefore, in alphabetizing, all those compound names with a common first part are grouped together, even though the first letter of the second part of the name may succeed the corresponding letter in a simple name. The three examples shown below are offered to illustrate this system in comparison with the less convenient alternate system of indexing.

### INDEXING SYSTEM USED IN THIS ATLAS

| | | |
|---|---|---|
| San Cristobal | La Ceiba | Bac Kan |
| San Francisco | La Spezia | Bac Lieu |
| San Jose | Labe | Bac Linh |
| Sanchez | Lachlan | Bacabal |
| Sandakan | | Backang |

### ALTERNATE INDEXING SYSTEM

| | | |
|---|---|---|
| Sanchez | Labe | Bacabal |
| San Cristobal | La Ceiba | Bac Kan |
| Sandakan | Lachlan | Backang |
| San Francisco | La Spezia | Bac Lieu |
| San Jose | | Bac Ninh |

As a special feature translations of foreign geographical terms have been incorporated directly into the body of the index. For example: Rio will be found in the index with its English translation. All physical features are listed under their proper names and not according to their generic terms; that is to say, Rio Negro will be found under Negro and not under Rio Negro.

# INDEX OF THE WORLD

Capitals of Countries, States and Provinces are designated by asterisks (*).          Dagger (†) designates Population figure including suburbs.

| | Index Ref. | Plate No. |
|---|---|---|
| Berndorf, Austria, 8,992 | C 3 | 20 |
| Beroun, Czech., 15,946 | B 2 | 20 |
| Berthierville, Quebec, 3,708 | F 4 | 41 |
| Berwick, Nova Scotia, 1,282 | G 4 | 41 |
| Berwick-on-Tweed, Eng., 12,178 | F 2 | 10 |
| Berwyn (mountains), Wales | D 5 | 10 |
| Besançon, France, 90,203 | G 4 | 16 |
| Beşiktaş, Turkey, 93,647 | D 6 | 28 |
| Besni, Turkey, 11,194 | G 4 | 28 |
| Bet-Pak-Dala (steppe), U.S.S.R. | H 5 | 23 |
| Bethanie, S.W. Africa, 1,053 | K17 | 35 |
| Bethlehem, Jordan, 15,777 | C 4 | 24 |
| Bethlehem, O.F.S., 24,176 | M17 | 35 |
| Béthune, France, 22,530 | E 2 | 16 |
| Bettegiri (Gadag), India, 76,614 | C 5 | 29 |
| Bettiah, India, 39,990 | D 3 | 29 |
| Betul, India, 19,860 | C 4 | 29 |
| Beuel, Germany, 31,836 | B 3 | 14 |
| Beuthen (Bytom), Poland, 182,500 | B 4 | 24 |
| Beverley, Australia, 851 | B 2 | 36 |
| Beverley, England, 16,031 | G 4 | 10 |
| Beverwijk, Neth., 8,602 | F 4 | 15 |
| Bexhill-on-Sea, England, 28,941 | H 7 | 10 |
| Beykoz, Turkey, 45,679 | D 5 | 28 |
| Beyoğlu, Turkey, 216,425 | D 6 | 28 |
| Béziers, France, 57,601 | E 6 | 16 |
| Bezwada (Vijayavada), India, 233,634 | D 5 | 29 |
| Bhadrakh, India, 25,285 | E 4 | 29 |
| Bhadravati, India, 24,495 | C 6 | 29 |
| Bhadreswar, India, 35,489 | E 1 | 29 |
| Bhagalpur, India, 143,850 | E 4 | 29 |
| Bhamo, Burma, 9,821 | C 1 | 30 |
| Bhandara, India, 27,710 | D 4 | 29 |
| Bharatpur, India, 49,776 | C 3 | 29 |
| Bhatinda, India, 52,253 | B 2 | 29 |
| Bhatkal, India, 15,070 | B 6 | 29 |
| Bhatpara, India, 147,630 | E 1 | 29 |
| Bhavnagar, India, 171,039 | B 4 | 29 |
| Bhawanipatna, India, 14,300 | D 5 | 29 |
| Bhera, Pakistan, 16,632 | B 2 | 29 |
| Bhilwara, India, 43,499 | B 3 | 29 |
| Bhimavaram, India, 43,821 | D 5 | 29 |
| Bhiwandi, India, 47,630 | B 5 | 29 |
| Bhiwani, India, 58,194 | C 3 | 29 |
| Bhopal, India, 185,374 | C 4 | 29 |
| Bhuj, India, 38,953 | A 4 | 29 |
| Bhusawal, India, 73,994 | C 4 | 29 |
| Biafra (bay), Africa | H11 | 35 |
| Biała Podlaska, Poland, 19,200 | F 2 | 24 |
| Białogard (Belgard), Poland, 17,700 | B 2 | 24 |
| Białystok, Poland, 120,800 | F 2 | 24 |
| Biancavilla, Italy, †20,010 | E 6 | 18 |
| Biarritz, France, 24,273 | C 6 | 16 |
| Bibai, Japan, 87,345 | L 2 | 33 |
| Biberach, Germany, 21,524 | C 4 | 14 |
| Bic, Quebec, 1,177 | G 4 | 41 |
| Bida, Nigeria, 50,000 | H10 | 34 |
| Bidar, India, 32,420 | C 5 | 29 |
| Biel (Bienne), Switz., 59,216 | D 2 | 19 |
| Bielawa, Poland, 27,000 | C 3 | 24 |
| Bielefeld, Germany, 174,642 | C 2 | 14 |
| Biella, Italy, †50,209 | B 2 | 18 |
| Bielsko-Biała, Poland, 71,600 | D 4 | 24 |
| Bien Hoa, S. Vietnam, 33,820 | E 5 | 30 |
| Bienfait, Sask., 842 | K 5 | 40 |
| Bienne (Biel), Switz., 59,216 | D 2 | 19 |
| Big Beaver, Saskatchewan, 100 | J 5 | 40 |
| Big River, Saskatchewan, 896 | J 4 | 40 |
| Biga, Turkey, 10,845 | B 2 | 28 |
| Biggar, Saskatchewan, 2,702 | J 4 | 40 |
| Bighorn (mountains), Wyoming | G 3 | 42 |
| Bighorn (river), U.S. | G 3 | 42 |
| Bihać, Yugoslavia, 15,763 | B 3 | 21 |
| Bihar, India, 78,581 | E 3 | 29 |
| Bijapur, India, 78,854 | C 5 | 29 |
| Bijar, Iran, 7,920 | E 3 | 27 |
| Bijeljina, Yugoslavia, 17,340 | D 3 | 21 |
| Bijnor, India, 33,821 | C 3 | 29 |
| Bikaner, India, 150,634 | B 3 | 29 |
| Bikini (island), Marshall Is. | G 4 | 37 |
| Bilaspur, India, 86,706 | D 4 | 29 |
| Bilbao, Spain, †297,942 | E 1 | 17 |
| Billiton (Belitung) (island), Indonesia, 102,375 | D 6 | 31 |
| Bilma, Niger, 1,300 | J 8 | 34 |
| Bilston, England, 33,067 | E 5 | 10 |
| Bindjai, Indonesia, 45,235 | B 5 | 31 |
| Bingara, Australia, 1,485 | H 5 | 36 |
| Bingen, Germany, 20,210 | B 4 | 14 |
| Bingerville, Ivory Coast, 2,500 | F10 | 34 |
| Binghamton, N.Y., 75,941 | P 4 | 43 |
| Bingöl (Çapakçur), Turkey, 8,526 | J 3 | 28 |
| Binh Dinh, S. Vietnam, 18,350 | F 4 | 30 |
| Bintuhan, Indon., 1,918 | C 6 | 31 |
| Binyamina, Israel, 2,950 | B 2 | 24 |
| Biograd, Yugoslavia, 2,491 | B 4 | 24 |
| Bir (Bhir), India, 33,066 | C 5 | 29 |
| Bird (isl.), Australia | K 4 | 36 |
| Birecik, Turkey, 13,110 | G 4 | 28 |
| Birjand, Iran, 13,934 | L 4 | 27 |
| Birkenhead, England, 141,813 | D 4 | 10 |
| Bîrlad, Rumania, 32,040 | H 2 | 21 |
| Birmingham, Ala., 340,887 | M 6 | 43 |
| Birmingham, England, 1,107,187 | F 5 | 10 |
| Birobidzhan, U.S.S.R., 40,667 | O 5 | 23 |
| Birsk, U.S.S.R., 24,837 | J 3 | 22 |
| Birtle, Man., 846 | K 4 | 40 |
| Biscay (bay) | B 5 | 16 |
| Bisceglie, Italy, †41,451 | F 4 | 18 |
| Bischofshofen, Austria, 8,287 | B 3 | 20 |
| Biscotasing, Ontario, 200 | D 4 | 41 |
| Bishop Auckland, England, 35,314 | F 3 | 10 |
| Bishops Falls, Newf., 3,393 | K 4 | 41 |
| Biskra, Algeria, †66,563 | H 5 | 34 |
| Bislig, Philippine Isls., 1,968 | H 4 | 31 |
| Bismarck,* N. Dak., 27,870 | H 3 | 42 |
| Bismarck (archipelago), Terr. N.G., 145,000 | E 6 | 37 |
| Bissagos (isls.), Port. Guinea, 9,763 | C 9 | 34 |
| Bissau,* Port. Guinea, 47,251 | D 9 | 34 |
| Bissett, Manitoba, 770 | L 4 | 40 |
| Bistriţa, Rumania, 20,292 | G 2 | 21 |
| Bitlis, Turkey, 16,636 | J 3 | 28 |
| Bitola (Bitolj), Yugo., 49,001 | E 5 | 21 |
| Bitonto, Italy, †37,395 | F 4 | 18 |
| Bitterfeld, Germany, 30,882 | E 3 | 14 |
| Bitterroot (mt. range), U.S. | E 3 | 42 |
| Biwa (lake), Japan | H 6 | 33 |
| Biysk, U.S.S.R., 162,000 | J 4 | 23 |
| Bizerte, Tunisia, 44,681 | J 4 | 34 |
| Bjelovar, Yugoslavia, 15,761 | C 3 | 21 |
| Björneborg (Pori), Finland, 54,024 | M 6 | 13 |
| Black (hills), United States | H 3 | 42 |
| Black (sea) | H 4 | 9 |
| Black (Schwarzwald) (forest), Germany | C 5 | 14 |
| Black Diamond, Alberta, 1,043 | H 4 | 40 |
| Black River, Jamaica, 2,612 | B 3 | 45 |
| Black Rock (desert), Nevada | D 4 | 42 |
| Black Volta (river), Africa | F 9 | 34 |
| Blackall, Australia, 2,217 | G 4 | 36 |
| Blackburn, England, 106,242 | E 4 | 10 |
| Blackpool, England, 153,185 | D 4 | 10 |
| Blacktown, Australia, 86,295 | K 3 | 36 |
| Blackwater (river), Ireland | D 7 | 12 |
| Blagodarnoye, U.S.S.R. | F 5 | 22 |
| Blagoveshchensk, U.S.S.R., 94,746 | N 4 | 23 |
| Blagoyevgrad, Bulgaria, 14,066 | F 5 | 21 |
| Blaine Lake, Saskatchewan, 641 | J 4 | 40 |
| Blair Athol, Australia, 405 | H 4 | 36 |
| Blairmore, Alberta, 1,980 | H 5 | 40 |
| Blaj, Rumania, 8,731 | G 2 | 21 |
| Blanc (cape), Africa | C 7 | 34 |
| Blanc (mountain), France | G 5 | 16 |
| Blanca Peak (mountain), Colo. | G 5 | 42 |
| Blanco (cape), Oregon | B 4 | 42 |
| Blankenburg, Germany, 19,385 | D 3 | 14 |
| Blantyre-Limbe, Malawi, †40,498 | N15 | 35 |
| Blasket (isls.), Ireland | A 7 | 12 |
| Blaydon-on-Tyne, England, 30,292 | F 3 | 10 |
| Blaze (point), Australia | D 2 | 36 |
| Blenheim, New Zealand, 11,956 | L 6 | 36 |
| Blida, Algeria, 38,067 | G 4 | 34 |
| Blind River, Ontario, 4,093 | D 4 | 41 |
| Blitar, Indonesia, 62,972 | K 2 | 31 |
| Bloemfontein,* O.F.S., †140,924 | L17 | 35 |
| Blois, France, 30,081 | D 4 | 16 |
| Bloody Foreland (prom.), Ireland | D 1 | 12 |
| Blora, Indonesia, 49,296 | K 2 | 31 |
| Bludenz, Austria, 11,127 | B 4 | 20 |
| Blue (mountains), U.S. | D 3 | 42 |
| Blue Mountains, Aust., 28,119 | J 6 | 36 |
| Blue Mud (bay), Australia | F 2 | 36 |
| Blue Nile (river), Africa | N 9 | 34 |
| Blue River, Br. Columbia, 352 | G 4 | 40 |
| Bluefields, Nicaragua, 12,293 | F 4 | 39 |
| Bluff, New Zealand, 3,042 | L 7 | 36 |
| Blumenau, Brazil, 22,627 | L 9 | 47 |
| Blyth, England, 35,921 | F 2 | 10 |
| Bôa Vista, Brazil, 10,180 | H 3 | 46 |
| Bobbili, India, 25,592 | D 5 | 29 |
| Bobo-Dioulasso, Upper Volta, 56,100 | F 9 | 34 |
| Bobruysk, U.S.S.R., 104,000 | C 4 | 22 |
| Bôca do Acre, Brazil, 2,994 | G 5 | 46 |
| Bochnia, Poland, 11,800 | E 4 | 24 |
| Bocholt, Germany, 45,675 | B 3 | 14 |
| Bochum, Germany, 361,382 | B 3 | 14 |
| Bodaybo, U.S.S.R., 18,226 | M 4 | 23 |
| Bodensee (Constance) (lake) | H 1 | 19 |
| Bodhan, India, 30,929 | C 5 | 29 |
| Bodjonegoro, Indonesia, †61,749 | J 2 | 31 |
| Bodö, Norway, 12,618 | J 3 | 13 |
| Boggeragh (mountains), Ireland | D 7 | 12 |
| Bognor Regis, England, 28,064 | G 7 | 10 |
| Bogor, Indonesia, 154,092 | H 2 | 31 |
| Bogotá,* Colombia, †1,123,600 | F 3 | 46 |
| Bogra, Pakistan, 24,996 | E 4 | 29 |
| Boguchar, U.S.S.R. | F 5 | 22 |
| Bohemian (forest) | B 2 | 20 |
| Boise,* Idaho, 34,481 | E 4 | 42 |
| Boissevain, Manitoba, 1,303 | L 5 | 40 |
| Bojador (cape), Sp. Sahara | C 6 | 34 |
| Boké, Guinea, 6,000 | D 9 | 34 |
| Bolama, Port. Guinea, 4,895 | D 9 | 34 |
| Bolangir, India, 18,663 | D 4 | 29 |
| Bolbeck, France, 11,922 | D 3 | 16 |
| Bolesławiec, Poland, 20,300 | B 3 | 24 |
| Bolívar, Argentina, 14,010 | H11 | 44 |
| Bolívar, Colombia, 2,495 | E 3 | 46 |
| Bolívar (peak), Venezuela | F 2 | 46 |
| Bolligen, Switz., 14,914 | E 3 | 19 |
| Bologna, Italy, †444,872 | C 2 | 18 |
| Bologoye, U.S.S.R., 30,301 | D 3 | 22 |
| Bol'shevik (island), U.S.S.R. | K 2 | 23 |
| Bolsón de Mapimí (dep.), Mexico | G 3 | 44 |
| Bolton, England, 160,789 | E 4 | 10 |
| Bolu, Turkey, 13,745 | D 2 | 28 |
| Bolus Head (cape), Ireland | A 8 | 12 |
| Bolvadin, Turkey, 16,026 | D 3 | 28 |
| Bolzano, Italy, †88,799 | C 1 | 18 |
| Boma, R.o.t. Congo, 33,143 | J13 | 35 |
| Bombala, Australia, 1,389 | H 7 | 36 |
| Bombay, India, †4,152,056 | B 8 | 29 |
| Bomu (river), R.o.t. Congo | L11 | 34 |
| Bonaire (island), Neth. Antilles, 5,812 | C 1 | 46 |
| Bonaventure, Que., 1,000 | G 4 | 41 |
| Bonavista, Newfoundland, 4,186 | K 4 | 41 |
| Bondoukou, Ivory Coast, 5,216 | F10 | 34 |
| Bondowoso, Indonesia, †44,215 | L 2 | 31 |
| Bondy, France, 38,032 | B 1 | 16 |
| Bône, Algeria, 88,920 | H 4 | 34 |
| Bong Son, S. Vietnam | F 4 | 30 |
| Bonin-Volcano (islands), Pacific, 210 | E 3 | 37 |
| Bonn,* West Germany, 143,850 | B 3 | 14 |
| Bonne Bay, Newfoundland, 509 | J 4 | 41 |
| Bonnyville, Alberta, 1,736 | H 4 | 40 |
| Bonthain, Indonesia, †48,289 | F 7 | 31 |
| Bontoc, Philippine Isls., 5,472 | G 2 | 31 |
| Boom, Belgium, 17,468 | E 6 | 15 |
| Boothia (gulf), N.W. Terrs. | B14 | 8 |
| Boothia (peninsula), N.W. Terrs. | B14 | 8 |
| Bootle, England, 82,773 | D 4 | 10 |
| Bor, Turkey, 13,169 | F 4 | 28 |
| Bor, Yugoslavia, 18,496 | E 3 | 21 |
| Borah Peak (mountain), Idaho | E 3 | 42 |
| Borås, Sweden, 67,272 | H 8 | 13 |
| Borazjun, Iran, 10,233 | G 6 | 27 |
| Borba, Brazil, 1,030 | J 4 | 46 |
| Bordeaux, France, 246,186 | C 5 | 16 |
| Bordertown, Australia, 1,546 | G 7 | 36 |
| Borgerhout, Belgium, 51,182 | E 6 | 15 |
| Borisoglebsk, U.S.S.R., 54,415 | F 4 | 22 |
| Borisov, U.S.S.R., 59,280 | C 4 | 22 |
| Borlänge, Sweden, 26,334 | J 6 | 13 |
| Bornholm (island), Denmark, 48,217 | J 9 | 13 |
| Borovichi, U.S.S.R., 44,123 | D 3 | 22 |
| Borzya, U.S.S.R., 23,680 | M 4 | 23 |
| Bosanska Gradiška, Yugo., 6,363 | C 3 | 21 |
| Bosaso, Somali Rep., 6,359 | R 9 | 34 |
| Bosporus (Karadeniz) (strait), Turkey | C 2 | 28 |
| Boston, England, 24,915 | H 5 | 10 |
| Boston,* Mass., 697,197 | R 2 | 43 |
| Botany, Australia, 28,904 | L 3 | 36 |
| Bothnia (gulf) | N 4 | 13 |
| Botoşani, Rumania, 29,569 | H 2 | 21 |
| Bottrop, Germany, 111,548 | B 3 | 14 |
| Botucatu, Brazil, 33,878 | L 8 | 47 |
| Botwood, Newfoundland, 3,680 | J 4 | 41 |
| Bouaké, Ivory Coast, 45,340 | F10 | 34 |
| Boucaut (bay), Australia | E 2 | 36 |
| Bougainville (cape), Australia | D 2 | 36 |
| Bougainville (reef), Australia | H 3 | 36 |
| Bougainville (island), Territory N.G., 37,000 | F 6 | 37 |
| Bougie, Algeria, 29,748 | G 4 | 34 |
| Bougouni, Mali, 5,000 | E 9 | 34 |
| Boulder, Australia, 5,773 | C 6 | 36 |
| Boulia, Australia, 179 | G 4 | 36 |
| Boulogne-Billancourt, France, 106,559 | A 2 | 16 |
| Boulogne-sur-Mer, France, 49,036 | D 2 | 16 |
| Boundary Peak (mountain), U.S. | D 5 | 42 |
| Bourem, Mali, 1,732 | G 8 | 34 |
| Bourg-en-Bresse, France, 28,813 | F 4 | 16 |
| Bourges, France, 55,216 | E 4 | 16 |
| Bourke, Australia, 3,001 | H 6 | 36 |
| Bourlamaque, Quebec, 3,344 | E 4 | 41 |
| Bournemouth, England, 154,296 | F 7 | 10 |
| Boutilimit, Mauritania, 3,000 | C 8 | 34 |
| Bow (river), Alta. | H 4 | 40 |
| Bow Island, Alberta, 1,122 | H 5 | 40 |
| Bowen, Australia, 5,160 | H 3 | 36 |
| Bowling Green (cape), Australia | H 3 | 36 |
| Boyne (river), Ireland | J 4 | 12 |
| Bozen (Bolzano), Italy, †88,799 | C 1 | 18 |
| Bozhüyük, Turkey, 9,101 | C 3 | 28 |
| Bra, Italy, †12,742 | A 2 | 18 |
| Bracebridge, Ontario, 2,927 | D 4 | 41 |
| Brackwede, Germany, 25,999 | C 3 | 14 |
| Bradford, England, 295,922 | F 4 | 10 |
| Braga, Portugal, 41,023 | B 2 | 17 |
| Bragado, Argentina, 16,104 | M12 | 47 |
| Bragança, Brazil, 12,848 | L 4 | 46 |
| Bragança, Portugal, 8,554 | C 2 | 17 |
| Brahmaputra (river) | F 3 | 29 |
| Braich-y-pwll (cape), Wales | B 5 | 10 |
| Brăila, Rumania, 102,500 | H 3 | 21 |
| Braintree, England, 10,732 | H 6 | 10 |
| Brake, Germany, 15,939 | C 2 | 14 |
| Bralorne, Br. Columbia, 613 | F 4 | 40 |
| Branco (river), Brazil | H 3 | 46 |
| Brandenburg, Germany, 87,993 | E 2 | 14 |
| Brandon (mountain), Ireland | A 7 | 12 |
| Brandon, Manitoba, 28,166 | K 5 | 40 |
| Brandon and Byshottles, England, 19,868 | F 3 | 10 |
| Brandvlei, C. of G. Hope, 1,417 | E19 | 35 |
| Brantford, Ontario, 55,201 | D 5 | 41 |
| Brasília,* Brazil, 180,000 | L 7 | 46 |
| Braşov, Rumania, 123,834 | G 3 | 21 |
| Bratislava, Czech., 257,856 | D 2 | 20 |
| Bratsk, U.S.S.R., 51,455 | L 4 | 23 |
| Braunau, Austria, 14,449 | B 2 | 20 |
| Braunschweig (Brunswick), Germany, 246,085 | D 2 | 14 |
| Brava (Barawa), Somali Rep., †7,160 | P11 | 35 |
| Bravo (river), Mexico | H 2 | 44 |
| Bray (Brí Chualann), Ireland, 11,680 | K 6 | 12 |
| Brazos (river), Texas | J 7 | 42 |
| Brazzaville,* R.o. Congo, 135,638 | K12 | 35 |
| Brčko, Yugoslavia, 12,290 | D 3 | 21 |
| Brebes, Indonesia, †72,971 | H 2 | 31 |
| Brecon Beacons (mt.), Wales | D 6 | 16 |
| Breda, Netherlands, 107,875 | F 5 | 15 |
| Bregenz, Austria, 21,428 | A 3 | 20 |
| Breidhifjördhur (fjord), Iceland | B 2 | 9 |
| Brejo, Brazil, 3,084 | M 4 | 46 |
| Bremen, Germany, 564,517 | C 2 | 14 |
| Bremerhaven, Germany, 141,849 | C 2 | 14 |
| Brentwood, England, 49,242 | H 6 | 10 |
| Brescia, Italy, †172,744 | C 2 | 18 |
| Breslau (Wrocław), Poland, 429,200 | C 3 | 24 |
| Bressay (island), Scotland, 269 | N 3 | 11 |
| Brest, France, 130,867 | A 3 | 16 |
| Brest, U.S.S.R., 73,557 | B 4 | 22 |
| Brewarrina, Australia, 1,225 | H 5 | 36 |
| Brí Chualann (Bray), Ireland, 11,680 | K 5 | 12 |
| Bridgend, Wales, 15,174 | D 6 | 10 |
| Bridgeport, Conn., 156,748 | O 2 | 43 |
| Bridgetown,* Barbados, 11,304 | G 4 | 45 |
| Bridgewater, Nova Scotia, 4,497 | H 5 | 41 |
| Bridgwater, England, 25,600 | D 6 | 10 |
| Bridlington, England, 26,023 | G 3 | 10 |
| Bridlington (bay), England | G 3 | 10 |
| Brighouse, England, 30,804 | F 4 | 10 |
| Bright, Australia, 803 | H 7 | 36 |
| Brighton, Australia, 41,302 | L 2 | 36 |
| Brighton, England, 163,159 | G 7 | 10 |
| Brindisi, Italy, †70,657 | G 4 | 18 |
| Brisbane, Australia, †621,550 | J 5 | 36 |
| Bristol, England, 437,048 | E 6 | 10 |
| Bristol (channel), England | C 6 | 10 |
| Britstown, C. of G. Hope, 2,834 | L18 | 35 |
| Britt, Ontario, 225 | D 4 | 41 |
| Brive-la-Gaillarde, France, 38,105 | D 5 | 16 |
| Brno (Brünn), Czech., 323,309 | D 2 | 20 |
| Broach, India, 73,639 | B 4 | 29 |
| Broad (sound), Australia | H 4 | 36 |
| Broadstairs-Saint Peter's, Eng., 16,991 | J 6 | 10 |
| Brockville, Ontario, 17,744 | E 5 | 41 |
| Brod, Yugoslavia, 28,810 | D 3 | 21 |
| Brodeur (peninsula), N.W. Terrs. | B14 | 8 |
| Brodnica, Poland, 14,500 | D 2 | 24 |
| Broken Hill, Australia, 31,267 | G 6 | 36 |
| Broken Hill, N. Rhodesia, †33,890 | M14 | 35 |
| Bromberg (Bydgoszcz), Poland, 231,500 | D 2 | 24 |
| Bromsgrove, England, 34,497 | E 5 | 10 |
| Bronte, Italy, †21,619 | E 6 | 18 |
| Brooks, Alberta, 2,827 | H 4 | 40 |

*Index Ref. Plate No.*
Jarocin, Poland, 15,500...C 3 24
Jaroměř, Czech., 11,853...C 1 20
Jarosław, Poland, 26,200...F 3 24
Jarrow, England, 28,811...F 3 10
Jarvis (island), Pacific, 3...K 6 37
Jask, Iran, 1,078...K 8 27
Jasper, Alberta, 2,360...G 4 40
Jasper (park), Alberta, 2,902...G 4 40
Jassy (Iaşi), Rumania, 112,977...H 2 21
Jászárokszállás, Hung., 11,131...E 3 20
Jaszberény, Hungary, 30,322...E 5 20
Játiva, Spain, †19,896...F 3 17
Jaú, Brazil, 31,229...L 8 46
Jauf, Saudi Arabia, 7,500...C 4 26
Jauja, Peru, 12,673...E 6 46
Jaunpur, India, 61,851...D 3 29
Java (island), Indonesia, 60,909,381...D 7 31
Java (sea)...D 6 31
Javarí (Yavarí) (river), S.A. ...F 4 36
Jawor (Jauer), Poland, 12,900...C 3 24
Jaworzno, Poland, 49,500...D 3 24
Jedrzejów, Poland, 11,900...E 3 24
Jefferson City,* Mo., 28,288...K 5 43
Jelenia Góra, Poland, 47,900...B 3 24
Jelgava, U.S.S.R., 36,300...B 3 22
Jemappes, Belg., 13,092...D 8 15
Jena, Germany, 82,113...D 3 14
Jenin, Jordan, 13,854...C 3 24
Jequié, Brazil, 40,158...M 6 46
Jérémie, Haiti, 12,456...A 6 48
Jerez de la Frontera, Spain, 96,209...C 4 17
Jerez de los Caballeros, Spain, 12,349...C 3 17
Jericho (Ariha), Jordan, 10,284...C 4 24
Jerusalem (New City),* Israel, 166,301...C 4 24
Jerusalem (Old City), Jordan, 60,337...C 4 24
Jesenice, Yugoslavia, 15,726...A 2 21
Jesselton,* Sabah, 21,719...F 4 31
Jessore, Pakistan, 23,867...E 4 29
Jette, Belgium, 34,927...B 9 15
Jever, Germany, 9,382...B 2 14
Jeypore, India, 25,291...D 5 29
Jhang-Maghiana, Pak., 73,397...B 2 29
Jhansi, India, 140,217...C 3 29
Jhelum, Pakistan, 38,567...B 2 29
Jhunjhunu, India, 24,962...C 3 29
Jibhalanta (Uliassutai), Mongolia, 6,000...E 2 32
Jidda, Saudi Arabia, 80,000...C 5 26
Jihlava, Czech., 36,487...C 2 20
Jijiga, Ethiopia, 11,000...P10 34
Jimma, Ethiopia, 8,000...O10 34
Jind, India, 24,216...C 3 29
Jinja, Uganda, 29,741...N11 35
Jinotepe, Nicaragua, 17,239...D 5 39
Jinsen (Inch'ŏn), S. Korea, 402,009...C 5 33
Jiparaná (river), Brazil...H 6 46
Jirgalanta (Kobdo), Mongolia, 10,000...D 2 32
João Pessoa (Paraíba), Brazil, 89,517...O 5 46
Jódar, Spain, 14,289...E 4 17
Jodhpur, India, 224,760...B 3 29
Jogjakarta (Djokjakarta), Indonesia, 312,698...J 2 31
Johannesburg, Transv., †1,096,541...M17 35
Johnston (island), Pacific, 69...K 4 37
Johnstone, Scotland, 18,434...B 2 11
Johore Bahru, Malaya, 75,080...B 2 11
Joinville, Brazil, 20,951...L 9 47
Joliet, Ill., 66,780...K 2 43
Joliette, Quebec, 18,088...F 4 41
Jones (cape), Quebec...D 3 41
Jönköping, Sweden, 50,522...H 8 13
Jonquière, Quebec, 28,588...F 4 41
Jordan (river)...D 3 24
Jorhat, India, 24,953...F 3 29
Jos, Nigeria, 11,854...H10 34
Joseph Bonaparte (gulf), Australia...D 2 36
Juan de Fuca (strait), No. Amer. ...B 2 42
Juan Fernández (islands), Chile...D10 47
Juárez (Ciudad Mante), Mexico, 22,919...K 5 44
Juàzeiro do Norte, Brazil, 53,421...N 5 46
Juba, Sudan, 10,660...N11 34
Juba (river), Somali Rep. ...P11 35
Jubbulpore, India, 295,375...D 4 29
Juchitán, Mexico, 3,459...M 8 44
Judenburg, Austria, 9,869...C 3 20
Juiz de Fora, Brazil, 124,979...M 8 46
Jujuy, Argentina, 31,091...G 8 46
Juli, Peru, 3,816...G 7 46
Juliaca, Peru, 20,786...F 7 46
Julianehaab, Greenland, 1,741...D12 8
Jülich, Germany, 14,687...B 3 14
Jullundur, India, 222,569...C 2 29
Jumet, Belgium, 28,713...E 8 15
Jumilla, Spain, 15,703...F 3 17
Jumna (river), India...C 3 29
Junagadh, India, 74,298...B 4 29
Juncos, Puerto Rico, 6,247...G 1 45
Jundiaí, Brazil, 79,536...L 8 47
Juneau,* Alaska, 6,797...G 8 42
Junee, Australia, 3,980...H 6 36
Junín, Argentina, 36,149...M12 47
Juquiá, Brazil, 2,573...L 8 47
Jur (river), Sudan...M10 34
Jura (island), Scotland, 258...E 8 11
Jura (mountains)...F 4 16
Juruena (river), Brazil...J 5 46
Jutaí (river), Brazil...G 4 46
Jüterbog, Germany, 13,715...E 3 14
Jutiapa, Guatemala, 7,914...B 3 39
Jyväskylä, Finland, 39,636...O 5 13

# K

K 2 (Godwin Austen) (mt.), India...C 1 29
Kabale, Uganda, 10,919...N12 35
Kabul,* Afghanistan, 224,134...J 3 26
Kadayanallur, India, 41,249...C 7 29
Kadiköy, Turkey, 129,918...D 6 28
Kadina, Australia, 1,866...F 6 36
Kadiri, India, 24,307...C 6 29
Kadiyevka, U.S.S.R., 191,000...E 5 22
Kadjang, Indonesia, †30,304...G 7 31
Kaduna, Nigeria, 10,628...H 9 34
Kaédi, Mauritania, 8,037...D 8 34
Kaesŏng, N. Korea, 139,900...C 5 33
Kafr Kanna, Israel, 3,530...C 2 24
Kafue (river), N. Rhodesia...M15 35
Kagan, U.S.S.R., 21,103...G 6 23
Kagoshima, Japan, 296,003...E 8 33
Kagul, U.S.S.R., 16,223...C 5 22
Kaiapit, Terr. N.G. ...B 7 31
Kaiapoi, New Zealand, 3,110...L 7 36
Kaifeng, China, 299,100...J 5 32
Kaikoura, New Zealand, 1,328...L 6 36
Kairouan, Tunisia, 33,968...H 4 34
Kairuku, Papua...B 7 31
Kaiserslautern, Germany, 86,259...B 4 14
Kaitaia, New Zealand, 2,706...L 5 36
Kaizuka, Japan, 61,067...H 8 33
Kajaani, Finland, 14,687...P 4 13
Kakabeka Falls, Ontario, 422...B 4 41
Kakhk, Iran, 4,978...L 3 27
Kakhovka, U.S.S.R., 19,107...D 5 22
Kakhovka (res.), U.S.S.R. ...D 5 22
Kakinada, India, 122,865...D 5 29
Kalachinsk, U.S.S.R., 18,987...H 4 23
Kalámai, Greece, 38,211...F 7 21
Kalamazoo, Mich., 82,089...M 4 43
Kalannie, Australia, 114...B 6 36
Kalat, Pak., 2,009...A 3 29
Kalbe (Calbe), Germany, 15,161...D 3 14
Kalewa, Burma, 2,230...B 2 30
Kalgan, China, 229,300...J 3 32
Kalgoorlie, Australia, †21,773...C 6 36
Kalianda, Indonesia, †31,073...D 7 31
Kalinin, U.S.S.R., 279,000...D 3 22
Kaliningrad, U.S.S.R., 226,000...B 4 22
Kalisz, Poland, 67,300...D 3 24
Kalmar, Sweden, 30,802...K 8 13
Kalmykovo, U.S.S.R. ...F 5 23
Kaluga, U.S.S.R., 145,000...E 4 22
Kalutara, Ceylon, 20,354...C 7 29
Kalyan, India, 73,482...B 5 29
Kálymnos, Greece, 10,211...H 7 21
Kama (river), U.S.S.R. ...H 3 22
Kamaishi, Japan, 87,511...L 4 33
Kamakura, Japan, 98,617...O 3 33
Kamarhati, India, 125,457...E 1 29
Kambove, R.o.t. Congo, 14,517...M14 35
Kamchatka (peninsula), U.S.S.R., 220,000...Q 4 23
Kamenets-Podol'skiy, U.S.S.R., 40,299...C 5 22
Kamensk-Shakhtinskiy, U.S.S.R., 57,525...E 5 22
Kamensk-Ural'skiy, U.S.S.R., 151,000...G 4 23
Kamenskoye, U.S.S.R. ...R 3 23
Kamenz, Germany, 15,461...F 3 14
Kamienna Góra, Poland, 16,000...C 3 24
Kamina, R.o.t. Congo, 20,915...L13 35
Kamloops, British Col., 10,076...F 4 40
Kamo, Japan, 39,292...J 5 33
Kampala,* Uganda, 46,735...N11 35
Kampar, Malaya, 24,611...D 6 30
Kampen, Netherlands, 25,498...H 3 15
Kampot, Cambodia, 12,558...E 5 30
Kamptee, India, 40,859...C 4 29
Kamsack, Saskatchewan, 2,968...K 4 40
Kamyshin, U.S.S.R., 56,511...F 4 22
Kamyshlov, U.S.S.R., 30,137...G 4 23
Kanash, U.S.S.R., 32,897...G 3 22
Kanazawa, Japan, 298,972...H 5 33
Kanchanaburi, Thailand, 12,957...C 4 30
Kanchenjunga (mt.), Asia...E 3 29
Kanchipuram, India, 92,714...D 6 29
Kanchow, China, 98,600...H 6 32
Kandahar, Afghan., 114,981...J 3 26
Kandalaksha, U.S.S.R., 37,045...D 1 22
Kandangan, Indonesia, 9,774...F 6 31
Kandi, Dahomey, 5,100...G 9 34
Kandukur, India, 12,436...C 5 29
Kandy, Ceylon, 57,359...D 7 29
Kangaroo (island), Australia, 3,285...F 7 36
Kangavar, Iran, 6,251...F 3 27
Kanggye, N. Korea, 30,013...C 3 33
Kanggyŏng, S. Korea, 24,554...C 5 33
Kanghwa (bay), S. Korea...B 5 33
Kangnŭng, S. Korea, 58,703...D 5 33
Kaniapiskau (river), Quebec...G 2 41
Kanin (peninsula), U.S.S.R. ...G 1 22
Kanjiža, Yugoslavia, 10,722...D 2 21
Kankan, Guinea, 25,000...E 9 34
Kannauj, India, 24,646...C 3 29
Kano, Nigeria, 130,173...H 9 34
Kanoya, Japan, 72,498...E 8 33
Kanpur, India, 881,177...D 3 29
Kansas (river), Kans. ...J 5 42
Kansas City, Kans., 121,901...K 5 43
Kansas City, Mo., 475,539...K 5 43
Kansk, U.S.S.R., 73,814...K 4 23
Kanuma, Japan, 77,927...J 5 33
Kanye, Bech. Pr., 22,922...L16 35
Kaohsiung, China, 371,225...J 7 32
Kaokoveld (mts.), S.W. Africa...J15 35
Kaolack, Senegal, 69,560...C 9 34
Kapfenberg, Austria, 23,859...C 3 20
Kapingamarangi (Greenwich) (atoll), Pacific, 454...F 5 37
Kaposvár, Hungary, 43,428...D 3 20
Kapsan, N. Korea, 58,077...C 3 33
Kapuskasing, Ontario, 6,870...D 4 41
Kara (sea), U.S.S.R. ...G 2 23
Kara-Kum (canal), U.S.S.R. ...G 6 23
Kara-Kum (des.), U.S.S.R. ...F 5 23
Karabük, Turkey, 31,440...E 2 28
Karacabey, Turkey, 15,969...C 2 28
Karachayevsk, U.S.S.R. ...F 6 22
Karachi, Pakistan, †2,062,000...A 4 29
Karad, India, 33,772...B 5 29
Karadeniz (Bosporus) (strait), Turkey...C 2 28
Karaganda, U.S.S.R., 441,000...H 5 23
Karaginskiy (island), U.S.S.R. ...R 4 23
Karaikudi, India, 43,698...C 7 29
Karakoram (mts.), Asia...C 1 29
Karaköse (Ağri), Turkey, 19,776...K 3 28
Karaman, Turkey, 21,668...E 4 28
Karanja, India, 26,440...C 4 29
Karapinar, Turkey, 10,767...E 4 28
Karasburg, S.W. Africa, 2,233...K17 35
Karasuk, U.S.S.R., 19,961...H 4 23
Karatsu, Japan, 77,825...D 7 33
Karauli, India, 23,696...C 3 29
Karbala, Iraq, 71,163...D 2 27
Karcag, Hungary, 26,035...F 3 20
Kardítsa, Greece, 23,708...E 6 21
Kargopol', U.S.S.R. ...E 2 22
Kariba (lake), Africa...M15 35
Karibib, South-West Africa, 1,395...K16 35
Karikal, India, 22,252...D 6 29
Karimata (strait), Indonesia...D 6 31
Karisimbi (mt.), Africa...M12 35
Karkal, India, 15,536...B 6 29
Karkaralinsk, U.S.S.R., 6,874...H 5 23
Karkur, Israel, 3,100...C 3 24
Karl-Marx-Stadt, Ger., 15,237...E 4 14
Karlö (Hailuoto) (island), Finland, 1,369...O 4 13
Karlovac, Yugoslavia, 40,180...B 3 21
Karlovy Vary, Czech., 46,877...B 1 20
Karlshamn, Sweden, 11,597...J 9 13
Karlskoga, Sweden, 35,343...J 7 13
Karlskrona, Sweden, 33,010...K 8 13
Karlsruhe, Germany, 241,929...C 4 14
Karlstad, Sweden, 42,924...H 7 13
Karnal, India, 72,109...C 3 29
Karonga, Malawi, 2,310...N13 35
Karpogory, U.S.S.R. ...F 2 22
Kars, Turkey, 32,141...K 2 28
Karshi, U.S.S.R., 19,709...G 6 23
Karskiye Vorota (str.), U.S.S.R. ..J 1 22
Karur, India, 50,564...C 6 29
Karviná, Czech., 53,729...E 2 20
Karwar, India, 23,906...B 6 29
Kasai (river), R.o.t. Congo...L13 35
Kasama, N. Rhodesia, 1,796...N14 35
Kasaragod, India, 27,635...B 6 29
Kasba (lake), N.W. Terrs. ...K 2 40
Kaschau (Košice), Czech., 79,581...F 2 20
Kasganj, India, 37,559...C 3 29
Kashan, Iran, 45,955...G 3 27
Kashgar, China, 91,000...C 7 32
Kashing, China, 78,300...K 5 32
Kashiwazaki, Japan, 74,139...J 5 33
Kashmar, Iran, 13,299...K 3 27
Kasimov, U.S.S.R., 27,855...F 4 22
Kaslo, British Columbia, 646...G 4 40
Kassa (Košice), Czech., 79,581...F 2 20
Kassala, Sudan, 40,612...O 8 34
Kassel, Germany, 207,507...C 3 14
Kastamonu, Turkey, 20,307...E 2 28
Kastoría, Greece, 10,162...E 5 21
Kastrup, Denmark, 20,305...H 9 13
Kasur, Pakistan, 63,086...B 2 29
Katahdin (mountain), Maine...R 3 43
Katanga (prov.), R.o.t. Congo, 1,742,719...M13 35
Katanning, Australia, 3,360...B 6 36
Katerínē, Greece, 28,046...F 5 21
Katha, Burma, 7,648...B 1 30
Katherine, Australia, 606...E 2 36
Katihar, India, 46,837...E 3 29
Katmandu,* Nepal, 122,507...D 3 29
Katni (Murwara), India, 46,159...D 4 29
Katowice, Poland, 268,900...B 4 24
Katrineholm, Sweden, 19,004...K 7 13
Katsena Ala, Nigeria, 1,138...J10 34
Katsina, Nigeria, 52,672...H 9 34
Kattegat (strait)...G 8 13
Kattowitz (Katowice), Poland, 268,900...B 4 24
Katwijk aan Zee, Netherlands, 22,013...E 4 15
Kau, Indonesia, †7,497...H 5 31
Kauai (island), Hawaii, 29,683...G 7 42
Kaufbeuren, Germany, 34,686...D 5 14
Kaunas, U.S.S.R., 232,000...B 4 22
Kaura Namoda, Nigeria, 13,068...H 9 34
Kavadarci, Yugoslavia, 11,409...E 5 21
Kavaje, Albania, 14,195...D 5 21
Kavali, India, 20,544...D 6 29
Kávalla, Greece, 44,517...G 5 21
Kavieng, Terr. N.G., 715...E 6 37
Kavir (desert), Iran...J 3 27
Kawagoe, Japan, 107,523...O 2 33
Kawaguchi, Japan, 170,066...O 2 33
Kawasaki, Japan, 632,975...O 2 33
Kaya, Upper Volta, 10,304...F 1 34
Kayes, Mali, 24,218...D 9 34
Kayseri, Turkey, 102,596...F 3 28
Kazalinsk, U.S.S.R., 7,697...G 5 23
Kazan (river), N.W. Terrs. ...K 2 40
Kazan', U.S.S.R., 711,000...G 3 22
Kazandzhik, U.S.S.R. ...F 6 23
Kazanlŭk, Bulgaria, 19,386...G 4 21
Kazbek (mtn.), U.S.S.R. ...F 6 22
Kazerun, Iran, 30,641...G 6 27
Kazvin, Iran, 66,420...F 2 27
Kebumen, Indonesia, †64,874...J 2 31
Kecskemét, Hungary, 66,842...E 3 20
Kediri, Indonesia, 158,918...K 2 31
Kédougou, Senegal, 1,938...D 9 34
Kędzierzyn, Poland, 18,000...D 3 24
Keele (peak), Canada...E 2 40
Keelung, China, 197,029...K 6 32
Keeper (mountain), Ireland...E 6 12
Keerweer (cape), Australia...G 2 36
Keetmanshoop, S.W. Afr., 7,989...K17 35
Keewatin, Ontario, 2,197...B 3 41
Kefar Ata, Israel, 14,245...C 2 24
Kefar Sava, Israel, 17,935...B 3 24
Keighley, England, 55,845...F 4 10
Keijo (Seoul),* S. Korea, 2,444,883...C 5 33
Kelliher, Saskatchewan, 461...K 4 40
Kelmscott, Aust., 1,270...B 2 36
Kelowna, Br. Columbia, 13,188...G 5 40
Kelvington, Saskatchewan, 885...K 4 40
Kem', U.S.S.R., 18,127...D 2 22
Kemerovo, U.S.S.R., 298,000...J 4 23
Kemi, Finland, 28,040...O 4 13
Kemi (river), Finland...O 3 13
Kempsey, Australia, 8,016...J 6 36
Kempten, Germany, 43,116...D 5 14
Kenadsa, Algeria, 7,131...F 5 34
Kendal, England, 18,599...E 3 10
Kendal, Indonesia, 23,129...J 2 31
Kendari, Indonesia, †21,065...G 6 31
Kendawangan, Indonesia, 6,845...D 6 31
Kendrapara, India, 15,830...E 4 29
Keng Tung, Burma...C 2 30
Kenitra (Port-Lyautey), Morocco, 88,533...E 5 34

| | Index Ref. | Plate No. |
|---|---|---|
| Kenmare (river), Ireland | A 8 | 12 |
| Kenn (reef), Australia | K 4 | 36 |
| Kennedy (Canaveral) (cape), Fla. | N 7 | 43 |
| Kennet (river), England | F 6 | 10 |
| Keno Hill, Yukon, 100 | C 2 | 40 |
| Kénogami, Quebec, 11,816 | F 4 | 41 |
| Kenora, Ontario, 10,904 | B 4 | 41 |
| Kensington, P.E.I., 884 | H 4 | 41 |
| Kensington and Norwood, Australia, 13,476 | D 8 | 36 |
| Kentville, Nova Scotia, 4,612 | H 4 | 41 |
| Kenya (mountain), Kenya | O12 | 35 |
| Keonjhargarh, India, 12,624 | E 4 | 29 |
| Kepsut, Turkey, 3,980 | C 3 | 28 |
| Kerang, Australia, 3,727 | G 7 | 36 |
| Kerch', U.S.S.R., 104,000 | E 5 | 22 |
| Kerema, Papua, 292 | B 7 | 31 |
| Keren, Ethiopia, 8,000 | O 8 | 34 |
| Kerintji (mountain), Indonesia | C 6 | 31 |
| Kerki, U.S.S.R. | G 6 | 23 |
| Kerkrade, Netherlands, 49,144 | J 7 | 15 |
| Kérkyra (Corfu), Greece, 26,991 | D 6 | 21 |
| Kerman, Iran, 62,157 | K 5 | 27 |
| Kermanshah, Iran, 125,439 | E 3 | 27 |
| Kerrobert, Saskatchewan, 1,220 | J 4 | 40 |
| Kersbrock, Australia, 402 | D 7 | 36 |
| Kerulen (river), Mongolia | H 2 | 32 |
| Keşan, Turkey, 15,061 | B 2 | 28 |
| Keta, Ghana, 16,719 | G10 | 34 |
| Ketapang, Indonesia, 4,385 | E 6 | 31 |
| Ketapang, Indonesia, †46,245 | K 2 | 31 |
| Kete Krakye, Ghana, 3,928 | F10 | 34 |
| Kettering, England, 38,659 | G 5 | 10 |
| Kew, Australia, 33,341 | L 2 | 36 |
| Khabarovsk, U.S.S.R., 349,000 | O 5 | 23 |
| Khachmas, U.S.S.R. | G 6 | 22 |
| Khairpur, Pakistan, 18,184 | A 3 | 29 |
| Khalturin, U.S.S.R. | G 3 | 22 |
| Khamgaon, India, 44,432 | C 4 | 29 |
| Khammam, India, 35,888 | C 5 | 29 |
| Khan Yunis, Egypt, 11,220 | A 5 | 24 |
| Khanabad, Afghanistan, 30,000 | J 2 | 26 |
| Khandwa, India, 63,505 | C 4 | 29 |
| Khanewal, Pakistan, 37,915 | B 2 | 29 |
| Khaniá (Canea), Greece, 38,467 | G 8 | 21 |
| Khanka (lake) | P 5 | 23 |
| Khanpur, Pakistan, 15,197 | B 3 | 29 |
| Khanty-Mansiysk, U.S.S.R., 20,677 | H 3 | 23 |
| Kharagpur, India, 147,253 | E 4 | 29 |
| Khardah, India, 28,362 | E 1 | 29 |
| Khârga (oasis), Egypt, 11,155 | N 6 | 34 |
| Khar'kov, U.S.S.R., 990,000 | E 4 | 22 |
| Kharmanlii, Bulgaria, 9,240 | H 5 | 21 |
| Kharovsk, U.S.S.R. | F 3 | 22 |
| Khartoum,* Sudan, 93,103 | N 8 | 34 |
| Khartoum, North, Sudan, 39,082 | N 8 | 34 |
| Khaskovo, Bulgaria, 27,394 | G 5 | 21 |
| Khatanga, U.S.S.R. | L 2 | 23 |
| Khenifra, Morocco, 18,503 | E 5 | 34 |
| Kherson, U.S.S.R., 174,000 | D 5 | 22 |
| Khilok, U.S.S.R., 15,855 | M 4 | 23 |
| Khingan, Great (mt. range), China | K 2 | 32 |
| Khmel'nitskiy, U.S.S.R., 62,473 | C 5 | 22 |
| Khodzheyli, U.S.S.R., 20,525 | F 5 | 23 |
| Khoi, Iran, 34,491 | D 1 | 27 |
| Kholm, U.S.S.R. | D 3 | 22 |
| Kholmsk, U.S.S.R., 31,541 | P 5 | 23 |
| Khon Kaen, Thailand, 19,591 | D 3 | 30 |
| Khong, Laos, 1,750 | E 4 | 30 |
| Khorat (Nakhon Ratchasima), Thailand, 41,037 | D 4 | 30 |
| Khorog, U.S.S.R., 8,218 | H 6 | 23 |
| Khorramshahr, Iran, 43,850 | F 5 | 27 |
| Khotan (Hotien), China | B 4 | 32 |
| Khulna, Pakistan, 128,000 | E 4 | 29 |
| Khurja, India, 41,491 | C 3 | 29 |
| Khurramabad, Iran, 38,676 | F 4 | 27 |
| Khushab, Pakistan, 20,467 | B 2 | 29 |
| Khyber (pass), Pakistan | B 2 | 29 |
| Kiamusze, China, 146,000 | L 2 | 32 |
| Kian, China, 52,800 | J 6 | 32 |
| Kiaochow (bay), China | K 4 | 32 |
| Kidal, Mali, 800 | G 8 | 34 |
| Kidderminster, England, 41,671 | E 5 | 10 |
| Kiel, Germany, 273,284 | C 1 | 14 |
| Kielce, Poland, 83,000 | E 3 | 24 |
| Kienteh, China | J 6 | 32 |
| Kieta, Terr. New Guinea, 242 | F 6 | 37 |
| Kiev, U.S.S.R., 1,208,000 | D 4 | 22 |
| Kiffa, Mauritania, 2,600 | D 8 | 34 |
| Kigali,* Rwanda, †4,055 | N12 | 35 |
| Kigoma, Tanganyika, 1,000 | N12 | 35 |
| Kikinda, Yugoslavia, 34,059 | E 3 | 21 |
| Kikori, Papua, 113 | B 7 | 31 |
| Kikwit, R.o.t. Congo, 16,101 | K13 | 35 |
| Kilimanjaro (mountain), Tanganyika | O12 | 35 |
| Kilis, Turkey, 33,005 | G 4 | 28 |
| Kilkenny, Ireland, 10,158 | G 6 | 12 |
| Kilkís, Greece, 10,963 | F 5 | 21 |
| Killarney, Ireland, 6,824 | C 7 | 12 |
| Killarney, Manitoba, 1,729 | L 5 | 40 |
| Kilmarnock, Scotland, 47,509 | G 8 | 11 |
| Kilosa, Tang., 4,500 | O13 | 35 |
| Kilwa Kivinje, Tang., 3,000 | P13 | 35 |
| Kimberley, Br. Columbia, 6,013 | G 5 | 40 |
| Kimberley, C. of G. Hope, †77,180 | L17 | 35 |
| Kimry, U.S.S.R., 41,243 | E 3 | 22 |
| Kinabalu (mountain), Sabah | F 4 | 31 |
| Kincardine, Ontario, 2,841 | D 5 | 41 |
| Kindersley, Saskatchewan, 2,990 | J 4 | 40 |
| Kindia, Guinea, 17,000 | D 9 | 34 |
| Kindu-Port Empain, R.o.t. Congo, 19,385 | M12 | 35 |
| Kineshma, U.S.S.R., 85,418 | F 3 | 22 |
| King (island), Tas., Australia, 2,784 | G 7 | 36 |
| King (sound), Australia | C 3 | 36 |
| King Leopold (mt. range), Australia | D 3 | 36 |
| King William's Town, C. of G. Hope, 14,646 | M18 | 35 |
| Kingaroy, Australia, 4,914 | J 5 | 36 |
| Kingoonya, Australia, 112 | E 6 | 36 |
| King's Lynn, England, 27,536 | H 5 | 10 |
| Kings Peak (mountain), Utah | F 4 | 42 |
| Kingscote, Australia, 739 | F 7 | 36 |
| Kingsgate, Br. Columbia, 35 | G 5 | 40 |
| Kingston, Australia, 963 | F 7 | 36 |
| Kingston,* Jamaica, †380,757 | C 3 | 45 |
| Kingston, Ontario, 53,526 | E 5 | 41 |
| Kingston-upon-Thames, Eng., 36,461 | G 6 | 10 |
| Kingston-upon-Hull (Hull), England, 303,261 | G 4 | 10 |
| Kingstown,* St. Vincent, 16,141 | G 4 | 45 |
| Kingstown (Dún Laoghaire), Ireland, 47,803 | K 5 | 12 |
| Kingsville, Ontario, 3,041 | D 5 | 41 |
| Kingswood, England, 25,417 | E 6 | 10 |
| Kingtehchen, China, 92,000 | J 6 | 32 |
| Kinhwa, China, 46,200 | K 6 | 32 |
| Kinistino, Saskatchewan, 764 | J 4 | 40 |
| Kinnairds Head (prom.), Scotland | N 4 | 11 |
| Kinsale, Ireland, 1,587 | D 8 | 12 |
| Kintampo, Ghana, 4,678 | F10 | 34 |
| Kintyre (peninsula), Scotland, 11,670 | E 9 | 11 |
| Kinuso, Alberta, 323 | G 3 | 40 |
| Kioga (lake), Uganda | N11 | 35 |
| Kirchheim, Germany, 25,007 | C 4 | 14 |
| Kirensk, U.S.S.R. | L 4 | 23 |
| Kirikkale, Turkey, 42,904 | E 3 | 28 |
| Kirin, China, 435,400 | L 3 | 32 |
| Kirkağaç, Turkey, 11,345 | B 3 | 28 |
| Kirkby-in-Ashfield, England, 21,686 | F 4 | 10 |
| Kirkcaldy, Scotland, 52,390 | K 7 | 11 |
| Kirkee, India, 58,496 | B 5 | 29 |
| Kirkintilloch, Scotland, 18,270 | C 2 | 11 |
| Kirkland Lake, Ontario, 17,329 | D 4 | 41 |
| Kirklareli, Turkey, 20,196 | B 2 | 28 |
| Kirkuk, Iraq, 147,806 | D 3 | 27 |
| Kirkwall, Scot., 4,315 | K 2 | 11 |
| Kirov, U.S.S.R., 269,000 | G 3 | 22 |
| Kirov, U.S.S.R., 16,647 | D 4 | 22 |
| Kirovabad, U.S.S.R., 123,000 | G 6 | 22 |
| Kirovakan, U.S.S.R., 49,423 | F 6 | 22 |
| Kirovograd, U.S.S.R., 134,000 | D 5 | 22 |
| Kirovsk, U.S.S.R., 39,047 | D 1 | 22 |
| Kirsanov, U.S.S.R., 15,654 | F 4 | 22 |
| Kirşehir, Turkey, 20,248 | F 3 | 28 |
| Kiruna, Sweden, 26,703 | L 3 | 13 |
| Kiryu, Japan, 123,010 | J 5 | 33 |
| Kisarazu, Japan, 52,689 | P 3 | 33 |
| Kiselevsk, U.S.S.R., 141,000 | J 4 | 23 |
| Kishangarh, India, 25,244 | C 3 | 29 |
| Kishinev, U.S.S.R., 244,000 | C 5 | 22 |
| Kishiwada, Japan, 120,265 | J 8 | 33 |
| Kishorganj, Pakistan, 19,034 | F 4 | 29 |
| Kiskundorozsma, Hungary, 8,679 | E 3 | 20 |
| Kiskunfélegyháza, Hungary, 33,126 | E 3 | 20 |
| Kiskunhalas, Hungary, 26,226 | E 3 | 20 |
| Kiskunmajsa, Hungary, 13,012 | E 3 | 20 |
| Kislovodsk, U.S.S.R., 79,097 | F 6 | 22 |
| Kismayu, Somali Rep., 10,386 | P12 | 35 |
| Kississing, Manitoba, 500 | K 3 | 40 |
| Kisújszállás, Hungary, 13,756 | F 3 | 20 |
| Kisumu, Kenya, 23,200 | N12 | 35 |
| Kita, Mali, 5,230 | E 9 | 34 |
| Kitakyushu, Japan, 986,401 | E 7 | 33 |
| Kitale, Kenya, 6,338 | O11 | 35 |
| Kitami, Japan, 66,932 | L 2 | 33 |
| Kitchener, Ontario, 74,485 | D 5 | 41 |
| Kitchener (greater), Ontario, 154,864 | D 5 | 41 |
| Kitimat, Br. Columbia, 8,217 | E 4 | 40 |
| Kitwanga, Br. Columbia, 175 | E 3 | 40 |
| Kitzbühel, Austria, 7,744 | B 3 | 20 |
| Kitzingen, Germany, 17,784 | D 4 | 14 |
| Kiuchüan, China, 246,873 | E 4 | 32 |
| Kiukiang, China, 64,600 | J 5 | 32 |
| Kivu (lake), Africa | M12 | 35 |
| Kizel, U.S.S.R., 60,687 | J 3 | 22 |
| Kizlyar, U.S.S.R., 25,573 | G 6 | 22 |
| Kizyl-Arvat, U.S.S.R. | F 6 | 23 |
| Kjölen (mt. range) | K 3 | 13 |
| Kladno, Czech., 51,698 | C 1 | 20 |
| Klagenfurt, Austria, 69,218 | C 3 | 20 |
| Klaipėda, U.S.S.R., 100,000 | B 3 | 22 |
| Klamath (river), U.S. | C 4 | 42 |
| Klang, Malaya, 75,649 | D 7 | 30 |
| Klar (river), Sweden | H 6 | 13 |
| Klatovy, Czech., 14,273 | B 2 | 20 |
| Klemtu, Br. Columbia, 150 | E 4 | 40 |
| Kleve (Cleves), Germany, 21,483 | B 3 | 14 |
| Klin, U.S.S.R., 53,322 | E 3 | 22 |
| Klintsy, U.S.S.R., 42,033 | D 4 | 22 |
| Kłodzko (Glatz), Poland, 21,900 | C 3 | 24 |
| Kloppenburg, Germany, 15,214 | C 2 | 14 |
| Kluane (lake), Yukon | C 2 | 40 |
| Kluang, Malaya, 31,183 | D 7 | 30 |
| Kluczbork, Poland, 13,300 | D 3 | 24 |
| Klukhori (Karachayevsk), U.S.S.R., 2,848 | F 6 | 22 |
| Klyuchevskaya Sopka (volcano), U.S.S.R. | Q 4 | 23 |
| Knittelfeld, Austria, 14,259 | C 3 | 20 |
| Knoxville, Tenn., 111,827 | N 6 | 43 |
| Knurów, Poland, 14,100 | A 4 | 24 |
| Knysna, Cape of Good Hope, 11,085 | L18 | 35 |
| Kobayashi, Japan, 43,894 | E 8 | 33 |
| Kobdo, Mongolia, 10,000 | D 2 | 32 |
| Kobe, Japan, 1,113,977 | H 7 | 33 |
| København (Copenhagen), *Denmark, 721,381 | G 9 | 13 |
| Koblenz, Germany, 99,240 | B 3 | 14 |
| Kobrin, U.S.S.R., 13,686 | B 4 | 22 |
| Kocaeli (Izmit), Turkey, 73,488 | C 2 | 28 |
| Kochevo, U.S.S.R. | H 3 | 22 |
| Kochi, Japan, 196,288 | F 7 | 33 |
| Koesfeld, Germany, 20,348 | B 3 | 14 |
| Koforidua, Ghana, 34,856 | G10 | 34 |
| Kofu, Japan, 160,963 | J 6 | 33 |
| Kogaluk (river), Quebec | E 2 | 41 |
| Kogarah, Australia, 46,600 | L 3 | 36 |
| Köge, Denmark, 12,294 | H 9 | 13 |
| Kohat, Pakistan, 40,534 | B 2 | 29 |
| Koi (Coi) (river), N. Vietnam | E 2 | 30 |
| Kokchetav, U.S.S.R., 39,694 | H 4 | 23 |
| Kokiu, China, 159,700 | F 7 | 32 |
| Kokkola (Gamlakarleby), Finland, 16,195 | N 5 | 13 |
| Koko Nor (lake), China | E 4 | 32 |
| Kokoda, Papua | C 7 | 31 |
| Kola (peninsula), U.S.S.R. | E 1 | 22 |
| Kolaka, Indonesia, †18,671 | G 6 | 31 |
| Kolar, India, 32,587 | C 6 | 29 |
| Kolar Gold Fields, India, 146,811 | C 6 | 29 |
| Kolarovgrad (Shumen), Bulgaria, 41,670 | H 4 | 21 |
| Kolding, Denmark, 35,101 | F 9 | 13 |
| Kolguyev (island), U.S.S.R. | G 1 | 22 |
| Kolhapur, India, 187,442 | B 5 | 29 |
| Kolín, Czech., 23,137 | C 1 | 20 |
| Köln (Cologne), Germany, 809,247 | B 3 | 14 |
| Kołobrzeg, Poland, 13,200 | B 1 | 24 |
| Kolomna, U.S.S.R., 124,000 | E 4 | 22 |
| Kolonodale, Indonesia | G 6 | 31 |
| Kolozsvár (Cluj), Rumania, 154,723 | F 2 | 21 |
| Kolpashevo, U.S.S.R., 22,595 | J 4 | 23 |
| Kolwezi, R.o.t. Congo, 45,192 | M14 | 35 |
| Kolyma (river), U.S.S.R. | Q 3 | 23 |
| Kolyma (Gydan) (mt. range), U.S.S.R. | Q 3 | 23 |
| Komandorskiye (islands), U.S.S.R. | R 4 | 23 |
| Komárno (Komorn), Czech., 24,975 | D 3 | 20 |
| Komatsu, Japan, 89,085 | H 5 | 33 |
| Kommunarsk, U.S.S.R., 107,000 | E 5 | 22 |
| Komotinē, Greece, 28,355 | G 5 | 21 |
| Kompong Chhnang, Cambodia, 12,847 | E 4 | 30 |
| Kompong Speu, Cambodia, 7,453 | E 5 | 30 |
| Komsomol'sk, U.S.S.R., 189,000 | O 4 | 23 |
| Konakry (Conakry),* Guinea, 38,000 | D10 | 34 |
| Konan (Hungnam), N. Korea, 143,600 | C 4 | 33 |
| Kondopoga, U.S.S.R., 16,060 | D 2 | 22 |
| Kongju, S. Korea, 27,071 | C 5 | 33 |
| Kongmoon, China, 85,000 | H 7 | 32 |
| Kongolo, R.o.t. Congo, 10,434 | M13 | 35 |
| Kongsberg, Norway, 9,703 | F 7 | 13 |
| Königgrätz (Hradec Králové), Czech., 55,147 | C 1 | 29 |
| Königsberg (Kaliningrad), U.S.S.R., 226,000 | B 4 | 22 |
| Königshütte (Chorzów), Poland, 146,700 | B 4 | 24 |
| Konin, Poland, 16,700 | D 2 | 24 |
| Köniz, Switzerland, 27,243 | D 3 | 19 |
| Konnagar and Rishra, India, 29,443 | E 1 | 29 |
| Konotop, U.S.S.R., 54,097 | D 4 | 22 |
| Konstanz, Germany, 52,651 | C 5 | 14 |
| Kontum, S. Vietnam, 14,358 | E 4 | 30 |
| Konya, Turkey, 119,841 | E 4 | 28 |
| Köpenick, Germany, 52,294 | F 4 | 14 |
| Kopeysk, U.S.S.R., 168,000 | G 4 | 23 |
| Koppal, India, 19,530 | C 5 | 29 |
| Koprivnica, Yugoslavia, 11,842 | C 2 | 21 |
| Korat (Nakhon Ratchasima), Thai., 41,037 | D 4 | 30 |
| Korbach, Germany, 15,084 | C 3 | 14 |
| Korçë, Albania, 39,386 | E 5 | 21 |
| Korea (peninsula) | C 4 | 33 |
| Korea (strait) | L 5 | 32 |
| Korhogo, Ivory Coast, 10,139 | E10 | 34 |
| Koriyama, Japan, 102,636 | K 5 | 33 |
| Korkino, U.S.S.R., 84,962 | G 4 | 23 |
| Korneuburg, Austria, 8,276 | D 2 | 20 |
| Kornwestheim, Germany, 26,296 | C 4 | 14 |
| Koror,* Palau Islands, 1,207 | D 5 | 37 |
| Korosten', U.S.S.R., 38,041 | C 4 | 22 |
| Korsakov, U.S.S.R., 32,914 | P 5 | 23 |
| Korsør, Denmark, 14,276 | G 9 | 13 |
| Kortkeros, U.S.S.R. | H 2 | 22 |
| Kortrijk (Courtrai), Belgium, 43,606 | C 7 | 15 |
| Koryak (mtn. range), U.S.S.R. | R 3 | 23 |
| Kościan, Poland, 15,200 | C 2 | 24 |
| Kosciusko (mountain), Australia | H 7 | 36 |
| Košice, Czech., 87,529 | F 2 | 20 |
| Koslan, U.S.S.R. | G 2 | 22 |
| Köslin (Koszalin), Poland, 41,000 | C 1 | 24 |
| Kosovska Mitrovica, Yugoslavia, 26,721 | E 4 | 21 |
| Kosti, Sudan, 22,688 | N 9 | 34 |
| Kostroma, U.S.S.R., 184,000 | F 3 | 22 |
| Koszalin (Köslin), Poland, 41,000 | C 1 | 24 |
| Kota, India, 120,345 | C 3 | 29 |
| Kota Bharu, Malaya, 38,096 | D 6 | 30 |
| Kotaagung, Indonesia, †25,314 | C 7 | 31 |
| Kotabaharu, Indonesia | E 6 | 31 |
| Kotabaru, Indonesia, 3,756 | F 6 | 31 |
| Kotabaru (Hollandia),* West Irian, 15,153 | K 6 | 31 |
| Kotamobagu, Indonesia | G 5 | 31 |
| Kotel'nich, U.S.S.R., 27,640 | G 3 | 22 |
| Kothen, Germany, 38,611 | E 3 | 14 |
| Kotka, Finland, 30,293 | P 6 | 13 |
| Kotlas, U.S.S.R., 39,162 | G 2 | 22 |
| Kotor, Yugoslavia, 4,764 | D 4 | 21 |
| Kotovsk, U.S.S.R., 25,511 | F 4 | 22 |
| Kotri, Pakistan, 15,154 | A 3 | 29 |
| Kotrung, India, 31,031 | E 1 | 29 |
| Kottayam, India, 52,685 | C 7 | 29 |
| Kottbus (Cottbus), Germany, 69,472 | F 3 | 14 |
| Kotto (river), Cent. Afr. Rep. | L10 | 34 |
| Koudougou, Upper Volta, 7,940 | F 9 | 34 |
| Koulikoro, Mali, 6,144 | E 9 | 34 |
| Kouroussa, Guinea, 5,500 | E 9 | 34 |
| Koutiala, Mali, 8,047 | F 9 | 34 |
| Kouvola, Finland, 18,245 | P 6 | 13 |
| Kovel', U.S.S.R., 24,666 | C 4 | 22 |
| Kovrov, U.S.S.R., 103,000 | F 3 | 22 |
| Kovur, India, 14,580 | D 6 | 29 |
| Kowloon, Hong Kong, 725,177 | H 7 | 32 |
| Kozan, Turkey, 15,159 | F 4 | 28 |
| Kozáne, Greece, 21,537 | F 5 | 21 |
| Kozhikode (Calicut), India, 192,521 | C 6 | 29 |
| Kraaifontein, C. of G. Hope, 4,832 | D19 | 35 |
| Kragan, Indonesia, 23,786 | K 2 | 31 |
| Kragujevac, Yugoslavia, 52,792 | E 3 | 21 |
| Kraków (Cracow), Poland, 479,000 | E 3 | 24 |
| Kraksaan, Indonesia, †29,466 | K 2 | 31 |
| Kraljevo (Rankovićevo), Yugoslavia, 20,490 | E 4 | 21 |
| Kramatorsk, U.S.S.R., 123,000 | E 5 | 22 |
| Kranj, Yugoslavia, 21,477 | B 2 | 21 |
| Kraśnik, Poland, 12,500 | F 3 | 24 |
| Krasnoborsk, U.S.S.R. | G 2 | 22 |
| Krasnodar, U.S.S.R., 343,000 | E 6 | 22 |
| Krasnokamsk, U.S.S.R., 54,715 | H 3 | 22 |
| Krasnoslobodsk, U.S.S.R., 18,993 | F 4 | 22 |
| Krasnotur'insk, U.S.S.R., 61,990 | G 3 | 23 |

| | Index Ref. | Plate No. |
|---|---|---|
| Krasnoural'sk, U.S.S.R., 39,245 | G 4 | 23 |
| Krasnovishersk, U.S.S.R., 15,207 | J 2 | 22 |
| Krasnovodsk, U.S.S.R., 30,000 | F 5 | 23 |
| Krasnoyarsk, U.S.S.R., 468,000 | K 4 | 23 |
| Krasnystaw, Poland, 11,300 | F 3 | 24 |
| Krasnyy Liman, U.S.S.R., 28,911 | E 5 | 22 |
| Kratié, Cambodia, 11,908 | E 4 | 30 |
| Krefeld, Germany, 213,104 | B 3 | 14 |
| Kremenchug, U.S.S.R., 86,569 | D 5 | 22 |
| Krems, Austria, 21,046 | C 2 | 20 |
| Krētē (Crete) (island), Greece, 483,075 | G 8 | 21 |
| Kribi, Cam., 3,000 | J11 | 35 |
| Krichev, U.S.S.R., 19,028 | D 4 | 22 |
| Krishna (river), India | C 5 | 29 |
| Krishnagar, India, 70,440 | E 4 | 29 |
| Kristiansand, Norway, 27,900 | F 8 | 13 |
| Kristianstad, Sweden, 25,763 | J 9 | 13 |
| Kristiansund, Norway, 17,204 | E 5 | 13 |
| Kristinehamn, Sweden, 21,604 | H 7 | 13 |
| Krivoy Rog, U.S.S.R., 436,000 | D 5 | 22 |
| Križevci, Yugoslavia, 6,642 | C 2 | 21 |
| Krnov, Czechoslovakia, 22,506 | D 1 | 20 |
| Kroměříž, Czechoslovakia, 21,990 | D 2 | 20 |
| Kronshtadt, U.S.S.R. | C 3 | 22 |
| Kroonstad, O.F.S., 42,331 | M17 | 35 |
| Kropotkin, U.S.S.R., 53,997 | F 5 | 22 |
| Krosno, Poland, 19,600 | E 4 | 24 |
| Krotoszyn, Poland, 17,900 | C 3 | 24 |
| Krui, Indonesia, 3,860 | C 7 | 31 |
| Krung Kao (Ayutthaya), Thailand, 24,597 | D 4 | 30 |
| Krung Thep (Bangkok),* Thailand, †1,299,528 | D 4 | 30 |
| Kruševac, Yugoslavia, 21,957 | E 4 | 21 |
| Ksar es Souk, Morocco, 7,039 | F 5 | 34 |
| Kuala Lumpur,* Fed. of Malaysia, 316,230 | D 7 | 30 |
| Kuala Trengganu, Malaya, 29,436 | D 6 | 30 |
| Kualakapuas, Indonesia, 8,682 | E 6 | 31 |
| Kuandang, Indonesia, †15,379 | G 5 | 31 |
| Kuban' (river), U.S.S.R. | E 5 | 22 |
| Kubeno (lake), U.S.S.R. | E 3 | 22 |
| Kuching,* Sara., 50,579 | E 5 | 31 |
| Kudat, Sabah, 3,660 | F 4 | 31 |
| Kudus, Indonesia, 62,130 | J 2 | 31 |
| Kudymkar, U.S.S.R., 21,801 | H 3 | 22 |
| Kufra (oasis), Libya, 4,600 | L 7 | 34 |
| Kufstein, Austria, 11,215 | B 3 | 20 |
| Kukawa, Nigeria, 20,000 | J 9 | 34 |
| Kukmor, U.S.S.R. | H 3 | 22 |
| Kuldja, China, 108,200 | B 3 | 32 |
| Kulebaki, U.S.S.R., 44,720 | F 3 | 22 |
| Kulmbach, Germany, 23,467 | D 3 | 14 |
| Kuma (river), U.S.S.R. | G 5 | 22 |
| Kumagaya, Japan, 98,168 | J 5 | 33 |
| Kumamoto, Japan, 373,922 | E 7 | 33 |
| Kumanovo, Yugoslavia, 22,985 | E 4 | 21 |
| Kumasi, Ghana, †218,172 | F10 | 34 |
| Kumbakonam, India, 92,581 | C 6 | 29 |
| Kumta, India, 16,223 | B 6 | 29 |
| Kungur, U.S.S.R., 64,796 | J 3 | 22 |
| Kuningan, Indonesia, †77,181 | H 2 | 31 |
| Kunlun (mt. range), China | B 4 | 32 |
| Kunming, China, 698,900 | F 6 | 32 |
| Kunsan, S. Korea, 90,481 | C 6 | 33 |
| Kuolayarvi, U.S.S.R. | D 1 | 22 |
| Kuopio, Finland, 44,911 | Q 5 | 13 |
| Kupang, Indonesia, 7,171 | G 8 | 31 |
| Kupino, U.S.S.R., 23,185 | H 4 | 23 |
| Kupyansk, U.S.S.R., 25,644 | E 5 | 22 |
| Kurashiki, Japan, 125,097 | F 6 | 33 |
| Kŭrdzhali, Bulgaria, 10,480 | G 5 | 21 |
| Kure, Japan, 210,032 | F 6 | 33 |
| Kuressaare, U.S.S.R. | B 3 | 22 |
| Kurgan, U.S.S.R., 164,000 | G 4 | 23 |
| Kurgan-Tyube, U.S.S.R., 23,560 | G 6 | 23 |
| Kuria Muria (islands) (Br.), 100 | G 6 | 26 |
| Kuril (isls.), U.S.S.R., 12,000 | P 5 | 23 |
| Kurnool, India, 100,815 | C 5 | 29 |
| Kursk, U.S.S.R., 222,000 | E 4 | 22 |
| Kurume, Japan, 155,041 | E 7 | 33 |
| Kurunegala, Ceylon, 17,319 | D 7 | 29 |
| Kusaie (island), Caroline Is., 1,865 | G 5 | 37 |
| Kushiro, Japan, 150,624 | M 2 | 33 |
| Kushka, U.S.S.R. | G 6 | 23 |
| Kuskokwim (river), Alaska | F 8 | 42 |
| Kustanay, U.S.S.R., 86,382 | G 4 | 23 |
| Kut, Iraq, 81,388 | E 4 | 27 |
| Kütahya, Turkey, 39,663 | C 3 | 28 |
| Kutaisi, U.S.S.R., 137,000 | F 6 | 22 |
| Kutaradja, Indonesia, 40,067 | A 4 | 31 |
| Kutna Hora (Kuttenberg), Czech., 16,740 | C 2 | 20 |
| Kutno, Poland, 25,500 | D 2 | 24 |
| Kutoardjo, Indonesia, 44,962 | J 2 | 31 |
| Kuybyshev, U.S.S.R., 882,000 | H 4 | 22 |
| Kuybyshev (res.), U.S.S.R. | G 4 | 22 |
| Kuznetsk, U.S.S.R., 56,880 | G 4 | 22 |
| Kuzomen', U.S.S.R. | E 1 | 22 |
| Kwajalein (island), Marshall Is., 1,971 | G 5 | 37 |
| Kwando (river), Africa | L15 | 35 |
| Kwangju, S. Korea, 315,124 | C 6 | 33 |
| Kweilin, China, 145,100 | G 6 | 32 |
| Kweisui (Huhehot), China, 148,400 | H 3 | 32 |
| Kweiyang, China, 270,900 | G 6 | 32 |
| Kwilu (river), R.o.t. Congo | K13 | 35 |
| Kyaikto, Burma, 13,154 | C 3 | 30 |
| Kyakhta, U.S.S.R., 10,000 | L 4 | 23 |
| Kyangin, Burma, 6,073 | B 3 | 30 |
| Kyaukpadaung, Burma, 5,480 | B 2 | 30 |
| Kyaukpyu, Burma, 7,335 | B 3 | 30 |
| Kyaukse, Burma, 8,659 | C 2 | 30 |
| Kyŏmip'o, N. Korea, 53,035 | C 4 | 33 |
| Kyŏngju, S. Korea, 76,032 | D 6 | 33 |
| Kyŏngsŏng (Seoul),* S. Korea, 2,444,883 | C 5 | 33 |
| Kyoto, Japan, 1,284,818 | J 7 | 33 |
| Kyushu (island), Japan, 12,903,515 | E 7 | 33 |
| Kyustendil, Bulgaria, 19,309 | F 4 | 21 |
| Kywebwe, Burma, 3,150 | C 3 | 30 |
| Kyzyl, U.S.S.R., 34,462 | K 4 | 23 |
| Kyzyl-Kum (desert), U.S.S.R. | G 5 | 23 |
| Kzyl-Orda, U.S.S.R., 65,902 | G 5 | 23 |


## L


| | Index Ref. | Plate No. |
|---|---|---|
| L'Aquila, Italy, †56,019 | D 3 | 18 |
| La Barca, Mexico, 16,330 | H 6 | 44 |
| La Carolina, Spain, 10,915 | E 3 | 17 |
| La Ceiba, Honduras, 24,880 | D 3 | 39 |
| La Chaux-de-Fonds, Switz., 38,906 | C 2 | 19 |
| La Chorrera, Panama, 13,696 | H 6 | 39 |
| La Ciotat, France, 17,552 | F 6 | 16 |
| La Coruña, Spain, †177,502 | B 1 | 17 |
| La Flèche, France, 9,257 | C 4 | 16 |
| La Gloria, Colombia, 1,331 | F 2 | 46 |
| La Grand-Combe, France, 10,333 | E 5 | 16 |
| La Guaira, Venezuela, 20,681 | G 1 | 46 |
| La Línea, Spain, 35,446 | D 4 | 17 |
| La Malbaie, Quebec, 2,580 | F 4 | 41 |
| La Orotava, Canary Is., Spain, 8,019 | B 4 | 17 |
| La Paz, Argentina, 15,006 | J10 | 47 |
| La Paz,* Bolivia, 350,142 | G 7 | 46 |
| La Paz, Mexico, 24,253 | D 5 | 44 |
| La Pérouse (strait), Asia | O 2 | 32 |
| La Piedad, Mexico, 24,337 | H 6 | 44 |
| La Plata, Argentina, †330,310 | O12 | 47 |
| La Quiaca, Argentina, 6,768 | G 8 | 46 |
| La Rioja, Argentina, 23,164 | G 9 | 47 |
| La Roche-sur-Yon, France, 22,231 | C 4 | 16 |
| La Rochelle, France, 65,581 | C 4 | 16 |
| La Romana, Dom. Rep., 24,058 | F 6 | 48 |
| La Ronge, Saskatchewan, 707 | J 3 | 40 |
| La Serena, Chile, 46,689 | F 9 | 47 |
| La Seyne-sur-Mer, France, 22,471 | F 6 | 16 |
| La Solana, Spain, 14,948 | E 3 | 17 |
| La Spezia, Italy, †121,923 | B 2 | 18 |
| La Tuque, Quebec, 13,023 | F 4 | 41 |
| La Unión, Chile, 11,558 | F12 | 47 |
| La Unión, El Salvador, 10,687 | D 4 | 39 |
| La Vega, Dominican Rep., 19,884 | E 5 | 48 |
| Labé, Guinea, 12,500 | D 9 | 34 |
| Łabedy, Poland, 13,800 | A 4 | 24 |
| Labelle, Quebec, 1,224 | E 4 | 41 |
| Laboulaye, Argentina, 9,032 | H10 | 47 |
| Labrador (terr.), Newf., 13,534 | H 3 | 41 |
| Lábrea, Brazil, 2,080 | H 5 | 46 |
| Labuan (isl.), Sabah, 14,904 | E 4 | 31 |
| Labuha, Indonesia | H 6 | 31 |
| Labuhan, Indonesia, †22,259 | G 2 | 31 |
| Labuhanbilik, Indonesia | C 5 | 31 |
| Lac-au-Saumon, Quebec, 1,548 | G 4 | 41 |
| Lac-Bouchette, Quebec, 911 | F 4 | 41 |
| Lac-Edouard, Quebec, 250 | F 4 | 41 |
| Lac-Frontière, Quebec, 619 | G 4 | 41 |
| Lac-la-Biche, Alberta, 1,314 | H 4 | 40 |
| Laccadive, Minicoy and Amindivi (isls.), India, 24,108 | B 6 | 29 |
| Lacepede (bay), Australia | F 7 | 36 |
| Lacepede (islands), Australia | C 3 | 36 |
| Lachine, Quebec, 38,630 | F 4 | 41 |
| Lachlan (river), Australia | G 6 | 36 |
| Lachute, Quebec, 7,560 | F 4 | 41 |
| Lacombe, Alberta, 3,029 | H 4 | 40 |
| Ladoga (lake), U.S.S.R. | D 2 | 22 |
| Ladysmith, Br. Columbia, 2,173 | F 5 | 40 |
| Ladysmith, Natal, 22,997 | N17 | 35 |
| Lae, Terr. N. Guinea, 4,146 | B 7 | 31 |
| Laflèche, Saskatchewan, 749 | J 5 | 40 |
| Laghouat, Algeria, 20,344 | G 5 | 34 |
| Lagos, Mexico, 23,636 | J 6 | 44 |
| Lagos,* Nigeria, 394,000 | G10 | 34 |
| Lagos, Portugal, 10,008 | B 4 | 17 |
| Laguna, Brazil, 9,459 | L 9 | 47 |
| Laham, Indonesia | F 5 | 31 |
| Lahat, Indonesia, †25,781 | C 6 | 31 |
| Lahej, South Arabia, 11,000 | E 7 | 26 |
| Lahore, Pakistan, 1,297,000 | B 2 | 29 |
| Lahr, Germany, 22,599 | B 4 | 14 |
| Lahti, Finland, 66,802 | O 6 | 13 |
| Lais, Indonesia, †13,201 | C 6 | 31 |
| Laiwui, Indonesia | H 6 | 31 |
| Lajes, Brazil, 14,596 | L 9 | 47 |
| Lake Cargelligo, Australia, 1,118 | H 6 | 36 |
| Lake Louise, Alberta, 113 | G 4 | 40 |
| Lakhdenpokh'ya, U.S.S.R. | C 2 | 22 |
| Lal'sk, U.S.S.R. | G 2 | 22 |
| Lambay (island), Ireland | K 4 | 12 |
| Lamego, Portugal, 10,236 | C 2 | 17 |
| Lamía, Greece, 21,509 | F 6 | 21 |
| Lammermuir (hills), Scotland | L 8 | 11 |
| Lamongan, Indonesia, †34,825 | K 2 | 31 |
| Lampang, Thai., 36,488 | C 3 | 30 |
| Lampertheim, Germany, 19,218 | C 4 | 14 |
| Lamphun, Thailand, 10,602 | C 3 | 30 |
| Lamu, Kenya, 5,868 | P12 | 35 |
| Lanai (island), Hawaii, 3,136 | H 8 | 42 |
| Lanark, Scotland, 8,441 | J 8 | 11 |
| Lancaster, England, 48,235 | E 3 | 10 |
| Lancaster (sound), N.W. Terrs. | B14 | 8 |
| Lanchow, China, 397,400 | F 4 | 32 |
| Lanciano, Italy, †27,624 | E 3 | 18 |
| Łańcut, Poland, 9,106 | F 3 | 24 |
| Lândana, Angola, 819 | J13 | 35 |
| Landau, Germany, 28,725 | C 4 | 14 |
| Landerneau, France, 11,278 | B 3 | 16 |
| Landeshut (Kamienna Góra), Poland, 16,000 | C 3 | 24 |
| Land's End (cape), England | B 7 | 10 |
| Landsberg, Germany, 13,413 | D 4 | 14 |
| Landsberg (Gorzów Wielkopolski), Poland, 50,700 | B 2 | 24 |
| Landshut, Germany, 49,514 | E 4 | 14 |
| Landskrona, Sweden, 28,820 | H 9 | 13 |
| Lang Son, N. Vietnam | E 2 | 30 |
| Langenbielau (Bielawa), Poland, 27,000 | C 3 | 24 |
| Langenburg, Saskatchewan, 757 | K 4 | 40 |
| Langsa, Indonesia, †47,044 | B 5 | 31 |
| Lansing,* Mich., 107,807 | M 4 | 43 |
| Lanús, Argentina, 381,561 | O12 | 47 |
| Lao Kay, N. Vietnam | E 2 | 30 |
| Laoag, Philippine Is., 25,105 | F 2 | 31 |
| Laon, France, 23,528 | E 3 | 16 |
| Lappeenranta, Finland, 21,627 | P 6 | 13 |
| Laptev (sea), U.S.S.R. | N 2 | 23 |
| Lar, Iran, 14,188 | J 7 | 27 |
| Larache, Morocco, 31,504 | E 4 | 34 |
| Laramie (mt. range), Wyo. | G 4 | 42 |
| Larantuka, Indonesia | G 7 | 31 |
| Larder Lake, Ontario, 1,894 | E 4 | 41 |
| Lárisa, Greece, 55,391 | F 6 | 21 |
| Larkana, Pakistan, 33,247 | A 3 | 29 |
| Larnaca, Cyprus, 19,824 | E 5 | 28 |
| Larne, N. Ireland, 16,341 | K 2 | 12 |
| Larvik, Norway, 10,603 | C 4 | 13 |
| Las Flores, Argentina, 9,287 | J11 | 47 |
| Las Lomitas, Argentina, 4,000 | H 8 | 47 |
| Las Palmas,* Canary Is., Spain, 166,236 | B 4 | 17 |
| Las Vegas, Nev., 64,405 | E 5 | 42 |
| Lascahobas, Haiti, 2,356 | C 6 | 48 |
| Lashio, Burma | C 2 | 30 |
| Lassen Peak (mountain), Calif. | C 4 | 42 |
| Latacunga, Ecuador, 14,936 | E 4 | 46 |
| Latakia, Syria, 67,799 | F 5 | 28 |
| Latouche Treville (cape), Australia | C 3 | 36 |
| Latur, India, 40,913 | C 5 | 29 |
| Lauban (Lubań), Poland, 14,300 | B 3 | 24 |
| Launceston, Australia, †56,721 | H 8 | 36 |
| Lauria, Italy, †12,644 | E 4 | 18 |
| Lauritsala, Finland, 11,647 | Q 6 | 13 |
| Lausanne, Switzerland, 126,328 | C 3 | 19 |
| Laval, France, 35,835 | C 3 | 16 |
| Lavello, Italy, †13,745 | E 4 | 18 |
| Laverton, Australia, 57 | C 5 | 36 |
| Lavongai (island), Territory N.G., 5,500 | F 6 | 37 |
| Lawang, Indonesia, †40,239 | K 2 | 31 |
| Lawrence, Mass., 70,933 | R 1 | 43 |
| Le Chesnay, France, 13,223 | A 2 | 16 |
| Le Creusot, France, 33,002 | F 4 | 16 |
| Le Havre, France, 182,504 | C 3 | 16 |
| Le Locle, Switzerland, 13,762 | C 2 | 19 |
| Le Mans, France, 128,814 | C 3 | 16 |
| Le Port, Réunion, 7,232 | P20 | 35 |
| Le Puy, France, 22,396 | F 5 | 16 |
| Leader, Saskatchewan, 1,211 | J 4 | 40 |
| Leaf (river), Quebec | F 2 | 41 |
| Leamington, England, 42,561 | F 5 | 10 |
| Leamington, Ontario, 9,030 | D 5 | 41 |
| Leatherhead, England, 35,582 | G 6 | 10 |
| Lębork (Lauenburg), Poland, 21,100 | C 1 | 24 |
| Lebrija, Spain, 12,903 | D 4 | 17 |
| Lecce, Italy, †75,297 | G 4 | 18 |
| Lecco, Italy, †48,230 | B 2 | 18 |
| Ledo, India | G 3 | 29 |
| Leduc, Alberta, 2,356 | H 4 | 40 |
| Lee (river), Ireland | D 8 | 12 |
| Leech (lake), Minn. | K 3 | 43 |
| Leeds, England, 510,676 | F 4 | 10 |
| Leek, England, 19,182 | E 4 | 10 |
| Leer, Germany, 20,524 | B 2 | 14 |
| Leeuwarden, Netherlands, 82,899 | H 2 | 15 |
| Leeuwin (cape), Australia | A 6 | 36 |
| Legaspi, Philippine Is., 21,887 | G 3 | 31 |
| Leghorn, Italy, †161,077 | C 3 | 18 |
| Legionowo, Poland, 18,900 | E 2 | 24 |
| Legnica (Liegnitz), Poland, 61,500 | C 3 | 24 |
| Lehrte, Germany, 21,257 | D 2 | 14 |
| Leiah, Pakistan, 14,913 | B 2 | 29 |
| Leicester, England, 273,470 | G 5 | 10 |
| Leichhardt (river), Australia | F 3 | 36 |
| Leiden, Netherlands, 96,592 | E 4 | 15 |
| Leigh, England, 46,174 | E 4 | 10 |
| Leipzig, Germany, 587,226 | E 3 | 14 |
| Leiria, Portugal, 7,477 | B 3 | 17 |
| Lekitobi, Indonesia | G 6 | 31 |
| Lemgo, Germany, 21,365 | C 2 | 14 |
| Lēmnos (island), Greece, 21,808 | G 6 | 21 |
| Lena (river), U.S.S.R. | N 3 | 23 |
| Leninabad, U.S.S.R., 77,465 | G 5 | 23 |
| Leninakan, U.S.S.R., 113,000 | F 6 | 22 |
| Leningrad, U.S.S.R., †3,498,000 | C 3 | 22 |
| Leninogorsk, U.S.S.R., 66,812 | J 5 | 23 |
| Leninsk, U.S.S.R. | G 5 | 22 |
| Leninsk-Kuznetskiy, U.S.S.R., 138,000 | J 4 | 23 |
| Lenkoran', U.S.S.R., 30,800 | G 7 | 22 |
| Lens, France, 42,508 | E 2 | 16 |
| Lentini, Italy, †32,389 | E 6 | 18 |
| Leoben, Austria, 36,257 | C 3 | 20 |
| Léogane, Haiti, 3,922 | C 6 | 48 |
| León, Mexico, 209,870 | J 6 | 44 |
| León, Nicaragua, 55,347 | D 4 | 39 |
| León, Spain, 73,483 | D 1 | 17 |
| Leonforte, Italy, †17,927 | E 6 | 18 |
| Leonora, Australia, 970 | C 5 | 36 |
| Léopold II (lake), R.o.t. Congo | K12 | 35 |
| Léopoldville,* R.o.t. Congo, 402,492 | K12 | 35 |
| Leoville, Saskatchewan, 416 | J 4 | 40 |
| Lepel', U.S.S.R. | C 4 | 22 |
| Lerdo, Mexico, 17,682 | H 4 | 44 |
| Lérida, Spain, 50,047 | G 2 | 17 |
| Les Cayes, Haiti, 13,088 | B 6 | 48 |
| Les Méchins, Quebec, 1,049 | G 4 | 41 |
| Les Sables d'Olonne, France, 18,267 | B 4 | 16 |
| Lesbos (island), Greece, 117,371 | G 6 | 21 |
| Leskovac, Yugoslavia, 34,396 | E 4 | 21 |
| Lesozavodsk, U.S.S.R., 32,124 | O 5 | 23 |
| Lesser Antilles (islands) | E 4 | 45 |
| Lesser Slave (lake), Alta. | G 3 | 40 |
| Leszno, Poland, 28,900 | C 3 | 24 |
| Letchworth, England, 25,511 | G 6 | 10 |
| Lethbridge, Alberta, 35,454 | H 5 | 40 |
| Leticia, Colombia, 1,898 | F 4 | 46 |
| Letpadan, Burma, 15,896 | C 3 | 30 |
| Leuser (mountain), Indon. | B 5 | 31 |
| Leuven (Louvain), Belgium, 32,524 | F 7 | 15 |
| Levack, Ontario, 3,178 | D 4 | 41 |
| Levádeia, Greece, 12,609 | F 6 | 21 |
| Levallois-Perret, France, 61,801 | A 1 | 16 |
| Lévêque (cape), Australia | C 3 | 36 |
| Leverkusen, Germany, 94,641 | B 3 | 14 |
| Levice, Czech., 13,770 | E 2 | 20 |
| Lévis, Quebec, 15,112 | F 4 | 41 |
| Levskigrad, Bulgaria, 8,862 | G 4 | 21 |
| Levuka, Fiji Islands, 1,944 | H 7 | 37 |
| Lewis (dist.), Scotland, 21,937 | C 3 | 11 |
| Lewisporte, Newf., 2,702 | K 4 | 41 |
| Lhasa, China, 50,000 | D 6 | 32 |
| Lhokseumawe, Indonesia, 2,043 | B 4 | 31 |
| Liaoyang, China, 150,000 | K 3 | 32 |
| Liaoyüan, China, 120,100 | L 3 | 32 |
| Liard (river), Canada | E 3 | 40 |
| Liberec, Czech., 67,180 | C 1 | 20 |
| Libourne, France, 15,050 | C 5 | 16 |
| Libreville,* Gabon, 31,027 | H11 | 35 |

## M

N

# Illustrated GEOGRAPHY and GAZETTEER of the WORLD

**THE HEADLINE EVENTS** of the last half-century have made the average person acutely curious of the vast world beyond the national borders of his homeland. Constant repetition has tended to make this thought a cliche, yet it is one of the most significant truths of our times. This new national concern for the external world and its problems is one of the hopeful signs pointing to a better future for mankind. However, no matter how well-intentioned our concern for international relations may be, it is of no value unless it is grounded on an intelligent appreciation for the great diversity of social, economic and political forms extant throughout the globe.

On the following pages the editors have presented a treasure-trove of information on the world's nations, resources, peoples and governments. Salient facts regarding the many countries of our Mother Earth have been arranged in easily-found tabular form. This arrangement by tables makes comparison between political units a simple task. Striking photographs lend a sense of immediacy to the equally engaging text descriptions of countries and continents. Highlighting the gazetteer and geography are the Resource-Relief maps which locate at a glance the major relief and resource features of the continental land masses.

Canadian National Railways

Small fishing fleets like this one in Prince Rupert, British Columbia, support Canada's important fishing industry.

**NORTH AMERICA** — Lying across the wide expanse of the Atlantic Ocean, was a new World waiting discovery and recognition. Europe was completely unaware of its existence for many centuries. Its discovery was destined to change the whole course of history and affect the fortunes of men and nations the world over. More than that, its discovery ushered in a whole new era of civilization, and marked the first faltering steps towards the exploration and charting of all lands and waters of the world.

No discovery, before or since, has added more to man's opportunities and the wealth of the world; or played a more important part in shaping a world's destiny.

Compared with the other continents of the world, North America is perhaps the most favored for natural wealth, climate and position on the earth. Being situated between the two largest oceans has protected the people of North America from enemy invasion, and also enabled them to develop an extensive commerce. The millions of square miles of fertile soil and untold mineral wealth has provided a standard of living unknown elsewhere in the world.

The principal geographical features of North America are its two mountain ranges and the intervening central plains. The high and rugged mountains to the westward extend from the tip of Alaska to the base of the Isthmus of Panama, or from the northern to the southern extremity of the continent. These mountain ranges include the coastal system that hugs the Pacific Coast, and the Rocky Mountains that branch out eastward and southward across the United States to become, in Mexico and Central America, the Sierra Madres. The Cascade Mountains, which farther south become the Sierra Nevada, are separate ranges that work inland from the coastal mountains. These diverging mountain chains in the east and west form the bulwark for a number of high plateaus that lie between. The land adjoining the Cascade Mountains is the Columbia Plateau, while farther south lies the Colorado Plateau. In between is the arid region of the Great Basin. The Great Salt Lake is a remnant of an inland sea which once covered this vast area.

In the east, extending from the Gulf of Saint Lawrence to the Gulf of Mexico is the Appalachian Range. These mountains are older and less rugged than the Rockies. Time has worn them down and rounded their peaks. On the side toward the Atlantic Ocean, they merge with the Piedmont Plateau, which slopes off into a coastal plain.

The great central plains that slope towards the center, and lie between the Rocky Mountains and Appalachian Highlands describe a giant "V" which extends from the Arctic Ocean to the Gulf of Mexico.

North America exhibits striking contrasts in its patterns of temperature and rainfall. The greater part of the continent, however, enjoys a temperate and invigorating climate. The inhabitants of the far north must adjust themselves to the rigors of Arctic weather,

Mexico endures sub-tropical temperatures, and Central America a tropical heat. Even from east to west there is a wide variety of climate due to difference in altitude and prevailing winds.

On the western coast, the great Pacific Ocean, generally a protective barrier, separating most of North America from the shores of Asia, offers little promise of isolation at its far northwest corner. While eight thousand miles separate the peoples of China from the United States, Russia and Alaska almost meet at the Bering Strait, which is only fifty-five miles wide.

Quidi Vidi Gut, Newfoundland, is typical of the many inlets along Canada's eastern coast.

Trans Canada Airlines

**CANADA**—The over 5,000 mile boundary between the United States and Canada is convincing proof that two great nations may live side by side in peace and harmony. For over a hundred years this boundary line —the longest in the world—has been free from fortification of any kind by either nation.

Canada is the largest domain of the British Commonwealth. It extends from the icy waters of the Arctic to the borders of the United States, and from east to west its greatest distance is 3,700 miles. Its area, partly unsuited for habitation, is nearly as large as the continent of Europe. Like the United States, Canada can be roughly divided into three sections: the eastern highlands, a great level central plain, and mountain ranges extending from the Rockies to the Pacific.

In the east are the beautiful Maritime Provinces with their hilly or mountainous terrain with very heavily forested sections and fertile farm lands. Just west of the highlands lies the St. Lawrence Valley including the Ontario peninsula, the hub of Canada's industry. In this area, rich in minerals, forests, water power and fertile land is the highest concentration of population. Invigorating climate combined with valuable accessible resources have made this a section of the greatest economic importance. Northwest of the Valley is the Canadian Shield, an area characterized by low hills, countless lakes connected by streams and rapids. Here is Canada's greatest store of resources, minerals, forests, furs and water power. In the interior Plains is the great wheat belt. In the west, parallel to the Pacific, is the magnificent mountain country formed by the Cordilleran Mountain System. In addition to minerals and valuable forests, this area, in the fertile valleys, produces much of Canada's fruit and vegetable crops.

Wheat is the principal crop of the prairie provinces, and Canada is one of the biggest producers and exporters of this grain. Lumbering is of great importance, which is to be expected, for the forests of Canada are among the largest in the world. Furs have been a great source of wealth since the early

U.S. Air Forces
Like a wide river of ice with side-streams, Ribbon Glacier descends from high peaks near Mt. McKinley, Alaska.

Drumlins, elongated mounds of glacial drift, as seen from the air over Labrador.

Walter Nebiker

days of the Hudson's Bay Company, and the fishing grounds of Canada are large and highly productive.

Canada possesses a wide variety of precious mineral resources, such as uranium, petroleum, gold, nickel, iron, lead, zinc and copper. Since the expansion of railroads and, more recently, the development of air service, their exploitation is rapidly increasing. As over six per cent of Canada's area is water, the country's potential hydroelectric power is almost limitless.

About half of the population is of British origin and one third is French. The rest are Germans, Russians, Scandinavians and others. Indians number some hundred thousands; in the Arctic region live a few thousand Eskimo.

**UNITED STATES** — Bordered on the east and west by the Atlantic and Pacific Oceans, on the north by Canada, and on the south by Mexico and the Gulf of Mexico, the United States also includes the outlying states of Alaska and Hawaii. Lying mostly in the temperate zone, its climate and land surfaces are varied. The three principal geographical features are a continuation of those in Canada; the eastern highlands, comprising the Appalachian Range, the broad central plains, and the Rockies and the coastal ranges in the far west.

The Appalachian highlands, which dominate the eastern United States, rise directly from the sea in the northeast. This region of hills and poor soil is part of the manufacturing belt which crosses the northeastern and north-central part of the nation. It is also known for its educational institutions and commercial activities. Boston, the largest city of the region, is its seaport. From the central and southern portions of the highlands come coal and lumber to feed the industries of the east.

Where the sea drowned the rivers, the New York, Delaware and Chesapeake Bays were formed. Around their port cities cluster smaller manufacturing cities and their suburbs, making the Middle Atlantic region the most heavily populated area of the country. New York is the largest city of the United States, its chief port, and a leading manufacturing center. Philadelphia, the third largest city, is also a major port and manufacturing center. Washington, the capital, is located on the Potomac River, which empties into lower Chesapeake Bay.

In the warmer south, on the broad and fertile coastal plain, peanuts are grown. On the piedmont behind these plains tobacco and cotton are cultivated. The Florida penin-

TWA-Trans World Airlines
Modern, many-storied office buildings characterize the sky line of New York City.

ton. Here there are important deposits of oil and sulphur. New Orleans, a port city on the Mississippi Delta, is the southern outlet of the Mississippi River Valley. Houston is the center of an oil-producing and live-stock-raising area.

The mountain region which covers the western third of the nation includes the Rocky Mountains, an area of plateaus and basins, and the high Sierra Nevada-Cascade Range, whose foothills extend to the Pacific. Here is an area of beautiful mountain scenery, spectacular canyons, broad expanses of deserts, all of which attract large numbers of tourists. The mountains of the northwest are an important source of lumber and throughout the area there is considerable mining of copper, silver, gold, lead, zinc, and other minerals. In the basins farming is carried on, particularly in the irrigated areas of the south where citrus fruits, cotton, and winter vegetables are grown, and the north where fruits, sugar beets and grain are grown.

West of the Sierra Nevada-Cascade mountains, the coastal ranges drop to the sea, interrupted in places by fertile valleys. In the north is Puget Sound, on which is Seattle, the chief port for Alaskan trade. The Great Central Valley of California is one of the country's richest garden spots. Citrus and other fruits, nuts and winter vegetables thrive in the mild sunny climate. The Sacramento and San Joaquin Rivers which water the valley, empty into San Francisco Bay, on which are the city of spectacular views, San Francisco, and her sister city, Oakland. On the southern California coast are Los Angeles and San Diego, major industrial centers and Pacific ports.

A peninsula jutting from the northwestern

Walter Nebiker
Spanish-style church on Watling I., Bahamas, where Columbus first landed in 1492.

corner of the continent, Alaska is the largest of the fifty states. It has a wide area of equable climate, but in the extreme north the ground thaws only a few inches at the surface during the summer, and there is comparatively little life or vegetation able to survive the rigors of the frigid climate. In the more temperate area, mining, lumbering and fishing are the chief industries. The Aleutian Islands are strung out in a broad arc off the tip of Alaska for a thousand miles, separating the Bering Sea from the north Pacific.

Hawaii, the last state to enter the Union, is a group of eight large islands, and many smaller ones located in the Pacific Ocean some two thousand five hundred miles from the mainland. These tropical islands, the peaks of volcanic mountains rising from the ocean's floor, produce sugar, pineapple, coffee and cut flowers for export.

sula is an important citrus fruit-growing region and a popular vacationland.

Beyond the Appalachians, a vast plain is drained by a major river system, the Mississippi-Missouri. In the north is a dairying region; in the center is the corn and wheat growing belt. Chicago, on the southern edge of Lake Michigan, one of the five great inland seas which border Canada, is the second largest city of the country, and an important manufacturing center standing at the center of a vast web of railroads. Manufacturing cities spread across the north-central plains and the Appalachians into the northeast.

In the south the coastal area of the Gulf of Mexico grows rice, sugarcane and cot-

Small towns like Peacham, Vermont, add to the rural charm of the New England countryside.

Winston Pote

**MEXICO** — Beyond the southern border of the United States and across the Rio Grande, where North America begins to taper sharply to a point, lies Latin America. It is difficult to conceive of the contrast to be found beyond this man-made boundary with the rest of the continent. It is another world, with a totally different culture, another language, and traditions and customs which set it apart from its northern neighbors.

From its nearly 2,000 mile-long northern border, Mexico swings south for about eighteen hundred miles, ending in the narrow hook of the peninsula of Yucatan.

While half of Mexico lies in the torrid zone, its climate is determined more by elevation than latitude. Along the coast the weather is hot and humid, with luxuriant

Picturesque Taxco, in Mexico, founded by Cortes in 1529.

Constance Larson

Charles Perry Weimer

Farm and farmhouse in El Salvador.

between. The average altitude of this plateau is about 6,500 feet. Mexico's highest concentration of population is here where the fertile land, ideal climate and favorable rainfall afford excellent conditions for agricultural crops. Although industrial development has increased rapidly in recent years and most of Mexico's wealth is derived from her mines and petroleum, the great majority of the people are still employed in agricultural pursuits. Except for the coastal plain bordering the Gulf of Mexico, mountains and plateaus occupy the greater part of Mexico. Lying in both the temperate and torrid zones allows the country to produce a greater variety of crops than is possible in most other countries.

Mexico is a beautiful and picturesque country with ancient ruins of pyramids and temples still standing as mute evidence of a flourishing civilization that existed before the coming of the Spanish invaders in the early fifteenth century.

bors on both coasts, with the principal seaports on the Caribbean Sea. Most of the rivers that flow into the Caribbean are navigable.

Charles Perry Weimer

Volcano Santiago near Managua, Nicaragua.

tropical vegetation. As the land rises the climate changes to temperate and the mountain peaks are snow-clad. Two mountain chains, that are a continuation of those in the United States, converge and meet at the southern tip, leaving a high plateau

Guatemalan Indians, descendants of the Mayas, selling their wares in Chichicastenango.

E. L. Jordan

**CENTRAL AMERICA** — As North America decreases in size from a land of magnificent distance to a slender neck of land where the Isthmus of Panama joins South America, the sizes of its nations shrink to even greater extent. In Central America six small countries: Guatemala, Honduras, El Salvador, Nicaragua, Costa Rica and Panama are confined to an area slightly greater than 200,000 square miles. Their total population is somewhat more than 12,000,000.

The Cordilleras, a continuation of the mountain chains starting far north in Alaska, extend the entire length of the land. Many of the peaks are volcanic and frequent eruptions occur. These mountains have formed many high and fertile plateaus which provide fine pasturage for livestock and rich soil for a diversity of crops. As in Mexico, the tropical climate of the lower regions is tempered by the elevation of the high plateaus. There are a number of har-

These agricultural nations have become increasingly important in the past few years. With the organizing of the Pan American Union, the growth of air travel, and the fostering of a new spirit of co-operation between the republics of North and South

Natives displaying their attractive woven goods in Santiago Atitlán, Guatemala.

E. L. Jordan

El Morro fortress, centuries-old sentinel guarding the harbor of San Juan, Puerto Rico.

Hamilton Wright

America, Central America's future became one of promise. When global war shut off supplies of many important crops to the Western world from the East, it was found that here in the Americas could be grown many necessities that formerly had been imported from afar. Great variation in soils, rainfall, and terrain afford an enormous variety of tropical, semi-tropical and temperate crops. Experiments have successfully produced important quantities of spices, fibers, and essential oils for medicinal and industrial purposes that were introduced from the East. Among the important crops exported almost exclusively to the United States are bananas, natural rubber, coffee, rope fibers, cacao and sugar.

Although there is potential mineral wealth in most of the countries of Central America, this resource, for the most part, has been unexploited. Much of the land is heavily forested and some of the world's most valuable woods such as mahogany, rosewood, teak and ebony are found here. However, only a very small part of the forests have been as yet cut for commercial purposes.

**ISLANDS OF THE CARIBBEAN**—The Caribbean Sea is a vital water link between the Americas and the West Indies. With the opening of the Panama Canal it took on added importance as a trade route for the ships of the world.

The Caribbean islands, which Columbus named the Indies in the belief he had reached India, extend in a wide arc beginning near southern Florida and ending off the coast of Venezuela. The upper part of this arc is called the Greater Antilles and includes Jamaica, Cuba, Hispaniola, Puerto Rico and some smaller islands. The lower part of the arc from Virgin Islands to Curaçao and Aruba is made up of many small islands known as the Lesser Antilles.

Cuba (the largest island of the Greater Antilles), Haiti and the Dominican Republic (which share Hispaniola — the second largest of this island group), Jamaica, and Trinidad and Tobago are independent countries; Puerto Rico is a free commonwealth associated with the United States. East of Puerto Rico are the Virgin Islands, part of which are British; the rest form a territory of the United States. Most of the remaining islands of the area are British dependencies; a few are French, and a few belong to the Netherlands Antilles, an island group lying off the coast of Venezuela.

Although most of the Caribbean islands are mountainous, there is sufficient arable land to permit the raising of a great variety of tropical products. The climate is hot but tempered by the trade winds. All the islands are subject to hurricanes and in many regions occur occasional volcanic eruptions.

The original Carib Indians have for the most part disappeared from the islands. In Cuba, Puerto Rico and the Dominican Republic, the descendants of the white Spanish settlers form a large part of the population. In the other islands, the majority of the peoples are Negro or of mixed descent.

All the Caribbean islands depend on farming, and since they are very densely populated, the available crops are insufficient. Many of the natural resources are underdeveloped. In recent years a more extensive utilization of the natural wealth has set in, as modern agricultural planning helps to improve the crops, industrial manufacture is encouraged, and better transportation opens up wider markets.

**CUBA** — This largest of the Caribbean islands is also the most fertile, often called the "Pearl of the Antilles." Its actual name is of Indian origin. After its discovery by Columbus in 1492, it was ruled by Spain until 1898 and in 1902 became a republic under United States direction, which ended in 1934. The population contains minorities of Negroes, native Indians and mixed groups, but the majority (about 66%) are white, of Spanish descent. Customs and traditions have a distinctly Spanish flavor.

In Central and South America, sugar cane is cut by hand and large numbers of seasonal workers are required for its harvest.

Hamilton Wright

In recent years, Cuba has undergone great political changes, and it follows today in many ways the example of the Soviet Union.

Only one of Cuba's rivers is navigable, but it has many excellent harbors and an extensive rail and road system. It is fringed with several coral reefs and islands, the largest of which is the Isle of Pines, once the seat of pirates and reputed to be the original of Stevenson's "Treasure Island." Cuba is the world's largest producer of cane sugar. Minerals are found in the Sierra Maestra range, where especially iron, copper and gold are mined.

**HAITI** — The western portion of the island of Hispaniola, where the Gulf of Gonaives reaches far inland, is occupied by Haiti. This

Dominican Information Center

Central American countries produce sugar mainly for export. This sugar factory is in the Dominican Republic.

United Fruit Co.

The raising and export of tropical fruit is an important activity in Central America.

was the first of the Latin American countries to gain independence. In 1804 it shook off French rule, retaining, however, one important heritage, the French language; it is the only French-speaking republic in the Americas. The majority of the population is Negro.

Trade winds from the northeast bring rain and fertility to Haiti's tropical valleys. Coffee, which grows wild on its slopes, is the chief product for export. Haiti is also known for its sisal fiber, obtained from the leaves of the agave plant, which is used for lariats and other tough cordage, and its logwood, which furnishes an important dye.

**DOMINICAN REPUBLIC** — This comprises the eastern and larger part of the island of Hispaniola, bordering on the Atlantic Ocean and the Caribbean Sea. During its turbulent past, the country saw Spanish and Haitian rule and was temporarily occupied by the

United States (1916-1924). Its beautiful capital, the seaport city of Santo Domingo, was founded by Columbus' brother, Bartholomew, and is the oldest surviving European town in the Americas.

The island's Pico Duarte, 10,417 feet high, is the highest peak in the Caribbean. The country is mainly agricultural, cattle are extensively raised, the mineral resources include gold, and the forests abound in valuable timber. The most important products for export are sugar and molasses.

**PUERTO RICO** — This island, crisscrossed by craggy mountains and deep valleys, rises close to the greatest known depth of the Atlantic Ocean, and its southern shore is washed by the Caribbean Sea. In the West Indies group, it is the easternmost island of the Greater Antilles, of which Cuba, Hispaniola and Jamaica are the other larger units. Roughly rectangular in shape, it is about 100 miles long by 35 miles wide.

Puerto Rico was discovered by Columbus in 1493. Morro Castle, which guards the entrance to the harbor of San Juan, the capital, was built by the Spaniards, who ruled the island until 1898, when it was ceded to the United States. Puerto Rico has been a free commonwealth associated with the United States since 1952.

The island has over 2 million inhabitants and an area of 3,421 square miles; it is thus very densely populated with more than 687

inhabitants to the square mile. Its major agricultural crop is sugar. Tobacco, coffee and fruits are also extensively raised. By 1956, manufacturing had gained ground and the income from it exceeded that from agriculture. The climate is mild the year around with a mean winter temperature of 73° and a summer temperature of about 79°. This fine climate and excellent shipping and air connections attract many tourists.

**JAMAICA** — The English-speaking island country of Jamaica lies south of Cuba and west of the island of Hispaniola. This large and mountainous island produces coffee, bananas, cocoa and cabinet woods. Rum and the sugar from which it is manufactured are other highly profitable exports. Bauxite deposits, among the greatest in the world, are being worked in the interior. Kingston, the capital, has a large and particularly fine harbor. Montego Bay and Ocho Rios are but two of the many tourist resorts for which the island is famous.

**TRINIDAD AND TOBAGO** — The British islands of Trinidad and Tobago lie close to the continent of South America, of which, geologically speaking, they are an extension. Through the capital of Trinidad, Port of Spain, pass its valuable exports of asphalt, oil, sugar and cacao. Tobago, to the northeast of Trinidad, produces coconuts and cacao.

Air view of English Harbour, Antigua, in the West Indies.

Hamilton Wright
Children in native costume in Medellín, Colombia.

**SOUTH AMERICA** — Roughly triangular in shape, South America is joined to North America by the Isthmus of Panama. It tapers southward from its long Caribbean coast a distance of several thousand miles to its narrow tip where Cape Horn overlooks the Drake Passage, disturbed by fierce Antarctic storms. Most of South America lies well to the east of North America; its easternmost point in Brazil is slightly less than two thousand miles from the west coast of Africa. A theory has been advanced though never proved that at one time Africa and South America were joined.

Smaller than North America by over two million square miles, and representing one-seventh of the world's total land area, South America is the fourth largest continent.

With the equator crossing South America on a line with the Amazon River, two thirds of this southern neighbor is in the tropics and the balance in the temperate zone. In

common with other lands situated in the Southern Hemisphere, it has the further disadvantage of being far removed from the principal world markets. These factors, together with the history of the continent, explain why it has not developed as rapidly as the United States, although discovered at the same time. But in spite of the handicaps of climate, position and history, South America has an extensive trade with the United States and Europe. And, although for centuries the Spaniards robbed it of its buried treasures, South America still possesses great mineral wealth.

South of the Isthmus of Panama, the great line of mountains which extends the entire length of North America becomes the mighty Andes. Second only to the Himalayas, they follow the western coast to Cape Horn, rising steeply from the Pacific in long ranges of snow-capped peaks and wide plateaus. Mount Aconcagua is the highest peak in the Americas and rises to nearly twenty-three thousand feet. Several lesser peaks are active volcanos. To the south the range begins to narrow and the coast is bordered by a tattered fringe of islands clothed with pines and swept by fierce northwesterly winds.

In the east are two broad plateaus, the Guiana and Brazilian highlands, which might be compared with the Laurentian highlands and the Appalachian chain of North America. Between the eastern slope of the Andes and these plateaus lie broad lowlands. The grassy, tree-dotted plains, or *llanos,* of the Orinoco Basin in Venezuela and Colombia, provide fine pasturage between the dry and rainy seasons. In the dry season they practically revert to desert. To the south are the dry plains, or *pampas,* of Northern Argentina, which is the great cattle country of the continent.

The Amazon — largest river system in the world — drains over one-third of the continent, an immense area of over two million square miles. This mighty river is four thousand

Charles Perry Weimer
Sparkling bays and jagged hills form Rio de Janeiro's impressive natural setting.

sand miles long and in some places is over fifty miles wide. It flows through the densest tropical forest in the world and much of it is unexplored.

The La Plata River is actually the estuary for three rivers, the Paraná, the Uruguay and the Paraguay which drain a huge, little developed region, difficult of access.

Don Murray
Native children in Brazil doing their share of the farmwork.

Buenos Aires, metropolis of the Southern Hemisphere, is situated on the south bank of the La Plata 175 miles from the Atlantic.

The only important indentations on the Pacific are found along the rugged coast of southern Chile and the Gulf of Guayaquil in Ecuador.

The high temperature and humidity of the tropical regions, together with many insects and diseases, discourage the activity of white people and even sap the strength of the natives. Large areas of swamp and rugged mountains have made the development of transportation difficult and expensive. Only with the growth of air travel has it been possible for the Andean countries to contact one another with relative ease.

In the main, South America is sparsely settled, with the greatest density of popula-

The backdrop for Caracas' baroque churches and modern apartment buildings is formed by the slopes of an eastern spur of the Andes.

Hamilton Wright

Moore-McCormack

Its extensive port facilities have helped to make Buenos Aires one of the largest and most important trade centers in the western hemisphere.

tion along the coasts. The original inhabitants were Indians, but, due to the early colonization by the Spanish and Portuguese, many of the present inhabitants are *mestizos,* a mixture of Indian and Spanish or Portuguese blood. The remainder is largely composed of Italian and German immigrants. Except in Brazil, where the official language is Portuguese, Spanish is spoken in all the other independent countries.

Since the early coming of the Spaniards, South America has continued to yield great stores of precious metals. The Andes are rich in minerals, and the eastern highlands contain iron, gold, and diamonds. Some coal is found in Brazil, Chile and Colombia, but

Charles Perry Weimer

Llamas in the highlands of Bolivia serving as beasts of burden.

Charles Perry Weimer

Ruins of an ancient Indian citadel at Machu Picchu high in the Peruvian mountains.

not in great quantity. Water-power and oil are being utilized to make up for this lack.

Ecuador, Peru and Chile are all west coast countries, which, until the opening of the Panama Canal, were practically isolated from the rest of the world. Bolivia, having no outlet to the sea, moves nearly all of her exports through the seaports of Chile and Peru.

**CHILE** — Sometimes called the "Shoestring Republic," Chile stretches along the west coast for twenty-six hundred miles, from the borders of Peru to Cape Horn. It has a

variety of climate ranging from frigid to torrid. This long, narrow and mountainous country is one of the most progressive in South America. It is one of the three republics where there are more white people than natives. The other two are Argentina and Uruguay.

From north to south Chile is divided into three regions: the desert, a dry sub-tropical region which is densely populated, and a section that is forested. The greatest mineral region lies between Santiago and the Peruvian border. In the northern half of this area are the nitrate fields which have produced almost the entire world's supply of this important fertilizer. The nitrate beds located in the Pacific coastal desert (Atacama) were wrested from Peru during the War of the Pacific (1879-83) from which Chile emerged victorious. Chile's fame as a nitrate region has waned with the introduction of synthetic nitrate into world industry. The country is now seeking to stimulate the export of wine, honey and livestock. In the southern half there are deposits of copper, iron, gold and silver. Chile ranks next to the United States in the mining of copper and supplies about 20 per cent of the world's output.

**PERU**—This country is an extension of the narrow and arid coastal plain in northern Chile, with the Andes occupying fully half of the land. A densely wooded tropical region drops down in the east to meet the low plains of Brazil.

About a fourth of the population is white, most of whom are Spanish. The balance are *mestizos* (mixed) or Indians. Descendants of the ancient Incas, the Indians of Peru are found principally living on the high mountain slopes of the Andes, and sailing their strange fiber craft on Lake Titicaca. These Indians have domesticated the llama and the alpaca, two animals which are native to this region, and which have never been raised successfully elsewhere. The llama is a sure-footed animal upon which the Indians depend for food, clothing and transportation. Used as a beast of burden in this lofty arid country, the llama, like the camel, can go several days without water. The alpaca is too small to carry loads and is raised for its very long wool.

Once famous for its precious metals, Peru today produces in its mountains besides silver and gold other important minerals such as copper, zinc and vanadium. In the coastal lowlands, cotton and sugar are grown on

Not Panama but Ecuador is the place where the original, hand-woven "Panama" hats are made.

Hamilton Wright

large plantations (haciendas). In the headlands of the Amazon River, shut off from the
rest of the country by the Andes, oil has recently been discovered, which may hasten
their development.

**ECUADOR**—Peru and Ecuador have a
similar climate and topography except for
the northern part of the coastal plain of
Ecuador. This plain is as fertile as any area
in South America and is the principal agricultural section of Ecuador. The chief crops
are cacao, coffee and bananas. Ecuador's
coffee and bananas have been increasing in
importance since its cacao, blighted by
witches'-broom, has suffered an appreciable
decrease in export. Tagua, a substitute for
ivory, is produced in limited quantities. Ecuador is world-famous for its amazing variety
of wild birds. The country contains one-
fourth of all recorded species in South
America.

**BOLIVIA** — Shut off from the sea by Chile
and Peru, Bolivia is one of the most sparsely
populated countries in the world. It consists of a high plateau in the southwest that
is cold and dry, and wet tropical lowlands
in the north and east. Though Bolivia's surface is three fifths lowlands, the country includes one of the highest inhabitable regions
in the world. The Andes spread out into two
great chains of mountains which enclose a
plateau nearly as high as the peaks themselves. On this plateau, on the border between Peru and Bolivia, lies Lake Titicaca,
the highest navigable lake in the world.

Oil refinery at Cochabamba, second largest city in Bolivia. Bolivia's young oil industry promises to become
important.

While its scenery is tropical, Brazil's climate
is tempered in many parts by altitude and sea
breezes.
Brazilian Government Trade Bureau

Bolivia ranks next to the Malay Peninsula
and the Indonesian islands in its tin deposits,
and is well supplied with nearly all the
known metals. Strangely enough, although
having local supplies of coal, necessary in
smelting, it is usually cheaper to import coal.

Lack of capital, the high cost of transportation, and the scarcity of labor, have re-
tarded mining in all the countries of the
Andes. Only the natives can do manual
labor in the high altitudes and the people
are not inclined toward mining.

**BRAZIL**—Covering nearly half the continent
and with about one-half the population,
Brazil lies almost entirely in the tropics. This
republic spreads over 3,286,170 square
miles and has three times the area of Argentina.

The Amazon and its tributaries have a
total length of over nineteen thousand miles,
of which thirteen thousand are navigable.
This huge system extends through more than
half the country's area.

The Brazilian Highlands, a great plateau
country, extend to the south and east of the
Amazon River. The capital, Brasília, is located in this region. At the Atlantic shore
lies Rio de Janeiro with its famous harbor. It
is the second largest city on the continent.

Brazil at one time was the greatest rubber-
producing country. Brazil has embarked on
a program of intensified manufacturing. Silk,
cotton and woolen mills have sprung up all
over the eastern seaboard. Shoes and hats

are becoming major products. Many paper
mills are being built to utilize some of the
billion acres of forests that cover half the
land area. Its greatest mineral wealth has
yet to be exploited, though one of the
largest estimated deposits of iron ore in the
world is now being developed. The country
produces nearly fifty percent of the world's
coffee. Efforts to do away with the one-crop
system are gaining success and coffee is no
longer the economic tyrant that it was. A
growing cacao industry now ranks second in
the world, while tobacco, rice, cotton and
sugar are attaining commercial significance.

**URUGUAY** — This is the smallest republic
in South America. It has a fine climate with
the winds of the ocean modifying the
temperature.

Since the Spanish brought sheep and
cattle to the grassy plains of Uruguay in the
17th century, it has been a stock raising
country. Today it is one of the leading meat
exporters of the world. Only a small per-
centage of the arable land is devoted to the
raising of crops and it is limited in both
minerals and manufacturing.

**PARAGUAY**—One of the two republics of
South America that is completely surrounded
by other nations. Little has been done to
develop its natural resources.

Most of the surface of western Paraguay
is a low, swampy and unhealthy plain. The
climate in the north is hot and unsuited to

the white man. Most of the people live in the southern area east of the Paraguay River. It is a country of small villages, grazing and farm lands, which depends upon the rivers for means of transportation.

Extending from Bolivia across the western third of Paraguay and south into Argentina, is the Gran Chaco, a great plain.

**THE ARGENTINE REPUBLIC** — The early colonists' anticipation of finding silver and gold in Argentina prompted them to name the country for the Latin word meaning silver. Although the colonists' search for great mineral wealth was in vain, the fertile soil and temperate climate have fostered the country's great economic progress. The Republic is the second largest of the South American countries.

The Gran Chaco, in the northern part, is a land of forests, lakes and swamps, which is largely unexplored. The grassy plains of the *Pampas* occupy a large area of Argentina. This cattle country and farm land extends from the Atlantic coast to the Andes in the west, and northwest to the highlands which reach into Brazil. The rich grazing lands, which have led to Argentina becoming a large exporter of meat and wool,are in the center of the *Pampas*.

Argentina is an agricultural and commercial, rather than an industrial country. It has been hindered in the development of manufacture by a shortage of coal, the lack of water power, and an inadequate supply of minerals.

Descendants of the Spanish settlers are the leaders of the country, with most of the farm population consisting of Italians. Immigrants from the British Isles have taken to sheep raising, and many Germans have migrated to Argentina. Today most of the

population are foreign-born or descendants of immigrants.

**COLOMBIA**—The only South American country having a coastline along both the Atlantic and Pacific oceans. Half the country is high in the rugged Andes; the other half lies in unhealthy tropical plains. Three cordilleras of the Andes traverse it in parallel lines from north to south forming a barrier between the seacoast and the rich inland valleys. The chief source of wealth is coffee. Colombian coffee is the finest in the world and the bean is jealously guarded. Ninety percent of the exported coffee is shipped to the United States. A type from the area around Medellín commands the highest price per pound in the world. Surpassed by Brazil in quantity, Colombia's coffee yields to none in quality. Next to coffee in export value is oil. The fields are to a large extent a continuation of those in Venezuela. Other resources include gold, platinum, emeralds and coal.

**VENEZUELA**—One of the most productive oil regions in the world is on the coast of the Caribbean. Easy access to this coast from the interior affords great possibilities for commercial and industrial development. Venezuela's land area is distinguished by its llanos or wide lowlands along the Orinoco River. The river is navigable for a course of 700 miles and is connected to the Amazon system by the Casiquare River, a natural canal. Coffee, chiefly from the basin of the Maracaibo, is second only to that of Colombia. A ranking producer of petroleum, Venezuela's exploitation of oil is fraught with difficulties which have never been successfully surmounted. Virgin forests cover the country and include about 600 species of wood. At Margarita is located a profitable pearl in-

The large oil deposits beneath the waters of Lake Maracaibo make Venezuela one of the most productive oil regions in the world.

dustry. Iron, asphalt, coal and gold figure as the main mineral resources.

**THE GUIANAS** — On the north coast of South America are the only European possessions on the continent. The climate is tolerable except in the south where the northeast trade winds do not prevail. Mineral resources in the form of gold and diamonds are about equally divided among the three Guianas.

Long stretches of the Pan American Highway pass through elevated highlands in sight of snow-capped peaks and extinct volcanoes.

Hamilton Wright

Walter Nebiker

The Rock of Gibraltar guards the western entrance to the Mediterranean Sea.

the Balkan Peninsula is surrounded by the Black Sea and the Adriatic, Ionian and Aegean Seas of the Mediterranean.

Great Britain is prevented from being a peninsula only by the narrow English Channel, and was once a part of the mainland. The entire course of history has been changed by this strip of water which made England an island. The same may be said for the Straits of Gibraltar separating Europe from Africa. But for this eight-mile passage, the Mediterranean would have had no outlet to the Atlantic.

Europe may be divided into five natural regions: (1) the Northwest Highlands, (2) the Central Plains, (3) the Central Highlands, (4) the Southern Mountains and Plateaus, and (5) the Southern Lowlands.

Most of the British Isles, a section of France, and a good part of the Scandinavian Peninsula are included in the Northwest Highlands. This is the coastal region with excellent harbors where men have made

E. L. Jordan

On the Balearic Islands, as elsewhere in Europe, windmills were an important source of power before motors were invented.

**EUROPE** — Eurasia is the world's largest land mass and includes both Europe and Asia. Europe occupies about a third of the western end of Eurasia, and, with the exception of Australia, is the smallest continent.

E. L. Jordan

The world's northernmost city, Hammerfest in Norway, lies in the region of the midnight sun. A warm ocean drift keeps the port ice-free.

It is the most densely populated for its size and no other continent has so many separate nations. Nearly all of these countries have distinctive customs and speak different languages. This does much to explain Europe's turbulent history.

Actually Europe is a huge peninsula, subdivided into a number of lesser peninsulas, caused by the oceans and inland seas which encroach upon it. Its irregular form, together with the mountain barriers, and the presence of important islands near the continent, have contributed to the growth of individual nations.

In the northwest, two peninsulas are formed by the Baltic Sea. The countries of Norway and Sweden occupy the Scandinavian Peninsula. Denmark is on the Jutland Peninsula between the Baltic and North Seas. To the south, Portugal and Spain comprise the Iberian Peninsula. The peninsular boot of Italy thrusts out into the Mediterranean, and

their living by the sea, and commerce has become most important. In those places where coal and iron are found it has led to an industrial life. This highland region enjoys

a cool, temperate climate and people are energetic.

The great Central Plains extend from the British Isles to the Ural Mountains that separate Europe from Asia. These plains range from the tundra regions of the Far North to the Caspian Sea, the Caucasus Mountains, and the Black Sea of the Southeast. In the Southwest they reach into southern France. Within such an extensive area there are naturally great differences in climate. There is also great diversity of vegetation and the occupations of the people.

The Central Highlands include the plateau in central France and take in parts of Belgium, southern Germany, Austria, and the Czecho-Slovakian area. It is the region of forest, water-power, and varied mineral resources. The industrial districts of Central Europe are the outgrowth of the great deposits of coal and iron found here.

The impressive peaks of the Alps rise south of the Central Highlands, forming one of the many ranges of Southern Europe. The Apennines extend the length of Italy, and other ranges follow the eastern coast of the Adriatic through Yugoslavia and Albania to the southern tip of Greece. Spreading out to the east they include most of the Balkan Peninsula. To the north the Carpathian Mountains swing northeast and then southeast around

Rome is the seat of the Vatican City State with the beautiful Renaissance basilica of St. Peter's.

TWA-Trans World Airlines

the valley of the Danube, forming with the Transylvanian Alps in Rumania a kind of semicircle around the Plain of Hungary. Farther to the east, the Caucasus Mountains reach from the Black to the Caspian Sea. Separating France and Spain are the Pyrenees, and the Sierra Nevadas are in southern Spain bordering the Mediterranean.

The Southern Lowlands of the Danube Valley and the Plain of Hungary represent some of the finest farming and grazing land in the world.

The extreme irregularity of the European coastline has been of great importance to the life of the people. With the North and Baltic Seas, the Mediterranean and Black Seas penetrating far into the interior, only Central Europe and Eastern Russia are very far from the coast. Although the combined areas of South America and Africa are nearly five times that of Europe, the coastline of Europe is longer.

The soil yields little and rural life is simple on the Isle of Skye, Scotland.

British Information Services

The Arch of Triumph, begun by Napoleon I, is a landmark of Paris.

TWA-Trans World Airlines

A majority of the great seaports of the world are in Western Europe. Its people have led the world in seafaring.

Europe has a generally mild, temperate climate, particularly in the western areas,

Canals thread their way through the center of Amsterdam, capital of the Netherlands.

Karletta

which are warmed by ocean currents and the winds blowing over these waters. Even the British Isles have a mild climate in spite of being in the same latitude as Labrador. Greater extremes of temperature exist in eastern Europe where these winds lose their moderating effect.

Due to the Alps blocking the cold north winds, and the influence of the warm waters of the Mediterranean, the southern shores of Europe enjoy a mild year-round climate. Except in eastern Europe, where the rainfall is light, there is generally sufficient moisture for agriculture.

**GREAT BRITAIN AND NORTHERN IRELAND**—The British Isles and the British Commonwealth of Nations owe much of their commercial and industrial growth to the daring and initiative of their early mariners. Although we usually think of the British Isles as comprising Great Britain and Ireland, it actually consists of nearly five thousand islands. Within the small compass of the islands there is a considerable variety of topography.

In Northern Ireland there are many lakes, including the largest one of the island, Lough Neagh, as well as a range known as the Mourne Mountains. A large portion of the country consists of the basalt plateau of Antrim.

Northern Ireland, or Ulster, as the six counties are sometimes called, is the seat of a very extensive lace and linen industry. In County Down and County Antrim there are highgrade deposits of granite and bauxite which are being exploited. Shipbuilding is a major industry centered in the capital, Belfast.

In Scotland the three well-marked divisions stand out, the highlands, the southern uplands, and between these two, the central lowlands, into which four fifths of the population is crowded. The lowlands contain the richest agricultural land as well as the coal fields. They are penetrated by three great estuaries, the Firths of Tay and Forth on the east, and of Clyde on the west, so that communication coastwise or overseas is everywhere easy.

Scotland has some of the largest shipbuilding yards in the world on the Firth of Clyde. Sheep and cattle are raised in large numbers since the land is not well suited to agriculture.

The Welsh cliffy upland is flanked to the north and east by small coal fields, but the greatest field lies to the south. A belt of limestone running from Bill of Portland to Tees Bay, and bearing at many points valuable iron ores, serves as a rough boundary of industrial England, for to the south and east of it, apart from the metropolis, agricultural interests predominate. Lying to the west of the limestone band is the Devon-Cornwall peninsula, where great bosses of granite and slate form the famous moors.

Wales, after 700 years as a part of the English kingdom, retains its individuality and is nationalistic in speech, dress and customs. The Welsh language is Celtic, akin to the Gaelic of Ireland. It is the only speech of nearly one tenth of the people.

Because of the density of population Great Britain is far from self-sustaining and must depend upon the raw materials and products

The colorful uniforms of the "Yeomen of the Guard," also called "Beefeaters," attest to England's tendency to preserve old customs.

British Information Services

Typical Irish landscape in County Donegal, Ireland.

of other countries. This has led to the development of her world-wide commerce, a large part of which is carried on with the other members of the British Commonwealth. Agriculture is intensive with much importance placed on livestock. Many of the world's most valuable breeds of farm animals have been developed on English farms.

**IRELAND**—Except for coastal hills and mountains, the country is largely an ill-drained plain dotted with lakes and peat-bogs, and crossed by the sluggish Shannon. In the southwest is the beautiful Killarney Lakes region which attracts many tourists each year. Although little of the land is suitable for large scale agriculture, grass and fodder crops are abundant and provide stockraising needs which is the major in-

dustry of the country. The Shannon River, Royal Canal, anc the Grand Canal provide an excellent inland waterway system of transportation. Shannon airport, near Limerick, is a major international airway terminal. Horse-breeding is the most famous of Irish farm industries. A prosperous tourist trade is developing.

**NORWAY AND SWEDEN**—With its saw-toothed coast, great fiords, and neighboring islands, it is natural that Norway, occupying the western part of the Scandinavian peninsula, would be a maritime country. Norway's long coast line, facing the Atlantic, is edged with lofty cliffs and seamed with deep fiords. Islands, countless in number, fringe the coast. Most of the country is a rocky, rugged and barren land, about 20 per cent of which is forested. The rivers are short and torrential, but provide the finest salmon fishing in Europe. The Kjolen Mountains which form the backbone of the peninsula separate Norway from Sweden. These mountains rise in many parts to over 6,000 feet, the highest peaks being over 8,000 feet.

Norway is the land of the "midnight sun". From Trondheim northward at least a part of the disk of the sun is visible from May through July. But the winter nights are 17 hours long and midday seems like twilight during the winter months. Another striking feature is that much of the area above the Arctic Circle is warmer than some regions further south. Northeast Norway is the warmest part of the country in the summer.

Sweden consists primarily of a table-land sloping from the Kjolen Range to the Baltic. No less than 8 per cent of the surface of Sweden is water, the immense number of lakes covering almost 15,000 square miles. The two largest, Vänern and Vättern, in the southern portion of the country, are connected by a system of canals. Besides the

large number of small islands which fringe the coast, Sweden includes the two large Baltic islands of Gotland and Oland.

In Sweden, iron deposits are among the richest in the world. Swedish steel is universally famous for its fine qualities. The making of machinery for export is a major industry. Swedish agriculture is in a very high state of development, and exports wheat, bacon and butter in large quantities. In forestry and sawmilling the nation has evolved advanced methods and nearly half of her exports are in pulp and paper products.

**DENMARK** — Denmark occupies a peninsula and numerous islands lying at the entrance to the Baltic. It is a lowland country characterized by many lakes, ponds and short rivers. Its sandy shores are shallow, with lagoons shut in by shifting sand bars. Most of Denmark is farm land, about half of which is used for grazing. The Faeroe Islands produce fish, mutton and wool for the homeland.

Dairy farming is the country's chief industry, the products of which comprise nearly all her exports. Greenland, the largest island in the world, is a part of Denmark.

**ICELAND** — The republic is an island in the north Atlantic consisting of a great tableland averaging 2,000 feet above sea level. Of its whole area barely a quarter is habitable. The surface is dotted by over 100 volcanic peaks. There are many boiling springs and the geysers are world-famous. It is too cold for agriculture but has rich grazing land for sheep and cattle. Fishing provides the chief products for export.

**FINLAND**—Finland consists of a great plateau, ranging from 400 to 600 feet in elevation. The southern half of the plateau has about 25 per cent of its area occupied by thousands of shallow lakes, many of them linked by short natural or artificial channels, providing many miles of navigable waterways. Forests cover the greater part of the country which has led to lumbering, paper-making and the manufacture of woodenware. Over half the population is engaged in agricultural pursuits which are carried on under great difficulties.

**THE NETHERLANDS** — The tiny kingdom of the Netherlands, lacking natural resources, has been largely a nation of seafarers for centuries. Along the canals, the meadows are often ten or twelve feet below the water line, and between the land and the sea at high tide there may be a difference of twenty-five feet or more. The land is protected by embankments and dikes, and it may be pictured as a great trough, the floor of which slopes down from east and southeast toward the North Sea. The rivers which flow across the country from the

The picturesque old part of Stockholm lies on an island in Lake Mälaren.

Swedish National Travel Office

Belgian Government Information Center

Some of the atmosphere of the Middle Ages can still be felt in Bruges, Flanders.

higher continent beyond, are at their mouths frequently below the level of the sea, into which they have to be lifted by canals and locks across the dams or dikes. A large part of the land has been reclaimed from the sea and little by little it has become a fertile country.

**BELGIUM** — Smaller than Holland, Belgium is one of Europe's most densely populated countries. Situated between England, Holland, France and Germany, it is in the very center of industrial Europe. The country is well watered, and has two principal rivers, the Scheldt and the Maas. The country does not raise sufficient food to feed her people. Belgium's intensive industrialization has been at the expense of its agriculture, for the valley of the Sambre-Meuse, the chief industrial center, is also the richest farming land. Besides coal mining, steel manufacturing, and iron milling, Belgium's industrial output is increased by the age-old textile industry (once noted for tapestries and lace) which produces synthetic fabrics, wool and linen. The nation furnishes a great variety of farm products and a world-famous breed of horses. Little wildlife remains except in the Ardennes where deer still roam.

**LUXEMBOURG**—The Grand Duchy of Luxembourg, smaller than the state of Rhode Island, is one of Europe's oldest states. An abundant store of iron ore has encouraged mining, smelting and some manufacturing. International trade of the duchy has been carried on through a customs union with Belgium.

**LIECHTENSTEIN**—Only 27 miles larger than San Marino, Liechtenstein is a part of the Swiss customs union. Switzerland also administers its postal facilities.

**FRANCE**—France is largely an agricultural country where the farmers, instead of living on their farms usually live in nearby villages. Although rich in minerals, it has lagged behind both England and Germany as an industrial country. France does not mine sufficient coal to make full use of its large iron ore deposits. The country's supply of energy has recently been supplemented by hydroelectric power obtained mainly in the alpine regions. It is a leading producer of textiles and has an important silk and rayon industry at Lyon. The business and traffic center of the entire country is Paris.

A large part of southeastern France is taken up by the Massif Central, a roughly triangular plateau with peaks reaching above 6,000 feet. Its eastern edge is formed by the Cévennes, and from them to the Vosges extend other mountain ranges. There is a mountainous area in Brittany, but the greatest heights are on the frontiers, the Jura, the Pyrenees, and the Alps separating France respectively from Switzerland, Spain and Italy. The Ardennes in the northeast are less lofty. The Seine drains the north, the Loire and the Garonne the west, and the Rhône the east and south. France has an extensive network of canals and much of its freight travels by waterway.

France enjoys a delightful climate. Only in the region of the Alps is real winter encountered. Protected by the mountains to the north, the balmy area along the Mediterranean is a magnet that has drawn countless vacationers. Many semi-tropical plants and fruits are grown in this section. Here also lies Grasse, an important center of the French perfume industry. In other parts of the country, notably around Paris and in Flanders, an abundant wheat crop is obtained. A great number of livestock are raised in many regions, particularly in Normandy and the Massif Central. Favored by a mild climate and fertile soils, French

viticulture has reached a high standard of excellency. France produces more wine than any other country, and the names of many of its vineyards and wine cellars have become famous throughout the world.

**MONACO**—The Principality of Monaco is one of the smallest states in the world. It possesses the administrative organs and institutions of larger nations in miniature. It has no taxes for it is supported by the gambling casino of Monte Carlo from which its own citizens are barred. The most striking feature of this 370 acre state is the Monagasque Acropolis on a headland 200 feet above the water. The Prince's Palace, a magnificent structure, is located on it.

**SWITZERLAND**—This rugged little country is a completely land-locked republic nestling among the beautiful Alps. It has succeeded in maintaining its neutrality and independence while the rest of Europe engaged in costly and devastating wars. Capitalizing upon its wonderful mountain and lake scenery, Switzerland has been the playground of Europe for many years. Although it has only very limited natural resources, the country has harnessed its great water power and is producing high-quality manufactured goods. On the slopes of the Alps and in the high valleys, dairying and cattle raising provide the chief occupation.

**GERMANY**—There are two natural regions in Germany, the low northern plains and the central and southern highlands. During the glacial period, sand was deposited over the plains region and the soil in many parts is not fertile, requiring the heavy use of fertilizers. Potatoes, sugar beets and rye are the chief crops, and cattle and horses are raised on large farms. In the central and southern highlands, a variety of fruits, vege-

River traffic on Rhine near St. Goar. On terraced hillsides are famous vineyards.

Walter Nebiker

Rapallo on the Italian Riviera attracts vacationers from many parts of the world.

tables and grains are grown on small farms. In Bavaria, where the Alps reach German soil, dairy farming prevails.

Germany's major rivers flow from the southern highlands northward, emptying into the North and Baltic Seas. Long stretches of them are navigable, and their lower courses are connected by canals providing cheap river traffic across the country and to the ocean. The Rhine carries more than half of this traffic, being the only river whose water supply remains adequate during the summer months. A system of canals enables German Rhine shipping to reach the ocean at a German seaport, Emden. Ships from the Baltic have a short route to the North Sea through the Kiel canal.

Germany is devoid of many important natural resources. However, she has an exceptionally large supply of coal. This formed the basis for the development of the country into one of the world's leading industrial nations. The chief coal fields are in the Ruhr Basin. Together with the adjacent part of

Mittenwald, Bavaria, is typical of places in the Bavarian and Austrian Alps.

Karletta

the Rhine valley, it is Germany's main industrial center. Germany also has sizable supplies of potash and petroleum and possesses some iron ore. The hydroelectric power obtained mainly in the southern highlands furnishes energy to a growing number of industries.

Germany's location in the center of Europe has meant both cultural stimulation and political tension. After the Second World War, the country was divided into an eastern and western part, each belonging to a different political sphere. This division upset the balance between Germany's various industrial and agricultural regions and required a far-reaching economic reorientation.

**AUSTRIA AND HUNGARY** — Austria is characterized by its beautiful mountain scenery, over 90 percent of the land is classified as mountainous, which has contributed to development of one of its largest industries—tourist and resort trade. However, over 80 per cent of the land is productive and half of this is under cultivation. In contrast, Hungary is largely comprised of a low fertile plain. The country is primarily agricultural and is a great grain and wine producer.

**CZECHOSLOVAKIA** — This land-locked country contains strategic routes between north and south Europe of economic and political value. The country has two large mountain ranges, the Carpathian in the east and the Sudeten in the west. Czechoslovakia is famous for its subterranean caverns and its spas and mineral springs. The people are energetic and progressive and there are valuable forest resources, fertile soil and varied mineral deposits.

**THE BALKANS**—They include Rumania, Yugoslavia, Bulgaria, Albania, Greece and European Turkey. Located at the gateway to Asia, and on a natural route connecting the two continents, this region has been a battleground for centuries. Repeated invasions from various directions have resulted in a

number of racial groups and religious beliefs. The rugged nature of the country has isolated the people into many rival factions with intense racial and national spirit.

**YUGOSLAVIA**—It consists essentially of a mountainous core, which stretches from the Dinaric Alps in the northwest to the Balkan Mountains on the Bulgarian frontier. The only valley which cuts the mountains and forms a passageway is that of the Marava River, which, with that of the Vardar, leads from Belgrade to Salonika. Beyond the Sava-Danube, as far as the northern boundary, the land is low and swampy near the rivers, with a few minor elevations. The chief concentrations of people are around Zagreb and Belgrade. Yugoslavia's greatest problem is the lack of communications between its regions. The more highly developed coastal areas have access to outside markets, but further inland the mountains impose a rugged barrier between the provinces.

E. L. Jordan

Canals lined with trees are frequently seen in many European countries.

**RUMANIA**—In eastern Rumania the Carpathian Mountains from the northwest and the Transylvanian Alps from the southwest meet in the center to form a crescent. To the north and west of this crescent is the Transylvanian plateau; to the south and east are

The sounds of the Alphorn, a peculiar Swiss instrument, carry far across the valleys.

E. L. Jordan

The gleaming marbles of the Parthenon temple crown the Acropolis above Athens, Greece.

E. L. Jordan

Italy's colorful history, scenery and balmy climate have attracted many tourists which has in some measure offset an unfavorable balance of trade.

**SAN MARINO**—San Marino is one of the oldest republics in the world and is the smallest. It has always been on good terms with its big neighbor, Italy, by whom it is surrounded. The state was founded in the fourth century by Marinius of Dalmatia, a stonecutter. Except for a few invasions, its liberty has been respected, even by Napoleon. Much of its revenue is obtained through the sale of its postage stamps issued for the benefit of collectors.

**SPAIN AND PORTUGAL** — About three fourths of the Iberian Peninsula is a granite plateau with a range of mountains dividing it in the center. The rivers that flow through this region through deep gorges block transportation and are unsuited for navigation, waterpower or irrigation. The dry climate, lack of water, a rugged land formation, poor soil and an absence of transportation have been great obstacles standing in the way of the economic development of both Spain and Portugal. A portion of the land in the valleys and plains has been made fertile through irrigation, and farming is the main industry. Fishing is important along the Portugal coast, although a great part of the coast is too rugged for harbors. There are forests in most of the higher areas where half the world's supply of cork is produced.

the plains of Moldavia and Walachia. The principal rivers are the Danube in the south which enters the Black Sea at Sulina, and the Prut in the northeast and the Siret in the southeast—both of which connect with the Danube. At the southern and eastern edge of the Carpathian Mountains are Rumania's rich oil fields.

**BULGARIA** — The country is hilly and well watered by numerous streams, of which the Isker, Struma and Maritza are the most important. Although nearly one third of the country's area is in forests, only a small part of the wood is used commercially since about one fourth of the forest area is completely unproductive. Many of the forests consist of scrub timber and a sizeable portion of the good forests are inaccessible. Eighty percent of Bulgaria's population is employed in agriculture, the chief crops being tobacco and cereals. Attar of roses and silk are important products.

**ALBANIA**—Albania is a mountainous country on the western side of the Peninsula. In the center, part of the plateau is cultivable,

The donkey, once its chief beast of burden, is seen less often in modern, motorized Italy.

Hamilton Wright

and in the south there is fertile alluvial soil with grazing land on the slopes.

**GREECE**—With a very long coast line on the Aegean and Ionian Seas, and a large number of islands, including Crete, Mitylene, Chios, and the Dodecanese islands, the area is generally mountainous. The mountains, though not very high, divide the country into a number of small districts, between which communication is difficult. It is the sea which links the different regions of Greece.

**ITALY**—Once the hub of the known world, Italy's importance declined as the age of exploration and discovery opened up the ocean routes of the world. Taking no part in this period of conquest and empire building, she did not acquire colonies. Lacking unity she was in no position to demand her share of the rich prizes of newly discovered land being acquired by other European nations.

With the opening of the Suez Canal and tunnels through the Alps, her trade somewhat improved, but the absence of the necessary minerals prevented her from keeping pace with industrial development elsewhere in Europe.

The south slope of the Alps belongs to Italy. At the point where the Alps reach the Mediterranean, the Apennines begin. These mountains follow the length of Italy and form a rugged backbone which extends through the island of Sicily. The southern and western parts of the peninsula have been subjected to volcanic eruptions, and Vesuvius, Etna, and Stromboli are still active volcanoes. The chief lowlands are in the Po Valley with narrow coastal plains east and west of the Apennines. The majority of the people, and most of the agriculture and manufacturing, are located in the Po Valley. Consequently Northern Italy does not experience the poverty to be found in Southern Italy. Many Italians emigrated to the Western Hemisphere.

The beautiful Alhambra, rising above Granada in Spain, was a fortress-palace of the Moors.

E. L. Jordan

The High Tatra, on the Polish-Czechoslovakian border, is famous for its alpine scenery.

**ANDORRA** — Tiny Andorra is in the Pyrenees Mountains between France and Spain. It is not a republic, as is often supposed, but a joint dependency of France and the Bishops of Urgel in Spain. Its mountains are high and arid, and its valleys contain poor soil so that the people are nearly all engaged in pastoral pursuits. The one product of the soil is tobacco.

**POLAND** — Lying between the western European nations and Russia, Poland has changed its boundaries many times. It was for centuries a chiefly agricultural country. More recently, her resources of coal, iron, lead and zinc have helped her industrial progress. Since World War II the rich coal fields of Upper Silesia, formerly German, have become a part of Poland. Most of the land is comprised of a plain. The lower regions of the Vistula have marshes, sand dunes and lakes. The central plain of Poland with an elevation of about 500 feet is traversed by great rivers, the most important being the Oder and the Vistula. The Baltic seaports, Szczecin and Gdansk, were joined to Poland after World War II. In the south, the country reaches into the Sudeten and Carpathian mountains.

**U.S.S.R.** — More than eight and one-half million square miles in area and comprising more than one seventh of the world's land surface, the Union of Soviet Socialist Republics sprawls across two continents. A large part of European Russia and western Siberia is a great plain. Russia's position in northern latitudes and the absence of protecting barriers result in an extreme climate with long, cold winters. The port of Murmansk to the north of Finland, lying within the Arctic Circle, is kept ice-free throughout the year by warm ocean currents. Kaliningrad on the

The courtyard of ancient Wawel Castle, Cracow, Poland, reconstructed in Renaissance style by King Sigismond in the 16th century.

Baltic Sea is also ice-free the year around. All other northern seaports of Russia are frozen for many months each year. Vladivostok on the Pacific coast, however, is kept open by icebreakers. In no part of the land is the rainfall heavy, and there are frequent and widespread droughts.

To the east of the Ural mountains is Siberia, Russia's Asiatic part. In the far north the ground has been found to be frozen to a depth of over six hundred feet. This presents peculiar problems which make it difficult to exploit the resources in the Arctic region. Here in the tundra country the moss, upon which the reindeer of the nomadic tribes feed, is often five feet thick.

South of the tundra belt is a great evergreen forest covering billions of acres, where lumbering and fur-trapping are the chief occupations.

Russia's supply of minerals is so great and widely scattered that the extent of many of the deposits is still unknown. There are immense reserves of coal in both European and Asiatic Russia. Copper, platinum, iron, gold, manganese and other minerals are found in the Urals. Some of the richest petroleum deposits in the world are located in the Baku region of the Caspian Sea and the Urals.

Great strides have been made in industrial development, with the manufacture of iron and steel, machinery, textiles and leather goods in the lead.

In spite of climate, high cost of manufacture and difficulties of transportation, the U. S. S. R. is a country that is largely self-sustaining. Its rapidly expanding industrialization and advancement in modern science have made it one of the leading world powers.

Within the walls of the Kremlin in Moscow stands the bell tower of Ivan the Great. Its construction was begun by Boris Godunov in 1600.

Catharine de Bary

Rocky hills rising from the desert sands near Wadi Halfa, Sudan.

**AFRICA**—In its steady conquest of the world, the technical age has reached Africa, and across the second largest continent great changes are taking place. As the difficulties of climate, communications and diseases are overcome and education increases, Africa with its rich natural resources and its remarkably vital peoples is rapidly joining the modern world.

Lying astride the equator, large parts of Africa extend through the torrid zone. Its coastline is steep and regular, offering few places for ships to anchor. The rivers, although numerous and many of them large, are not so important to transportation as the great rivers of Europe, Asia and the Americas.

The deltas of the Niger and the Zambezi are choked by silt, and on nearly all the other rivers navigation is impeded by shoal or cataract. Nevertheless, the Congo and the Nile with their tributaries have many thousands of miles of navigable waterways, as have the Niger, the Benue and the Zambezi.

To the north, the Sahara Desert proved an effective barrier of sand and intense heat, which for hundreds of years prevented any important exchange of ideas or trade between the north and the south. Extending from the Atlantic to the River Nile, and reaching from the Mediterranean to the Sudan, the dry Sahara is a region of desolation. What trade existed between Asia, Europe and Africa followed caravan routes which led from oasis to oasis. The only life to be found there is at these scattered oases.

Africa is a great plateau, about five thousand miles long from north to south. The average height of the entire continent is over two thousand feet above sea level. Its loftiest peak is nearly twenty thousand feet high (Mount Kilimanjaro in Tanganyika), while the Qattara Depression in the Libyan Desert sinks to four hundred feet below sea level.

The Atlas Mountains parallel the north coast of Africa, with their southern slopes dropping down to the Sahara. The Sudan belt, which extends south from the Sahara to the Gulf of Guinea, is a lower region of hills, valleys and plains. To the south is the Cameroon Massif and in the East rise the Ethiopian Highlands and the mountain ridges of the lake region.

The geological formation of the Great Rift, which on the Asian continent caused the deep trench of the Dead Sea, has its continuation in East Africa. Here a series of deep trenchlike valleys extend from the Red Sea into Mozambique, and between the mountain ridges lie Africa's large lakes. Lake Victoria is the second largest body of fresh water, Lake Tanganyika the second deepest in the world. In this lake region rise three of Africa's great rivers. The Nile flows north toward the Mediterranean, the Congo twists and turns to finally reach the Atlantic to the west, and the Zambezi flows east to empty into the Indian Ocean. Each river follows a winding course through the mountains before finding a way over the edge of the plateau to reach the sea. This results in many falls and rapids which interrupt transportation. The Victoria Falls on the Zambezi, the rapids of the Congo, and the cataracts of the Nile are typical.

The Congo, winding through the gloomy depths of fever-infested forests, is three thousand miles long. It is second only to the Amazon of South America in the volume of water it empties into the sea. The Nile, the longest river in the world, travels four thousand miles before reaching the Mediterranean, and today, as in ancient times, makes Egypt a habitable country. As the Nile winds slowly through the Sahara, the evaporation is so great that the river would dry up before reaching the sea were it not joined by rivers from the Ethiopian Highlands. It is these waters of the Blue Nile which bring the great Nile floods. They also supply water for irrigation, making Egypt a fertile strip of land hemmed in by cliffs and burning sands. Africa's fourth large river, the Niger, while rising only one hundred and fifty miles from the ocean, flows twenty-five hundred miles before reaching the Atlantic.

Africa is a land of climatic contradictions. At the equator the temperature ranges from typical jungle weather at the lower levels to a climate similar to that found well over a thousand miles to the north. This occurs in the high altitudes of the mountains. Along the Mediterranean, the weather compares with that of southern Europe. The weather in the Congo Basin is always hot and humid. However, to the east, in the mountain and lake region, it is tempered by the higher altitudes. In the far south, around Cape Town the weather is mild and sunny like the climate of southern California. The same extremes exist in rainfall. At the equator it is excessive, with periods of torrential rains. Traveling north or south from this wet center there is less and less rain, with parts of the Sahara never getting a drop.

Plant life varies with the rainfall. The dense, matted tropical jungles, which are exceeded only in size by the forests of the Amazon, give way to grassy plains and open forests, the savannas. The only vegetation in the Sahara is around the springs that nourish the oases. Because the hot winds of the south are blocked by the Atlas Mountains, the entire coastal area of North Africa from

Sailboats on the River Nile pass through the heart of modern Cairo.

Egypt. State Tourist Admin.

The giraffe, tallest of mammals, lives in the savannas of southeastern Africa.

East Africa Tourist Travel Assoc.

the Atlantic to the Nile River is agriculturally productive.

Sorghum and other grains are staple foods in Africa. Other important products, especially for export, are coffee, cocoa, tea and

Gezira cotton, the "white gold" of the Sudan.

Br. Information Services

Africa still has many wild animals, especially in its deep jungles. These teem with monkeys, among them gorillas and chimpanzees, and there are snakes and many birds. In the open woods and semi-arid grasslands of the savanna (called veldt in South Africa) live elephants, lions, giraffes, rhinoceroses, zebras and antelopes. Crocodiles and hippopotamuses are found in the rivers. The savanna is also the region for the raising of cattle. The desert has a very sparse animal population of a special kind, such as camels and jackals.

Some of Africa's mineral resources are of the richest in the world. Almost all gem diamonds for the world market are found here; gold is mined on a large scale, and one of the world's richest uranium mines, the Shinkolobwe of the Republic of the Congo,

Large-eared African elephants in Kruger National Park, South Africa. The young remain with their mothers for four years.

South African Tourist Corp.

tobacco. Cotton is grown in many places, and from various regions hides, ivory and timber are exported. The rain forests furnish rubber, mahogany and teakwood.

lies in this continent. Zinc, silver, tin, copper, chromium, vanadium and manganese are also found. There is very little oil, which poses a serious problem for modern transportation needs. However, Africa has a great potential source of industrial power in its mighty rivers.

**EGYPT**—Between the Arabian and the Libyan desert extends what might be called a huge river oasis, the valley and delta of the Nile. Here flourished the civilization of ancient Egypt, one of the oldest in the world. It was important in Greek and Roman times and became a stronghold of Islamic faith in the 7th century A.D. Mamelukes and Turks held it during the Middle Ages. In modern times, Egypt became important because of the Suez Canal, opened in 1869. This artificial waterway, used by almost all shipping between Europe and the Orient, lies in Egyptian territory. Since antiquity the Nile waters flooded this land during the summer

months, bringing fertile silt with the life-giving water. In recent years, several dams have been built on the river, and the large water reservoirs thus obtained make possible continuous irrigation. Crops can now be harvested three times a year. The exploitation of the hydroelectric power of the Nile has been started; it will increase the industrial and manufacturing possibilities of Egypt. In spite of the rich crops, the Egyptian farmer is very poor. Attempts are being made to improve farming methods, many of which have not changed since the time of the pharaohs. In 1958, Egypt and Syria formed the United Arab Republic (Syria withdrew in 1961).

**SUDAN** — Since 1899 under joint Anglo-Egyptian rule, the Sudan became independent in 1956. This land, inhabited in the north by Arabs, in the south by Negro tribes, embraces the Upper Nile basin to the borders of Uganda and Ethiopia. Its wild acacia trees furnish most of the world's supply of gum arabic, important in the manufacture of adhesives. Cotton is raised in the fertile areas between the Blue and the White Nile. Dates, ivory and livestock are also exported. Khartoum on the Blue Nile is capital and trade center.

**ETHIOPIA** — Three different zones of climate, depending on altitude, are typical for this mountainous country. The lowest zone, mainly comprising the lowlands in the west and the deep valleys, is tropical and unhealthy. The middle zone, of 6000-8000 feet elevation, favors agriculture and is most densely populated. In the higher regions, cattle are raised. In its federation with Eritrea in 1952, Ethiopia obtained access to the Red Sea, but its main outlet is Djibouti in Somaliland opposite Aden, where the railroad from the capital, Addis Ababa, terminates. An excellent coffee, growing wild on the slopes especially of the Jimma area, is chief export. With the exception of a few years of

Giant Protea, beautiful national flower of South Africa.

South African Tourist Corp.

East Africa Tourist Travel Assoc.

In contrast to its cooler uplands, Kenya's lowlands are tropically hot.

Italian occupation (1936-41), this country has always been independent. Its population is partly pagan, partly Moslem and partly Christian, belonging to the old Christian Coptic Church.

**FRENCH SOMALILAND**—At the entrance to the Red Sea lies this overseas territory of France.

**SOMALI REPUBLIC** — When British and Italian Somaliland joined in 1960, they became the independent republic of Somalia. Located on the eastern horn of Africa, it is a rugged country with river banks and swamps infested by reptiles. Elephants migrate through the brush where other wild game roam. Half of the country is a desert where nomadic peoples seek a precarious living. There are no really good harbors. Visited by ancient traders in search of aromatic plants, it still supplies half of the world's frankincense.

**KENYA** — This eastern gateway to Central Africa abounds in big game. The lowlands bordering the Indian Ocean are fertile, the climate is bearable. Western Kenya is a high plateau with isolated towering peaks, snowcapped the year around. The chief harbor is Mombasa. A large part of the Europeans and Asiatics in the country live in Nairobi, the capital, situated in the highlands.

Dancer at Shembe festival, Durban, South Africa.

South African Tourist Corp.

**UGANDA** — Between Mount Elgon (14,178 ft.) in the east and the Ruwenzori range (highest peak 16,795 ft.) in the west lie wide lakes and huge swamps, where rises the Nile River. Kampala, on Lake Victoria, is the capital of prosperous Uganda. Cotton, which is raised exclusively by the natives, is the main source of income. This land is the home of the Baganda people, who attained a higher degree of development before the white man came than any other African tribe. Their kings can be traced back through several centuries.

**TANGANYIKA AND ZANZIBAR** — Here ascends Kilimanjaro, Africa's highest peak. Also in the north, near Arusha, is Ngorongoro, a large inhabited crater with the

East Africa Tourist Travel Assoc.

Masai warriors, Tanganyika. The Masai, of Nilo-Hamitic origin, have a well-developed tribal organization.

strange appearance of a portion of the moon. Tanganyika's forests abound in wildlife of a greater number and variety than anywhere else in Africa. The capital, main harbor and largest city is Dar es Salaam, center for Ismaili Moslems in Africa. Here it has been the custom to give their leader (the Aga Khan) his weight in diamonds to distribute among charitable institutions. Lying off the coast to the east is the fertile island of Zanzibar, which, together with the island of Pemba, supplies most of the world's cloves. Zanzibar united with Tanganyika in 1964. During the Middle Ages, this island was ruled by Arabs and for a time by the Portuguese. The Germans occupied it in the 1880's but turned it over to England in 1890 in exchange for Helgoland.

**MOZAMBIQUE** — Several large rivers, among them the Zambezi, drain this Portuguese territory, which has a coast line of 1,500 miles along the Indian Ocean. Vasco

da Gama, the Portuguese who discovered the sea route to India around the Cape of Good Hope, visited it in 1498. Its natural resources have not been developed to any great extent. The country sends laborers to the South African mines. Mozambique's several harbors are important outlets for South African minerals. Because of malaria and yellow fever, a large part of the country is unhealthful. Few Europeans live there.

**SOUTH AFRICA** — Balmy temperate summers and mild winters make the southern tip of Africa an ideal land for European settlers. In the generally dry central tableland, crops are planted and cattle and sheep are raised. To the north extends the Witwatersrand with its rich gold mines. The

outlet for this mining region is Durban, an artificial port on the Indian Ocean. The only large natural harbor is at Cape Town. In the low veldt (savanna) of Transvaal is the

These fishermen near Cape Town are Afrikaners, of Dutch descent.

South African Tourist Corp.

TWA-Trans World Airlines
Rugged Rommel Gorge, Constantine, Algeria.

world famous Kruger National Park, an extensive reserve for African wildlife.

The population of South Africa consists of a white minority made up of English and Dutch stock, a considerable group of East Indians, a large Negro majority, and a small group of mixed people.

Dutch settlers came to this land in the 17th century; their descendants call themselves Afrikaners. When the English began to occupy the country, many Dutch left for the interior (in the so-called Boer Trek in 1836), where they founded the republics of Transvaal, the Orange Free State, and Natal. After the Boer War (1899-1902), these republics were combined with the Cape Colony to form the Union of South Africa. Today it is a republic.

**BECHUANALAND, BASUTOLAND AND SWAZILAND** — Three British Protectorates in southern Africa. Although most of the land is reserved for the natives, they have remained poor and many seek work in the South African mines.

**MALAGASY REPUBLIC**—The Malagasy Republic, which is co-extensive with the island of Madagascar, the fourth largest in the world, is separated from the east coast of Africa by the Mozambique Channel. In the mountains of the interior are found graphite, mica and other minerals, but only a small part of these resources has been developed. During the 19th century, Madagascar was ruled by the Howa, an educated tribe, many of whom became Christians. The numerous Negroes living on the island are mostly descendants of freed slaves. The French con-

quered Madagascar in 1896, but today it has regained its independence. Tananarive in the highlands is the capital. Main ports are Tamatave on the east coast and Diego-Suarez at the northern tip.

**MAURITIUS AND THE SEYCHELLES** — Negroes, East Indians and Chinese live on the fertile, very densely populated island of Mauritius in the Indian Ocean. The Seychelles Islands, long uninhabited, were used as a pirate base until the middle of the 18th century.

**RÉUNION AND THE COMORO ISLANDS** — Of volcanic origin, these French dependencies lie one to the east and the other to the northwest of Madagascar. They are important sources of rare essences used in the making of perfume.

**MALAWI** — Little Malawi (formerly Nyasaland), a long and narrow country, is crossed from north to south by the Great Rift Valley, which is occupied by huge Lake Nyasa, and the Shire river valley. Most of the country's population is to be found in the eastern highlands where the climate is pleasant. There is little industry or mining in Malawi, agriculture being the chief occupation, and cotton, tea and tobacco, the most important crops.

**ZAMBIA**—Lying between the forests of Central Africa and the wide plains of South Africa, it is separated from Southern Rhodesia by the Zambezi River and its famous Victoria Falls, which are more than twice as high as Niagara Falls. The mining of copper and lead, the raising of tobacco and corn, and the grazing of livestock are the principal sources of Zambia's wealth.

**SOUTHERN RHODESIA** — Most of the land consists of two plateaus ranging from 2,000 to 6,000 feet in altitude. It is suited to European settlement. Agriculture and mining are the chief occupations. The country's main resources are gold, asbestos and chrome.

**SOUTH-WEST AFRICA**—This territory, administered by South Africa, is engaged in the raising of livestock, the growing of grain, fishing, and the mining of such minerals as lead, zinc, copper, gold and diamonds. Germany held South-West Africa as a colony until 1919, when it became a mandate of the League of Nations.

**ANGOLA** — Although the central elevated plateau of Angola is a great African watershed, where rise important tributaries to the Congo and the Zambezi rivers, the country as a whole is arid and exposed to constant dry winds. Export of coffee, largely to the United States, provides the chief income. Luanda, the capital, near the mouth of the Cuanza was founded in 1575.

**REPUBLIC OF THE CONGO**—The exploration of this region by Stanley, Livingstone

British Information Services
The waters of the Zambezi River thunder nearly 400 feet into the gorge below at Victoria Falls, in Rhodesia.

and others roused the interest of Leopold II of Belgium, who became its sovereign in 1885, and under whom there were many abuses. These were corrected to some degree when in 1908 the Congo was formally annexed by Belgium, whose parliament administered the territory until 1960, when the Congo became independent. Stretching on either side of the equator, it has a large area of tropical rain forests which furnish valuable products, including cotton, coffee, palm oil and timber. The Katanga Province, enormously rich in mineral resources, yields copper, cobalt, zinc, cadmium, uranium, silver, gold, and other metals. Matadi, the major port, lies 100 miles inland below the last cataract of the Livingstone Falls on the Congo River. Leopoldville, the capital, is the largest city and a modern commercial and industrial center in which is located a noted institute for tropical medicine.

**RWANDA AND BURUNDI** — Two countries in the heart of Africa formerly administered by Belgium as a United Nations trust territory. Burundi's capital, Bujumbura, on the northern tip of Lake Tanganyika, is on the site where Stanley and Livingstone landed in 1871.

**CHAD AND THE CENTRAL AFRICAN REPUBLIC** — Due to a climate which ranges from humid to very arid, and the inaccessibility of vast parts of the land especially in Chad, these countries have not developed extensive industries or many of their resources. They are primarily agricultural, Chad being mainly engaged in cotton grow-

ing and livestock raising, while in the Central African Republic, cotton and coffee are grown and diamonds mined. In the northern parts the people are Islamic, while in the south animism prevails. These former French colonies gained their independence in 1960.

**REPUBLIC OF CONGO**—In past centuries raided for slaves and ivory, this country is the home of many varied peoples, including pygmies and many tribes of the Bantu group. The climate is tropical and there are some navigable rivers. Efforts are being made to develop agriculture and industry. Agricultural products are largely for domestic use, but the country exports palm oils and peanuts and lumber products. Its mineral resources have not been exploited to any extent. In 1960 the Republic of Congo became independent.

**GABON**—Like much of western Africa, Gabon was long the source of a flourishing slave trade in which the Portuguese, Dutch, English and French all played a part. In 1849, slaves freed from a ship engaged in this already outlawed trade settled Libreville, the present capital. Gabon's independence from France dates from 1960. Almost entirely a tropical rain forest, Gabon depends on its forest products for most of its income. Its recently discovered mineral resources (iron, petroleum, and uranium) promise to become future important sources of income.

**FERNANDO PO AND RÍO MUNI** — These provinces of Spain comprise the islands of Fernando Po and Annobón and a small area on the coast of the Gulf of Guinea.

**SÃO TOMÉ AND PRÍNCIPE**—These Portuguese islands which lie off the coast of Guinea are of volcanic origin. Climate and vegetation are tropical.

**CAMEROON**—A portion of the former German territory to the east of Nigeria, administered as a trust by France, Cameroon became a republic in 1960. The trust territory of Southern Cameroons, administered by Great Britain, voted in 1961 to join the Republic of Cameroon. It exports such tropical products as bananas, coffee, palm oil and cacao and possesses deposits of such minerals as gold and tin.

**NIGERIA** — From the forest-covered coast of the Gulf of Guinea at the huge delta of the Niger River, this country extends northward into dry savanna regions and finally to the desert around Lake Chad. Its highest elevation is the Bauchi plateau. The tin found there is approaching exhaustion. Nigeria is one of the most densely populated countries in Africa. Its capital and main port is Lagos. The largest town is Ibadan, seat

of an African university. Nigeria became an independent federation within the British Commonwealth in 1960. The British Trust Territory of the Northern Cameroons joined Nigeria in 1961.

**TOGO AND DAHOMEY** — These countries are small and densely populated. From a narrow coastal strip they rise to interior highlands. Both have agricultural economies, Togo exporting chiefly cocoa, and Dahomey the products of the palm tree. Once Portuguese plantations in Togo supplied slave ships with cassava, coconuts and other foods. Togo was in German hands from 1884 until World War I. The eastern part was administered by France after World War I until 1960, when it became independent. The western part, British Togoland, joined independent Ghana in 1957. Dahomey, which was for several decades a part of French West Africa, became independent in 1960.

**GHANA** — Independent within the British Commonwealth, this republic comprises the former Gold Coast and British Togoland. Once known for its gold alone, the country is today a leading producer of cocoa. Its manganese export, especially to the United States, is considerable. It is also an important producer of diamonds.

**IVORY COAST**—Trade in gold, ostrich feathers, gum arabic, pepper and ivory, which gave this country its name, once flourished in this area. Today its economy, which is being modernized, is based on the export of cocoa, fruit and wood. Industry in the Ivory Coast is largely concerned with the processing of its agricultural products. The Ivory Coast (like its neighbors, Mali and Upper Volta), was a part of French West Africa until it became a republic in 1960.

**LIBERIA** — This is the oldest independent African republic. In 1822 the American Colonization Society established a small settlement for freed American Negroes at the site of the present capital, Monrovia (named after President James Monroe). In 1847 Liberia became an independent state with its constitution modeled after that of the United States. The land is handicapped by a hot and unhealthful climate. Its economic condition was improved in recent years by American government aid and private enterprise. Rubber, mainly produced on plantations of the Firestone Company, is the chief export. A valuable iron ore is also exported.

**SIERRA LEONE** — The country was visited by early navigators and became a British possession in 1787. It became an independent member of the British Commonwealth of Nations in 1961. Rain forest covers the coastlands; savanna, the arid interior. The

Egyptian State Tourist Administration
The interior of the Mohammed Ali Mosque, Cairo, Egypt.

country has an excellent natural harbor. Here, Freetown, the capital is located. It began as an English settlement for freed slaves. Today it is an active trade center.

**GUINEA**—To the north and east of Sierra Leone stretches this land, which until 1958 was a part of French West Africa. Its main town and port is Conakry. Bananas, bauxite and iron ore are the chief exports.

**PORTUGUESE GUINEA**—A region of tropical forest and savanna, this territory has been in the hands of the Portuguese since the time of Prince Henry the Navigator (middle of 15th century).

**GAMBIA**—British possession since the early 17th century. Extends along both banks of the Gambia River. Capital is Bathurst on an island at the river's mouth. Peanuts are the chief crop.

**CAPE VERDE ISLANDS** — Over 300 miles west of Cape Verde, these Portuguese islands have been a stopping place on the route to the Western Hemisphere since the days of exploration.

**SENEGAL**—Although agriculture is its principal source of income — peanuts, gum arabic, animal products — Senegal has oil mills and soap factories, and various chemical industries, most of which are concentrated around Dakar. This city, the capital, is a

British Information Services

Mosque at Kano, Nigeria. Mohammedan influence is strong in northwestern and northeastern Africa.

major Atlantic seaport. Senegal has been independent since 1960.

**MALI**—The ancient, powerful and wealthy kingdom of Mali, from which this country

British Information Services

The Wana of Wa, a chieftain of Ghana.

Native weaving in Sierra Leone.

British Information Services

takes its name, flourished during the Middle Ages. Mali means hippopotamus, signifying strength. Formerly part of French West Africa and known as French Sudan, Mali became independent in 1960. This territory, whose topography ranges from desert and savanna to fertile land along the rivers, exports peanuts, gum arabic and kapok.

**NIGER AND UPPER VOLTA** — Immense, land-locked, limited in resources, Niger is underdeveloped — peanuts, cotton, and animal products being its chief cash crops. Upper Volta, much smaller than Niger, produces cotton, rice and peanuts for the market. Both countries were long the scene of contention between the Semitic and Hamitic peoples of the north, who came to trade with the already settled farming and fishing native peoples. They remained to colonize the area. These portions of the mammoth territory of French West Africa gained independence in 1960.

**MAURITANIA**—The major ethnic group in the Islamic Republic of Mauritania is a Caucasian Arab and Berber people known to us as the Moors whose ancestors conquered much of northern Africa and Spain in the eleventh century. Mauritania, which was a part of French West Africa, became independent in 1960. Agricultural production, still largely limited to subsistence farming, is expected to improve through the use of modern methods of farming and irrigation. The development of iron and copper mining has begun.

**SPANISH SAHARA AND IFNI**—These territories are Spanish provinces lying along the northwest coast of Africa.

**MOROCCO**—Three chains of the Atlas Mountains traverse this country from southwest to northeast. Although agriculture and manufacturing are handicapped in this rugged land, it is active in several industries. It has attractive old towns like Marrakesh

and Fez, seat of an old Islamic university, while Casablanca is one of the most modern cities on the African continent. At the northern shore of Morocco is the Strait of Gibraltar, separating Africa from Europe. At its narrowest point it is 8 miles wide.

For about half a century, Morocco was ruled by France, with a small portion under Spanish control. In 1956, it became independent and the former international city of Tangier was joined with it.

**ALGERIA**—The rugged, arid ranges of the Atlas Mountains divide Northern Algeria into three zones roughly parallel to the coast: the Tell Atlas, the High Plateaus and the Saharan Atlas. To the north of the Tell Atlas, the climate is Mediterranean and fruits and vegetables are abundantly grown. The High Plateaus form an arid region with several landlocked salt lakes. From the heights of the Saharan Atlas, the land falls off abruptly to the desert of the Sahara, where recently discovered fields of oil and natural gas are being developed.

**TUNISIA**—In ancient times, during Phoenician and later Roman rule, this land furnished grains and excellent fruits to the other countries around the Mediterranean. Then came centuries of neglect, and during the Middle Ages this coastal land was feared for its pirates. Today Tunisia is again very fertile. Olives grow along the coast; grains and tropical fruits, especially dates, are raised inland. There are several important towns, among them Tunis, the capital, and Bizerte, a naval base. Turkish rule over Tunisia was replaced by French protectorate in 1881. In 1956, Tunisia became independent.

**LIBYA** — This is the least valuable of the North African regions, being relatively unprotected from the scorching desert winds. However, the coastal areas are cultivated with the aid of artificial irrigation. The capitals are Tripoli and Benghazi.

Zebras roam Nairobi National Park, Kenya.

East African Tourist Travel Assoc.

E. L. Jordan

Arab street scene.

**ASIA** — Although there is no separating ocean between Europe and Asia, the great steppes and deserts of central and eastern Asia served as an effective barrier through thousands of years. Some of the oldest civilizations in the world developed in eastern and southeast Asia in almost complete isolation. In modern times, with the spreading of science and technology, Asia's old traditions and customs are receding as industrialization expands, based on the continent's rich resources and carried out by its great masses of populations.

This huge continent is the largest in the world. It is more than a million square miles larger than the combined areas of North and South America and covers one third of the world's land area. It extends from the ice-bound regions of the Arctic Circle to the sunburnt islands of the tropics. In the Himalayas it rises to the highest elevation in the world — Mount Everest — and in Palestine it sinks to the world's lowest surface —the Dead Sea.

Asia forms with Europe one continuous land mass, Eurasia. The boundary between Asia and Europe follows the Ural Mountains, the Ural River to the Caspian Sea, and the Greater Caucasus Mountains to the Black Sea. A man-made canal, the Suez Canal, separates the continent of Asia from Africa. Washed by three oceans, Asia has a coastline over thirty thousand miles in length. Deep indentations form seas, such as the Bay of Bengal and the Arabian Sea. Twisting and pointed peninsulas reach far out into the oceans, which are dotted with island groups. Among these are Japan, the Philippines, and Indonesia, all of which have become as important as mainland countries.

The belt of high mountains which extends across Europe from west to east finds its con-

tinuation in the high mountain ranges of Asia. They reach their greatest height in the Himalayas, which have been called "the roof of the world." These mountain chains extend eastward to the plateau of Tibet, then turn sharply south and traverse the Malay Peninsula in long mountain lines separated by deep, forested ravines. They terminate in the mountainous backbone of the Indonesian (Sunda) Islands.

The Himalayas represent the southern edge of Central Asia's high plateaus and mountain ranges. To the north extends the great tableland of northern Asia, which descends slowly to the Arctic Ocean. To the south are the peninsular plateaus of Arabia and India.

This enormous continent is drained by many large rivers. In Siberia, the Ob, Yenisei and Lena Rivers, rising in Central Asia, flow northward into the Arctic Ocean. They are blocked with ice for several months each year and flood the surrounding country in thaw. China's large rivers also have their headlands in the Central Asian mountains. They wind their way eastward to the sea through alluvial plains made fertile by the silt they carry. They are the Amur on the border between Siberia and China, the Hwang-Ho, or Yellow River, and the Yangtse Kiang or Blue River. These rivers often overflow in disastrous floods and have changed their courses many times.

India's holy river, the Ganges, rising in the western Himalayas, flows eastward through the plain which bears its name. Shortly before emptying into the Bay of Bengal, it receives another mighty river from the Himalayas, the Brahmaputra. In southwest Asia, two rivers, the Euphrates and Tigris, water the alluvial plain of ancient Mesopotamia in Iraq.

Covering so many degrees of latitude, the climate of Asia would naturally show great variation. Some of the coldest inhabited

Aramco

Onions growing in the irrigated Arabian desert.

Walter Nebiker

Where the Mediterranean reaches furthest east lies Iskenderun, Turkey.

Modern and traditional transportation—train and camel—meet in the desert of Arabia.

Aramco

TWA-Trans World Airlines
The state of Israel is commercially very active.

places on earth, Verkhoyansk and Oimyakon, lie in northeastern Siberia. Great areas in the center of the continent, far from the sea, are dry; tropical conditions prevail in the south. The heaviest rainfall anywhere in the world is in some localities of southeast Asia. In Assam, India, the rainfall averages about 40 feet a year.

The great continuous landmass of Asia cools off more in the winter and gets hotter in the summer than the surrounding oceans. The resulting changes in air pressure cause streams of air to flow from the continent to the oceans during the winter and from the oceans to the continent during the summer. In India and southeast Asia, these winds are known as monsoons; from April to October they bring the heavy, life-giving rains.

There is every type of vegetation, ranging from tundra mosses in the extreme north to tropical plant life in the south. There are extensive desert areas with very scant vegetation such as the famous Gobi desert in

The Dead Sea with the alluvial mouth of the Jordan.

Mongolia and the deserts in Arabia, Iran, south central U.S.S.R., and Sinkiang. Across Siberia stretches a wide belt of coniferous forest called the taiga. To the south of it are Siberia's steppelands. The slopes of the Himalayan foothills and the hills of the East Indian Islands are covered with tropical forest.

Of the many wild animals living in Asia, the giant panda is found only in Tibet. Here also lives one of the largest wild oxen, the black Yak. Another purely Asiatic animal, the tiger, is found over a wide range, from Persia (Iran) to the Amur, and from the island of Sakhalin to the forests of Bali. Birds of Paradise, who have the most brilliant plumage of any birds on earth, are confined to New Guinea and the Moluccas. In India and countries of southeast Asia, the Asiatic elephant has been tamed and is used for various types of work, such as hauling of logs. In agriculture, tamed water buffaloes are widely used.

Although Asia is very rich in resources, many of them have not yet been developed. They are unevenly distributed and often at great distances from trade and shipping centers. The greatest variety of resources has been found in the Ural Mountains on the borderline between Siberia and European Russia. Another important industrial center is the Kuznetsk Basin southeast of Novosibirsk in Siberia. In these regions, industrialization has attained a modern level. China's coal supply is one of the largest in the world. China is also rich in iron ore and other minerals, such as antimony and tungsten. Antimony is important in the making of steel, and tungsten is needed to harden metals. Japan has no ample mineral supplies, but water power obtained from its many swift rivers has helped manufacturing. India, long known for its wealth in precious stones, has an abundance of coal, copper, iron ore and sheet mica. There are large oil fields in southwest Asia—Arabia, Iran, Iraq and the Kuwait—as well as in southeast Asia—Burma, Indonesia and Borneo. Tin occurs in the Malay Peninsula in great amounts, and much of the world's natural rubber comes from

Malaya and Sumatra. Cotton and jute are exported by India, Pakistan and Japan, which also exports silk. Tea is grown in many parts of southern and southeastern Asia; the main exporting countries are India and Ceylon. Indochina produces great quantities of rice for export.

In the past, transportation in Asia was on rivers, canals and by coastwise shipping, or by slow caravan across the deserts and over the mountain passes. A great change was brought about when railroads were built, and today India, China and Japan have fairly extensive railroad systems. European Russia is connected with Siberia, Mongolia and Manchuria (China) by the Trans-Siberian Railroad, which has branches to the larger towns and industrial centers of adjacent regions. In the East Indies, transportation by bus and truck has become important in modern times. Many major cities in Asia are linked by airlines.

**TURKEY**—Once a vast empire, Turkey now comprises roughly the rectangular peninsula

B.O.A.C. photograph
The ancient city of Basra, Iraq.

between the eastern Mediterranean and the Black Sea. It is a dry plateau surrounded by mountain ranges, which reach to considerable heights. (Mt. Ararat, highest peak, 16,-945 ft.) Along the Mediterranean and Aegean seas, the land is fertile. The capital, Ankara, lies in the central highlands. Istanbul, on the European side of the Sea of Marmara, is an important seaport and a trade and university center. Another large port is Izmir (Smyrna). A republic since 1923, Turkey encourages modern industry and western style of life. At the same time, adhering to the Mohammedan religion, it retains many Turkish and Asiatic traits and traditions.

**LEBANON**—On the slopes along the coast and in the valley between the Lebanon and Anti-Lebanon mountains the country is fertile. It is mainly agricultural, and on its steep, terraced hillsides grow abundant crops. Besides the Philippines, Lebanon is the only country in Asia with a large Christian population (about 50 per cent). It obtained complete independence in 1946. The capital and

main port, Beirut, is one of the most important trade centers in the Near East.

**JORDAN**—When the Turkish empire broke apart after the First World War, Jordan became a British mandate. It gained its independence in 1946. Only a small area in the northwest of the country is fertile. Here lies Amman, the capital. The country has many relics from Biblical times.

**ISRAEL**—After 2000 years the Jewish people realized their dream of an independent homeland with the establishment of the new state of Israel in 1948. Lying between Egypt and Jordan on the eastern shores of the Mediterranean, the country is a hot and arid land. Modern irrigation, however, has made large regions fertile, and orchards and forests begin to give the land a green appearance. The new nation's economy is based on agriculture, but oil refining, chemical production and light industry are also important. Tel Aviv-Jaffa is the center of the manufacturing industries, while heavy industry is located at the seaport of Haifa. Many of the people, immigrants from all over the world, live together in modern cooperative settlements. The Hebrew language, formerly used only in religious rites and Bible studies, is the official language of the young republic. The frontier with Jordan divides Jerusalem; the modern part is Israel's capital and the old city belongs to Jordan.

**SYRIA** — Between Syria's mountain ranges in the west and its wide desert regions in the east lies a strip of land famous for its fertility. In ancient times, Syria was crossed by caravan trails connecting Mesopotamia with Egypt. In our time, it is an important passageway between the oil fields of Iraq and Arabia and the Mediterranean. The country is still mainly agricultural. The capital is Damascus, the oldest continuously inhabited city known today. Syria emerged from the First World War as a French mandate and became independent in 1946. On February 1, 1958, it joined with Egypt to form the United Arab Republic (withdrew in 1961).

**IRAQ**—The Euphrates and Tigris Rivers flow from the northwest to the southeast through the middle of Iraq. To the west and southwest extend the Syrian and Arabian deserts and to the north the mountains of Kurdistan. Agriculture depends on irrigation. Since the time of the ancient Babylonians, who had extensive irrigation systems, the land was neglected. In modern times, the income from the rich oil fields near Mosul permits extensive new efforts to irrigate the land. Important towns beside Baghdad, the capital, are Mosul, the oil center, and Basra, the country's port town near the mouth of the two rivers. Iraq was part of Turkey until after the First World War, when it became an independent constitutional monarchy. As a result of the revolution in July, 1958, it was declared a republic.

**IRAN (PERSIA)** — The seat of flourishing empires in antiquity and the Middle Ages,

An oasis watered by a mountain spring in central Iran.

Iran is today an independent monarchy. In the fertile region near the Caspian Sea, fruits, grains and vegetables are grown. In the Elburz Mountains which separate the coastal area from the interior is Mt. Demavend, Iran's highest peak. Tehran, the capital, lies to the southwest on the arid plateau which stretches in a vast belt through most of the interior. In this region, the raising of livestock is the chief occupation. Near the Persian Gulf are the country's rich oil fields. The oil refinery at Abadan is one of the largest in the world.

**ARABIA**—The Arabian Peninsula is a land composed almost entirely of desert, mostly of a barren and stony type, with an abundance of sand in the southeast. Besides scattered oases there are only a few small areas in Arabia with enough rainfall to permit the growing of crops. In the mountains of Yemen in the southwest corner of the peninsula, there is sufficient rain and the soil is fertile. A high-quality coffee is grown here. It received its name from the Red Sea port, Mocha, which used to handle its export. In some parts of Saudi Arabia, modern methods of irrigation are used. Recent discovery of immense oil fields along the Persian Gulf fostered new economic development, and many local sheikhs or tribal rulers have become suddenly rich. Roads are being built and cars and trucks are beginning to replace the camel. A railroad runs from Riyadh to the

Persian Gulf. Saudi Arabia, a unified kingdom since 1932, comprises about two thirds of the peninsula. It has two capitals, Riyadh and Mecca. Mecca is the center of worship for all Mohammedans.

**AFGHANISTAN** — Lying as a barrier between Siberia and India, Afghanistan has been the scene of many invasions and conquests but was never completely vanquished. Barren tablelands, deep ravines and snow-covered mountains leave it an unproductive country. However, the crops raised in small, irrigated areas are of high quality. The country is noted for its fine rugs and sheepskins, major export items. Attempts are made to develop water power and oil resources. Kabul is the capital.

**PAKISTAN**—In 1949 Pakistan was created to give the Mohammedans of India their own homeland. Its two sections are about 1000 miles apart and differ greatly. West Pakistan comprises the Indus valley and adjacent areas, stretching from the Himalaya to the Arabian Sea. It has vast desert regions and is not densely populated. Cereal raising and cotton growing are concentrated in the Indus valley, irrigated through an ancient but still efficient canal system and huge modern dams. East Pakistan occupies most of the Ganges-Brahmaputra delta and the foothills of the Assam highlands. It is very humid and densely populated. Here, rice

Looking across the Bombay Harbour, India.

TWA-Trans World Airlines

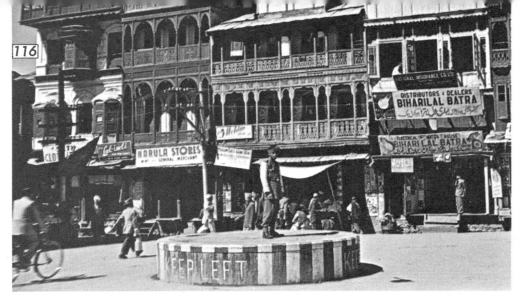

Remnant from British rule: traffic is "left-handed" in Indian lands. This traffic officer is at Srinagar, India.

E. L. Jordan

**CEYLON**—This island, whose capital is Colombo, lies in the Indian Ocean near India's southern tip. Ruled by kings since antiquity, Ceylon became an English colony in 1802 and obtained its independence in 1948. Mountains rise in the interior of the southern part of the island. Here is grown Ceylon's famous tea. In the lowlands of the north and along the coast, rice is the chief crop. Precious stones are found in the gravel of the rivers. Sea breezes temper the heat.

**INDOCHINESE PENINSULA** — Lying in South Asia between the Bay of Bengal and the South China Sea, it includes parts of Burma, Thailand, Vietnam, Laos, Cambodia and the Federation of Malaysia. Most of the peninsula is characterized by densely forested valleys and mountain ridges. Rainfall is heavy and the land is very productive. In

and jute are the chief crops. The separation from India entailed great human, economic and political problems which have only in part been solved.

Pakistan's people include many ethnic and language groups; its culture, related to that of its neighbors, is dominated by Islam, the major religion of the country.

**NEPAL**—This small independent state is shut off from the outside world by the Himalaya. Several of the world's highest mountains, including Mount Everest are in southern Nepal or on its border. The inhabitants are known for their courage. The Gurkhas of Nepal were famous soldiers in the Indian army, while the Nepalese Sherpas furnished reliable guides in the ascent of Himalayan peaks. Rich in mineral deposits which have not been developed, Nepal is chiefly engaged in agriculture.

**INDIA** — India has an average population density of 300 people per square mile. Although there are many large cities and some very sizeable industries, the majority of the people depend on agriculture. The Indian farmers live in small villages surrounded by tilled fields. In spite of primitive methods and equipment, crops are usually large. But India's harvest depends on seasonal rains (monsoons), and if they do not arrive in time,

disastrous droughts result. At such times, large groups of the population may be exposed to famine made more serious because transportation is often inadequate, so that food cannot be rushed to stricken areas. Within the last several decades, the government has sponsored irrigation works and the construction of railroads and motor roads to decrease the danger of famines.

For over four thousand years, India has been at the mercy of marauding and conquering races. Unlike many lesser countries, who have successfully thrown off the yoke of oppression, India has for many centuries been subject to foreign rule. As a result, it is a confusion of races and traditions. Throughout its history, the Hindu religion, especially the caste system, has had a strong influence on life in India, even under English rule. The caste system has prevented a gradual decrease in social differences, and great wealth and extreme poverty exist side by side.

India received its independence in 1947 and in 1950 became a republic. The capital is at New Delhi. By expanding its industries and modernizing its farming methods, it hopes to improve the lot of its people. To combine modern ideas and industrial requirements with age-old traditions in a densely populated country is India's major problem.

Hamilton Wright

Rice is cultivated throughout the lowlands of southeastern Asia.

the forests are valuable stands of prize woods, such as teak, ebony and other trees used for their wood or gum. Most of the world's natural rubber comes from this area. In the river plains and deltas, rice is harvested twice a year and much of it is exported. The villages are built on the dams between the rice fields. Chief harbors are the Burmese capital and great seaport, Rangoon, Bangkok (Krung Thep), the capital of Thailand, Saigon, capital of South Vietnam, and Singapore. The latter lies on an island at the tip of the peninsula and commands one of the most important sea routes in the world. A new port has been constructed at Sihanoukville, on Kompong Som Bay, in Cambodia.

**THE MALAY ARCHIPELAGO**—The world's largest group of islands extends from Su-

Busy docks at Singapore, one of the crossroads of the world.

British Information Services

matra to the Philippine islands off the coast of China and includes many thousands of islands. With the exception of the Philippines and parts of Timor, Borneo and New Guinea, the archipelago was ruled for hundreds of years by the Netherlands.

**INDONESIA** — Colonization and development begun by the Dutch in the seventeenth century has resulted in the richest and most important island group in the world.

Most of the islands are mountainous and of volcanic origin. At one time they were a part of the mainland connecting Asia with Australia. Java is the most productive and highly developed of the East Indies. It is one of the most densely populated regions in the world.

After Greenland, New Guinea and Borneo are the largest islands in the world. Sumatra and Celebes are next in size in the East Indies. Much of the mineral wealth of these islands is yet untouched. Borneo is crossed almost in the middle by the equator and few white people occupy the island because of the humidity and heat. Petroleum is an important resource of Borneo, Sumatra and Java, and two small islands adjoining Su-

Hamilton Wright

Spring and Autumn Temple at Kaohsiung, Taiwan. The city is a major port and industrial center of southern Taiwan.

E. L. Jordan

Floating market at Bangkok, Thailand.

Market scene at Kitakyushu, Japan.

Ronald Tolles

matra have valuable deposits of tin. Bali, one of the lesser islands, is known for its tropical charm.

After an extended struggle, Indonesia became independent in 1949. To mold the vast region of islands and islets into a unified country is no small task. An even greater problem lies in the fact that the education of the Indonesian people, neglected in the centuries of colonization, has as yet to be brought up to a more modern level.

**PHILIPPINE ISLANDS** — Numbering over seven thousand islands, the Philippines, like other islands of the Malay Archipelago, are the tops of drowned mountains protruding from the sea. There are well watered fertile plains between the mountains. The islands are near the equator and the temperature is never very low. Some of the many volcanoes in the Philippines are still active and the islands are subject to earthquakes.

Magellan, the great Portuguese sailor, discovered the Philippines in 1521. He was killed on Cebu Island. The Spaniards settled in the islands in 1565 and held them for 333 years. Their influence is still felt in many traditions. Most Filipinos are Christians (Catholics), but there are pagan tribes in the hills, and Mohammedans live on Mindanao and the Sulu Islands. During the nearly five decades of American rule (1898-1946), modern education, industry and land reform were introduced to the Philippines.

**CHINA** — The Chinese civilization is of greater antiquity than any other existent world culture. In the past it was able to absorb all foreign influences without changing basically. The Chinese people are patient, industrious and have great physical endurance. A large part of the country has a moderate climate. Agriculture supports the majority of the people. Few animals are raised, which conserves acreage for food crops. Rice is most widely grown, but almost every known crop is raised.

During the last three centuries, China's population increased from about 60 million in the 16th century to about 660 million to-

day. At the same time, the country remained almost completely agricultural, retaining its antiquated farming methods. As a result, famines were frequent and the living standard of the people as a whole remained low. In 1912, in an attempt to improve conditions, China became a democracy. However, quiet development was frustrated when Japan occupied Manchuria in 1931 and invaded China in 1937. When the Japanese were finally defeated, Communism had spread throughout the land, and in 1949 the mainland of China fell under Communist rule. Since then, industrialization and the establishment of cooperative farms on a large scale are changing the face of China.

Inner Mongolia, Tibet and Sinkiang are outer regions of China. These regions have extreme temperatures and are largely desert.

The island of Taiwan (Formosa) has remained free of Communist rule and is the seat of the Nationalist Chinese government. The central and eastern part of the island is mountainous, the highest peak, Mt. Morri-

Street scene in Hong Kong.

E. L. Jordan

The Temple of Dawn, a famous sanctuary opposite the Grand Palace, Bangkok, Thailand.

TWA-Trans World Airlines

son, rising to 13,595 feet. Valuable timber grows on the slopes and rivers furnish electrical power. The western part of the island is a fertile plain. Economically, Taiwan is almost self-supporting. Recently, a modern land reform has been introduced.

**SIBERIA**—The Asiatic part of Russia is a vast low plain in the west, rising to rugged plateaus and mountain chains in the east. Siberia has a "continental" (inland) climate, which means little rainfall and high temperatures in the summer, scant snow cover and low temperatures in the winter. In the Arctic region, the subsoil is permanently frozen. This land, where trees cannot grow, is called tundra. South of it is a wide belt of coniferous forests, the taiga, and these in turn merge into steppelands. Some of the steppe is dry, supporting only sheep and goats. But in southwestern Siberia, where the fertile "black soil" of the steppe receives sufficient rainfall, crops are abundant. The highest peak in Siberia is Klyuchevskaya Sopka, a volcano on Kamchatka peninsula. Lake Baikal, near the Mongolian border, is the deepest lake in the world (5,712 ft.).

For centuries, Russia sent its criminals and political exiles to Siberia to make up for the lack of voluntary settlers. In modern times, industry and large-scale agriculture have been developed in some regions, especially in the southwest, around Novosibirsk, and in the Kuznetsk basin. Huge dams are being built to furnish electrical power. The railway system is steadily expanded. Some isolated towns have air service. But the harsh climate, generally poor soil and enormous distances still remain major obstacles to a rapid development of the country.

**MONGOLIAN REPUBLIC** — The greater part of this country consists of an arid plateau composed mainly of the Gobi Desert. In the northwest are high mountains whose streams flow into numerous sizable lakes. The people are mostly nomads who wander from place to place seeking new pastures for their herds. In 1921, the country became a "People's Republic" and has since then been under the influence of Communist Russia. Attempts are being made to settle the nomads in cooperative farms. Ulan Bator is the capital.

**JAPAN**—Since Japan opened its doors to Western trade in the middle of the last century, it took over Western technical achievements and became in a very short time a modern industrialized state. Simultaneously, it increased its military power and was victorious in wars against China and Russia. Formosa (Taiwan today) and Korea were occupied in 1905, Manchukuo in 1932, and finally, in 1937, China was invaded. During the Second World War, Japan controlled Indonesia and Indochina. Defeat at the end of the war reduced the empire to the area of the Japanese islands.

Rising from great depths of the sea, the islands of Japan are largely mountainous (Fujiyama, 12,395 ft.). The Inland Sea or Japanese Mediterranean is almost entirely landlocked and surrounded by chains of volcanoes, of which few are now active. Because earthquakes are frequent, houses and factories are low structures mostly built of wood. The climate is temperate and healthful, with abundant rainfall. About 80 per cent of the land is too steep to be cultivated. Every effort is made to obtain large crops from the 20 per cent of arable land, as Japan is very densely populated. Fisheries

and canneries add to the food supply and are important for export.

The Japanese are a hardworking people with great technical ability who require little for themselves. They have been able to build up important textile, manufacturing and heavy industries, although most of the raw materials have to be imported. More recently, electrical power plants have been constructed to supplement available coal supplies. Japan's merchant fleet is one of the largest in the world.

For centuries, Japan had been controlled by a few powerful families. After the Second World War, it assumed a democratic constitution. The duties of the Emperor are merely ceremonial.

**KOREA** — Forming a kind of land bridge between the Asian mainland and Japan, Korea has been an historic pathway for invasion. Coveted at different times by China, Russia and Japan, it lost its independence early in the century to the Japanese. During the Second World War, Korea was promised independence. But the end of the fighting brought division and renewed conflict. Today, the country is divided by the 38th parallel into a northern Communist republic and a southern democracy following western ideas. Seoul is the capital of South Korea and Pyongyang is capital of North Korea.

In its climate the peninsula of Korea is influenced by the surrounding seas and the large continent of Asia, to which it is attached. In the summer, seasonal winds blow from the sea, bringing heat and humidity. In the winter, the winds blow from inner Asia, often bringing bitterly cold, dry weather.

Physically and economically, Korea is divided into two contrasting natural regions. The agricultural heart of the nation is south of the 38th parallel, producing rice, barley, cotton and other crops. North of the parallel, industry and mining of coal and iron predominate.

Seoul, capital of South Korea, lies in a setting of rocky hills.

I. L. P. Korea

## AUSTRALIA

**AUSTRALIA** — This island continent is the only one to lie entirely in the Southern Hemisphere. It was the last to be discovered, and is the only continent occupied in its entirety by one country. Australia lies at the opposite end of the earth from its parent country, Great Britain.

First sighted by the Dutch early in the seventeenth century, Australia was not settled by the British until late in the eighteenth. The early pioneers of the country had to conquer the wilderness before creating a nation. In less than two hundred years, it has become a highly developed country which, though it has thriving industries, exports a large number of agricultural products. Its exports include wool, wheat, meat and dairy products.

Of the people who came to Australia after 1787, almost all were of European origin, and the great majority came from Great Britain and Ireland. After World War II a program to stimulate population growth through increased immigration was inaugurated to provide manpower for future industrial growth. While manufacturing has increased and some manufactured goods are exported, most goods produced are for home consumption. Among the metal manufacturing industries, steel and machinery of various kinds are important. In addition, chemicals and plastics are manufactured in great variety.

A large part of the northern half of the continent lies within the tropics, while the southern portions of the continent in general enjoy a pleasantly mild climate. Snow normally falls only in the highlands in the winter. Since the seasons are the reverse of those in the northern hemisphere, this occurs in the months of June, July and August.

Australia is said to be most level in surface and regular in outline of all the continents. There is an entire absence of towering mountains. The highest peak is only about seventy-three hundred feet above sea level. The mountains parallel the east coast, with, by far, the greater part of the continent a vast, irregular, and undulating plateau.

Australia can be regarded as falling into four well-defined regions: (1) The Great Plateau in the west extends over about half of the continent; (2) The Eastern Highlands follow along the whole of the eastern coastline, rarely exceeding a distance of a hundred miles inland; (3) The Central Basin is a lowland area much of which was once a sea-bed; and (4) the Coastal Plains, which form a rim of varying width surrounding most of the continent.

Despite rich coastal lands and an immense grazing area in the interior, much of this interior is unsuited for agriculture. It includes large areas of desert and semi-desert which are sparsely settled and will never support a dense population. The heaviest rainfall is in the tropical regions of the north, and there is adequate moisture along the south coast and southern part of the highlands. Elsewhere there is insufficient rain.

One of the world's greatest bridges spans the harbor of Sydney, Australia.

But for the presence of numerous artesian wells scattered over wide areas, much more of the country would be without water. It is these wells that make stock-raising possible, but because of its mineral content, the water is seldom used for agriculture or human use.

The major rivers of Australia are of two types—those which flow toward the coast and are similar to such rivers in other parts of the world; and the inland rivers which gradually lose their water as they flow away from the coastal regions. The headwaters of most of these inland rivers are in the Eastern Highlands.

The Murray River with its tributaries is the main river system and flows into the ocean on the south coast. The Gilbert, Norman and Flinders are the principal streams flowing into the Gulf of Carpentaria in the north. On the west the Murchison, Gascoyne, Ashburton and Fitzroy empty into the Indian Ocean.

The rivers which flow inland vary greatly in volume during the year. For long periods they are mere strings of waterholes, but during floods their waters spread out over the flat country for many miles. Most of their waters evaporate or soak into the ground before they flow very far. In the center of the continent the rivers flow into Lake Eyre when there is sufficient water in them, but generally they are merely beds of dry sand.

The numerous natural lakes which appear to be scattered so liberally over the land are little more than shallow basins that carry water only after rains.

Great Barrier Reef, the largest of all coral formations, follows the northeast coast for twelve hundred miles of Australia's twelve-thousand-mile coastline. Except in a few places this reef is impassable to ships, but it does provide an inner passage for coastal navigation. There are good harbors on the southeastern coast.

Wherever there is sufficient moisture for grass to grow, the land is especially adapted to grazing. This land has proved the most suitable in the world for raising sheep. Merino sheep, which produce a very fine quality of wool, comprise most of the flocks. The heavy fleece from these sheep exceeds that of breeds raised elsewhere, so, although Australia produces less than one sixth of the world's sheep, the wool yield is more than a quarter of the world's requirement.

Melbourne, the capital of the State of Victoria, Australia, as seen from the River Yarra.

Australian News & Information Bureau

Australian News Bur.

Rawlinson Range, a flat tableland, typical of central Australia.

Lacking navigable rivers, most of the transportation is by railways. These have been of first importance in developing the country, but one great drawback of railroad transportation is that there are several gauges. During the last fifty years there has been a steady expansion of motor roads, and air routes are rapidly increasing.

In addition to the mainland and the island of Tasmania, Australia has extensive territorial interests. These include the Trust Territory of New Guinea, Papua, Nauru and Norfolk Island.

The Trust Territory of New Guinea includes the northeastern section of New Guinea, the Bismarck Archipelago, and the northern islands of the Solomon group. Scattered over a sea area of more than one million square miles, these islands are mountainous with limited coastal areas suitable for cultivation.

## NEW ZEALAND

**NEW ZEALAND** — Two large islands and several small ones make up New Zealand. Situated about twelve hundred miles southeast of Australia, New Zealand is a lonely

Queenstown, at Lake Wakatipu, lies in the shadow of the Remarkables, New Zealand.

N. Z. Gov't. Travel Comm.

member of the British Commonwealth of Nations.

The two principal islands, North and South Island are separated by Cook Strait which is ninety miles wide. Close as they are to each other, these islands have little in common except that they are both mountainous. North Island is of volcanic origin and consists chiefly of forested hills and plateaus. South Island is more rugged with glaciers and snow-clad peaks that rival the Alps of Switzerland.

**PACIFIC ISLANDS** — The Pacific Islands fall into three major regions: Polynesia, Micronesia and Melanesia.

Polynesia, or "many islands," consists of widely scattered groups and a few isolated islands forming a rough triangle. The Hawaiian Islands are at the northern point, twenty degrees north of the Equator. The Fiji Islands, at the western point of the triangle, are the meeting place of Polynesian and Melanesian cultures, the people being of mixed stock. The easternmost point lies in the Gambier group of the Tuamotu Archipelago, although isolated Pitcairn Island, inhabited by Anglo-Tahitian descendants of the mutinous crew of the "Bounty," is generally included geographically. Within this area lives the most highly developed group of Pacific peoples, a mixture of white, black and yellow racial stocks, the Polynesians. Famous as navigators, they crossed the Pacific from Asia hundreds of years ago, and sailed their canoes eastward to their present homes. For the most part, the islands are mountainous, volcanic and covered with dense vegetation, often fringed by coral reefs. Along the equator and in the southeast, low coral atolls predominate, often only a few feet above sea level, and frequently torn by hurricanes.

The people, often easy-going to the point of idleness, are not always used in local production, some Chinese having been hired to do manual work. Famous for dancing and feasting, the generally happy Polynesians strive to maintain their early customs against the inroads of European traders, missionaries and government regulations.

In the western Pacific, for the most part north of the equator, lies Micronesia, or "little islands," confined to the Marianas, Carolines, Marshall Islands, and Gilbert and Ellice Islands. Except for the latter islands, they are mostly volcanic and coral-fringed, and are peopled by a light-skinned group—the latest arrivals in the Pacific. These inhabitants show more evidence of a recent black and yellow mixture.

The earliest inhabited area of the Pacific, New Guinea and the islands spreading to the southeast of it, is known as Melanesia, the "black islands." Of early Negroid stock, this area was generally by-passed by the later Polynesians and Micronesians, as settlement was already established. Melanesia is a rapidly developing area, rich in minerals

Jean LeRoy

House with grass roof, Fiji Islands.

as well as the usual coconuts. Today the people range from Europeanized workers in the plantations of New Caledonia and Fiji, and the missions of the New Guinea coast, to half-naked savages in the higher regions of New Guinea. One island group has attained independence.

Colorful sailboat at Waikiki Beach, Hawaii, with Diamond Head in the background.

A. N. Dupay

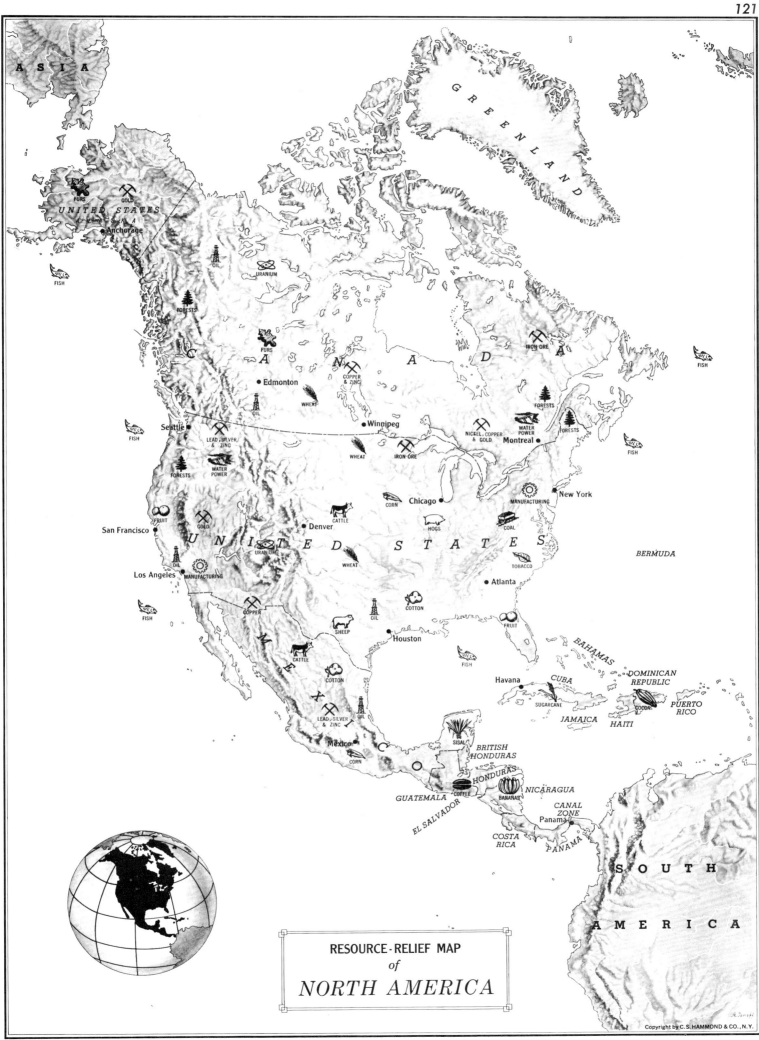

ASIA

GREENLAND

**FURS**
**GOLD**
**UNITED STATES ALASKA**
Anchorage
**FISH**
**OIL**
**URANIUM**
**FORESTS**

C A N A D A

**FURS**
Edmonton
**COPPER & ZINC**
**OIL**
**WHEAT**
Winnipeg
**IRON ORE**
**FISH**

Seattle
**FISH**
**LEAD, SILVER & ZINC**
**WATER POWER**
**FORESTS**
**WHEAT**
**IRON ORE**
**NICKEL, COPPER & GOLD**
**WATER POWER**
**FORESTS**
Montreal

**FORESTS**
**FISH**

**FRUIT**
**GOLD**
San Francisco
**URANIUM**
Denver
**CATTLE**
**CORN**
Chicago
**HOGS**
**MANUFACTURING**
New York

U N I T E D   S T A T E S

**OIL**
Los Angeles
**MANUFACTURING**
**WHEAT**
**COAL**
**TOBACCO**
Atlanta

BERMUDA

**FISH**
**COPPER**
**SHEEP**
**OIL**
**COTTON**
Houston
**FRUIT**

**CATTLE**
BAHAMAS

M E X I C O

**COTTON**
**FISH**
Havana
CUBA
**SUGARCANE**
DOMINICAN REPUBLIC
**COCOA**
PUERTO RICO
JAMAICA
HAITI

**LEAD, SILVER & ZINC**
**OIL**
México
**CORN**
**SISAL**
BRITISH HONDURAS
HONDURAS
**BANANAS**
NICARAGUA
GUATEMALA
**COFFEE**
EL SALVADOR
CANAL ZONE
Panama
COSTA RICA
PANAMA

S O U T H

A M E R I C A

**RESOURCE-RELIEF MAP**
*of*
**NORTH AMERICA**

RESOURCE-RELIEF MAP
of
SOUTH AMERICA

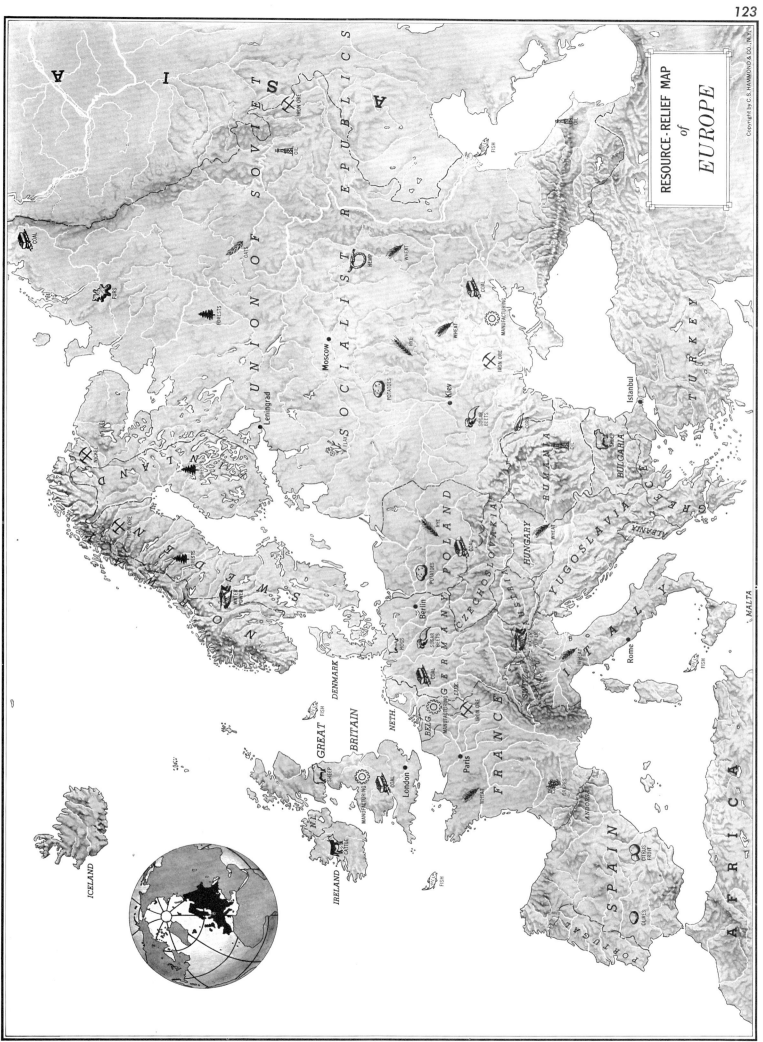

123

RESOURCE · RELIEF MAP
of
EUROPE

Copyright by C. S. HAMMOND & CO., N. Y.

A I S

UNION OF SOVIETS

SOCIALIST REPUBLICS

IRON ORE

OIL

OIL

FISH

COAL

FURS

OATS

FORESTS

HEMP

WHEAT

COAL

MANUFACTURING

Moscow

RYE

WHEAT

Kiev

IRON ORE

POTATOES

FLAX

SUGAR BEETS

CORN

OIL

SHEEP

BULGARIA

Istanbul

T U R K E Y

Leningrad

NICKEL

N

NICKEL

IRON ORE

FORESTS

FORESTS

WATER POWER

RYE

COAL

POTATOES

P O L A N D

HUNGARY

WHEAT

Y U G O S L A V I A

G R E E C E

ALBANIA

Berlin

SUGAR BEETS

HOGS

G E R M A N Y

CZECHOSLOVAKIA

AUSTRIA

WATER POWER

SWITZ.

WHEAT

MALTA

DENMARK

FISH

NETH.

BELG.

LUX.

COAL

MANUFACTURING

IRON ORE

F R A N C E

I T A L Y

Rome

FISH

GREAT BRITAIN

SHEEP

COAL

MANUFACTURING

London

Paris

WHEAT

GRAPES

ANDORRA

FISH

CATTLE

IRELAND

FISH

CITRUS FRUIT

S P A I N

P O R T U G A L

OLIVES

A F R I C A

ICELAND

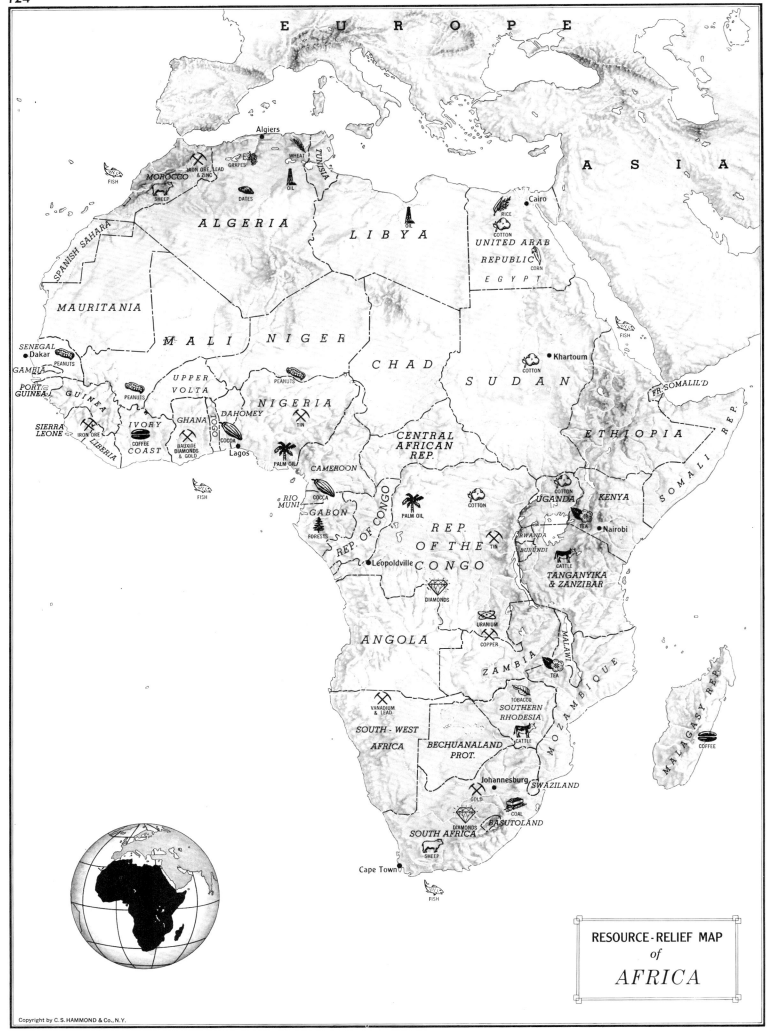

EUROPE

ASIA

FISH

Algiers

IRON ORE, LEAD & ZINC

GRAPES

WHEAT

TUNISIA

OIL

MOROCCO

SHEEP

DATES

OIL

Cairo

RICE

COTTON

UNITED ARAB

REPUBLIC

CORN

EGYPT

ALGERIA

LIBYA

SPANISH SAHARA

MAURITANIA

MALI

NIGER

CHAD

SUDAN

FISH

Khartoum

COTTON

FR. SOMALIL'D

SENEGAL

Dakar

PEANUTS

GAMBIA

PORT. GUINEA

GUINEA

PEANUTS

UPPER VOLTA

PEANUTS

NIGERIA

TIN

CENTRAL AFRICAN REP.

ETHIOPIA

SOMALI REP.

SIERRA LEONE

IRON ORE

LIBERIA

IVORY COAST

COFFEE

GHANA

BAUXITE DIAMONDS & GOLD

TOGO

DAHOMEY

COCOA

Lagos

PALM OIL

CAMEROON

COCOA

RIO MUNI

GABON

FORESTS

REP. OF CONGO

Léopoldville

REP. OF THE CONGO

PALM OIL

COTTON

UGANDA

COTTON

TEA

KENYA

Nairobi

RWANDA

BURUNDI

TIN

CATTLE

TANGANYIKA & ZANZIBAR

FISH

DIAMONDS

ANGOLA

URANIUM

COPPER

ZAMBIA

MALAWI

TEA

MOZAMBIQUE

MALAGASY REP.

COFFEE

VANADIUM & LEAD

TOBACCO

SOUTHERN RHODESIA

CATTLE

SOUTH - WEST AFRICA

BECHUANALAND PROT.

Johannesburg

SWAZILAND

GOLD

DIAMONDS

BASUTOLAND

COAL

SOUTH AFRICA

SHEEP

Cape Town

FISH

FISH

RESOURCE - RELIEF MAP

*of*

AFRICA

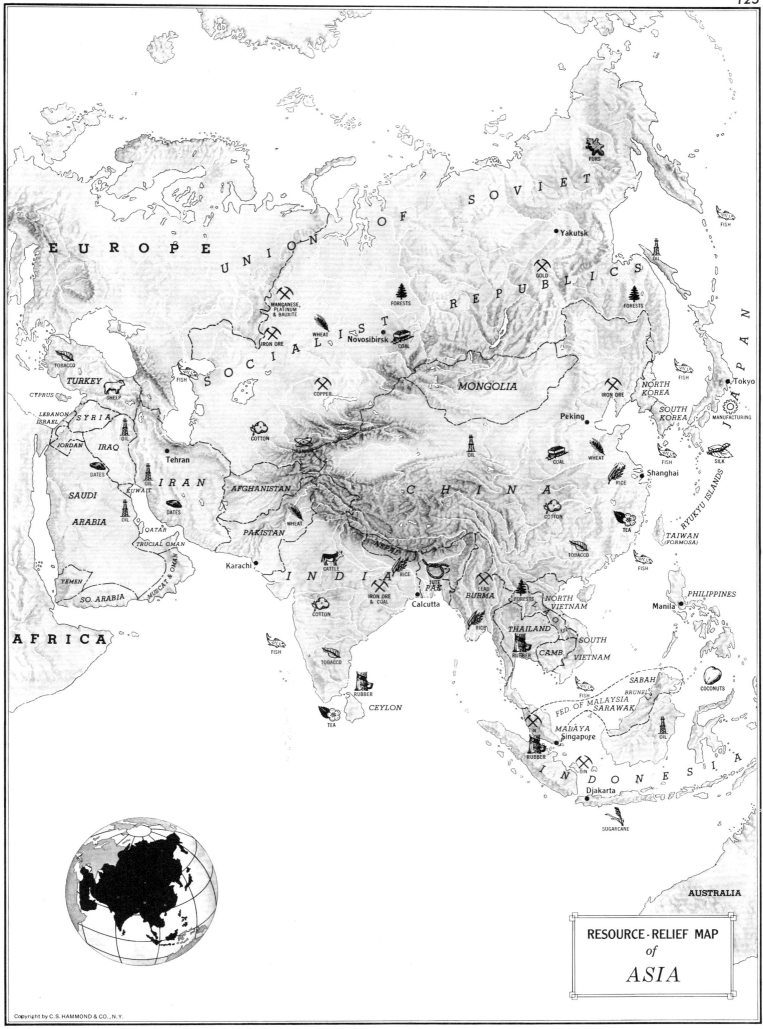

EUROPE

UNION OF SOVIET

SOCIALIST REPUBLICS

• Yakutsk

FURS

OIL

FISH

MANGANESE,
PLATINUM
& BAUXITE

FORESTS

FORESTS

IRON ORE

WHEAT

Novosibirsk

COAL

MONGOLIA

FISH

TOBACCO

TURKEY

CYPRUS

SHEEP

COPPER

IRON ORE

NORTH
KOREA

Tokyo

LEBANON
ISRAEL

SYRIA

OIL

COTTON

Peking

SOUTH
KOREA

MANUFACTURING

JORDAN

IRAQ

DATES

• Tehran

URANIUM

OIL

COAL

WHEAT

FISH

SILK

SAUDI

OIL

KUWAIT

IRAN

AFGHANISTAN

C  H  I  N  A

RICE

• Shanghai

DATES

COTTON

ARABIA

OIL

QATAR

PAKISTAN

WHEAT

TEA

RYUKYU ISLANDS

TRUCIAL OMAN

TAIWAN
(FORMOSA)

YEMEN

MUSCAT & OMAN

CATTLE

NEPAL

TOBACCO

SO. ARABIA

KARACHI •

I  N  D  I  A

RICE

FISH

AFRICA

COTTON

JUTE
PAK

IRON ORE
& COAL

Calcutta •

LEAD

BURMA

FORESTS

NORTH
VIETNAM

PHILIPPINES

FISH

COTTON

RICE

Manila •

TOBACCO

THAILAND

SOUTH
VIETNAM

FISH

RUBBER

CAMB.

TEA

RUBBER

CEYLON

SABAH

COCONUTS

FISH

BRUNEI

TEA

FED. OF MALAYSIA

SARAWAK

TIN

MALAYA

Singapore •

OIL

RUBBER

TIN

I  N  D  O  N  E  S  I  A

Djakarta •

SUGARCANE

AUSTRALIA

JAPAN

RESOURCE-RELIEF MAP
*of*
*ASIA*

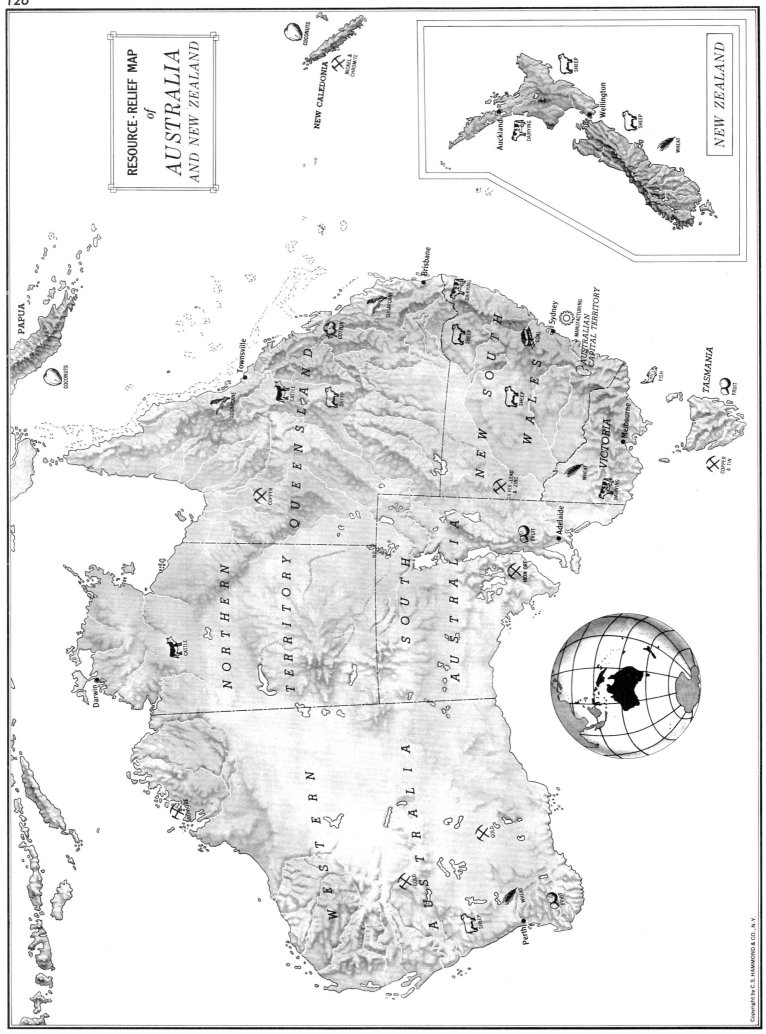

RESOURCE-RELIEF MAP
of
AUSTRALIA
AND NEW ZEALAND

NEW ZEALAND

COCONUTS

NEW CALEDONIA

NICKEL & CHROMITE

SHEEP

Wellington

SHEEP

Auckland

DAIRYING

WHEAT

PAPUA

COCONUTS

Brisbane

SUGARCANE

DAIRYING

Sydney

Townsville

COTTON

MANUFACTURING

SUGARCANE

CATTLE

SHEEP

SHEEP

COAL

AUSTRALIAN CAPITAL TERRITORY

Q U E E N S L A N D

SHEEP

NEW SOUTH WALES

FISH

TASMANIA

FRUIT

COPPER

NORTHERN TERRITORY

SOUTH AUSTRALIA

SILVER, LEAD & ZINC

WHEAT

VICTORIA

Melbourne

DAIRYING

COPPER & TIN

FRUIT

Adelaide

CATTLE

IRON ORE

Darwin

WESTERN AUSTRALIA

GOLD

KALGOORLIE

GOLD

WHEAT

FRUIT

SHEEP

Perth

Copyright by C. S. HAMMOND & CO., N.Y.

# Gazetteer of the World
## SOCIAL AND ECONOMIC TABLES

| POLITICAL DIVISION | GOVERNMENT | MONETARY UNIT | LANGUAGE | RELIGION | MAJOR PRODUCTS |
|---|---|---|---|---|---|
| AFGHANISTAN | A constitutional monarchy ruled by a king, a cabinet and a bi-cameral legislative assembly. | afghani | Afghan (Pushtu) Persian | Mohammedan | Wheat, barley, millet, corn, sorghum, lentils, vegetables, fruits, nuts, castor beans, madder, asafetida, cotton, tobacco, fat-tailed sheep (karakul), camels, zebus; wool, skins; sheepskin, textiles, leather, carpets, rugs; gold, iron, lapis lazuli, coal, copper, lead, silver. |
| ALBANIA | A Soviet-type republic with president, cabinet and one house legislature. Actually ruled by the Communist party politburo. | lek | Albanian | Moslem, Orthodox, Roman Catholic | Corn, tobacco, wheat, flax, oats, barley, rye, rice, olives, fruit; cattle, sheep; fish; wool, hides; dairy products, furs; bitumen, salt, lignite, aluminum, petroleum, copper, chromite; flour, olive oil, cheese, cement, leather. |
| ALGERIA | A one party constitutional republic, with a president and a national assembly. | dinar | Arabic French Berber | Mohammedan Roman Catholic Judaist | Wheat, barley, oats, corn, grapes, olives, tobacco, dates, figs, flax, pomegranates, prunes, apricots, legumes, potatoes; sheep, goats, cattle, mules, horses, pigs, camels; sardines, anchovies, tuna; forestry products; iron, phosphates, zinc, petroleum; wine, olive oil, distilling, flour, carpet weaving, alcohol, cotton weaving, tobacco products, wool, cork. |
| ANDORRA | A republic under the joint suzerainty of the French State and the Bishop of Urgel, with a council general of 24 elective members. Executive authority is vested in the First Syndic. | French franc and Spanish peseta | Catalan | Roman Catholic | Tobacco, potatoes, barley; sheep, cattle; lumber. |
| ANGOLA | Portuguese overseas province with a governor-general. | Portuguese escudo | Bantu languages Portuguese | Tribal religions | Coffee, corn, sugar, palm oil and kernels, cotton, sisal, wax, tobacco; diamonds; whale oil, fish oil, sugar, palm oil. |
| ANTIGUA | British colony with an administrator, an appointed chief minister, a legislative council and an executive council. | B.W.I. dollar | English | Protestant | Sugar cane, cotton, tropical fruits and vegetables, fish; barite; sugar, rum. |
| ARGENTINA | A republic with a president, vice-president, appointive cabinet, elective senate and house of deputies. | Argentine peso | Spanish | Roman Catholic | Wheat, corn, oats, barley, linseed, rye, grapes and other fruit, tobacco, vegetables; yerba maté; cattle, sheep; quebracho, lumber; petroleum, natural gas, gold, lead, silver, tungsten; vegetable oils, wines, hides, wool, meats, textiles, metal products, vehicles and machinery, chemicals, wood and paper products, leather, clothing and shoes. |
| ASCENSION ISLAND | Possession of Great Britain administered through the government of St. Helena by a resident magistrate and a Justice of the Peace. | pound sterling | English | Protestant | |
| AUSTRALIA | Member of the British Commonwealth of Nations with a governor-general, prime minister and cabinet. Parliament consists of a senate and house of commons. | Australian dollar | English | Protestant Roman Catholic | Wheat, oats, rice and other grains, fruits, vegetables, honey; sheep, cattle; gold, coal, copper, iron, lead, silver, tin, zinc; iron and steel, wool, textiles, electrical and radio equipment and appliances, drugs and chemicals, paints, optical instruments, agricultural implements and machinery, metal work and machinery, clothing, leather, furniture, airplanes, engines, ships, processed fruit and vegetables, building materials, confectionery, automobiles. |
| AUSTRIA | Republic with a president, chancellor and vice-chancellor, cabinet of ministers, and two-house assembly. | schilling | German | Roman Catholic | Rye, wheat, oats, barley, corn, potatoes, sugar beets, hops, grapes, rapeseed, flax, hemp, tobacco; iron, copper, lead, magnesite, graphite, coal, aluminum, petroleum, lignite, salt; timber, pulp, poultry and livestock; steel, machinery, machine tools, chemicals, textiles, paper, building materials, processed foods, leather. |
| BAHAMA ISLANDS | A constitutional self-governing British colony, with a governor, prime minister, a cabinet and a bicameral legislature. | Bahaman pound | English | Roman Catholic and Protestant | Tomatoes, pineapples, okra, vegetables, citrus fruits, bananas, sisal; crawfish, shells; lumber; salt; handcraft products. |
| BAHREIN | Arab sheikhdom protected by Great Britain and advised by British political agent. | Indian rupee | Arabic | Mohammedan | Pearl fishing, petroleum, boat building, fishing; reed mats, dates, lucerne; donkeys; textiles. |
| BARBADOS | An internally self-governing British colony, headed by a governor, a prime minister, a cabinet and a unicameral legislature. | B.W.I. dollar | English | Protestant | Sugar cane, cotton; flying fish; manjak (asphalt); sugar, molasses, rum, edible oil, margarine. |
| BASUTOLAND | A constitutionally governed British protectorate, with a resident commissioner, an executive and a national council. | pound sterling | Bantu languages Afrikaans English | Tribal religions Christian missions | Corn, wheat, sorghum, barley, oats, beans, peas; cattle, sheep, goats, horses, donkeys, pigs, mules; wool, mohair. |
| BECHUANALAND PROTECTORATE | British protectorate. Governed by a resident commissioner with a partly-elected legislative council. | pound sterling | Bantu languages Bushman English | Tribal religions Protestant | Kaffir, wheat and wheatmeal; cattle, sheep, goats, pigs; hides, gold. |
| BELGIUM | Constitutional, hereditary monarchy. King appoints a cabinet of ministers. Parliament consists of a senate and chamber of deputies. | Belgian franc | French (Walloon) and Flemish | Roman Catholic | Wheat, rye, oats, barley, potatoes, sugar beets, flax, tobacco, vegetables, fruit, hops, hemp, bulbs, livestock, fish; coal, iron, zinc, lead, copper, tin, silver; coke, steel, machinery, textiles, lace, glass, chemicals, uranium refining, sugar, margarine, cheese, vinegar, alcohol, beer, matches, paper, foods, beverages, wool, cut diamonds, dairy products. |
| BERMUDA | British colony with governor, executive and legislative council and house of assembly. | Bermuda pound | English | Protestant | Lily bulbs, onions, bananas, cabbage, tomatoes, beans; coral; fish; perfume. |
| BOLIVIA | A republic with a president, vice-president, appointive ministers of state, and an elective senate and chamber of deputies. | Bolivian peso | Spanish Indian | Roman Catholic | Potatoes, corn, barley, quinoa, nuts, coca, vanilla, rubber, quinine; tin, zinc, lead, copper, silver, antimony, tungsten, sulphur, petroleum; cattle; textiles, flour, cement, tobacco products, hides, beer, earthenware. |
| BONIN & VOLCANO IS. | Administered by the United States. | American dollar and Japanese Yen | Japanese | Shinto-Buddhist | Vegetables, sugar, coca; poultry, pigs, cattle; fish. |

| POLITICAL DIVISION | GOVERNMENT | MONETARY UNIT | LANGUAGE | RELIGION | MAJOR PRODUCTS |
|---|---|---|---|---|---|
| BRAZIL | Federal republic with a president, vice-president, appointive secretaries of state and a bicameral legislature. | cruzeiro | Portuguese | Roman Catholic | Coffee, corn, rice, cotton, cacao, sugar cane, cassava, beans, carnauba wax, medicinal plants, oranges, balata, tobacco, fibers, castor oil; livestock; timbo, brazil nuts; iron, manganese, gold, rutile, zirconium, diamonds, mica, bauxite, quartz, beryllium, chrome, tungsten, silver; foods, textiles, chemicals, pharmaceuticals, metallurgical products, paper and wood products, hides, vegetable oils, machinery. |
| BRITISH HONDURAS | A self-governing British colony with governor, prime minister, a cabinet and a bicameral legislature. | Br. Honduras dollar | English and Spanish | Protestant and Roman Catholic | Rice, maize, beans, bananas, coconuts, citrus fruits, sugar cane; mahogany, chicle, pine, cedar; fish; rum, food products. |
| BRUNEI | A sultanate with a chief minister, an executive council, a partly elected legislative assembly, and an advisory British high commissioner. | Malayan dollar | Malay English | Mohammedan | Rice, sago, rubber, jelutong, cutch, sugar cane, tapioca, bananas, pineapples; timber; domestic birds, buffalo, pigs, cattle; petroleum, natural gas; boat building, cloth, brass and silverware. |
| BULGARIA | Soviet-type republic with a one-house legislature, which elects a presidium whose president is the nominal chief of state. Actual power is Communist politburo. | lev | Bulgarian | Eastern Orthodox | Wheat, corn, barley, oats, rye, tobacco, fruit, cotton, sugar beets, potatoes; livestock, silkworm cocoons; fish; coal, salt, bauxite, copper, iron, lead, manganese, silver, kaolin; tobacco products, attar of roses, sugar, flour, textiles, leather goods, shoes, lead concentrates, wines and spirits. |
| BURMA, UNION OF | A republic with a president elected by a bicameral legislature. | kyat | Burmese Karen Shan | Buddhist Tribal religions | Rice, sesame, peanuts, corn, cotton, millet, tobacco, sugar, beans, fruit, vegetables, pulses, rubber; teak wood, lumber; cattle, buffalo, pigs, goats, sheep; petroleum, silver, lead, zinc, tin, copper, tungsten, rubies, sapphires, amber, jade, nickel, gold, antimony, cobalt, salt; textiles, hides, matches, lacquer ware. |
| BURUNDI | Constitutional kingdom, with a king, a prime minister, a cabinet and a legislative assembly. | Belgian franc | Bantu languages Flemish French | | Agricultural products; cattle; hides. |
| CAMBODIA | Constitutional monarchy with a national assembly. | riel | Khmer Lao | Buddhist | Rice, tobacco, kapok, cotton, pepper, coin, sugar, rubber; timber; cattle; fish; silk, cotton, textiles, pottery, rush mats, precious stones, phosphates. |
| CAMEROON | A federal state with a president, a national assembly and regional assemblies. | French franc | Sudanese and Bantu languages Arabic French | Tribal religions Mohammedan Christian | Cocoa, palm kernels, bananas, caoutchouc, coffee, cacao, palm oil; timber; cattle, sheep, pigs, horses, asses; rubber, tobacco. |
| CANADA | Member of the British Commonwealth with a governor-general, prime minister and cabinet. Parliament consists of a senate and house of commons. | Canadian dollar | English French | Protestant Roman Catholic | Wheat, oats, barley, flax, rye, potatoes, turnips, vegetables, sugar beets, tobacco, fruits, dairy products, livestock; fish; forestry products; furs; gold, copper, nickel, zinc, lead, silver, platinum, iron ore, titanium, cobalt, radium, uranium, petroleum, natural gas, coal, asbestos, salt, gypsum, quartz, sulphur, cement, clay; hydro-electric power; foods, beverages, transportation equipment, iron and steel products, aluminum, metal products, pulp, paper and wood products, textiles, electrical apparatus, chemicals. |
| CAPE VERDE ISLANDS | Portuguese overseas province, ruled by a governor. | Portuguese escudo | Portuguese | Roman Catholic | Coffee, castor beans, corn, fruit, grains, tobacco; goats, oxen, pigs, asses; hides, skins; preserved fish, salt, lime, sugar. |
| CAROLINE ISLANDS | A group in the United States trust Territory of the Pacific Islands and administered by a high commissioner. | American dollar | Micronesian dialects Malayo-Polynesian languages | Tribal religions Protestant Roman Catholic | Copra, breadfruit, cassava, taro, sweet potatoes; pigs, cattle, poultry, fish; phosphates. |
| CENTRAL AFRICAN REPUBLIC | Equatorial African republic within the French Community with a legislative assembly. | French franc | Bantu and Sudanese languages Arabic, French | Mohammedan Tribal religions Roman Catholic | Coffee, cotton, sisal, groundnuts, millet, sorghum; gold, diamonds; rubber; palm products, beeswax. |
| CEYLON | Independent member of the British Commonwealth ruled by a governor-general, a prime minister, a cabinet and a bicameral legislature. | Ceianese rupee | Singhalese Tamil | Buddhist Hindu | Tea, coconuts, rubber, rice, millet, tobacco, cacao, cinnamon, citronella, cloves, fruits, palmyra, fish; cattle, buffalo, goats, swine, sheep; graphite, plumbago, mica, ilmenite, monazite, iron ore; salt, pearls, zircon, glass sands, copra, plywood, leather, shoes, glass, steel, acetic acid, ceramics, quinine, strychnine, shark-liver oil, coconut oil, textiles. |
| CHAD | Equatorial African republic within the French Community with a legislative assembly. | French franc | Bantu and Sudanese languages Arabic, French | Mohammedan Tribal religions Roman Catholic | Millet, sesame, vegetables; livestock, hides; ivory, ostrich feathers; cotton, dates. |
| CHILE | A republic with a president, vice-president, appointive cabinet of ministers of state, elective senate and chamber of deputies. | Chilean escuco | Spanish | Roman Catholic | Wheat, potatoes, oats, rice, barley, corn, kidney beans, lentils, fruits; fish; livestock; copper, silver, nitrates, iodine, iron, sulphur, gold, manganese, coal; foods, textiles, leather, wood products, cement, chemicals and pharmaceuticals, wines and beer, wool. |
| CHINA: MAINLAND (COMMUNIST) | In theory, governmental power resides in the National People's Congress and the State Council. In practice, power resides in the Communist Party's Central Committee. | Chinese dollar | Chinese Mongol Turki | Confucianist Buddhist Taoist Mohammedan | Rice, wheat, sweet potatoes, corn, barley, millet, kaoliang, soybeans, cotton, tea, sugar cane, tobacco, peanuts, peas, beans, opium, tung, silk; pigs, oxen, sheep, goats, buffalo, donkeys, horses, mules, poultry; timber; fish; iron, coal, tungsten, tin, antimony, mercury, copper, lead, zinc, silver, salt, soda, gold, petroleum, bismuth, molybdenum; foodstuffs, textiles, chemicals, machinery, metal work, metallurgical products, bristles, cement, clothing, embroideries, ceramics. |
| CHINA: TAIWAN (NATIONALIST) | A republic whose supreme organ of government is the popularly elected National Assembly. The Assembly elects the president and vice-president. Legislative powers reside with the Legislative Yuan. | new Taiwan dollar | Chinese (Amoy dialect) Formosan | Confucianist Buddhist Taoist Christian Tribal religions | Rice, tea, sugar, sweet potatoes, ramie, jute, tumeric, pineapples, bananas, camphor; pigs, buffalo, cattle, goats, horses. |
| COLOMBIA | A centralized federal republic with a president, vice-president, appointive cabinet, elective senate and house of representatives. | Colombian peso | Spanish | Roman Catholic | Coffee, sugar cane, corn, rice, root crops, cotton, bananas, cacao, wheat, tobacco, cinchona; cattle; rubber, fibers; petroleum, gold, silver, platinum, emeralds, salt; textiles, beer, sugar, cement, flour, tobacco products. |
| COMORO ISLANDS | An overseas territory of France with an administrator, privy council and an elective general council. | French franc | Arabic French | Mohammedan | Sugar cane, vanilla, rice, sweet potatoes, yams, copra, sisal, cacao, perfume plants; rum distilling. |
| CONGO, REPUBLIC OF | Equatorial African republic within the French Community with a legislative assembly. | French franc | Bantu and Sudanese languages Arabic, French | Mohammedan Tribal religions Roman Catholic | Palm oil and kernels, hardwoods, kola nuts, copal, rubber, tobacco; lead, gold; livestock; rice. |
| CONGO, REPUBLIC OF THE | Independent republic, with a president and a national assembly. | Belgian franc | Bantu languages French Flemish | Tribal religions Roman Catholic | Palm oil and kernels, cotton, coffee, oil cakes, copal, rice, groundnuts; rubber, manioc, fibers; copper, cement, coal, silver, cassiterite (tin), diamonds, gold, cobalt, radium, uranium, tantalum, zinc. |

| POLITICAL DIVISION | GOVERNMENT | MONETARY UNIT | LANGUAGE | RELIGION | MAJOR PRODUCTS |
|---|---|---|---|---|---|
| COOK ISLANDS | Territory of New Zealand administered by a resident commissioner. | New Zealand pound | Polynesian dialects English | Protestant Tribal religions | Citrus fruits, coconuts, copra, tomatoes, arrowroot, pineapples, breadfruit, taro, kumaras, plantains, yams; mother-of-pearl. |
| COSTA RICA | Republic with president, cabinet and one-house legislature. | colón | Spanish | Roman Catholic | Coffee, bananas, cocoa, abaca, sugar cane, maize, rice, tobacco; cattle; tuna; gold; silver; cigars and cigarettes, textiles, furniture and woodwork, sugar. |
| CUBA | Formal republic with dictatorial aspects. Government by decree of Prime Minister. | Cuban peso | Spanish | Roman Catholic | Sugar cane, tobacco, coffee, pineapples, citrus fruits, bananas, henequen; cattle; cedar, mahogany and other woods; fish; chromite, iron, manganese, copper, nickel, asphalt; sugar, textiles, alcohol, molasses, chemicals, tobacco products, electrical goods, clothing. |
| CURACAO (NETH. ANTILLES) | Self-governing part of Netherlands Union with governor, executive council and one-house legislature. | Dutch guilder | Dutch and Papiamento | Protestant | Fish; dividivi (tannin), crude salt, phosphates; refined petroleum. |
| CYPRUS | Independent republic and member of British Commonwealth. | Cypriot pound | Greek Turkish | Greek Orthodox Mohammedan | Wheat, barley, oats, grapes, raisins, olives, fodder crops, potatoes, carobs, cotton, tobacco, linseed, hemp, flax, citrus fruits, bread beans, corn, sesame, melons; sponges, fish; sheep, goats, donkeys, cattle, pigs, horses, mules; copper pyrites, asbestos, chromite, gypsum, amber, copper concentrates; tobacco products, wines, spirits, false teeth, lace, gum, boots and shoes, dried fruits, cheese. |
| CZECHOSLOVAKIA | Soviet-type republic with a president and a one-house elective parliament. Actual power resides in politburo, highest body of Communist party. | koruna (crown) | Czech and Slovak | Roman Catholic | Wheat, rye, barley, oats, corn, hops, sugar beets, grapes, potatoes; poultry, livestock; timber; coal, lignite, iron, graphite, garnets, silver, copper, lead, salt, manganese, zinc; beer, spirits, malt, metals, munitions, machinery, iron and steel, porcelain, shoes, textiles, wood products, pulp and paper, sugar, leather, foods, chemicals, rubber products. |
| DAHOMEY | West African republic with a legislative assembly. | French franc | Sudanese languages French | Tribal religions Mohammedan | Palm oil, shea nuts, groundnuts, cotton fiber, copra, castor oil, kapok, millet; gold, diamonds, bauxite, iron ore. |
| DENMARK | Constitutional, hereditary monarchy with a two-house, elective legislature and an appointive council of ministers. | krone (crown) | Danish | Protestant | Barley, mixed grains, oats, rye, wheat, potatoes, sugar beets; livestock, fish; clay; ships and transportation equipment, butter, bacon, eggs, cheese, milk, footwear, clothing, machines, chemicals, tobacco products, metal goods, leather goods, beverages; stone, earthenware and glassware, electrical goods. |
| DOMINICAN REPUBLIC | Republic with president, cabinet and two-house legislature. | Dominican peso | Spanish | Roman Catholic | Sugar cane, cacao, coffee, tobacco, bananas, rice, corn; cattle; lumber; gold; starch, alcohol, molasses, sugar, chocolate, meats, cigars, cigarettes, leather. |
| ECUADOR | A centralized republic with a president, a cabinet and an elective bicameral legislature, the senate including representatives of various cultural groups. | sucre | Spanish, Indian | Roman Catholic | Rice, cacao, coffee, bananas, rubber, kapok, cotton, tagua (ivory) nuts, cinchona; livestock; gold, petroleum, salt, balsa wood; textiles, toquilla (panama) hats, buttons, sugar, flour, shoes, beer and liquors, chemicals, pharmaceuticals, cement, soap, candles. |
| EGYPT | Officially called the United Arab Republic, it is ruled by a president, a cabinet and a unicameral legislature. | Egyptian pound | Arabic | Mohammedan Christian minorities | Cotton, barley, wheat, rice, sugar cane, onions, corn, millet, fruits, vegetables; sheep, goats, cattle, buffalo, donkeys, pigs, horses, mules; fish; petroleum, cement, phosphates, asbestos, chromite, cotton ginning, milling, pottery, perfume, soap. |
| ENGLAND AND WALES | England is governed directly by the government of Great Britain and Northern Ireland. Executive power resides nominally in the Crown but actually in the prime minister and cabinet. Parliament consists of two houses. | pound sterling | English and Welsh (Celtic) | Protestant | Potatoes, turnips, beets, oats, wheat, barley, rye, hay, beans, peas, cabbage, vetches, hops, fruits; sheep, cattle, pigs, horses, poultry; fish; coal, coke, gas, iron, copper, lead, nickel, tin, clay; dairy products, wool, cotton and linen textiles; electrical goods, vehicles, steel, scientific instruments, cutlery, foods and beverages, tobacco products, clothing and shoes, chemicals, pottery, china, machinery, locomotives, carpets, knitwear, lace, pharmaceuticals. |
| ETHIOPIA | Constitutional monarchy with an emperor, a council of ministers and a bicameral legislature. | Ethiopian dollar | Amharic Hamitic languages Arabic | Coptic Christian Mohammedan | Coffee, teff, barley, durra, wheat, cotton, sugar cane; cattle, sheep, goats, horses, mules; hides, skins; wax, gold, rocksalt. |
| FALKLAND ISLANDS | British colony with a governor and an executive and a legislative council. | pound sterling | English | Protestant, Roman Catholic | Forage crops, sheep; wool, skins, tallow, whale oil, whale-meat meal. |
| FERNANDO PO | Internally autonomous Spanish province ruled by a governor. | Spanish peseta | Bantu languages Spanish | Tribal religions Roman Catholic | Cocoa, coffee, bananas, palm oil and kernels, copra; cabinet woods. |
| FIJI | British colony ruled by a governor with an executive and legislative council. | Fiji pound | English Fijian Hindustani Chinese | Protestant Roman Catholic Moslem Hindu | Sugar cane, coconuts, bananas, pineapples, rice, root vegetables, citrus fruits, cotton, rubber, castor oil seeds, taro, yams, cassava, sweet potatoes, groundnuts, pulses, corn, fodder crops, tobacco; cattle, pigs; tuna, bêche-de-mer, trochus shell; gold, silver; sugar, copra, coconut oil, soap, biscuits, molasses, paint, butter, ghee, candlenut oil. |
| FINLAND | A republic with a president, a one-house elective diet and appointive council of state. | markka (mark) | Finnish and Swedish | Protestant | Hay, potatoes, wheat, oats, barley, rye, sugar beets, flax, hemp, vegetables; cattle, horses, sheep, pigs, poultry, reindeer; wood and timber; fish; copper; lumber, plywood, furniture, pulp and paper, cardboard, textiles, butter, eggs, cheese, flour, leather, chemicals, china and glass, foodstuffs. |
| FRANCE | A republic with a president, a two-house elective parliament and an appointive council of ministers. | franc | French | Roman Catholic | Sugar beets, potatoes, wheat, oats, barley, rye; corn, turnips, fruits, nuts, wine grapes, buckwheat; cattle, sheep, pigs, horses; fish; coal, iron ore, lignite, salt, bauxite, pyrites, potash salts, leeks, kaolin, natural gas, iron and steel, chemicals; silk, cotton, rayon, wool and linen, textiles; clothing, lace, perfumes and cosmetics, automobiles, machinery, dairy products, beet sugar, wines, porcelain, aluminum, foods, leather, spirits. |
| GABON | Equatorial African republic within the French Community with a president and a national assembly. | French franc | Bantu and Sudanese languages Arabic, French | Mohammedan Tribal religions Roman Catholic | Mahogany, ebony, okumé wood; gold; fishing; cocoa; rubber, kapok, waxes, kola nuts; manioc, sweet potatoes, corn, plantains. |
| GAMBIA | Internal self-governing member of the British Commonwealth, headed by a Prime Minister. | West African pound | Sudanese languages English | Mohammedan Tribal religions Christian | Groundnuts, palm kernels; hides and skins; beeswax. |

| POLITICAL DIVISION | GOVERNMENT | MONETARY UNIT | LANGUAGE | RELIGION | MAJOR PRODUCTS |
|---|---|---|---|---|---|
| GERMANY | Country is divided between two governments—a democratic **Federal Republic of Germany** in the west and a Soviet-dominated **German "Democratic" Republic** in the east. **Federal Republic** has an elected federal diet and council who jointly elect the president. **German "Democratic" Republic** has a communist-controlled legislative branch which selects the president, cabinet and prime minister. | East German and West German Deutsch mark | German | Protestant Roman Catholic | Wheat, rye, barley, oats, potatoes, sugar beets, fruits, hops; pigs, cattle, poultry, horses; fish; forest products; coal, lignite, iron, copper, potash, sulphur, salt, uranium, lead, zinc, fluor spar, gypsum, vanadium, aluminum; automobiles, steel, cement, diesel oil, gasoline, cotton yarn, woolen yarn, rayon fiber, beet sugar, beer, wines, optical instruments, sulphuric acid, sodium bicarbonate, chemicals. |
| GHANA | Independent republic. Member of the British Commonwealth headed by a president and a national assembly. | cedi | Sudanese languages English | Mohammedan Tribal religions Christian | Cocoa, palm oil and kernels, sorghum, millet, corn, yams, cassava, groundnuts, cotton; gold, diamonds, manganese, bauxite. |
| GIBRALTAR | British Crown Colony administered by a governor, executive council, and a legislative council. | pound sterling | English and Spanish | Roman Catholic | Fish for export and processing of commodities for local consumption. |
| GILBERT AND ELLICE ISLS. | British colony administered by a resident commissioner. | Australian pound | English Gilbertese Samoan | Tribal religions Protestant Roman Catholic | Coconuts, copra, phosphate of lime; pearl shell, fish; hats, mats. |
| GREAT BRITAIN | See: England   Northern Ireland   Scotland | | | | |
| GREECE | A constitutional hereditary monarchy with a prime minister, cabinet of ministers and an elective assembly. | drachma | Greek | Greek Orthodox | Wheat, barley, corn, oats, rye, tobacco, currants, sultana raisins, olives, figs, grapes, cottonseed, sesame seed; sheep, goats, cattle, pigs, horses, mules; fish; iron ore, sulphur, emery, magnesite, zinc, lead, lignite, marble, bauxite; textiles, olive oil, foods, wines, chemicals, leather, wood and paper, metal products, machinery. |
| GREENLAND | An integral part of the Danish kingdom, with representation in Parliament and a provincial council. | Danish krone | Danish and Greenlandic | Protestant | Grass for fodder; cod and other fish; sheep, furs; cryolite; processed fish, hides. |
| GUADELOUPE | Overseas department of France with a prefect and elective general council. | French franc | French, French Patois | Roman Catholic | Sugar cane, bananas, coffee, cocoa, vanilla, cassava; fish; alcohol, rum. |
| GUAM | Territory of the United States administered by a governor and advisory and legislative bodies. | American dollar | English Chamorro Spanish | Roman Catholic | Coconut products, corn, taro, bananas, citrus fruits, mangoes, papayas, breadfruit, sweet potatoes, cocoa, cassava, sugar cane, pineapples; cattle, pigs, poultry, buffalo. |
| GUATEMALA | Republic with a president, cabinet and one-house legislature. | quetzal | Spanish | Roman Catholic | Coffee, bananas, sugar cane, rubber, chicle, cacao, abaca, cattle; mahogany and dye woods; essential oils; gold; textiles. |
| GUIANA, BRITISH | An internally self-governing British colony with a governor, a prime minister, a cabinet and a bicameral legislature. | B.W.I. dollar | English | Protestant | Sugar cane, rice, coconuts, coffee, citrus fruits, cacao; balata, rubber, green heart and other timber; livestock; bauxite, diamonds, gold; textiles, milled rice, beer and rum, lime rum and oil, sugar, woods, molasses, charcoal, matches. |
| GUIANA, FRENCH | Overseas department of France governed by a prefect, with an elective council-general. | French franc | French | Roman Catholic | Rice, cacao, bananas, sugar cane, corn, cassava, woods; gold; hides, rosewood essence, shoes, rum, fish glue. |
| GUINEA | Independent republic. | Guinea franc | Sudanese languages French | Tribal religions Mohammedan | Rice, groundnuts, palm oil and nuts, wax, honey, bananas, indigo, kola, orange products, coffee; cattle, sheep, goats, pigs; hides and skins; bauxite, iron ore, gold. |
| GUINEA, PORTUGUESE | Portuguese overseas province ruled by a governor. | Portuguese escudo | Sudanese languages Portuguese | Tribal religions Roman Catholic | Rice, palm kernels and oil, wax, groundnuts; hides. |
| HAITI | Republic with a president, cabinet and a two-house legislature. | gourde | Creole, French | Roman Catholic | Coffee, sugar, fig bananas, sisal, cotton, rice, cocoa; logwood; molasses, sisal products. |
| HONDURAS | Republic with a president, council of ministers and a one-house legislature. | lempira | Spanish | Roman Catholic | Bananas, coffee, coconuts, tobacco, grapefruit, rice, henequen; mahogany; cattle; gold, silver. |
| HONG KONG | A British colony ruled by governor assisted by executive and legislative council. | Hong Kong dollar | Chinese English | Confucianist Buddhist Christian | Rice, sugar, ginger; fish; poultry, pigs; kaolin, lead, iron, wolfram, granite, silver, cement; shipbuilding; enameled hollow-ware, textiles. |
| HUNGARY | Soviet-type republic with a president and a presidential council selected by the national assembly. Actual power in hands of politburo, highest organ of Communist party. | forint | Hungarian | Catholic Protestant | Wheat, corn, rye, barley, oats, potatoes, sugar beets, tobacco, grapes and other fruits, peppers, hemp, flax; pigs, cattle, sheep, horses, poultry; fish; coal, lignite, petroleum, natural gas, iron ore, bauxite, manganese; flour, distilling, brewing, iron and steel, wines, textiles, paprika, chemicals, leather, metal products, wood and paper products. |
| ICELAND | A republic with a president, an elective, two-house legislature and an appointive cabinet of ministers. | króna (crown) | Icelandic | Protestant | Hay, potatoes, turnips, hothouse fruits and vegetables; sheep, poultry, horses, cattle; fish; dairy products, meats, animal and vegetable oils, hides, skins, leather, clothing, textiles, frozen fish, herring oil, herring meal. |
| IFNI | Spanish province ruled by a governor. | Spanish peseta | Berber Arabic Spanish | Mohammedan | Barley, alfalfa, corn, tomatoes, argan oil, wheat; fish. |
| INDIA | An independent republic within the British Commonwealth with a president, cabinet and a bicameral legislature. | Indian rupee | Indo-Aryan (Hindi, Bengali, Urdu, Gujarati, Punjab, etc.) and Dravidian (Tamil, Kanarese, Telugan) English Bhutia Lepcha | Hindu Mohammedan Buddhist Animist Christian Sikh Jain Parsi Lamaist | Rice, wheat, legumes, groundnuts, oilseeds, tea, tobacco, jute, cotton, rubber, coffee, sugar cane, barley, millet, corn; cattle, goats, buffalo, sheep, pigs; fish; coal, manganese, gold, petroleum, salt, mica, iron, copper, chromite, ilmenite, diamonds, silver, bauxite; textiles, shawls, carpets, jute manufactures, wood-carving and metal work, leather, chemicals, shipbuilding, petroleum refining, sugar refining, cotton ginning, iron and steel mills, glass, soap, matches. |
| INDONESIA | Republic with president, cabinet and a People's Congress. | rupiah | Indonesian (Malay, Javanese, etc.) | Mohammedan Tribal religions Christian Hindu | Rice, sugar cane, rubber, palm oil, tobacco, corn, coconuts, copra, cassava, sweet potatoes, groundnuts, soya beans, cotton, kapok, coffee, cinchona, cocoa, pepper, fruits, vegetables; cattle, buffalo; tin, coal, petroleum, bauxite, manganese; rubber goods, chemicals, shipyards, textiles, paper. |

| POLITICAL DIVISION | GOVERNMENT | MONETARY UNIT | LANGUAGE | RELIGION | MAJOR PRODUCTS |
|---|---|---|---|---|---|
| IRAN | Constitutional monarchy governed by a shah, prime minister, cabinet and a bicameral legislature. | rial | Persian Arabic Kurdish | Mohammedan Parsi | Wheat, cotton, gums, opium, fruit, rice, barley, sugar beets, tobacco, tea, corn, millet, legumes, vegetables, nuts; sheep, goats, cattle, asses, horses, mules; fish; petroleum oil, red oxide, copper, sulphur, arsenic, coal, salt, marble, nickel, manganese, lead, cobalt, turquoise, iron ore; carpets, rugs, textiles, leather, glass, matches, chemicals, jute, tobacco products, oil refining, casings, wood, oils. |
| IRAQ | Independent republic. | Iraqi dinar | Arabic Turkish Kurdish | Mohammedan | Dates, other fruits, barley, wheat, rice, tobacco, cotton, beans, corn, sorghum, sesame; sheep, goats, asses, camels, horses, buffalo; oil, salt, wool, textiles, cigarettes, distilling. |
| IRELAND | A republic with a president, premier and an elective, two-house parliament. | Irish pound | English and Gaelic | Roman Catholic | Hay, potatoes, turnips, fodder, beets, sugar beets, oats, wheat, barley, cabbage, rye, flax; cattle, sheep, pigs, horses, poultry; fish; coal, peat, gypsum; tobacco, dairy products, foodstuffs, beer, malt, clothing, meats, textiles, boots and shoes, wood and paper products. |
| ISRAEL | Republic with president, prime minister, cabinet and elective unicameral legislature. | Israeli pound | Hebrew Arabic | Judaist Mohammedan | Dairy products, vegetables, eggs, fruits, green fodder, wheat, hay, barley, corn, durra; goats, sheep, cattle, camels, poultry; fish; textiles, clothing, foods, beverages, tobacco, diamond polishing, shoes, metal and woodwork, furniture, building materials, leather, dairy products, electrical products, paper, printing, false teeth, pharmaceuticals, chemicals, dyes, soap, radios, oil refining, wines. |
| ITALY | A republic with a president, a two-house, elective legislature and an appointive cabinet. | lira | Italian | Roman Catholic | Wheat, corn, oats, sugar beets, potatoes, tomatoes, rice, olives, grapes, lemons and other fruits, hemp, tobacco, nuts; fish; sheep and goats, cattle, pigs, horses, donkeys; iron ore, sulphur, zinc, bauxite, lead, mercury, barite, copper, marble, manganese, lignite; textiles, chemicals, wines, automobiles and machinery, electrical goods, beet sugar, olive oil, cheese, clothing, processed foods. |
| IVORY COAST | West African republic with a legislative assembly. | French franc | Sudanese languages French | Tribal religions Mohammedan | Coffee, cocoa, bananas, manioc, corn, rice, yams, kola, coconuts, palm oil, groundnuts, cotton, millet, tobacco; mahogany, caoutchouc; sheep, cattle, goats, pigs; gold, diamonds, manganese, iron ore, ilmenite. |
| JAMAICA | Independent member of the British Commonwealth of Nations. | Jamaican pound | English | Protestant, Roman Catholic | Sugar cane, bananas, tobacco, coconuts, cacao, pimentoes, coffee, ginger; bauxite; honey; logwood; rum, textiles, cigars. |
| JAPAN | Constitutional monarchy with the executive power vested in prime minister and cabinet, the legislative power residing in a two-house parliament. The duties of the emperor are merely ceremonial. | yen | Japanese | Buddhist Shinto | Rice, wheat, barley, mulberry trees, potatoes, sweet potatoes, fruits, rape, vegetables, oats, tobacco, soy beans, tea, flax, hemp, camphor; timber, bamboo; horses, cattle, sheep, goats, pigs, rabbits; fish, agar, pearl oysters; silk worms; coal, pyrites, gold, copper, pyrethrum, manganese, silver, sulphur, chromite, zinc, salt, tin, lead, iron, petroleum; textiles, steel, paper, porcelain, earthenware, lacquer ware, vegetable oil, toys, slippers, shoes, machinery. |
| JORDAN | Constitutional monarchy with cabinet and bicameral legislature. | Jordan dinar | Arabic | Mohammedan | Wheat, barley, legumes, vegetables, fruits, olives; sheep, goats, camels; salt, phosphate, potash; wool, tobacco products, flour milling, building materials, olive oil. |
| KENYA | Independent member of the British Commonwealth, headed by a president, a prime minister and a bicameral legislature. | East African shilling | Swahili English Sudanese Hamitic Bantu | Tribal religions Mohammedan | Sisal, wheat, tea, coffee, pyrethrum, cotton, corn, sugar cane, sesame, groundnuts, wattle; hides and skins; sodium carbonate, gold, kyanite, salt, silver, lime, bags, butter, sugar, sisal products. |
| KOREA | Divided into two parts by Armistice Line of August, 1953, pending final decisions of peace treaty. Communist "people's republic" in North Korea; South Korea headed by a president, a prime minister, a cabinet and a bicameral legislature. | hwan | Korean | Confucianist Buddhist Christian | Rice, barley, millet, wheat, soya beans, red beans, cotton, tobacco, hemp, ginseng, fruit, radishes; timber; draft cattle, pigs, horses, mules, donkeys, sheep, goats, rabbits; fish; gold, iron ore, coal, tungsten, copper, silver, graphite, salt, kaolin, talc, bismuth, flourite, minerals (N. Korea), textiles, fertilizer, chemicals, cement, heavy industries (N. Korea); textiles, cement, tobacco, silkworms, chemicals, machinery, metal, rubber, wood, paper and tobacco products (S. Korea). |
| KUWAIT | Constitutional sheikhdom, with a Sheikh, a cabinet and a unicameral national assembly. | Kuwaiti dinar | Arabic | Mohammedan | Petroleum, shipbuilding (dhows), pearls, skins, wool. |
| LAOS | Constitutional monarchy with a cabinet and a national assembly. | kip | Khmer (Annamese) Lao | Buddhist | Rice, coffee, tea, citrus fruits, corn, cinchona, gum, benzoin, cardamon; stick-lac; teak; tin. |
| LEBANON | Independent republic governed by a president, cabinet and an elective legislature. | Lebanese pound | Arabic French | Christian Mohammedan | Wheat, barley, corn, potatoes, citrus and other fruits, onions, olives, tobacco (Latakia); goats, asses, cattle, buffalo, sheep, horses, mules; iron, lignite; textiles, cement, olive oil, tobacco products, soap, matches, petroleum refining, gasoline, leather. |
| LIBERIA | Republic with president, cabinet, senate and house of representatives. | Liberian dollar | English Sudanese languages | Christian Tribal religions Mohammedan | Rubber, rice, coffee, cassava, sugar cane, cacao, palm oil and kernels, piassava, groundnuts; rum; iron ore. |
| LIBYA | A kingdom with a prime minister, a cabinet and a bicameral legislature. | Libyan pound | Arabic | Mohammedan | Barley, wheat, olives, grapes, dates, almonds, figs, tobacco, esparto; goats, sheep, camels, cattle, donkeys, mules and horses; sponge and tuna fishing; matting, carpets, leather articles, embroidered fabrics. |
| LIECHTENSTEIN | A principality headed by a prince and an elective, one-house legislature. | Swiss franc | German | Roman Catholic | Grain, fruit, grapes, wood; cattle, pigs, chickens; cotton textiles, wine, leather, false teeth, pottery, wood-carving. |
| LUXEMBOURG | A grand duchy and hereditary, constitutional monarchy with an elective chamber of deputies and appointive minister of state and cabinet. | Luxembourg franc | Mosel-frankisch (German dialect) | Roman Catholic | Oats, potatoes, wheat, rye, grapes; livestock; iron ore, slate, gypsum, sand and gravel; iron, steel and metal working; chemicals, non-metallic minerals, beverages, tobacco, leather, wines, dairy products, quarrying. |
| MACAO | Portuguese overseas province ruled by a governor. | pataca | Chinese Portuguese | Confucianist Buddhist Taoist Christian | Fish; preserves, firecrackers, vegetable oil, cement, metal work, lumber, tobacco (processed), matches, wine. |
| MALAGASY REPUBLIC | Independent republic. Member of the French Community. | French franc | French Malagasy and Bantu languages | Tribal religions Roman Catholic Protestant | Cassava, rice, corn, potatoes, coffee, sugar cane, haricot beans, groundnuts, sisal, castor oil, tobacco, raffia; cattle, pigs, goats, sheep; graphite, mica, gold, rock crystal, corundum, phosphates, agate; textiles, sugar and rice factories, tapioca. |
| MALAWI | An indepedent member of the British Commonwealth, with a prime minister, a cabinet and a unicameral legislature. | Malawi pound | Bantu languages English | Tribal religions | Tobacco, tea, cotton, pulses, tung oil, sisal, corn, cassava, wheat, rice, millet, groundnuts, rubber, beeswax, timber; goats, cattle, pigs, sheep; hides, skins, meat, ghee, soap; gold, mica, corundum. |

| POLITICAL DIVISION | GOVERNMENT | MONETARY UNIT | LANGUAGE | RELIGION | MAJOR PRODUCTS |
|---|---|---|---|---|---|
| MALAYSIA, FEDERATION OF | Independent federation of the British Commonwealth, with a head of state, a council of rulers, a bicameral legislature and 14 state assemblies. | Malayan dollar | Malay Chinese English Indonesian languages Hindi | Mohammedan Confucianist Tribal religions Buddhist Hindu Taoist | Rubber, rice, coconuts, coffee, pineapples, tapioca, pepper, sugar, tobacco, fibers, gambier, vegetables, tea; buffalo, swine, oxen, goats, sheep; fish; tin, coal, iron ore, bauxite, petroleum, antimony, manganese, copra, palm oil, timber, gold, rubber products, canning, shipping, milling, bricks, gasoline, wood products, textiles. |
| MALDIVE ISLANDS | An independent sultanate, with a bicameral legislature advised by the high commissioner in Ceylon. | Celanese rupee | Singhalese Arabic Dravidian | Mohammedan | Coconuts, copra, coir, fruit, nuts; fish, cowries; cloth, mats, boats. |
| MALI | West African republic with a legislative assembly. | French franc | Sudanese and Hamitic languages Arabic French | Mohammedan Tribal religions | Millet, rice, groundnuts, corn, sweet potatoes, cotton, manioc, tobacco, karite, shea nuts, yams, kopak, sisal; cattle, goats, sheep, horses, asses, camels; hides and skins; pottery, bricks, jewelry, weaving, leather, rice mills, soap. |
| MALTA | An independent member of the British Commonwealth, with a prime minister, a cabinet and a unicameral legislature. | Maltese pound | Maltese and English | Roman Catholic | Wheat, barley, potatoes, onions, grapes and other fruits, cumin seed, cotton; goats, sheep, pigs, cattle; fish; lace, filigree, wine, footwear, beer, cigarettes, buttons, pipes, gloves. |
| MARIANA ISLANDS | A group of islands in the United States trust Territory of the Pacific administered by a high commissioner. | American dollar | Micronesian dialects Spanish | Tribal religions | Fruits, corn, sweet potatoes, vegetables, breadfruit, cacao; fish; phosphates. |
| MARQUESAS ISLANDS | A group of islands in French Polynesia administered from Tahiti. | French franc | Marquesan French | Tribal religions Roman Catholic | Bananas, breadfruit, yams, bamboo, coconuts, sugar cane. |
| MARSHALL ISLANDS | A group of islands in the United States trust Territory of the Pacific administered by a high commissioner. | American dollar | Micronesian dialects | Tribal religions Protestant | Arrowroot, breadfruit, coconuts, pandanus, taro, vegetables, copra, bananas; poultry, pigs; fish. |
| MARTINIQUE | Overseas department of France with a prefect and elective general council. | French franc | Creole, French | Roman Catholic | Sugar cane, cocoa, pineapples, bananas, coffee; rum, sugar. |
| MAURITANIA | West African republic within the French Community with a legislative assembly. | French franc | Arabic Hamitic and Sudanese languages French | Mohammedan | Millet, gum, dates, corn, watermelons, wheat, henna; sheep and goats, cattle, camels, asses, horses; hides and skins; salt. |
| MAURITIUS | British colony ruled by a governor, an executive council and a legislative council. | Mauritius rupee | English Hindustani French | Roman Catholic | Sugar, aloe fiber, rice, vanilla beans, hemp, sisal, groundnuts, tea, yams, manioc, pineapples, tobacco, coconuts; alcohol, molasses, rum, copra. |
| MEXICO | Federative republic with a president, council of ministers and a two-house legislature. | Mexican peso | Spanish | Roman Catholic | Corn, wheat, beans, chick peas, sugar bananas, barley, cotton, coffee, vegetables; cattle; henequen; fish; silver, petroleum, lead, gold, zinc, copper; textiles, sugar, alcohol, foundry products. |
| MONACO | A principality. The prince's authority exercised through a state ministry and 3 government counsellors. The one-house legislative body is elective. | French franc | French | Roman Catholic | Principal revenue derived from Monte Carlo gambling casino. Tobacco, postage stamps, perfume, liqueurs, olive oil, oranges. |
| MONGOLIA | Communist republic, whose prime minister is also head of Communist party politburo, which is the actual ruler. | tugrik | Mongolian Russian | Lamaist Tribal religions | Stock raising (sheep, goats, cattle, horses, camels); milk, butter, cheese; wool, hides, skins, horns, bricks, machinery; coal, lead, gold. |
| MOROCCO | Constitutional monarchy with an appointed cabinet and a bicameral elected parliament. | dirham | Arabic Berber French | Mohammedan Roman Catholic Jewish | Wheat, barley, olives, almonds, citrus fruits, dates, beans, grapes, vegetables, linseed; cork, cedar; sheep, goats, cattle, asses, camels, horses, mules, pigs; fish; phosphate, iron ore, anthracite, manganese, lead, zinc, cobalt, copper, antimony; leather, carpets. |
| MOZAMBIQUE | Portuguese overseas province ruled by a governor and a government council. | Portuguese escudo | Bantu languages Portuguese | Tribal religions Roman Catholic | Sugar, corn, cotton, copra, sisal, cashew nuts, bananas, coffee, kapok, sorghum, manioc, beeswax, tea, tobacco, vegetable oils; mangrove bark, timber; oxen, goats, pigs, sheep, cattle; gold, silver, asbestos, uranium, bauxite, samerskite. |
| MUSCAT AND OMAN | An independent sultanate. | rupee (official) Maria Theresa dollar | Arabic | Mohammedan | Dates, pomegranates, limes and other fruits, sugar cane; dried fish. |
| NEPAL | An independent kingdom governed by a maharaja, prime minister and a national council acting as a unicameral elected legislature. | Nepalese rupee | Indo-Aryan languages Tibetan | Hindu Buddhist Lamaist | Rice, grains, jute, sugar cane, tea, vegetables, tobacco, cotton, potatoes, medicinal herbs; timber; cattle, hides, skins, ghee; iron, coal, copper, lead, zinc; cotton cloth, pottery, paper. |
| NETHERLANDS | A constitutional, hereditary monarchy governed by the queen, her ministers and a two-house legislature, partly elective and partly chosen by provincial councils. | guilder | Dutch | Roman Catholic Protestant | Potatoes, sugar beets, rye, wheat, oats, barley, flax, legumes, flower bulbs, seeds, vegetables, fruit; cattle, pigs, sheep, horses, poultry; fish; coal, petroleum, salt; leather, rubber, footwear; metal products, textiles, paper, building materials, chemicals, foods and beverages, clothing, shipbuilding, cheese and other dairy products, fertilizers, ceramics, cement, tobacco products. |
| NEW CALEDONIA | French overseas territory administered by high commissioner assisted by an appointive executive council and an elective general council. | French franc | Melanesian dialects French | Roman Catholic Tribal religions | Coconuts, copra, coffee, cotton, manioc, corn, tobacco, bananas, pineapples, wheat, rice, kauri logs; cattle, pigs, horses, goats, sheep, hides; guano, trochus shell; nickel, chrome, manganese, iron, cobalt, copper, lead, platinum; canned meat. |
| NEW GUINEA, TERR. OF | Trust territory of Australia governed by administrator of Papua. | Australian pound | Papuan Pidgin English English | Tribal religions Roman Catholic Protestant | Coconuts, copra, cocoa, dairying; timber; gold, silver, platinum; boat making. |
| NEW HEBRIDES | British and French condominium administered by British and French resident commissioners, with a partly elected advisory council. | Australian currency Bank of Indochina Notes | Melanesian dialects Pidgin English English French | Tribal religions Protestant Roman Catholic | Coconuts, copra, cocoa, coffee, yams, taro, manioc, fruits; kauri pine; cattle, pigs; trochus shells. |

| POLITICAL DIVISION | GOVERNMENT | MONETARY UNIT | LANGUAGE | RELIGION | MAJOR PRODUCTS |
|---|---|---|---|---|---|
| NEW ZEALAND | An independent member of the British Commonwealth governed by a governor-general, a prime minister, a cabinet and a uni-cameral assembly. | New Zealand pound | English Maori | Protestant | Wheat, oats, barley, seeds, kauri, gum; sheep, cattle, pigs, horses; hides, skins; fish; gold, silver, coal, copper, lime-stone, manganese, iron, tungsten; dairy products, meats, wool, clothing, lumber, woodwork, furniture, electrical and radio goods, motor assembly, printing, publishing, biscuits, confections, footwear, rubber products, chemical fertilizers, tobacco products, brewing. |
| NICARAGUA | Republic with a president, cabinet and a two-house legislature. | córdoba | Spanish | Roman Catholic | Coffee, sugar cane, sesame, corn, bananas, rice, cacao, cotton, beans; cattle; hardwoods; gold, silver; sugar, wood products. |
| NIGER | West African republic with a leg-islative assembly. | French franc | Sudanese Hamitic Arabic French | Mohammedan Tribal religions | Millet, manioc, groundnuts, rice, wheat, cotton, gum arabic, kapok, kidney beans, corn, onions, sorghum, dates, sugar cane; goats, sheep, cattle, asses, camels, horses; hides and skins, leather; natron, sodium sulphate, salt. |
| NIGERIA | Independent federal republic with-in British Commonwealth with a president, cabinet and a bicameral central legislature. | West African pound | Sudanese languages Arabic English | Mohammedan Christian | Palm oil and kernels, cacao, groundnuts, cotton, rubber, bananas, benni seeds, shea nuts, yams, cassava, corn, rice, fruits, millet, coffee; cattle, sheep, goats; hides and skins; timber; tin, coal, columbite, lead, gold, silver, zinc; cigarettes, soap, sugar. |
| NIUE | Dependency of New Zealand ad-ministered by a resident com-missioner. | New Zealand pound | Mixed Melanesian and Polynesian dialects English | Protestant | Copra, sweet potatoes, bananas; hats, baskets. |
| NORFOLK ISLAND | An Australian territory governed by an administrator. | Australian pound | English | Protestant | Citrus, passion fruits, bananas, cherry guavas; hides; fish. |
| NORTHERN IRELAND | Executive power vested in ap-pointed governor and cabinet re-sponsible to legislative two-house parliament. | pound sterling | English and Gaelic | Protestant Roman Catholic | Potatoes, oats, flax, turnips, hay; cattle, sheep, pigs, poul-try; basalt and igneous rocks, sand and gravel, grit and conglomerate, chalk, clays; linen, rayon, woolen goods, carpets, hosiery, cotton goods, shirts, collars, shipbuilding, aircraft, marine machinery, rope, tobacco, whiskey. |
| NORWAY | A constitutional, hereditary mon-archy headed by the king, his council of state and a two-house, elective legislature. | krone (crown) | Norwegian | Protestant | Hay, potatoes, oats, barley, wheat, rye, fruits, vege-tables; dairy products, livestock; herring, cod and other fish; sulphur, iron, copper, zinc, silver, nickel, molybdenum; timber, pulp, cellulose, paper, canned foods, electro-chemical products, transportation equipment, salted, dried and canned fish, leather, basic metals, textiles, fertilizers, shipbuilding. |
| PAKISTAN | Self-governing republic within the British Commonwealth ruled by a president, cabinet and unicameral legislature. | Pakistani rupee | Indo-Aryan languages (Urdu, Bengali, Punjabi, etc.) | Mohammedan Hindu Christian Sikh | Rice, wheat, corn, jute, cotton, sugar cane, fruit, oilseeds, tobacco, tea, fibers; timber; cattle, goats, sheep, horses, camels, poultry; hides, skins, wool; fish; salt, copper, pe-troleum, chromite, gypsum, magnisite, sulphur, antimony; textiles, flour milling, cement, iron and steel foundries, sugar, leather, chemicals, glass, sportsgoods, handicrafts, surgical instruments. |
| PALAU ISLANDS | A civil administrative district in the Western Carolines and part of the United States trust Territory of the Pacific Islands, with locally elected native councils. | American dollar | Micronesian dialects | Tribal religions Christian | Coconuts, manioc, taro, pineapples, sweet potatoes, papayas; poultry, pigs, goats; fish; phosphate; handcrafts. |
| PANAMA | A constitutional republic with a president, two vice-presidents, a cabinet of ministers and a one-house legislature. | balboa | Spanish | Roman Catholic | Bananas, cacao, abaca, coconuts, rice, sugar cane, coffee, pineapples; cattle; hardwoods; gold; hides, sugar, wood products. |
| PAPUA TERRITORY | Australian territory governed by an administrator and a house of assembly. | Australian pound | Papuan Pidgin English English | Tribal religions Protestant Roman Catholic | Coconuts, rubber, sweet potatoes, yams, taro, sago, rice, bananas, coffee, kapok, bamboo, sisal hemp, copra; shells, sponges; cattle, goats, poultry; gold, copper, manganese. |
| PARAGUAY | A centralized republic with a president, an appointed cabinet and a one-house legislature. | guaraní | Spanish, Indian | Roman Catholic | Cotton, tobacco, sugar cane, rice, cassava, yerba maté, corn, citrus fruits; cattle, hides; lumber, quebracho; iron, manga-nese, copper; canned meats, vegetable oils, petit-grain oil, tobacco products. |
| PERU | A republic with a president, two vice-presidents, appointive cabinet and a two-house legislature. | sol | Spanish, Indian | Roman Catholic | Cotton, sugar, potatoes, barley, corn, rice, wheat, coca, quinoa, cacao, tobacco, coffee, quinine, flax, rubber, balata, guano; fish; livestock; petroleum, lead, zinc, copper, silver, gold, vanadium; textiles, foodstuffs, cement, leather, wool, hides, pharmaceuticals, paper products, clothing, metal. |
| PHILIPPINES | Republic governed by a president, cabinet and a bicameral legis-lature. | Philippine peso | Malayan languages (Tagalog, Visayan, etc.) English Spanish | Roman Catholic Mohammedan Tribal religions | Rice, sugar cane, copra, manila hemp (abacá), corn, tobacco, maguey, rubber, bananas, pineapples, mangoes, papaya, citrus fruits, other fruits; hogs, carabaos, cattle, horses, goats, sheep; fish; timber; gum resins, tan and dye barks, dye woods; gold, iron, copper, chromite, silver, manganese, asbestos, asphalt, guano, silica, coal, petroleum; sugar, tex-tiles, distilling, dessicated coconuts, tobacco products, rice milling, cocoa, coconut oil, embroideries. |
| PITCAIRN ISLANDS | British colony administered by a chief magistrate responsible to the governor of Fiji. | Fiji pound | English Tahitian | Protestant (Seventh Day Adventist) | Fruits, vegetables, goats, poultry; handicraft. |
| POLAND | A Soviet-type "People's Republic" headed by a one-party legislative Sejm which elects an executive Council of Ministers. Actual power in the hands of politburo, highest organ of Communist party. | zloty | Polish | Roman Catholic | Potatoes, straw and hay, rye, sugar beets, mangolds, oats, barley, wheat, peas, beans, flax, hemp, rapeseed; livestock; fish; zinc, lead, coal, salt, iron ore, petroleum, natural gas, phosphates, lignite; iron and steel products, coke, foods and beverages, textiles, cement, lime, bricks, electrical goods, chemicals, wood, timber, paper, cellulose, leather and leather products, glass. |
| PORTUGAL | A "unitary corporative republic" with a president, premier, and a one-house elective legislature. | escudo | Portuguese | Roman Catholic | Wheat, corn, oats, barley, rye, rice, French beans, potatoes, grapes, olives; livestock; cork, lumber, resin; sardines, tuna and other fish; copper pyrites, coal, copper, tin, kaolin, cement, wolfram, sulphur, tungsten, iron; wines, olive oil, canned sardines, textiles, porcelain, tiles, embroideries, lace. |

| POLITICAL DIVISION | GOVERNMENT | MONETARY UNIT | LANGUAGE | RELIGION | MAJOR PRODUCTS |
|---|---|---|---|---|---|
| PUERTO RICO | A self-governing commonwealth associated with the United States, with a governor, an executive council and a bicameral legislature. | American dollar | Spanish, English | Roman Catholic | Sugar cane, tobacco, fruits, pineapples, grapefruit, coconuts, coffee, cotton, livestock, vegetables; molasses, embroideries, rum, canned fruit and juice, alcohol, cordials, tobacco products. |
| QATAR | British protected Sheikhdom. | rupee; riyal | Arabic | Mohammedan | Dates; pearl fishing, dried fish; camels; petroleum. |
| RÉUNION | French overseas department administered by a prefect. | French franc | French | Roman Catholic | Sugar, rum, vanilla, tapioca, essences, fruit and vegetable preserves. |
| RÍO MUNI | Internally autonomous Spanish province ruled by a governor. | Spanish peseta | Bantu languages Spanish | Tribal religions Roman Catholic | Cocoa, coffee, palm oil and kernels; cabinet woods. |
| RUMANIA | A Soviet-type "People's Republic" with a 17-member State Council, cabinet of ministers and a one-house legislature. Supreme power resides in Communist party politburo. | leu | Rumanian | Rumanian Orthodox | Wheat, barley, rye, corn, oats, potatoes, sugar beets, hemp, flax, grapes, fruits, tobacco; lumber; sheep, cattle, pigs, horses; petroleum, natural gas, salt, coal, lignite, iron and copper ores, gold, silver, bauxite, lead, manganese, zinc; flour, brewing and distilling, iron and steel, metal products, textiles, wood and paper products. |
| RWANDA | An independent republic with a president, a council of ministers and a legislative assembly. | Belgian franc | Bantu languages Flemish French | Tribal religions Roman Catholic | Foods; cattle; hides. |
| RYUKYU IS. | Administered by the United States. | American dollar | Luchuan Japanese English | Animistic Shinto | Sweet potatoes, sugar cane, rice, fruits, mulberries; swine, cattle, goats, horses, poultry; silkworms; fish; Panama hats, textiles, lacquer, pottery, china, glassware, tiles, plywood. |
| SABAH | State in the Federation of Malaysia, with a head of state, a cabinet and a unicameral legislature. | Malayan dollar | Malay Indonesian languages English Chinese | Tribal religions Mohammedan | Rubber, coconuts, copra, tobacco, manila hemp, sago, rice, cutch, sugar, pepper, kapok, groundnuts, derris root, vegetables, timber, fish. |
| ST. HELENA | British colony with a governor, an executive and an advisory council. | pound sterling | English | Protestant | Hemp, lily bulbs, potatoes, tow, rope and twine, lace; sheep, goats, cattle, donkeys, poultry. |
| ST. PIERRE AND MIQUELON | French overseas territory with a governor, privy council and elective general council. | French franc | French | Roman Catholic | Fish, silver fox; dried cod and cod liver oil; sienna earth, yellow ocher. |
| SALVADOR, EL | Republic with a president and a one-house legislature. | colón | Spanish | Roman Catholic | Coffee, cotton, corn, tobacco, henequen, sugar cane, rice; balsam and other woods; gold, silver; cotton textiles, henequen bags, sugar. |
| SAMOA, AMERICAN | U.S. territory with a governor and a bicameral legislature. | American dollar | English Samoan | Protestant | Copra, taro, breadfruit, yams, bananas, arrowroot, pineapples, oranges; mats. |
| SAMOA, WESTERN | Independent member of the British Commonwealth of Nations. | New Zealand pound | Samoan English | Protestant Tribal religions | Copra, cocoa beans, bananas, taro; fish; pigs, poultry. |
| SAN MARINO | Republic with two regents, council of state, one-house legislature. | lira | Italian | Roman Catholic | Cattle, hides, wines, quarrying. |
| SÃO TOMÉ AND PRÍNCIPE | Portuguese overseas province administered by a governor. | Portuguese escudo | Bantu languages Portuguese | Tribal religions Roman Catholic | Cacao, coffee, coconuts, copra, palm oil, cinchona, bananas. |
| SARAWAK | State in the Federation of Malaysia, with a governor, a chief minister, a cabinet and a unicameral legislature. | Malayan dollar | Malay Indonesian languages Chinese English | Mohammedan Tribal religions | Rice, rubber, sago, pepper, coconuts, pineapples, tobacco, coffee, fruits, vegetables; timber, rattan canes, guttas; buffalo, cattle, pigs, goats; fish; petroleum, gold, antimony, phosphates, cutch. |
| SAUDI ARABIA | Absolute monarchy, with premier and cabinet responsible to the king and advisory councils. | riyal | Arabic | Mohammedan | Dates, sorghum, wheat, rice, henna, coffee, fruits, nuts, vegetables, honey, gum, sesame oil; fish; camels, sheep, goats, cattle, donkeys, poultry, horses; hides, wool, clarified butter, charcoal, pottery, tile, salt, soap, weaving; petroleum, gold, pearls. |
| SCOTLAND | A secretary of state for Scotland in the British cabinet has in his charge four departments for Scotland (agriculture, education, health and home.) Authority in other matters is exercised by other members of the British cabinet. | pound sterling | English and Gaelic | Protestant | Turnips, potatoes, wheat, barley, sugar beets, flax, vegetables, forage crops, fruits; sheep, cattle, pigs, horses; coal, iron ore, granite, sandstone, limestone, slate, lead, clay; steel, machinery, tools, locomotives, electronic equipment, linoleum, shipbuilding and repair, watches, clocks, jute, bagging, burlap, textiles, hosiery, thread, lace, carpet, yarn, chemicals, whiskey, ale, paper, bricks and other clay products, preserves, boots and shoes, furniture. |
| SENEGAL | West African republic within the French Community with a president and an elected legislative assembly. | French franc | Sudanese languages Arabic French | Mohammedan Tribal religions Roman Catholic | Millet, groundnuts, manioc, rice, corn, gum arabic, palm nuts, honey, sweet potatoes, sisal, indigo; sheep, goats, cattle, asses, horses; fish; titanium, zircon; brick, pottery, weaving, jewelry, oil cakes. |
| SEYCHELLES | A British colony ruled by a governor and councils. | Seychelles rupee | English French | Roman Catholic | Coconuts, cinnamon, patchouli, copra, vanilla, corn; guano; salted fish, tortoise shell, calipee. |
| SIERRA LEONE | An independent member of the British Commonwealth with a prime minister, a cabinet, and a house of representatives. | leone | Sudanese languages English | Tribal religions Mohammedan Christian | Palm oil and kernels, kola nuts, ginger, piassava, groundnuts, cocoa; diamonds, iron ore, chrome ore. |
| SINGAPORE | State in the Federation of Malaysia, with a head of state, a prime minister, a cabinet and a unicameral legislature. | Malayan dollar | Chinese Malay Hindi English | Confucianist Buddhist Taoist Mohammedan Hindu Christian | Rubber, coconuts, fruits, vegetables, rice, coffee, tapioca, tobacco, sweet potatoes, pepper, pineapples; pigs, poultry, cattle; fish; tin; tin smelting, rubber milling, coconut milling, soap, beer, pineapple canning, biscuits, brick making, shipping, textiles, palm oil, cigarettes, gasoline, kerosene. |
| SOCIETY ISLANDS | Part of French Polynesia governed from Tahiti. | French franc | Polynesian French | Roman Catholic Tribal religions | Copra, vanilla, pearls, mother of pearl, vanilla, phosphates, sugar, rum. |
| SOLOMON ISLANDS | British protectorate, with appointed legislative and executive councils. | Australian pound | Melanesian Pidgin English English | Tribal religions Protestant Roman Catholic | Copra, pigs, poultry; trochus shell, turtle shell, bêche-de-mer. |

| POLITICAL DIVISION | GOVERNMENT | MONETARY UNIT | LANGUAGE | RELIGION | MAJOR PRODUCTS |
|---|---|---|---|---|---|
| SOMALI REPUBLIC | Independent republic with a prime minister, a parliament and territorial assemblies. | Somali shilling | Somali Arabic Italian | Mohammedan Roman Catholic | Sugar, cotton, tobacco, bananas, aromatic gums, resin, kapok, grains, beans; camels, goats, sheep, cattle; skins, hides; tunny, mother-of-pearl. |
| SOMALILAND, FRENCH | Overseas territory of France with a governor and an elective representative assembly. | Djibouti franc | Hamitic languages Arabic French | Mohammedan | Boats, sheep; salt. |
| SOUTH AFRICA | A republic with president, prime minister, cabinet, elective senate and house of assembly. | rand | Afrikaans English Bantu languages Bushman | Protestant Roman Catholic Mohammedan Hindu Buddhist | Corn, wheat, potatoes, oats, kaffir-corn, barley, tobacco, sugar cane, tea, citrus fruits, rye, groundnuts, grapes, pineapples; cattle, sheep, goats, pigs, horses, donkeys, mules; gold, coal, diamonds, copper, asbestos, manganese, lime, limestone, platinum, chrome, iron, silver, tungsten, mercury, vanadium, tin, antimony, silver, scheelite, talc; hides, chemicals, wool, footwear, rubber, machinery, clothing, textiles, food, vehicles, printing, furniture, building materials. |
| SOUTH ARABIA | British protectorate and federation, under a high commissioner and a supreme council, respectively. | East African shilling | Arabic | Mohammedan | Dates, gums, tobacco, salt, fish oil, butter; wheat, barley, sesame, millet, sorghum, aloes, ghee; goats, sheep, camels, cattle; dhow building, ship bunkering. |
| SOUTHERN RHODESIA | A self-governing state and member of Br. Commonwealth with governor and elective executive and legislative councils. | Rhodesian pound | Bantu languages English | Tribal religions Protestant | Corn, tobacco, groundnuts, wheat, potatoes, citrus and other fruits; cattle, sheep, pigs, goats; meats, hides; gold, asbestos, chromite, coal; footwear, apparel, cigarettes, flour, groundnut oil, wood products. |
| SPAIN | A nominal monarchy governed by a chief of state. The legislative Cortés prepares laws subject to the veto of the chief of state. A king is to be chosen by a regency council upon the death or incapacitation of the chief of state. | peseta | Spanish Catalan | Roman Catholic | Wheat, barley, potatoes, oranges, olives, oats, rye, rice, corn, peas, beans, grapes, onions, sugar beets, esparto, flax, hemp, pulse, cork, nuts; pigs, sheep, goats, donkeys, mules, horses, poultry; sardines, tuna, cod and other fish; coal, lignite, iron ore, lead, iron pyrites, potash, zinc, mercury, sulphur, copper; textiles, wines, olive oil, paper, cement, hides, preserved and canned fish and shellfish, paper. |
| SPANISH SAHARA | Spanish province with a high commissioner, a cabinet and a general assembly. | Spanish peseta | Arabic Spanish | Mohammedan | Barley, corn; goats, sheep, camels; fish. |
| SUDAN | A republic with a bicameral parliament and council of ministers. Executive power resides temporarily in a council of state. | Sudanese pound | Arabic Sudanese Hamitic languages English | Mohammedan Tribal religions | Cotton, cotton seed, gum arabic, Senna leaves and pods, groundnuts, sesame, millet, dates, dom nuts (vegetable ivory), wheat, shea nuts; sheep, goats, cattle, camels, asses; mahogany; hides and skins, ivory, gold, salt, trochus shell, mother-of-pearl. |
| SURINAM | Self-governing part of the Netherlands Union with an appointed governor, an appointive council of ministers, an advisory council and an elective legislative body. | Dutch guilder | Dutch | Christian Moslem Hindu | Rice, citrus fruits, coconuts, coffee, bananas, sugar cane, cacao, balata, corn, tobacco; lumber; gold, bauxite; sugar, rum, plywood, molasses. |
| SWAZILAND | British protectorate governed by a resident commissioner and a legislative council. | pound sterling | Bantu languages English | Tribal religions Christian missions | Tobacco, corn, groundnuts, kaffir-corn, wheat, oats, rye, barley, fruits; cattle, goats, sheep, pigs; butter; hides, skins; asbestos, gold, tin. |
| SWEDEN | A constitutional hereditary monarchy with a prime minister, council of state and a two-house elective legislature. | krona (crown) | Swedish | Protestant | Hay, sugar beets, potatoes, fodder crops, oats, wheat, rye, barley; forest products, cattle, pigs, sheep, horses, poultry; fish; iron ore, sulphur, arsenic, zinc, copper, silver, gold, lead, manganese; lumber and wood products, machinery, textiles, iron and steel and metal goods, chemicals, dairy products, electric power, tobacco products, brick, porcelain and glass, shipbuilding, matches. |
| SWITZERLAND | A republic with a president, vice-president, an executive federal council and a two-house, elective legislature. | Swiss franc | German French Italian Romansch | Protestant Roman Catholic | Wheat, potatoes, sugar beets, rye, oats, barley, fruits, tobacco; livestock; salt, iron, manganese; dairy products, textiles, watches and clocks, chemicals, foods, wines, dyes. |
| SYRIA | Independent republic. | Syrian pound | Arabic Turkish Kurdish | Mohammedan Christian | Wheat, barley, sorghum, corn, cotton, lentils, chickpeas, sesame, vegetables, olives, grapes, tobacco (Latikia); sheep, goats, cattle, donkeys, camels, horses, poultry; wool, hides, skins; gypsum; leather, textiles, food, tobacco, wine, flour. |
| TANGANYIKA AND ZANZIBAR | An independent united republic of the British Commonwealth, with a central parliament, a president and two vice-presidents. | East African shilling | Bantu languages Swahili English | Tribal religions Mohammedan Christian missions | Sisal, cotton, cloves, coffee, bananas, tobacco, papain, beeswax, grains, sugar; cattle, goats, sheep; hides, skins; wood, timber, wax, gum arabic; diamonds, gold, tin, mica, salt, camphor, tungsten. |
| THAILAND (SIAM) | Constitutional monarchy ruled by a king, prime minister and a legislative assembly. | baht | Thai Khmer | Buddhist Tribal religions | Rice, rubber, coconuts, tobacco, cotton, corn, beans; teak and other woods; bullocks, buffalo, horses, elephants; fish; tin, wolfram. |
| TIBET | Theocracy. Nominally independent but under effective Chinese Communist control. | sang | Tibetan | Lamaist | Barley, wheat, pulse, corn, vegetables, rice; yaks, asses, sheep, goats, donkeys; hides, wool, furs, musk; borax, salt, gold; cult objects. |
| TIMOR, PORTUGUESE | Portuguese overseas province ruled by a governor. | Portuguese escudo | Malay Portuguese | Mohammedan Tribal religions Roman Catholic | Coffee, copra, sandalwood, wax, cocoa; hides, shells. |
| TOGO | Independent republic. | French franc | Sudanese languages French | Tribal religions Mohammedan Roman Catholic | Palm oil and kernels, tapioca, cocoa, yams, coffee, plantains, corn, groundnuts, cotton, copra, kola, cassava, rubber; sheep, goats, pigs, cattle, asses, horses. |
| TOKELAU ISLANDS | An island territory of New Zealand with a high commissioner. | New Zealand pound | Samoan | Protestant Roman Catholic | Coconuts, fiber, taro, copra; pigs, chickens; fish; hats, mats. |
| TONGA | Constitutional monarchy ruled by queen with cabinet and legislative assembly, and advised by British Resident, with local autonomy. | Tongan pound | Tongan English | Protestant Roman Catholic | Copra, bananas, fungus, candlenuts; pigs, cattle, goats. |
| TRINIDAD AND TOBAGO | Independent member of the British Commonwealth. | B.W.I. dollar | English | Roman Catholic Protestant Hindu | Coffee, cocoa, sugar cane, citrus fruits; cattle; petroleum, asphalt; rum, canned grapefruit juice, sugar. |
| TRISTAN DA CUNHA | Possession of Great Britain governed by an administrator and an island council under St. Helena. | pound sterling | English | Protestant | Potatoes, fruit; cattle, sheep; fish. |

| POLITICAL DIVISION | GOVERNMENT | MONETARY UNIT | LANGUAGE | RELIGION | MAJOR PRODUCTS |
|---|---|---|---|---|---|
| TRUCIAL OMAN | Seven sheikhdoms under British protection with a British agent. | rupee riyal | Arabic | Mohammedan | Dates, grains, vegetables; fishing, pearl fishing. |
| TUNISIA | A republic with a president, a cabinet of secretaries of state, and an assembly. | Tunisian dinar | Arabic French Berber | Mohammedan Roman Catholic | Wheat, barley, oats, corn, sorghum, beans, grapes, olives, citrus fruits, dates, alfa grass, almonds, oranges, shaddocks, pistachios, cork; sheep, goats, cattle, horses, asses, mules, camels, pigs; fish, sponges; flour milling, oil refining, wool spinning, pottery, leather, silk weaving; phosphates, iron ore, lignite, lead, zinc. |
| TURKEY | A republic with a president and a two-house legislature. | Turkish pound (lira) | Turkish | Moslem | Tobacco, cereals, olives, cotton, figs, nuts, fruits; cattle, livestock; fish; chromium, iron ore, copper, coal, lignite, meerschaum, manganese; textiles, iron and steel, paper, rugs, olive oil. |
| UGANDA | An independent member of the British Commonwealth with a president, cabinet and a unicameral legislature. | East African shilling | Bantu and Sudanese languages English | Tribal religions Christian | Cotton, coffee, plantains, millet, cotton seed, tobacco, chilies, sugar cane, rubber; cattle, sheep, goats; hides, skins; tin; cigarettes. |
| U.S.S.R. | A federation of 15 socialist republics with a two-chamber legislative assembly (Supreme Soviet) which elects the executive presidium and council of ministers. The policy of the state is largely defined by the Central Committee of the Communist party, the only legal party. | ruble | Russian, Ukrainian, White Russian, Uzbek, Tatar, Azerbaidzhani, Georgian, Lithuanian, Armenian, Yiddish, Latvian, Mordvinian, Chuvash, Tadzhik, Estonian, Kazakh, etc. | Russian Orthodox | Wheat, rye, oats, barley, corn, sugar beets, sunflower seeds, cotton, forage crops, flax, hemp, potatoes, tobacco; cattle, sheep, goats, pigs, horses; lumber, furs; fish; coal, peat, petroleum, iron, lignite, copper, lead, zinc, nickel, aluminum, phosphates, manganese, gold, sulphur, potash, asbestos, platinum, salt, chromite; steel, machinery, textiles, sugar, flour, meats, automobiles, paper, synthetic rubber, foods, wines, chemicals. |
| UNITED ARAB REP. | See Egypt. | | | | |
| UNITED STATES | Federal republic with a president, vice-president and two-house legislature (senate and house of representatives), and an appointed cabinet. It consists of 50 states, each with a governor and state legislature. | dollar | English | Protestant, Roman Catholic | Corn, hay, tobacco, wheat, cotton, oats, soy beans, potatoes, barley, sorghums, peanuts, rye, rice, citrus fruits, fruits, sugar beets, sugar cane, vegetables, tree nuts, feed grains and hay; livestock; fish; lumber; petroleum, coal, cement, iron, natural gas, copper, sand and gravel, zinc, lead, stone, gold, silver, molybdenum, bauxite, phosphates, mica, sulphur; foods, transportation equipment, machinery, primary metal products, electrical machinery, textiles, chemicals, paper and wood products, beverages, dairy products. |
| UPPER VOLTA | West African republic with a legislative assembly. | French franc | Sudanese languages French | Tribal religions Mohammedan | Millet, groundnuts, corn, karite nuts and butter (shea nut), vegetables, rice, tapes, cotton, kapok, sesame, sorghum, tea; sheep, goats, cattle, asses, pigs; gold, manganese, copper, silver, chrome, lignite, iron. |
| URUGUAY | A republic governed by a National Council, an appointed cabinet and a two-house elective legislature. | Uruguayan peso | Spanish | Roman Catholic | Wheat, corn, linseed, oats, sunflower seeds, peanuts, barley, rice, citrus fruits, peaches, grapes, vegetables, tobacco; sheep, cattle; gold; meat, hides, wool, textiles, leather, boots and shoes, wines. |
| VATICAN CITY | The Pope, who is elected for life by the cardinals of the Roman Catholic Church, exercises absolute legislative, executive and judicial power. He appoints a governor of the state and delegates diplomatic and judicial power. | Italian lira | Italian Latin | Roman Catholic | |
| VENEZUELA | A republic with a president, appointive cabinet, and elective two-house legislature. | bolívar | Spanish | Roman Catholic | Coffee, cacao, sugar cane, cotton, tobacco, coconuts, tonka beans, balata, dividivi, rubber; livestock; fish and pearls; petroleum, iron, gold, coal, copper, phosphates, magnesite, asphalt, salt, diamonds; textiles, leather, sugar, cement, wood products, foodstuffs, beverages, soap, tobacco products, meats, milk; refined petroleum. |
| VIETNAM | Divided in two parts by Armistice Line Sept. 1954. North of 17th parallel is Communist controlled "republic". South is a republic with a president and an assembly. | piaster | Khmer (Annamese) Lao | Buddhist | Rice, corn, sugar, tobacco, coffee, fruits, manioc, betel nuts, arrowroot, tea, cotton, areca nut, medicinal plants, cardamom, soya, rubber, copra, groundnuts, haricots, sweet potatoes, cinnamon; mulberries, bamboo, silk; cattle, buffalo, pigs; lumber; gold, tin, copper, coal, zinc, iron, cement, limestone, calamine, tungsten, manganese, phosphate, lead, bauxite. |
| VIRGIN ISLANDS (BR.) | British colony with an administrator, an executive and a legislative council. | B.W.I. dollar | English, Creole | Protestant | Poultry and livestock, fish, fruit, vegetables. |
| VIRGIN ISLANDS (U. S.) | Territory of the U. S. with an appointed governor. | American dollar | English, Creole | Roman Catholic, Protestant | Sugar cane, vegetables, citrus fruits, coconuts; cattle; fish; rum, bay rum, bay oil, molasses, handicrafts, sugar, lime juice, hides, bitters. |
| WEST IRIAN | Former Dutch colony now under Indonesian administration, with independence to be scheduled before 1969. | Indonesian rupiah | Papuan Dutch Indonesian | Tribal religions | Sago, coconuts, sweet potatoes, wild nutmeg, mace, copra; bird of paradise plumes; petroleum. |
| YAP | Administered by a civil administrator of the Palau district as a part of the United States Trust Territory of the Pacific Islands. | American dollar | Micronesian dialects | Tribal religions Christian | Coconuts, breadfruit, sweet potatoes, taro, manioc, vegetables; poultry, pigs; fish. |
| YEMEN | Independent republic. | bakcha | Arabic | Mohammedan | Coffee, barley, wheat, millet, sesame; cattle, hides; fish. |
| YUGOSLAVIA | A Soviet-type republic combining six republics under a central government with a president, fed. executive council and two-house elective legislature. Actually ruled by Communist League. | Yugoslav dinar | Serbian-Croatian, Slovenian Macedonian | Eastern Orthodox Roman Catholic | Wheat, barley, rye, oats, corn, sugar beets, hemp, hops, opium, tobacco, flax, alfalfa, vegetables, fruits; sheep, cattle, pigs, goats, horses, poultry; coal, lignite, iron, copper, lead, salt, zinc, mercury, antimony, petroleum, bauxite, chrome, cement; lumber, textiles, foods, beverages, sugar, wood-distillates, wines. |
| ZAMBIA | Independent republic within the British Commonwealth, with a president, a cabinet and a unicameral legislature. | Zambia pound | Bantu languages English | Tribal religions | Corn, wheat, potatoes, tobacco, sorghum, millet, groundnuts, cassava, rice, beans, cowpeas, cotton; lumber; cattle; copper, lead, manganese, zinc, cobalt. |

# REFERENCE MAPS

## of the

# STATES of the UNITED STATES

THE STATES
OF THE
UNITED STATES

This map shows the states and the date each was admitted to the Union.

Note that many states were admitted in the same year or period.

1776-1790 Thirteen original states

1791-1819

1820-1850

1851-1876

1877-1912

1913-1959

Copyright by C. S. Hammond & Co., N. Y.

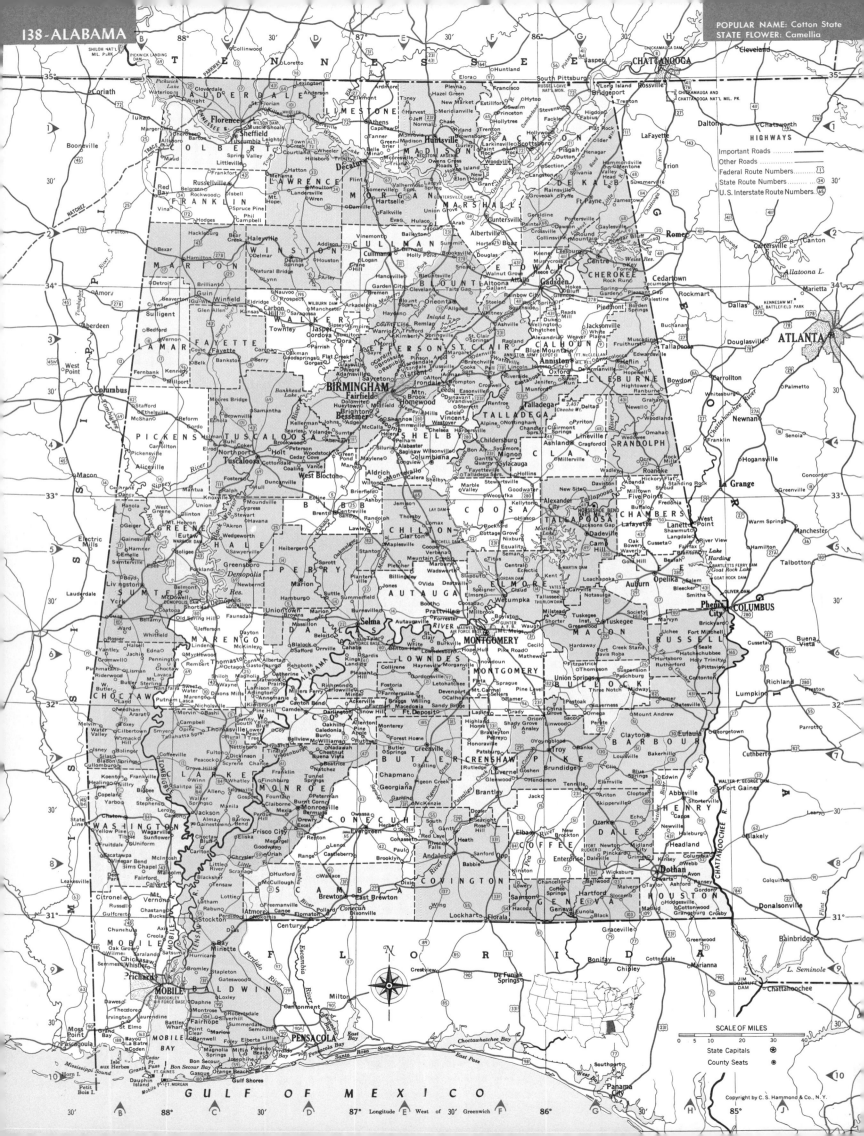

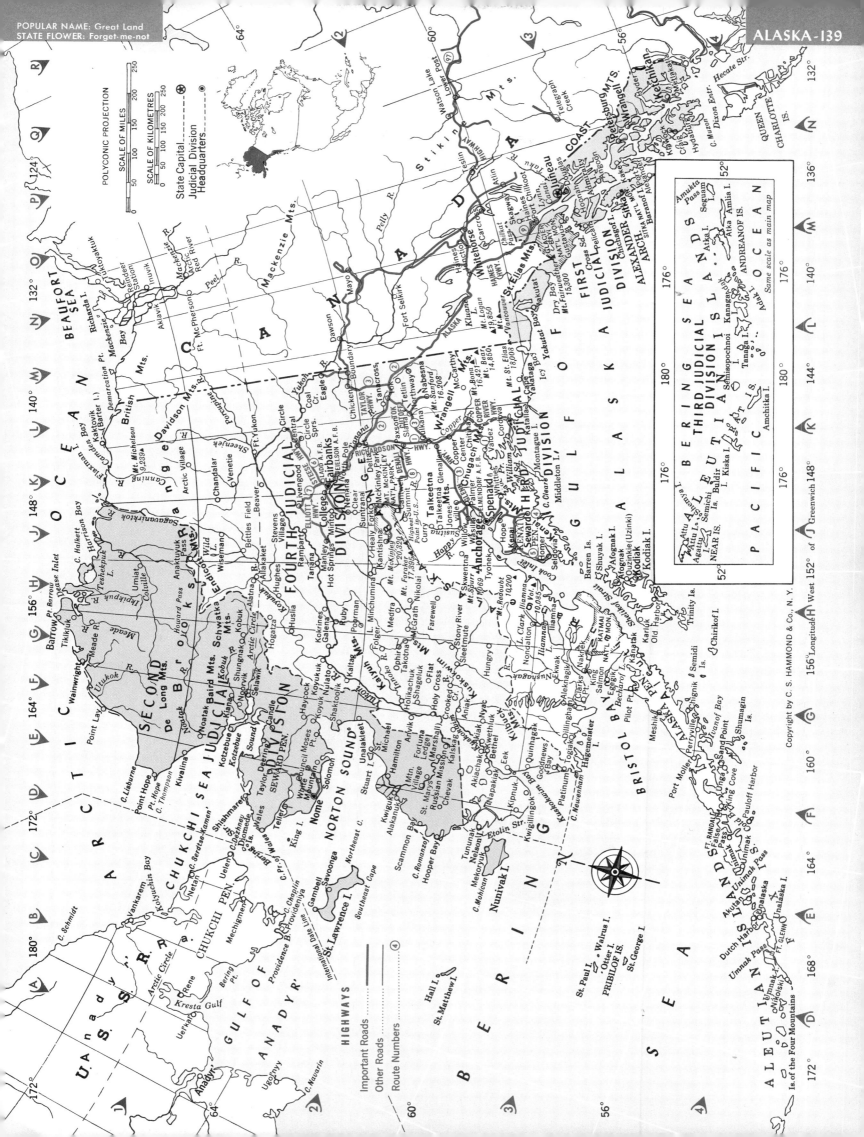

POPULAR NAME: Great Land
STATE FLOWER: Forget-me-not

POLYCONIC PROJECTION

SCALE OF MILES
0  50  100  150  200  250

SCALE OF KILOMETRES
0  50 100 150 200 250

State Capital ........⊛
Judicial Division
Headquarters..........⊙

HIGHWAYS

Important Roads .........
Other Roads .............
Route Numbers ......... ④

Copyright by C. S. HAMMOND & Co., N. Y.

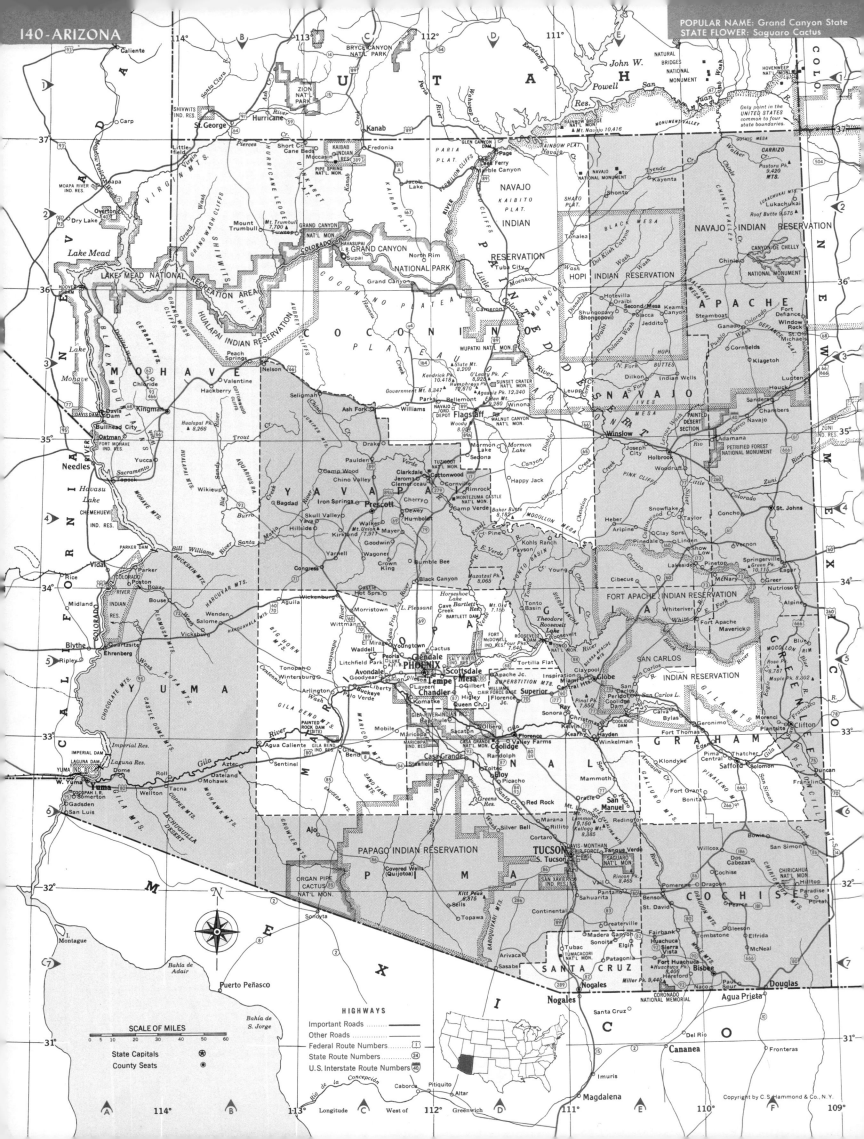

POPULAR NAME: Grand Canyon State
STATE FLOWER: Saguaro Cactus

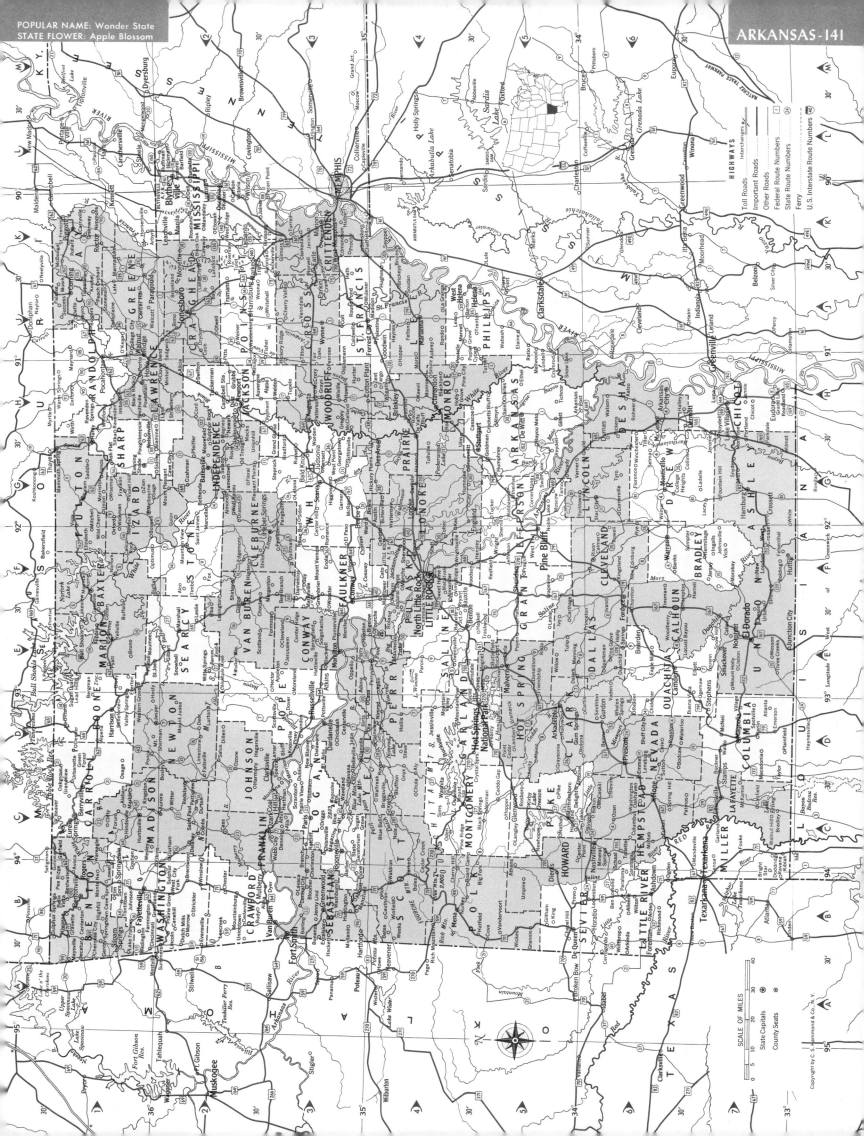

POPULAR NAME: Wonder State
STATE FLOWER: Apple Blossom

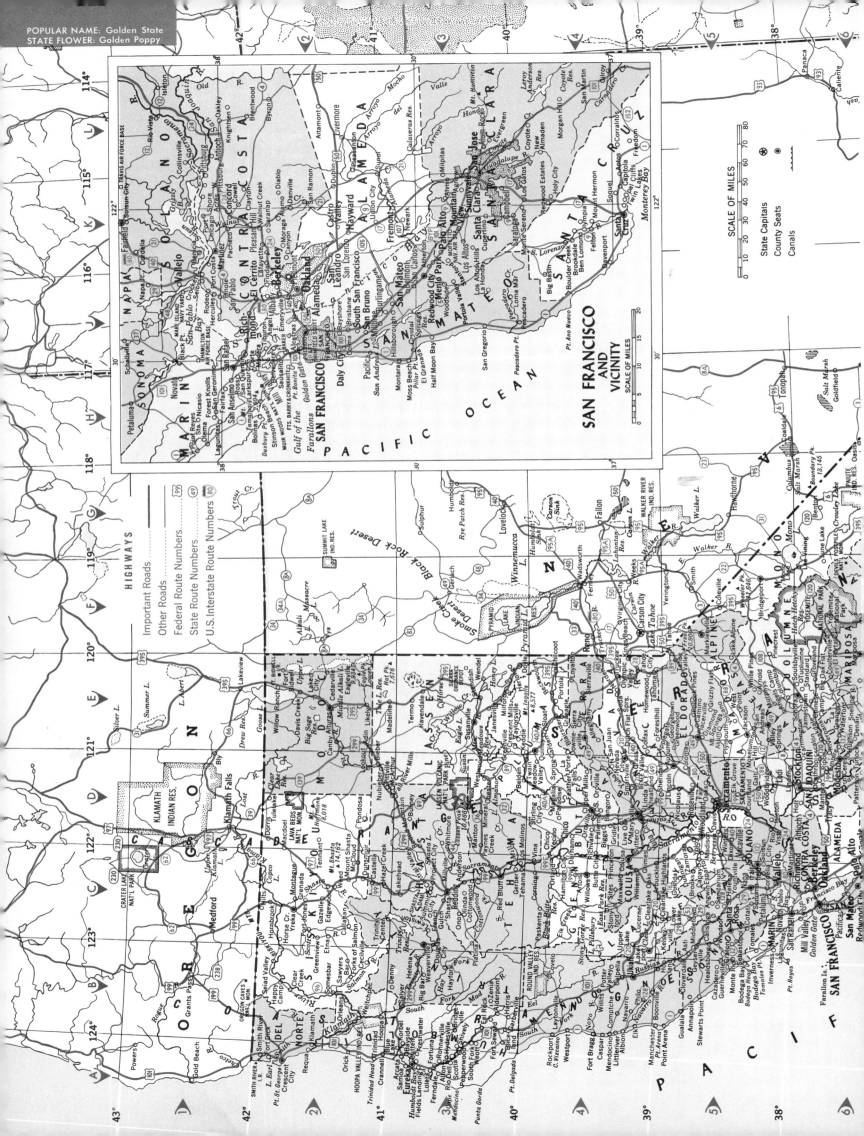

SAN FRANCISCO
AND
VICINITY

SCALE OF MILES

State Capitals
County Seats
Canals

HIGHWAYS

Important Roads
Other Roads
Federal Route Numbers
State Route Numbers
U.S. Interstate Route Numbers

PACIFIC OCEAN

SACRAMENTO
AND
VICINITY

LOS ANGELES
AND VICINITY

POPULAR NAME: Centennial State
STATE FLOWER: Mountain Columbine

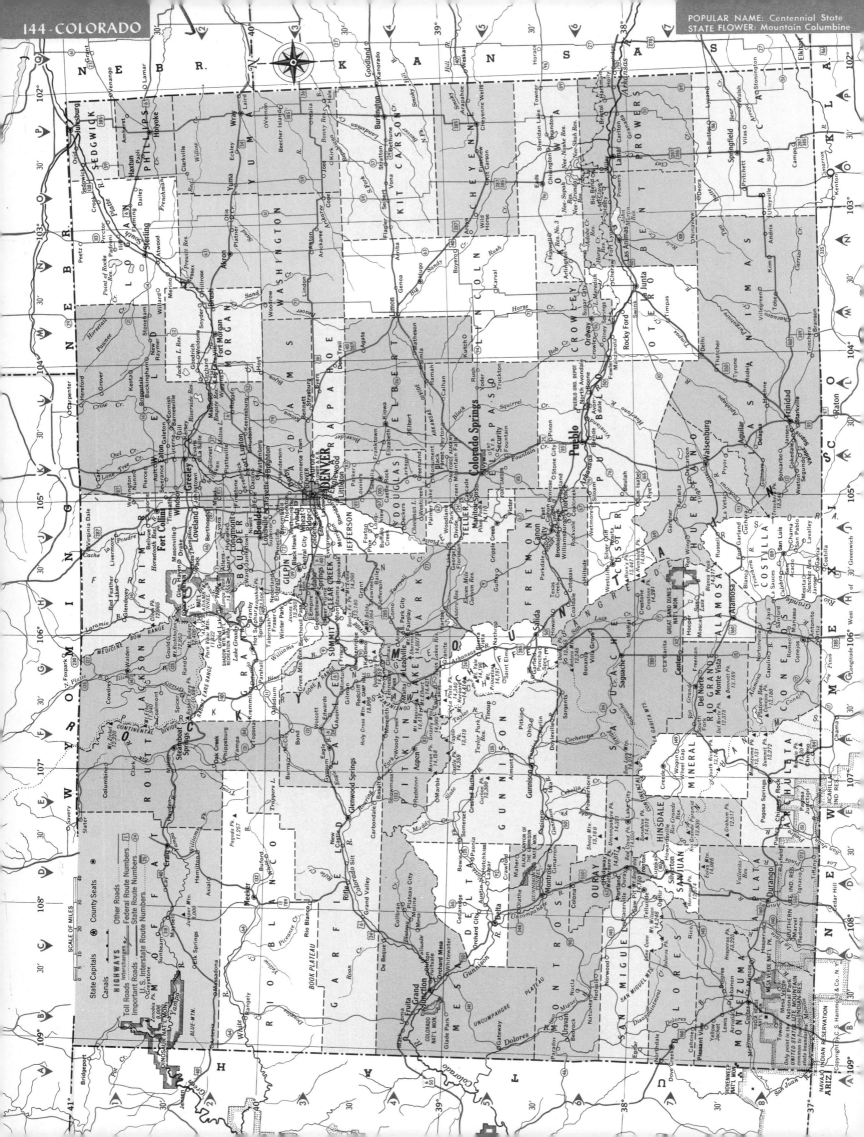

POPULAR NAME: Nutmeg State
STATE FLOWER: Mountain Laurel

POPULAR NAME: Sunshine State
STATE FLOWER: Orange Blossom

SCALE OF MILES
0   10   20   30   40   50

State Capitals ⊛
County Seats ◉
Canals ——

## HIGHWAYS

Toll Roads .............. Interchanges
Important Roads .........
Other Roads .............
Federal Route Numbers ... [17]
State Route Numbers ..... [24]
Ferry ...................
U.S. Interstate Route Numbers [10]

GULF OF MEXICO

ATLANTIC OCEAN

GEORGIA

ALA

Okefenokee Swamp

### Counties and places (selected)

JACKSON, CALHOUN, LIBERTY, GADSDEN, LEON, WAKULLA, FRANKLIN, GULF, MADISON, HAMILTON, SUWANNEE, COLUMBIA, TAYLOR, LAFAYETTE, DIXIE, GILCHRIST, ALACHUA, BRADFORD, UNION, BAKER, NASSAU, DUVAL, CLAY, ST. JOHNS, PUTNAM, FLAGLER, MARION, VOLUSIA, CITRUS, SUMTER, LAKE, SEMINOLE, ORANGE, HERNANDO, PASCO, OSCEOLA, BREVARD, PINELLAS, HILLSBOROUGH, POLK, INDIAN RIVER, MANATEE, HARDEE, OKEECHOBEE, ST. LUCIE, SARASOTA, DESOTO, HIGHLANDS, MARTIN, CHARLOTTE, GLADES, PALM BEACH, LEE, HENDRY, BROWARD, COLLIER, DADE, MONROE

Tallahassee, Jacksonville, St. Augustine, Gainesville, Ocala, Daytona Beach, Orlando, Tampa, St. Petersburg, Clearwater, Sarasota, Bradenton, Fort Myers, West Palm Beach, Fort Lauderdale, Hollywood, Miami, Miami Beach, Coral Gables, Homestead, Key West, Key Largo

STRAITS OF FLORIDA

FLORIDA KEYS

### WESTERN PART OF FLORIDA

*Same scale as main map*

ALABAMA

SANTA ROSA, OKALOOSA, WALTON, HOLMES, WASHINGTON, JACKSON, BAY, CALHOUN

Pensacola, Fort Walton Beach, Panama City, Marianna, Chipley, DeFuniak Springs

GULF OF MEXICO

Copyright by C. S. Hammond & Co., N.Y.

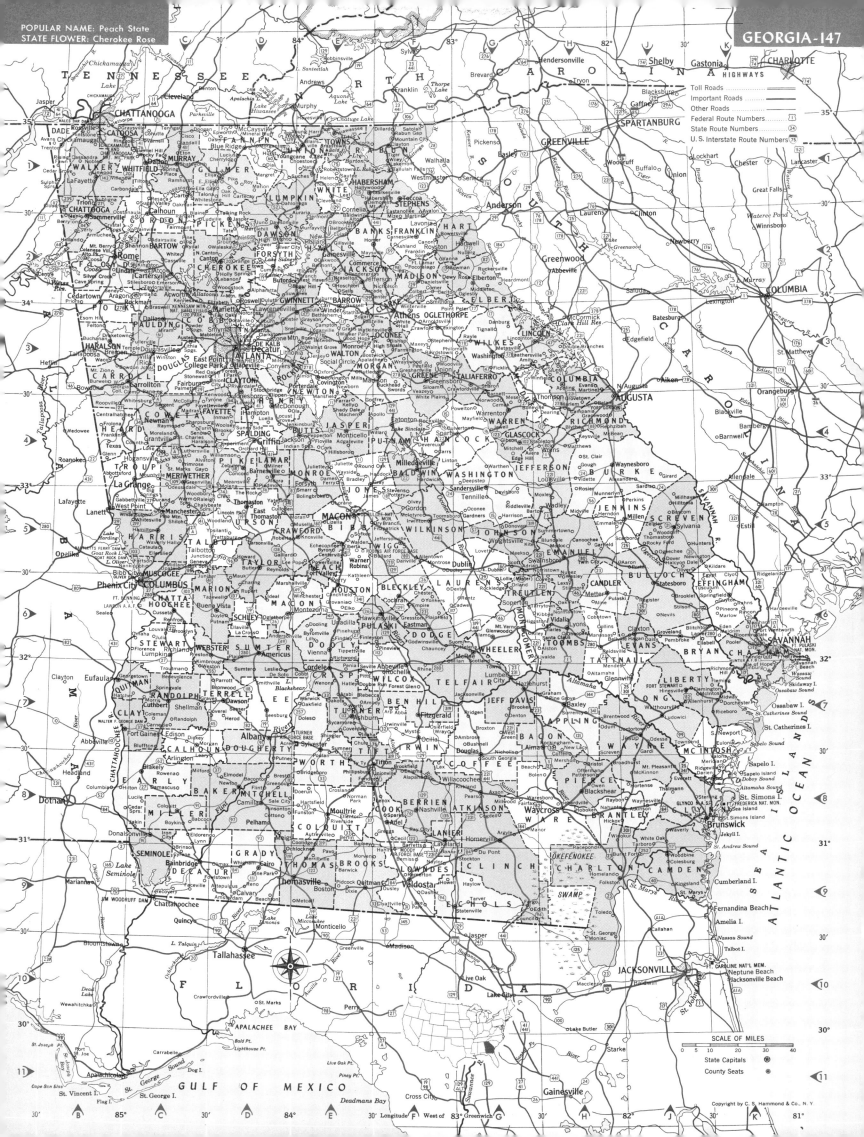

POPULAR NAME: Peach State
STATE FLOWER: Cherokee Rose

HIGHWAYS
Toll Roads
Important Roads
Other Roads
Federal Route Numbers
State Route Numbers
U.S. Interstate Route Numbers

SCALE OF MILES
0  5  10    20    30    40

State Capitals
County Seats

Copyright by C. S. Hammond & Co., N.Y.

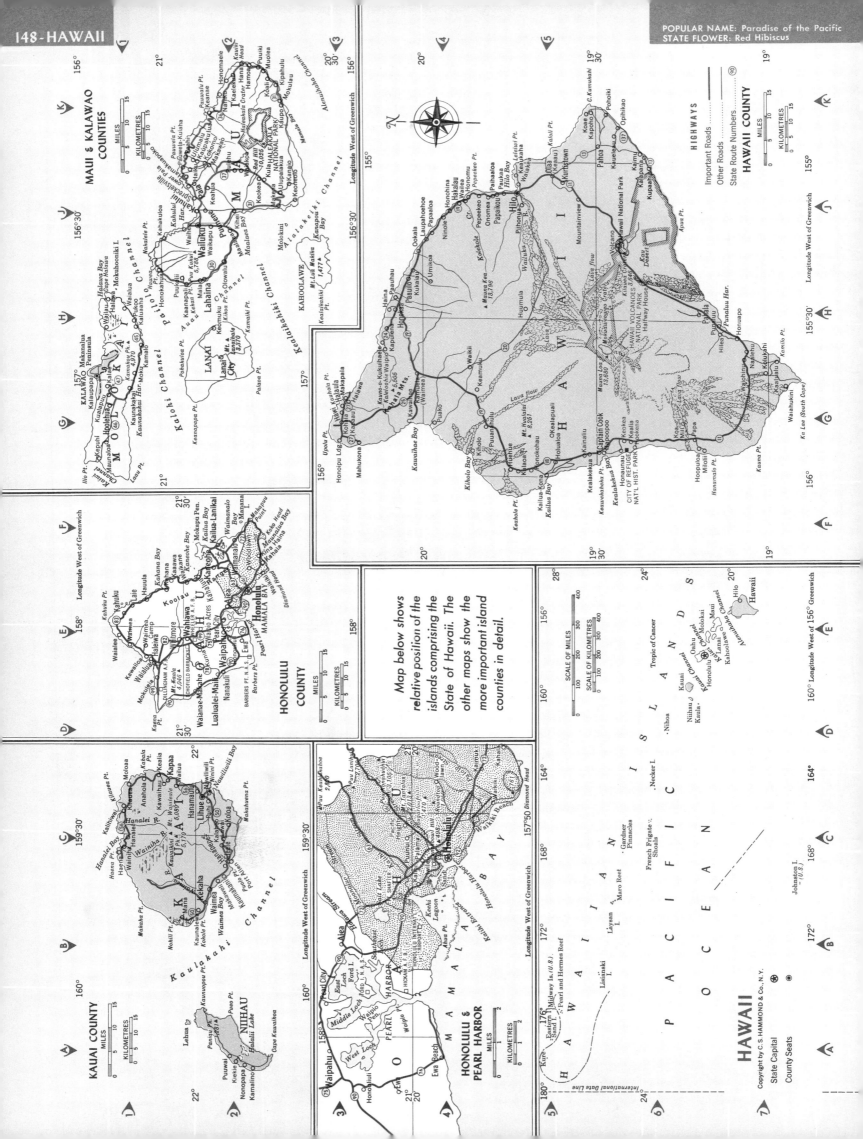

POPULAR NAME: Paradise of the Pacific
STATE FLOWER: Red Hibiscus

## MAUI & KALAWAO COUNTIES

## KALAWAO

## MOLOKAI

## LANAI

## KAHOOLAWE

## HAWAII

## HAWAII COUNTY

### HIGHWAYS
Important Roads
Other Roads
State Route Numbers

## KAUAI COUNTY

## NIIHAU

## HONOLULU COUNTY

*Map below shows relative position of the islands comprising the State of Hawaii. The other maps show the more important island counties in detail.*

## HONOLULU & PEARL HARBOR

## HAWAII

Copyright by C. S. HAMMOND & Co., N.Y.

✴ State Capital
◉ County Seats

HAWAIIAN ISLANDS

SCALE OF MILES

SCALE OF KILOMETRES

Tropic of Cancer

PACIFIC OCEAN

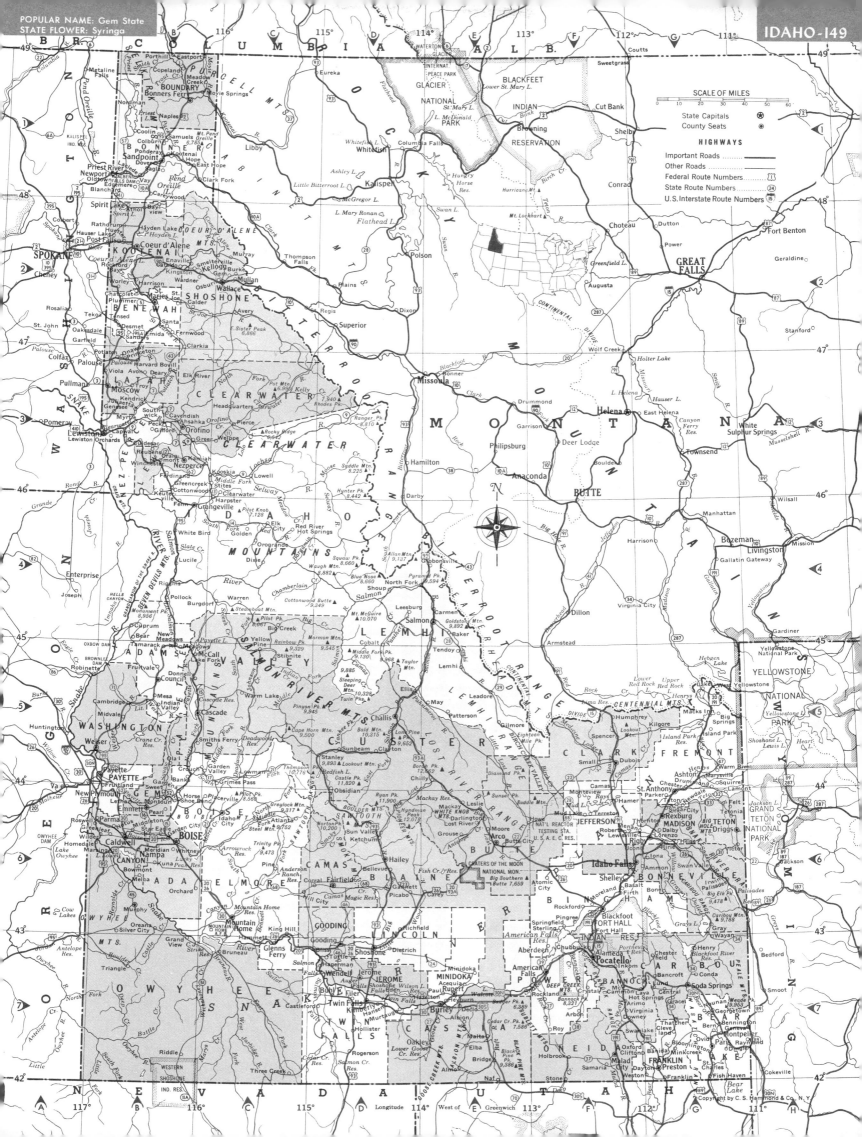

POPULAR NAME: Gem State
STATE FLOWER: Syringa

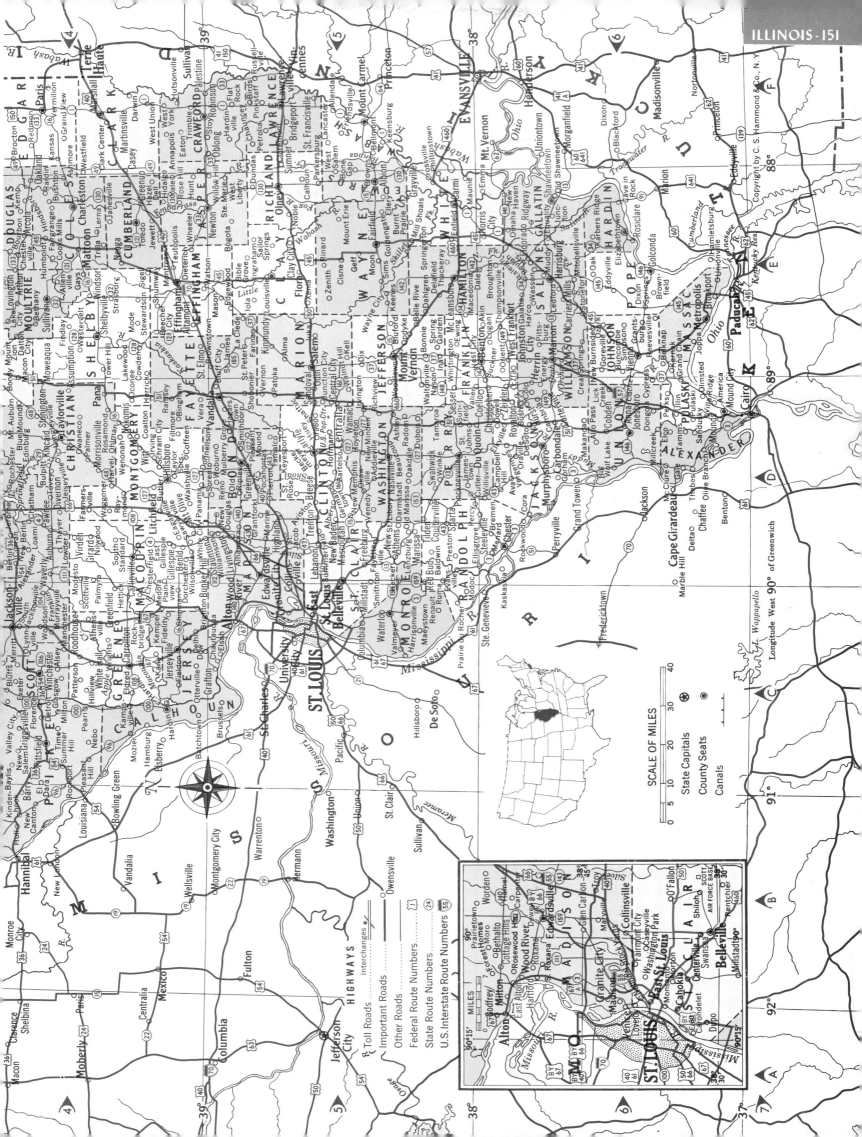

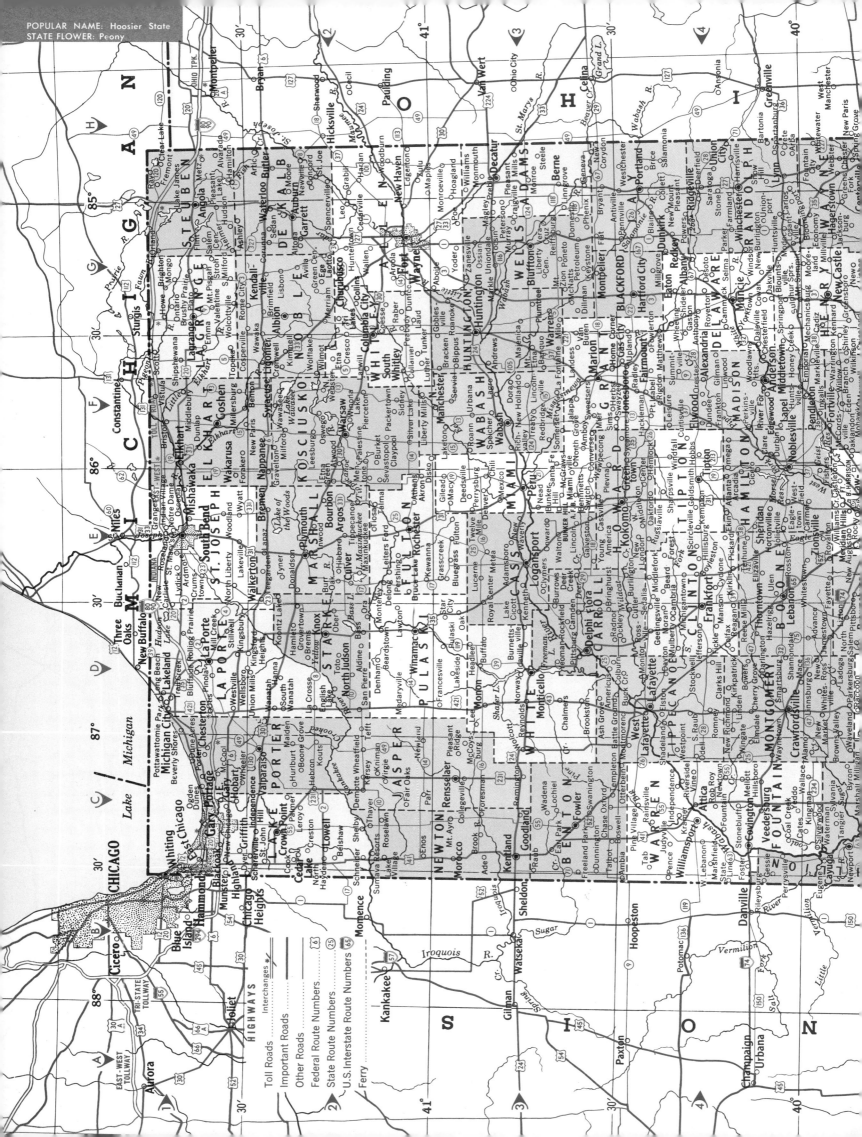

POPULAR NAME: Hoosier State
STATE FLOWER: Peony

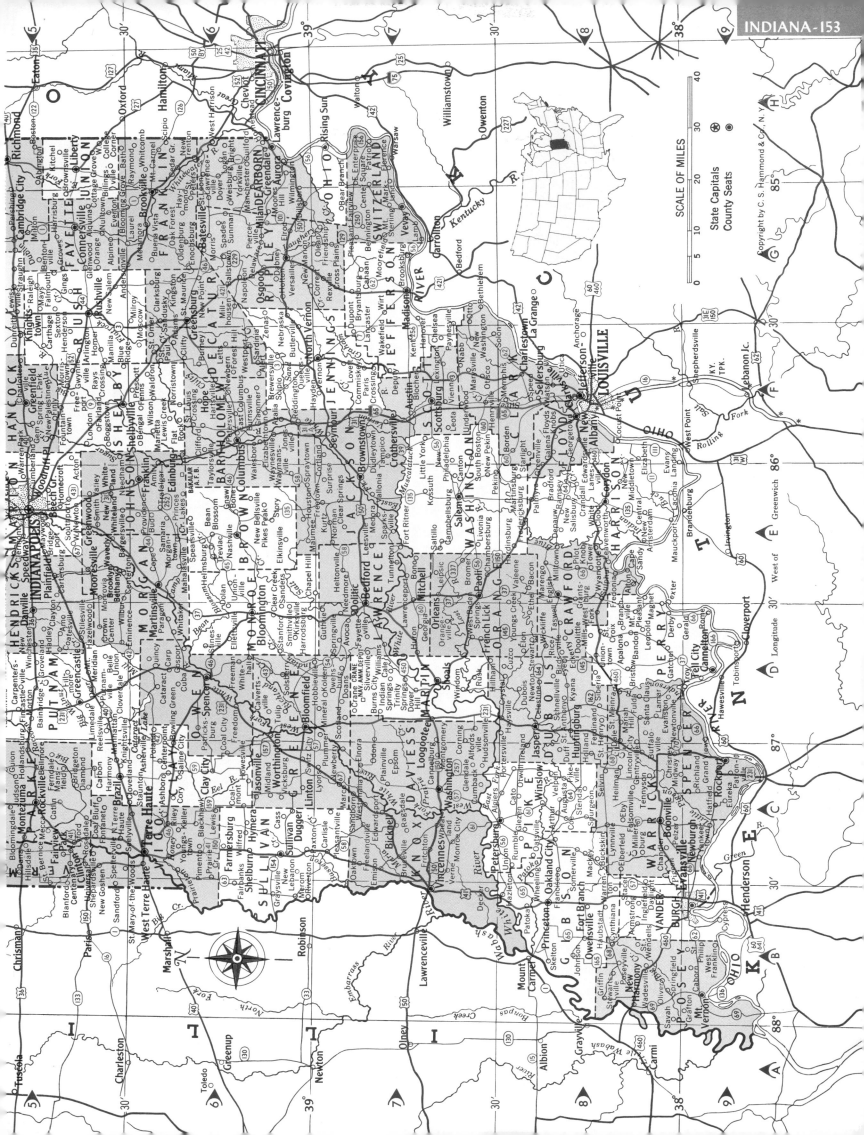

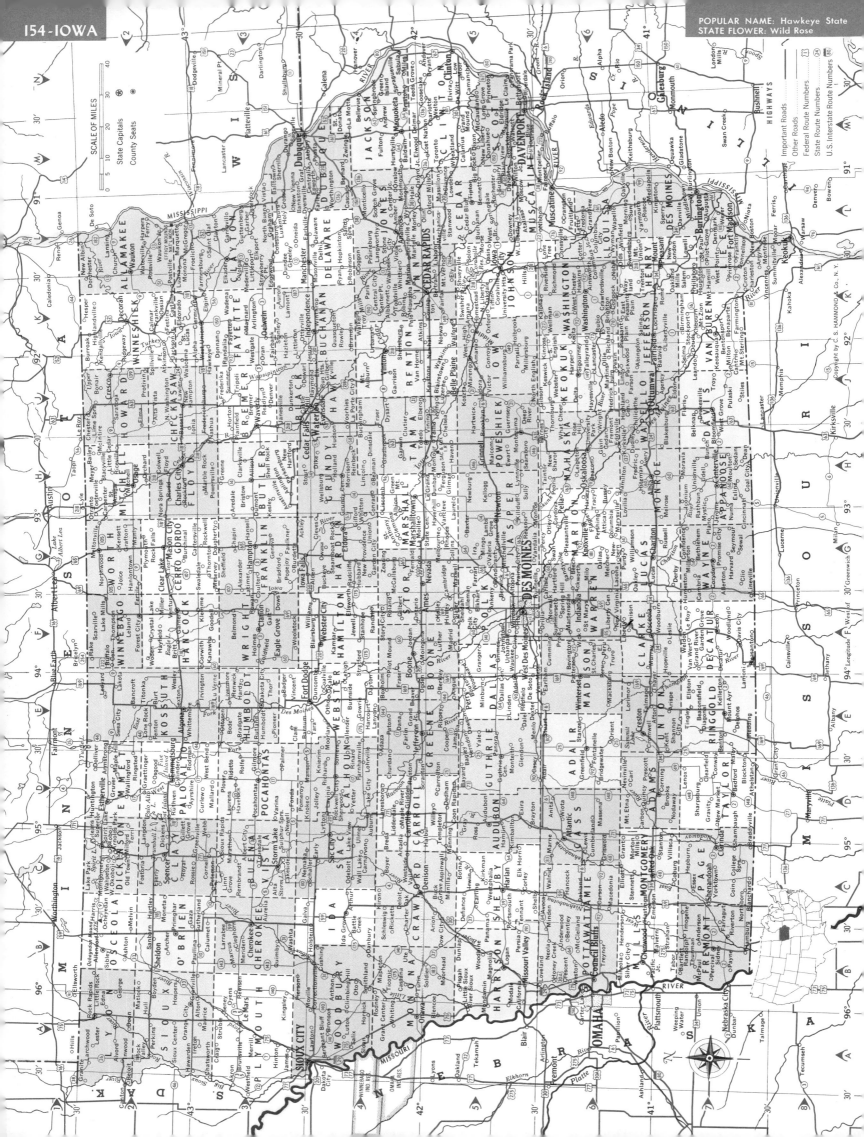

POPULAR NAME: Hawkeye State
STATE FLOWER: Wild Rose

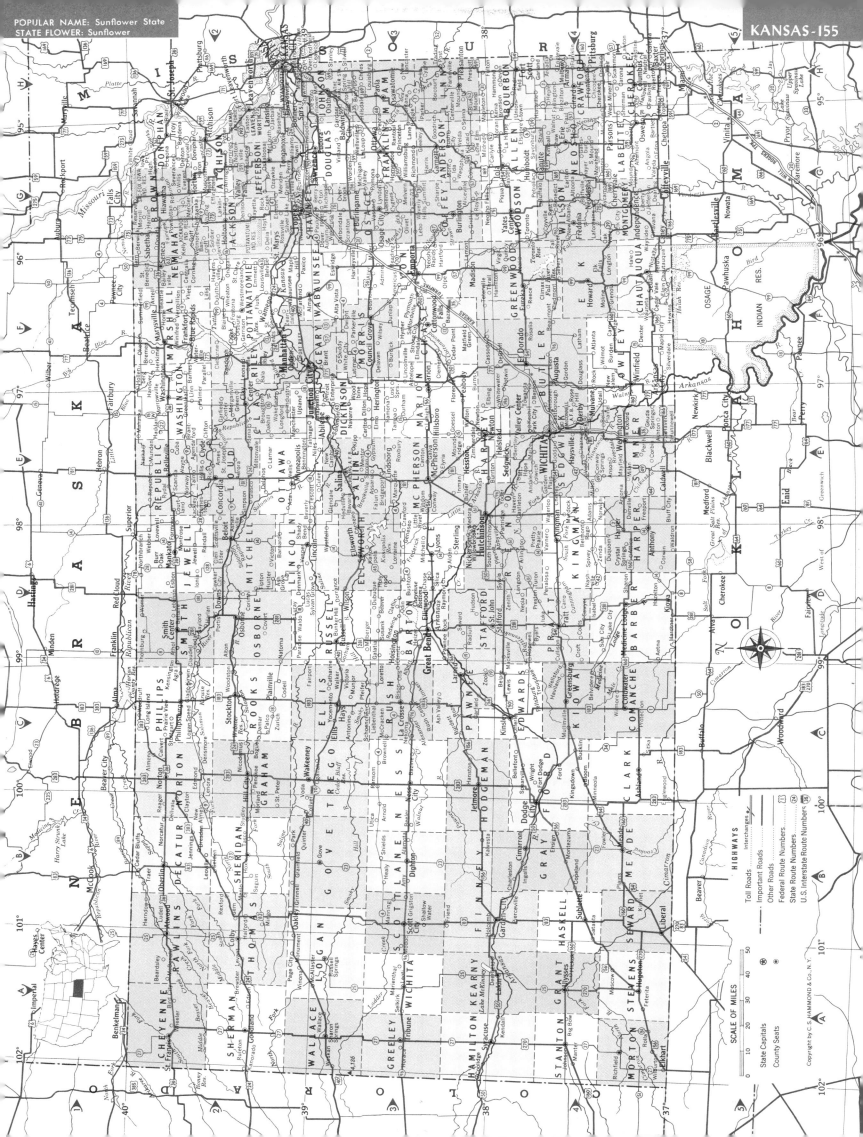

POPULAR NAME: Sunflower State
STATE FLOWER: Sunflower

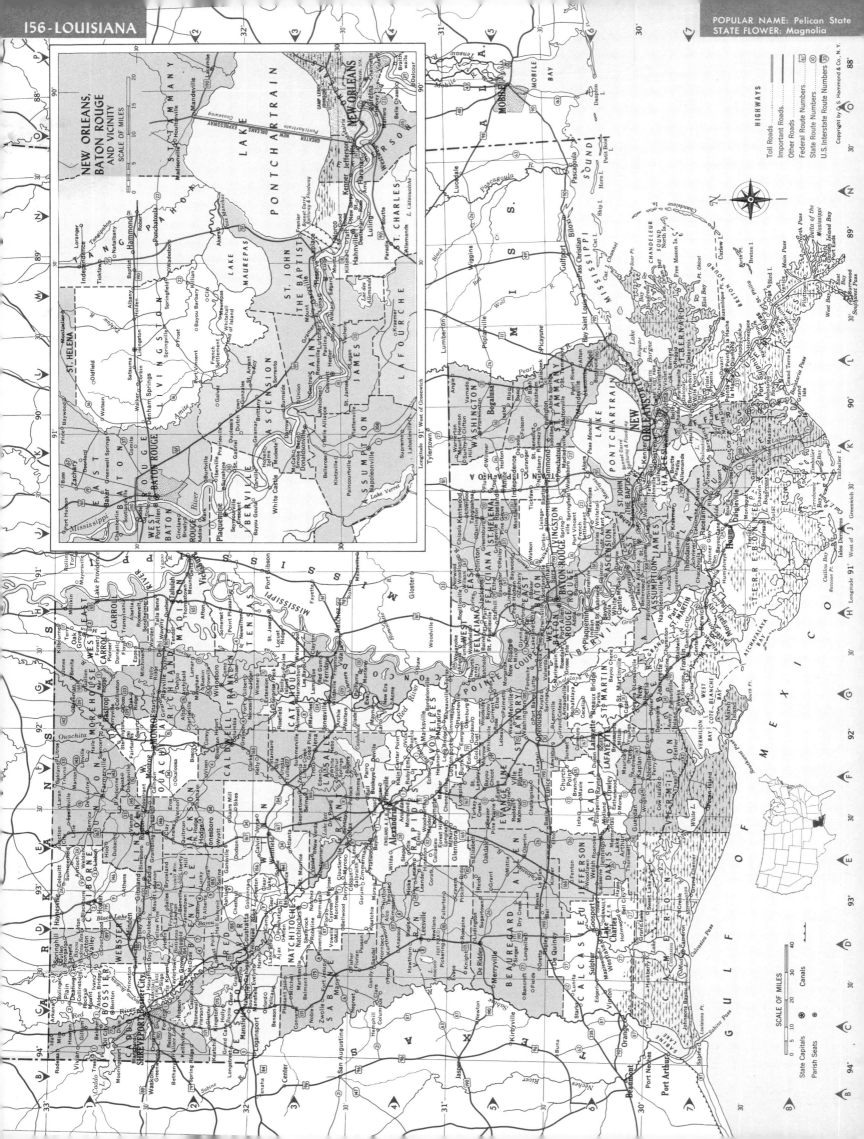

**POPULAR NAME: Pelican State**
**STATE FLOWER: Magnolia**

NEW ORLEANS, BATON ROUGE AND VICINITY
SCALE OF MILES

HIGHWAYS
Toll Roads
Important Roads
Other Roads
Federal Route Numbers
State Route Numbers
U.S. Interstate Route Numbers

Copyright by G.S. Hammond & Co., N.Y.

SCALE OF MILES
State Capitals
Parish Seats
Canals

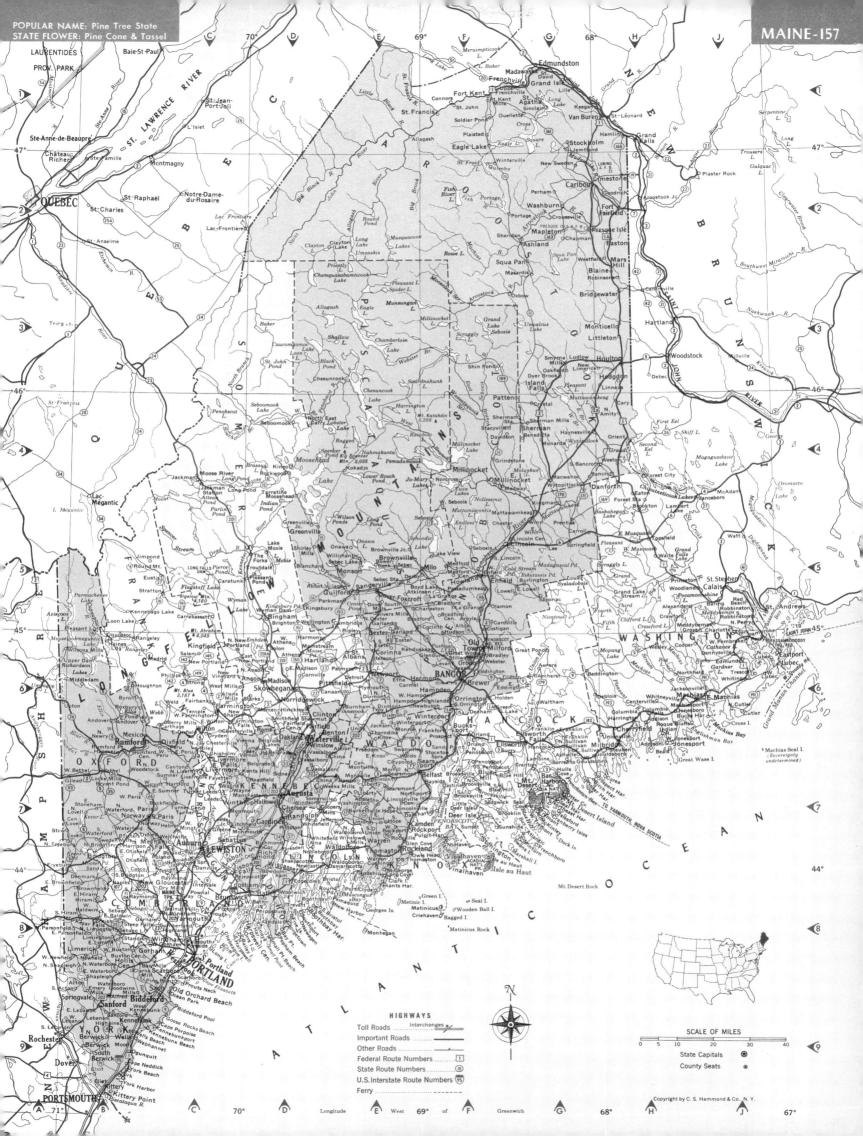

POPULAR NAME: Pine Tree State
STATE FLOWER: Pine Cone & Tassel

**HIGHWAYS**

Toll Roads ........... Interchanges
Important Roads .........
Other Roads ...........
Federal Route Numbers
State Route Numbers
U.S. Interstate Route Numbers
Ferry

SCALE OF MILES
0   5   10      20      30      40

⊛ State Capitals
⊛ County Seats

Copyright by C. S. Hammond & Co., N. Y.

POPULAR NAME: Old Line State  POPULAR NAME: Diamond State
STATE FLOWER: Black-eyed Susan  STATE FLOWER: Peach Blossom

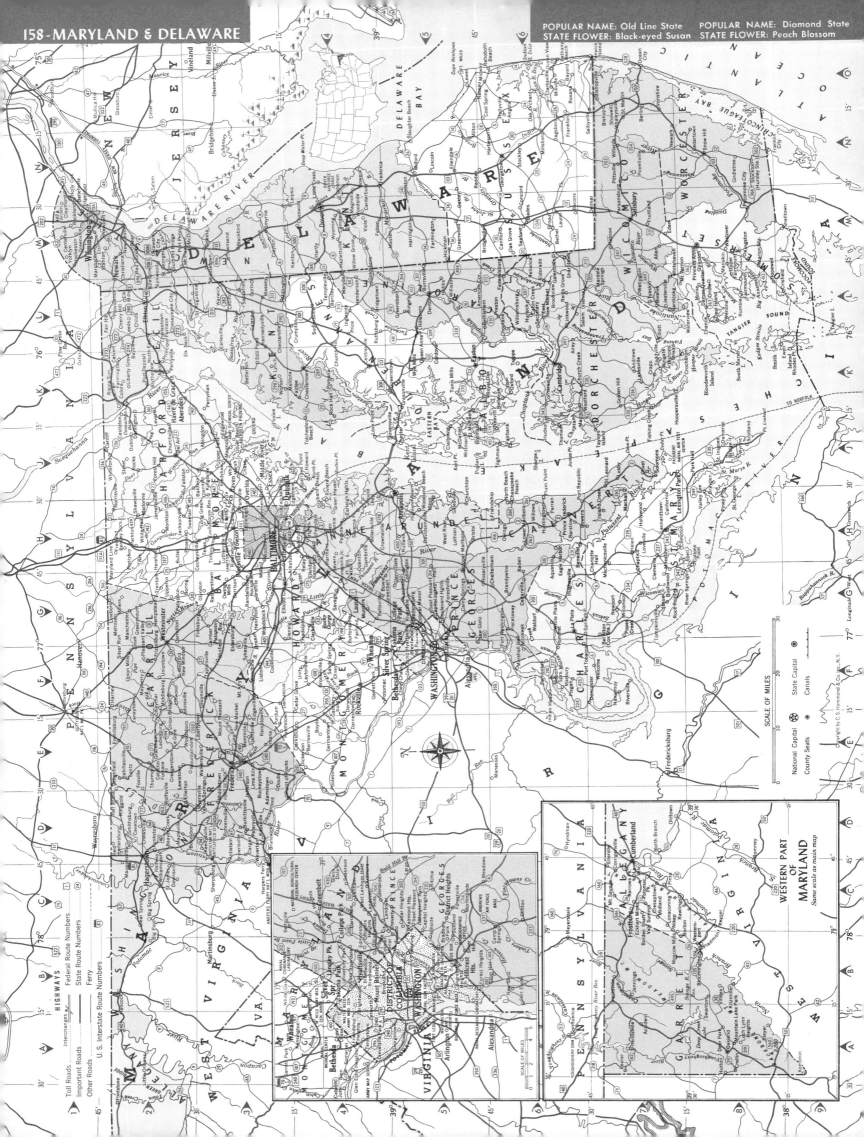

HIGHWAYS
Toll Roads ▷◁ Interchanges
Important Roads
Other Roads
Ferry
U.S. Interstate Route Numbers

Federal Route Numbers
State Route Numbers

SCALE OF MILES

⊗ State Capital
National Capital ⊛
County Seats • Canals

WESTERN PART OF MARYLAND
Same scale as main map

Copyright by C. S. HAMMOND & Co. Inc., N.Y.

POPULAR NAME: Bay State
STATE FLOWER: Mayflower

POPULAR NAME: Little Rhody
STATE FLOWER: Violet

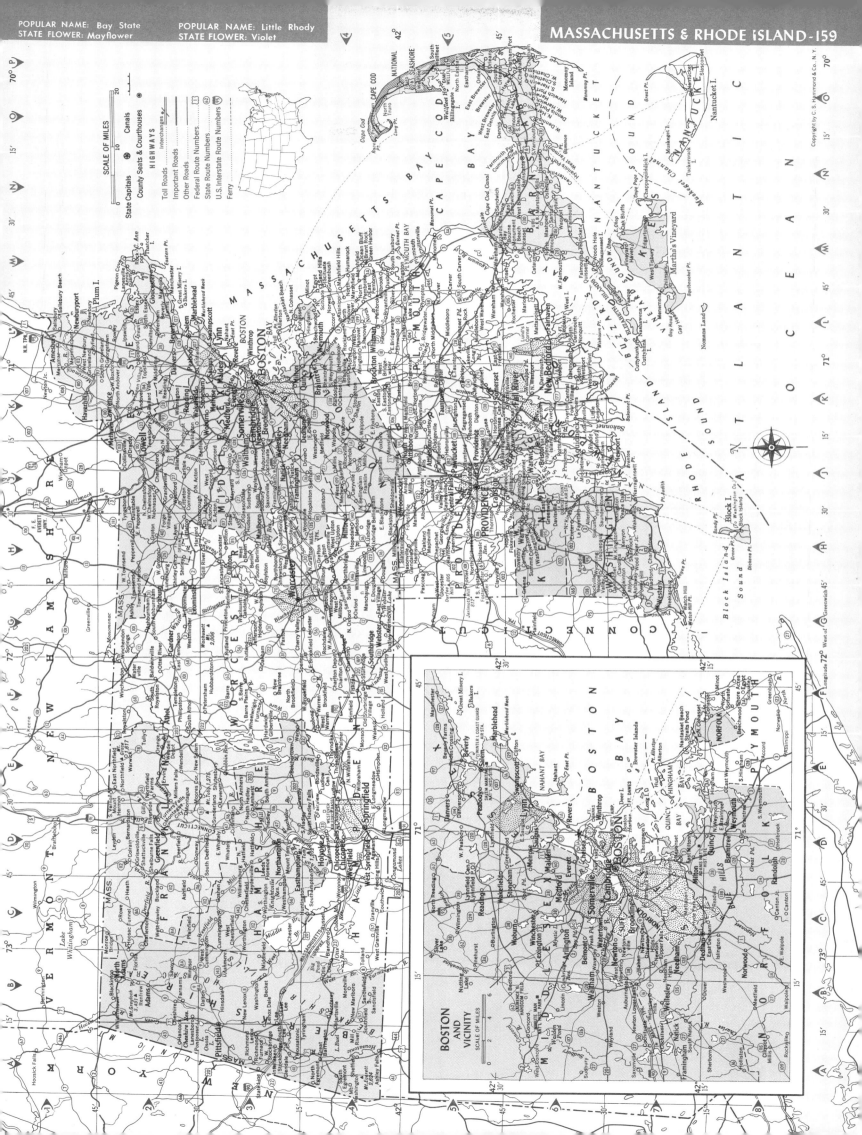

SCALE OF MILES

HIGHWAYS

State Capitals
County Seats & Courthouses
Canals
Toll Roads
Important Roads
Other Roads
Federal Route Numbers
State Route Numbers
U.S. Interstate Route Numbers
Interchanges
Ferry

BOSTON AND VICINITY
SCALE OF MILES

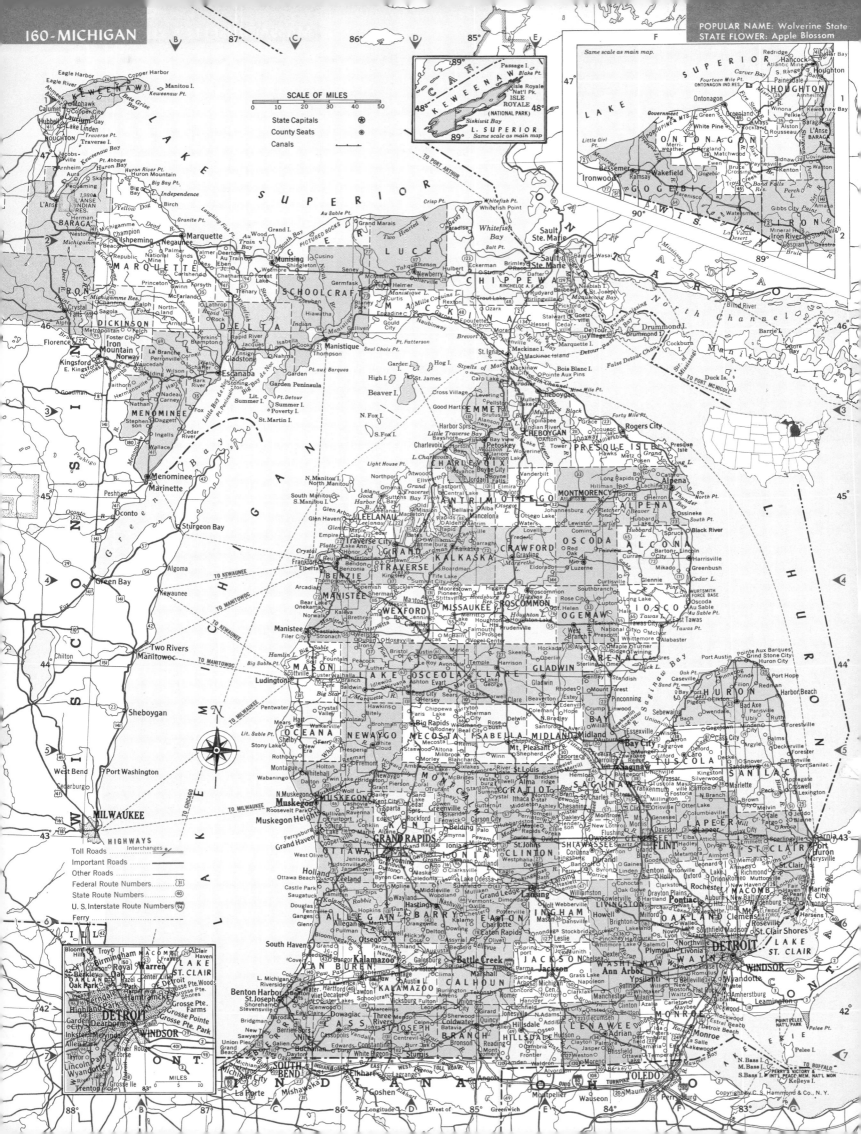

POPULAR NAME: Wolverine State
STATE FLOWER: Apple Blossom

SCALE OF MILES
0   10   20   30   40   50

State Capitals
County Seats
Canals

HIGHWAYS
Toll Roads ............... Interchanges
Important Roads .........
Other Roads .............
Federal Route Numbers ......... 31
State Route Numbers ............ 40
U. S. Interstate Route Numbers .. 94
Ferry

Copyright by C. S. Hammond & Co., N.Y.

POPULAR NAME: North Star State
STATE FLOWER: Ladyslipper

HIGHWAYS

Important Roads ..........
Other Roads ..............
Federal Route Numbers ........
State Route Numbers ........
U.S. Interstate Route Numbers ....

NORTHEASTERN PART OF MINNESOTA
Same scale as main map

SCALE OF MILES
0 10 20 30 40 50

State Capitals
County Seats

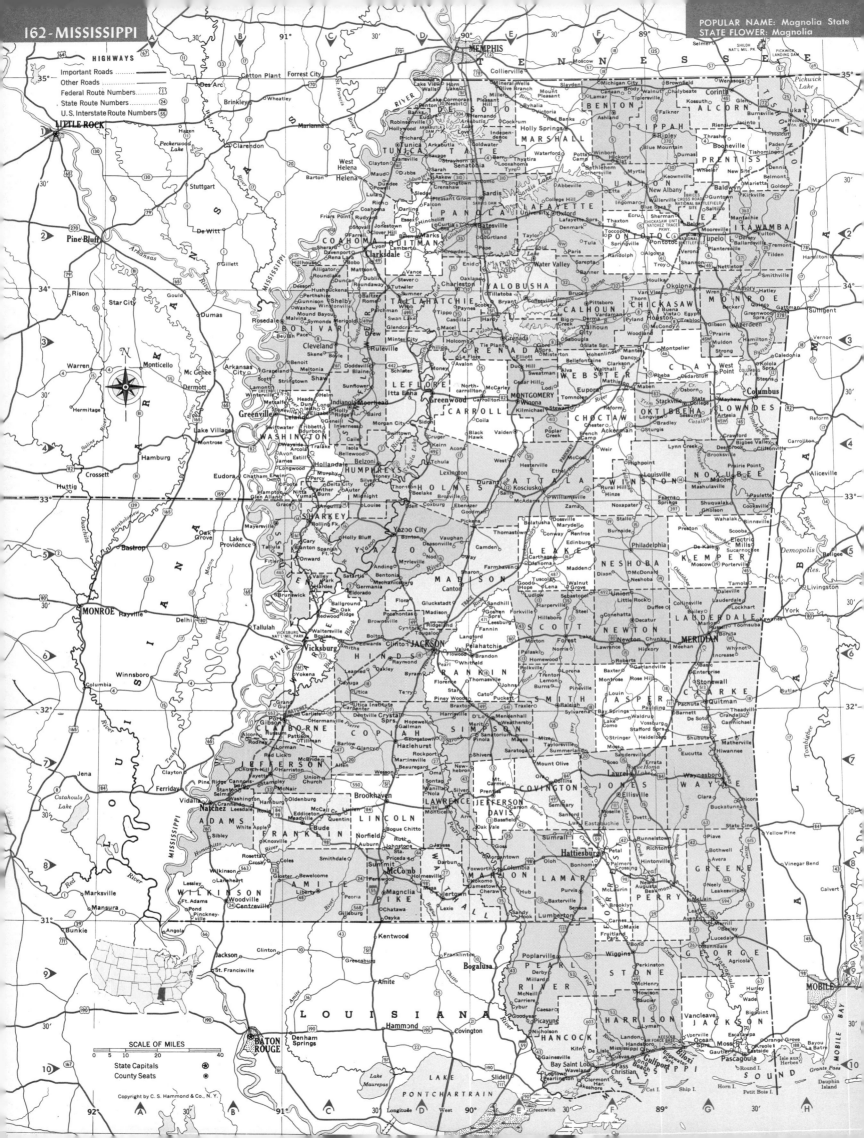

POPULAR NAME: Magnolia State
STATE FLOWER: Magnolia

HIGHWAYS
Important Roads ..........
Other Roads ..........
Federal Route Numbers .... 11
State Route Numbers .... 24
U.S. Interstate Route Numbers .... 55

SCALE OF MILES
0   5   10   20   30   40

● State Capitals
⊛ County Seats

Copyright by C. S. Hammond & Co., N.Y.

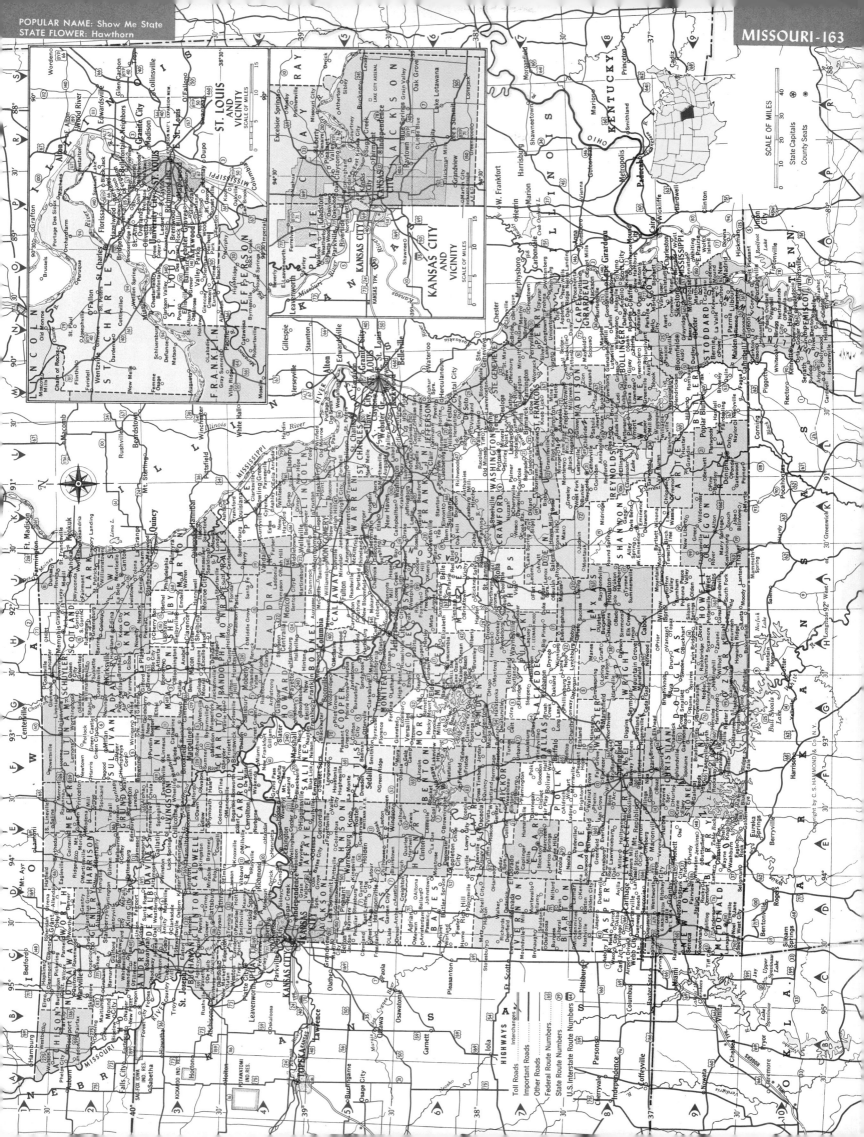

POPULAR NAME: Show Me State
STATE FLOWER: Hawthorn

ST. LOUIS AND VICINITY
SCALE OF MILES

KANSAS CITY AND VICINITY
SCALE OF MILES

SCALE OF MILES

HIGHWAYS
Toll Roads
Interchanges
Important Roads
Other Roads
Federal Route Numbers
State Route Numbers
U.S. Interstate Route Numbers

State Capitals
County Seats

Copyright by C. S. HAMMOND & Co., N.Y.

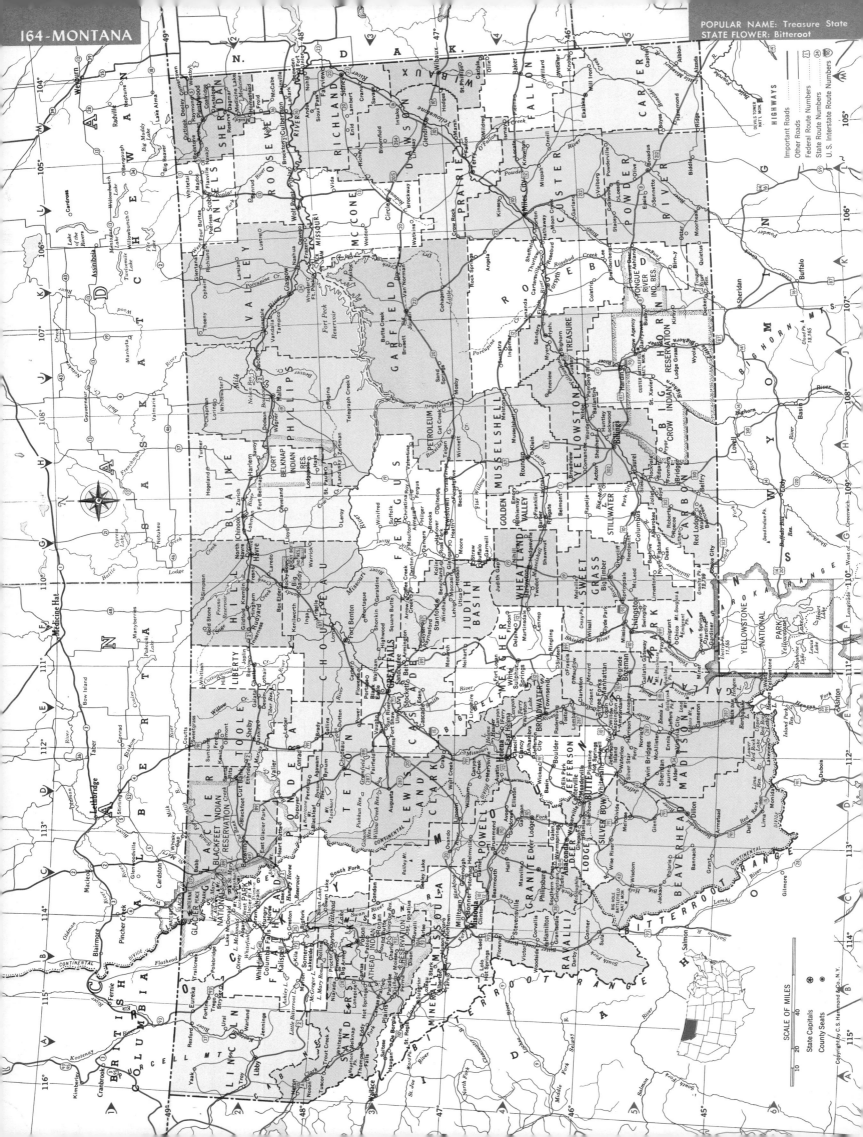

POPULAR NAME: Treasure State
STATE FLOWER: Bitterroot

HIGHWAYS
Important Roads
Other Roads
Federal Route Numbers
State Route Numbers
U.S. Interstate Route Numbers

SCALE OF MILES
10      20      30      40

State Capitals
County Seats

Copyright by C.S. Hammond & Co., N.Y.

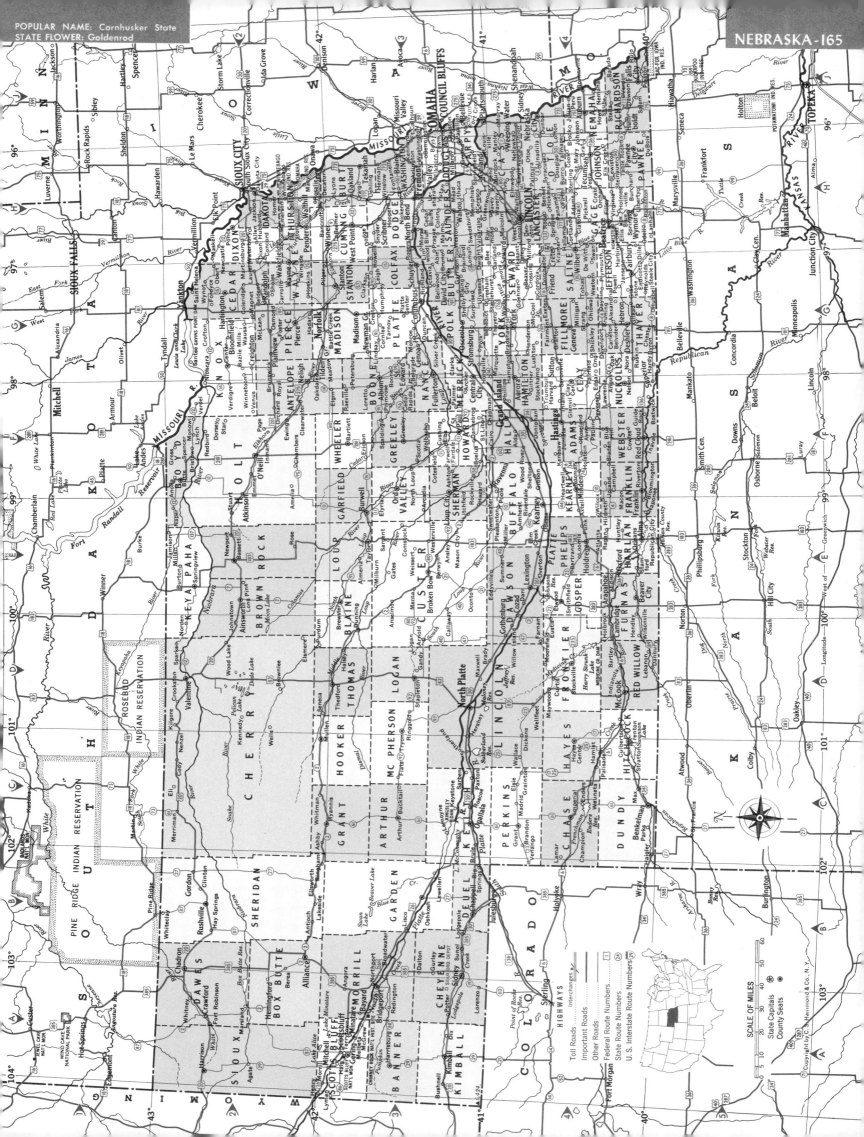

POPULAR NAME: Cornhusker State
STATE FLOWER: Goldenrod

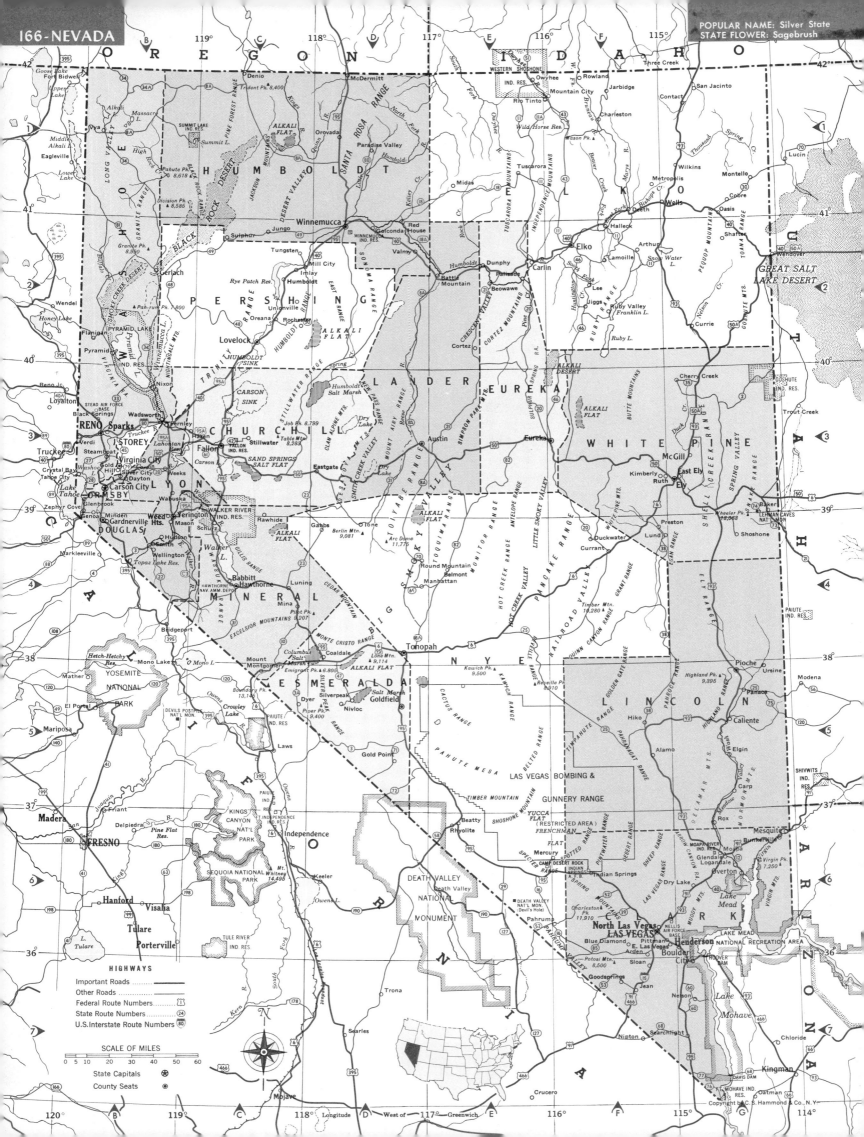

POPULAR NAME: Silver State
STATE FLOWER: Sagebrush

HIGHWAYS

Important Roads
Other Roads
Federal Route Numbers..........13
State Route Numbers..........24
U.S. Interstate Route Numbers..........80

SCALE OF MILES
0  5 10   20    30    40    50    60

State Capitals
County Seats

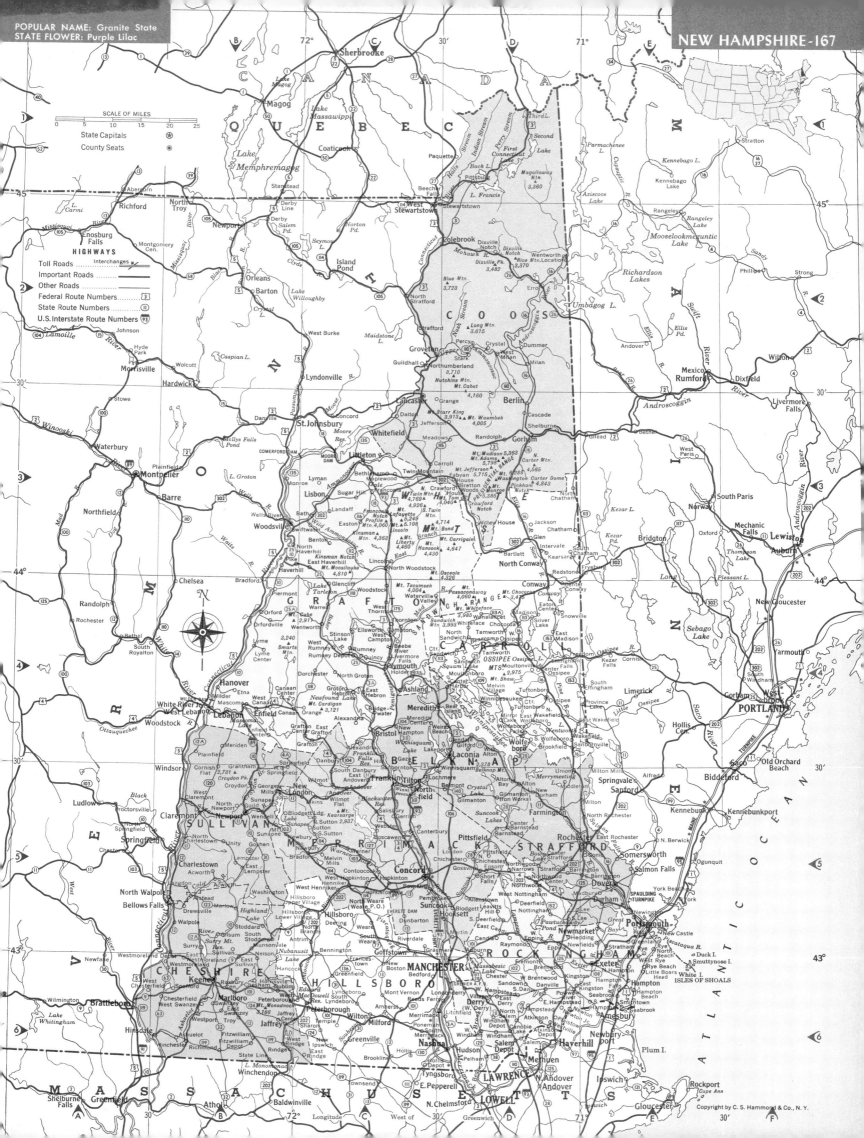

POPULAR NAME: Granite State
STATE FLOWER: Purple Lilac

SCALE OF MILES
0  5  10  15  20  25

⊛ State Capitals
⊙ County Seats

HIGHWAYS
Toll Roads ........... Interchanges
Important Roads ..........
Other Roads .............
Federal Route Numbers ...... ③
State Route Numbers .......... ⑪
U.S. Interstate Route Numbers ⑨③

Copyright by C. S. Hammond & Co., N.Y.

POPULAR NAME: Garden State
STATE FLOWER: Violet

PHILADELPHIA

CAMDEN

HIGHWAYS

Toll Roads          Interchanges
Important Roads
Other Roads
Federal Route Numbers............13
State Route Numbers............47
U.S. Interstate Route Numbers....80
Ferry

SCALE OF MILES
0   5   10   15   20

State Capitals          Canals
County Seats

Copyright by C. S. HAMMOND & CO., N.Y.

Longitude 75° West of Greenwich

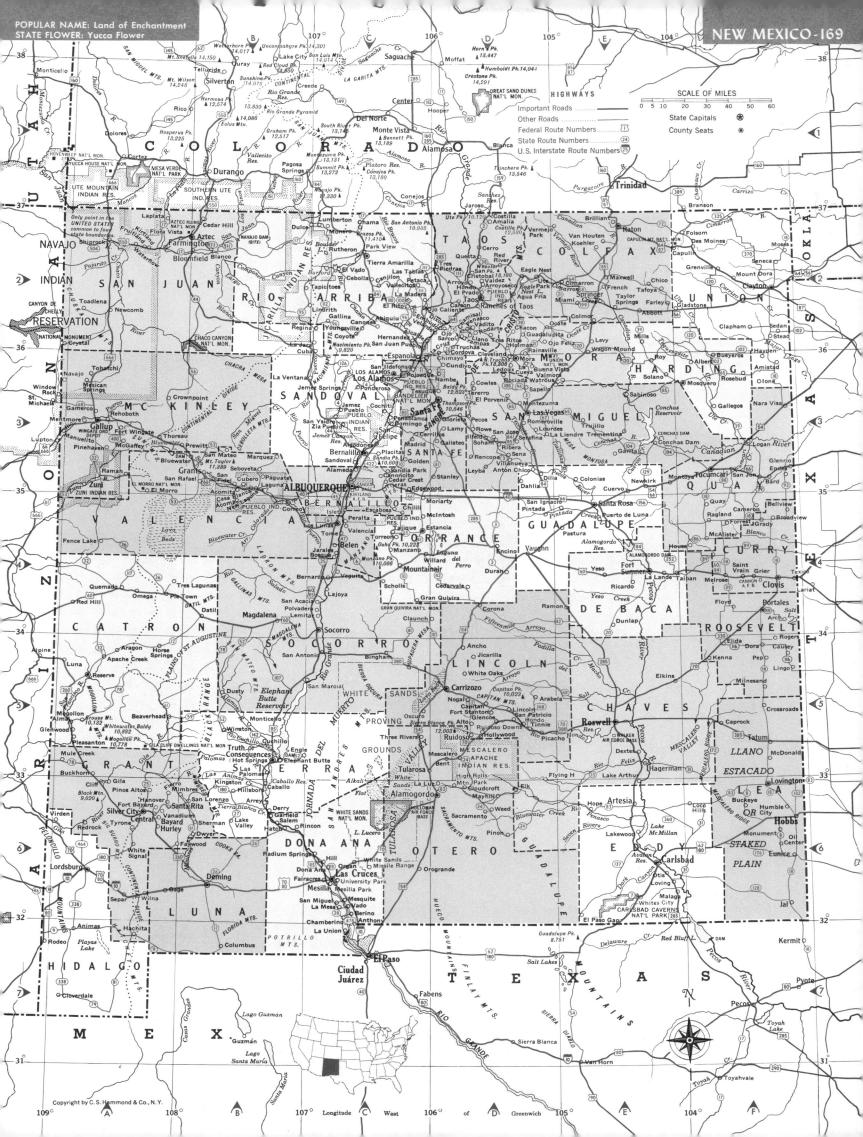

POPULAR NAME: Land of Enchantment
STATE FLOWER: Yucca Flower

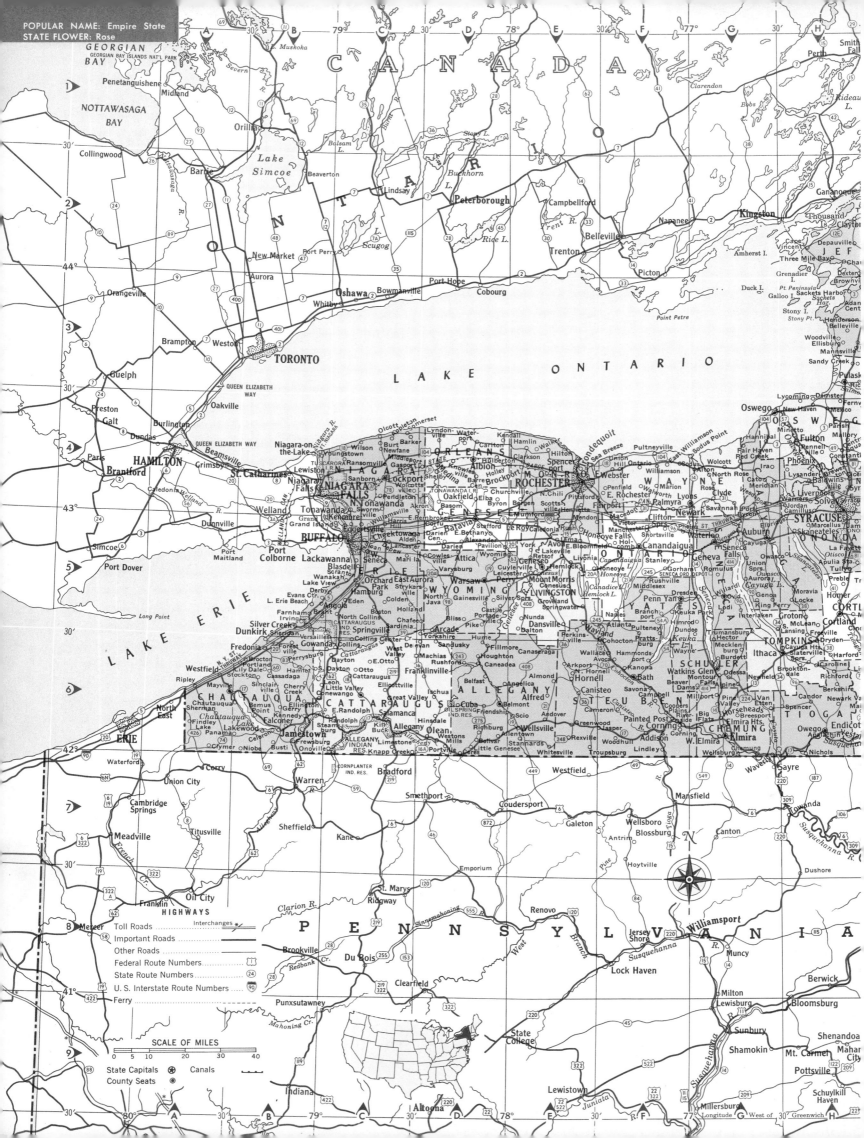

POPULAR NAME: Empire State
STATE FLOWER: Rose

HIGHWAYS

Toll Roads ............ Interchanges *
Important Roads ..............
Other Roads ..............
Federal Route Numbers ........
State Route Numbers ..........
U.S. Interstate Route Numbers .....
Ferry ..............

SCALE OF MILES
0  5  10   20   30    40

State Capitals ⊛       Canals
County Seats ◉

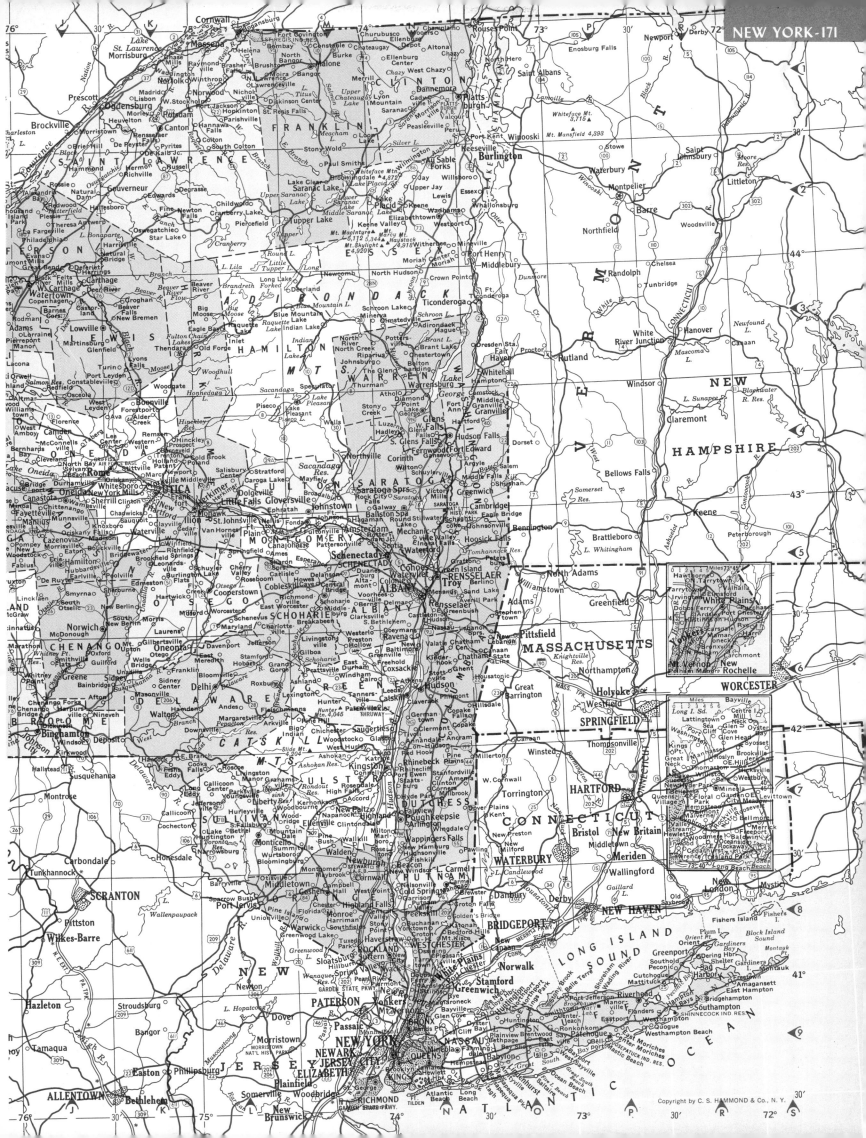

Copyright by C. S. HAMMOND & Co., N.Y.

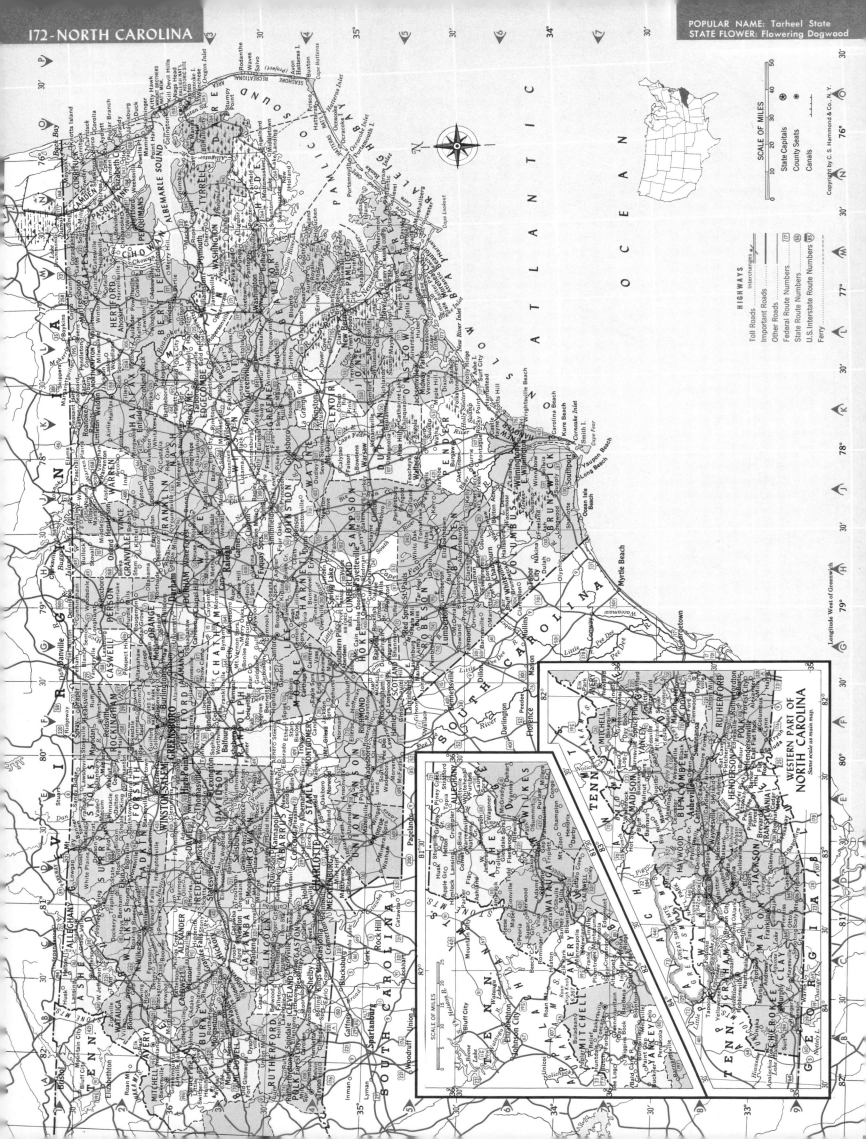

WESTERN PART OF
NORTH CAROLINA
Same scale as main map.

SCALE OF MILES

HIGHWAYS
Toll Roads .......... Interchanges
Important Roads ..............
Other Roads ..................
Federal Route Numbers ......
State Route Numbers .........
U.S. Interstate Route Numbers
Ferry .......................

State Capitals
County Seats
Canals

Copyright by C. S. Hammond & Co., N.Y.

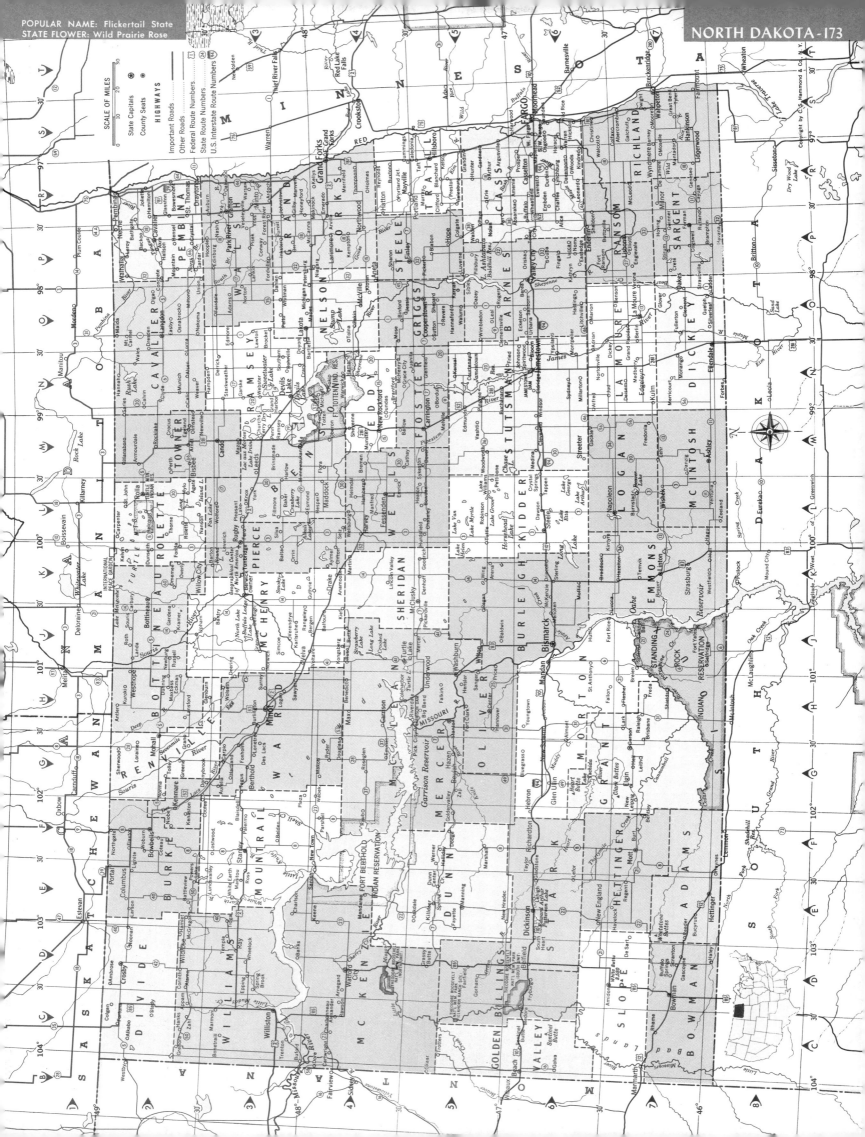

POPULAR NAME: Flickertail State
STATE FLOWER: Wild Prairie Rose

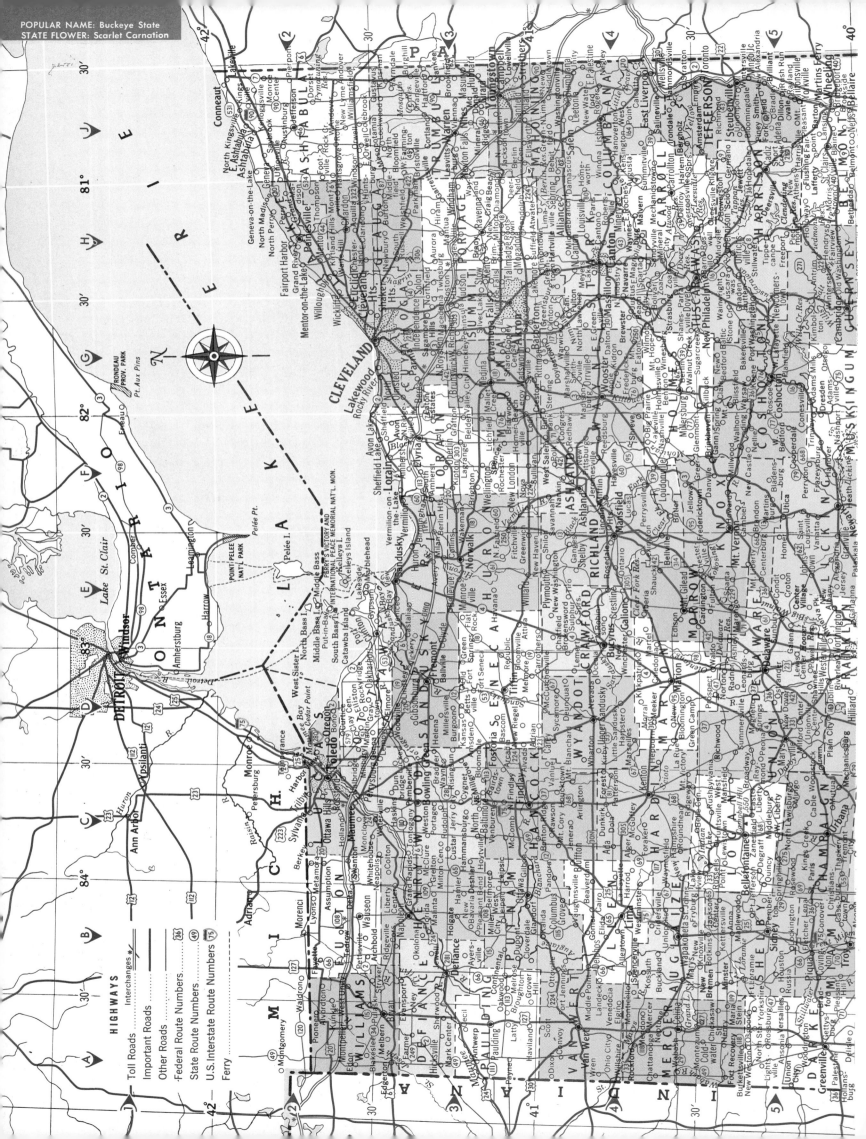

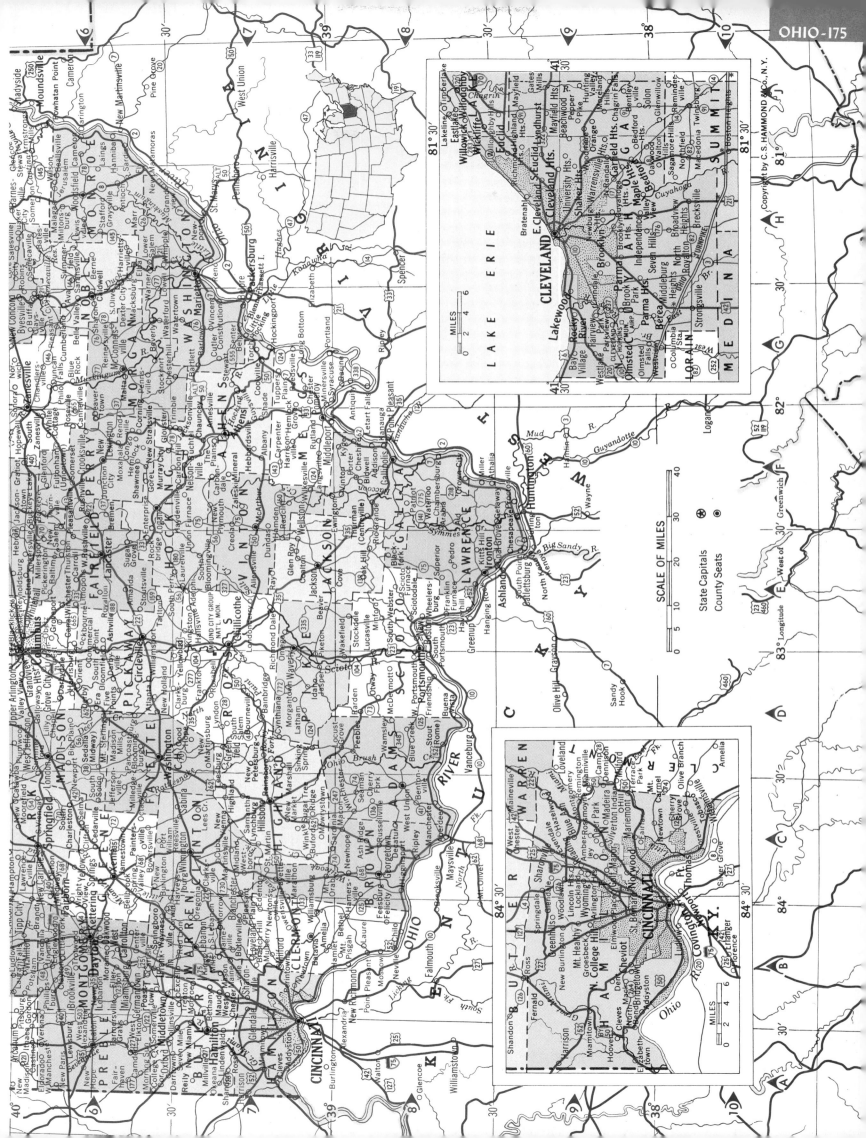

**CLEVELAND**

LAKE ERIE

**CINCINNATI**

SCALE OF MILES

State Capitals
County Seats

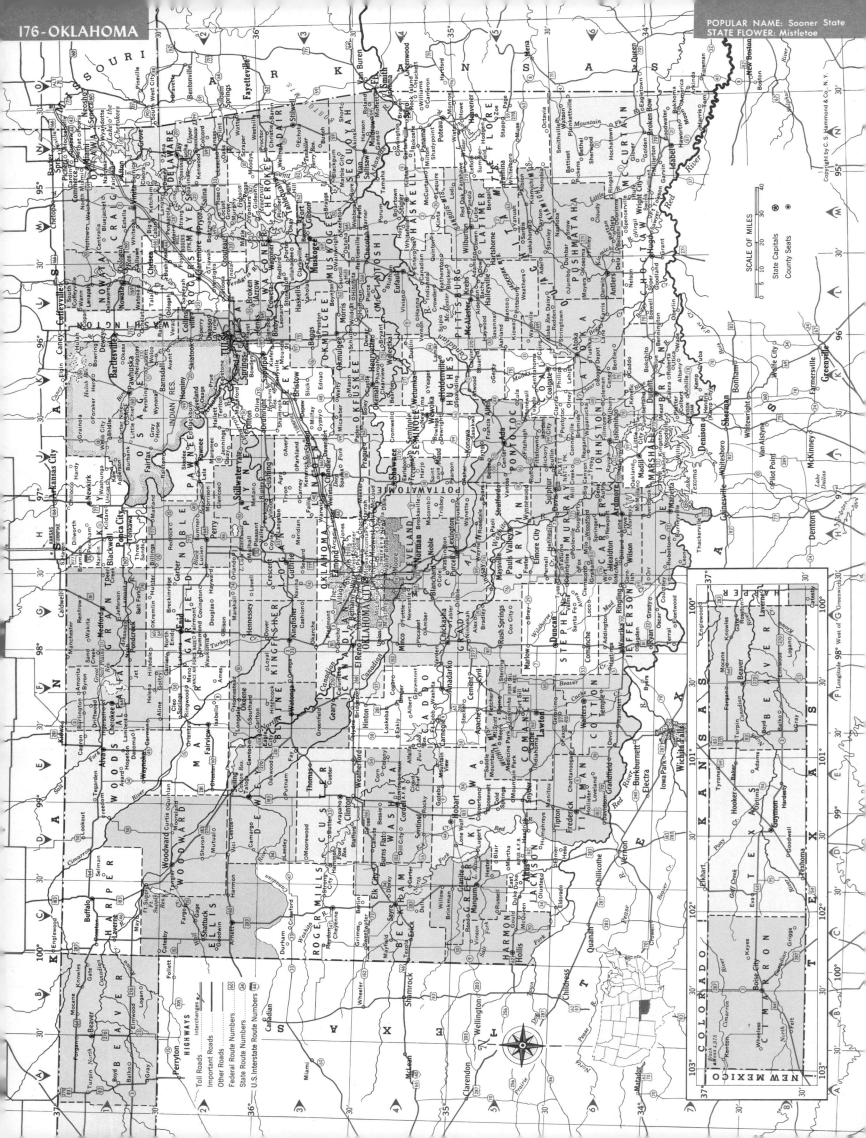

POPULAR NAME: Sooner State
STATE FLOWER: Mistletoe

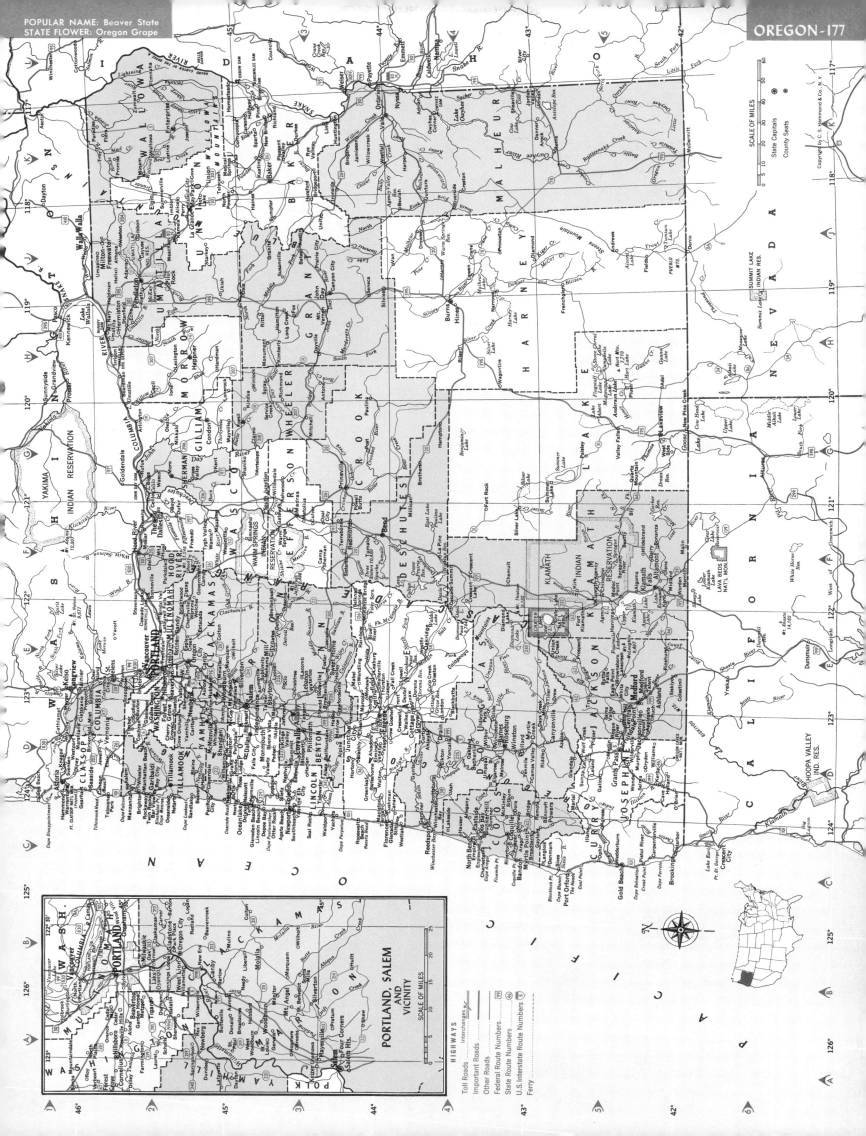

POPULAR NAME: Beaver State
STATE FLOWER: Oregon Grape

SCALE OF MILES

⊛ State Capitals
⊙ County Seats

Copyright by C. S. Hammond & Co., N.Y.

PORTLAND, SALEM AND VICINITY
SCALE OF MILES

HIGHWAYS
Toll Roads
Interchanges
Important Roads
Other Roads
Federal Route Numbers
State Route Numbers
U.S. Interstate Route Numbers
Ferry

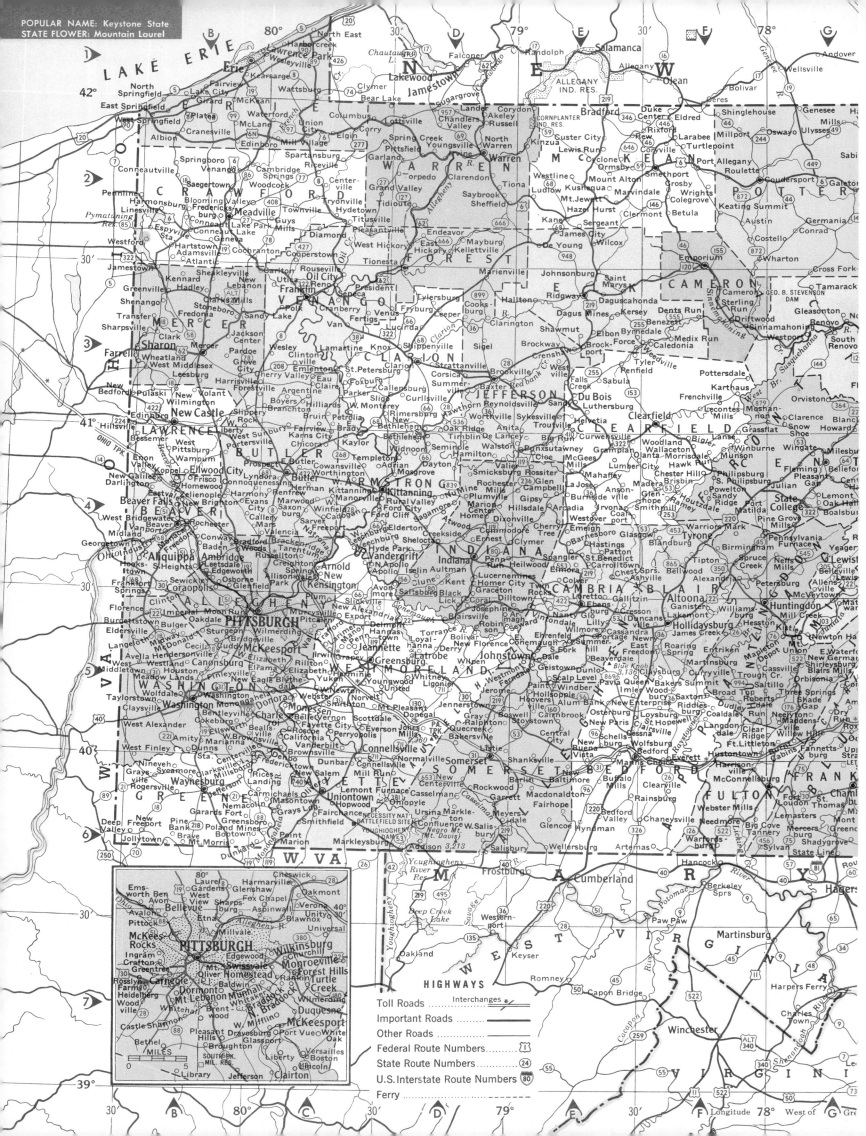

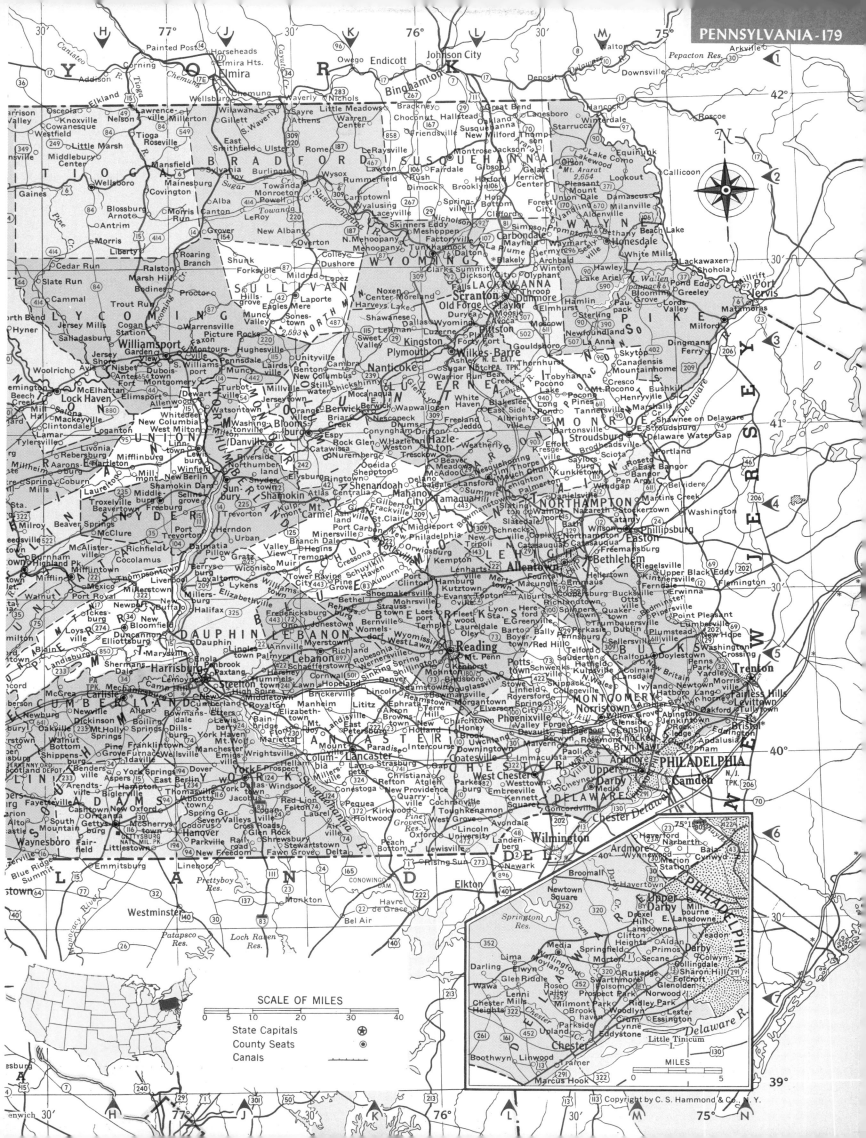

SCALE OF MILES

0  5  10      20        30        40

⊛ State Capitals

◉ County Seats

Canals

MILES

0        5

POPULAR NAME: Palmetto State
STATE FLOWER: Carolina Jessamine

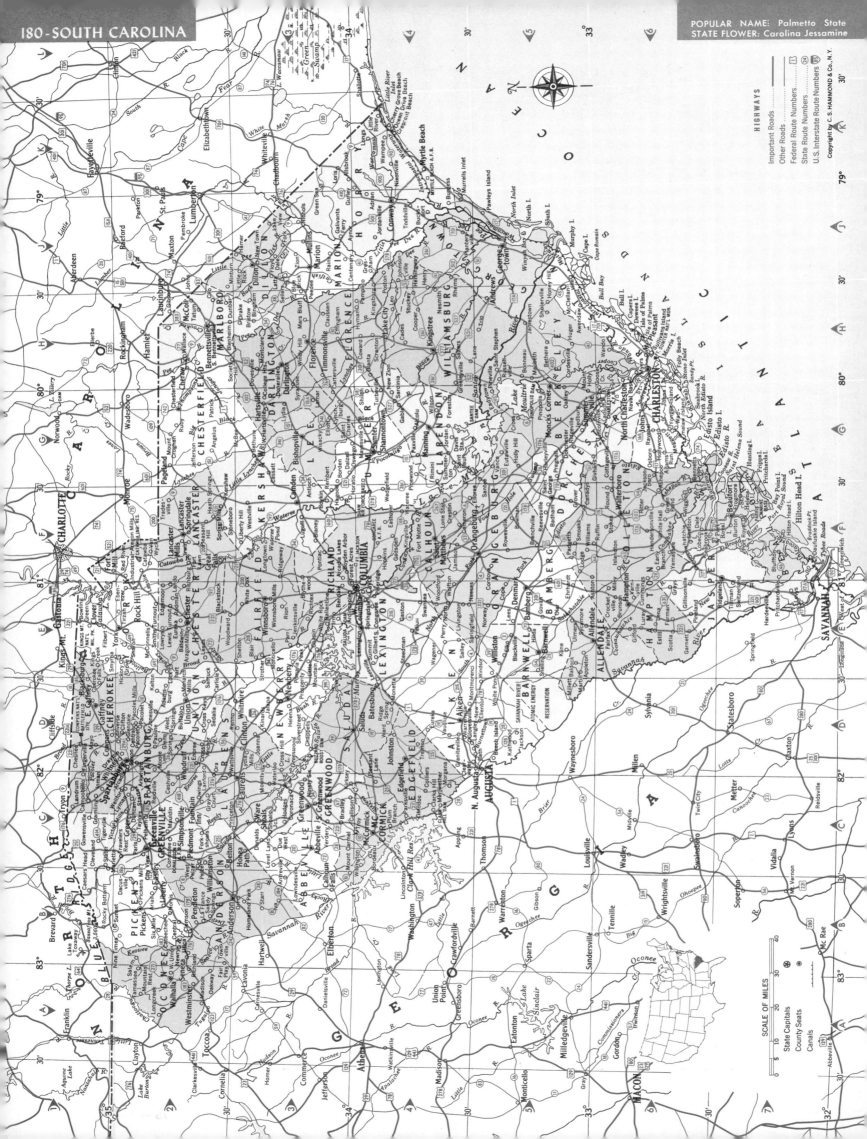

HIGHWAYS

Important Roads
Other Roads
Federal Route Numbers
State Route Numbers
U.S. Interstate Route Numbers

Copyright by C. S. HAMMOND & Co., N.Y.

SCALE OF MILES

State Capitals
County Seats
Canals

POPULAR NAME: Coyote State
STATE FLOWER: Pasque Flower

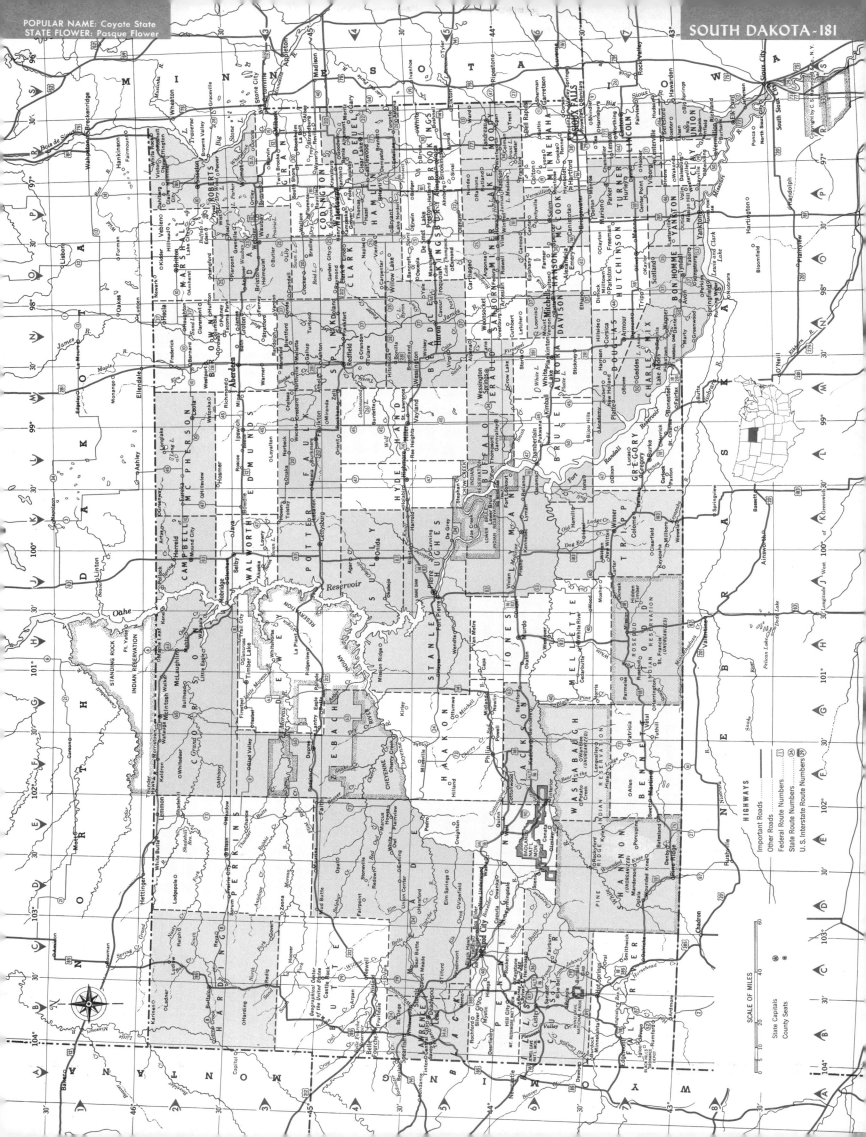

HIGHWAYS

Important Roads
Other Roads
Federal Route Numbers
State Route Numbers
U.S. Interstate Route Numbers

SCALE OF MILES

State Capitals
County Seats

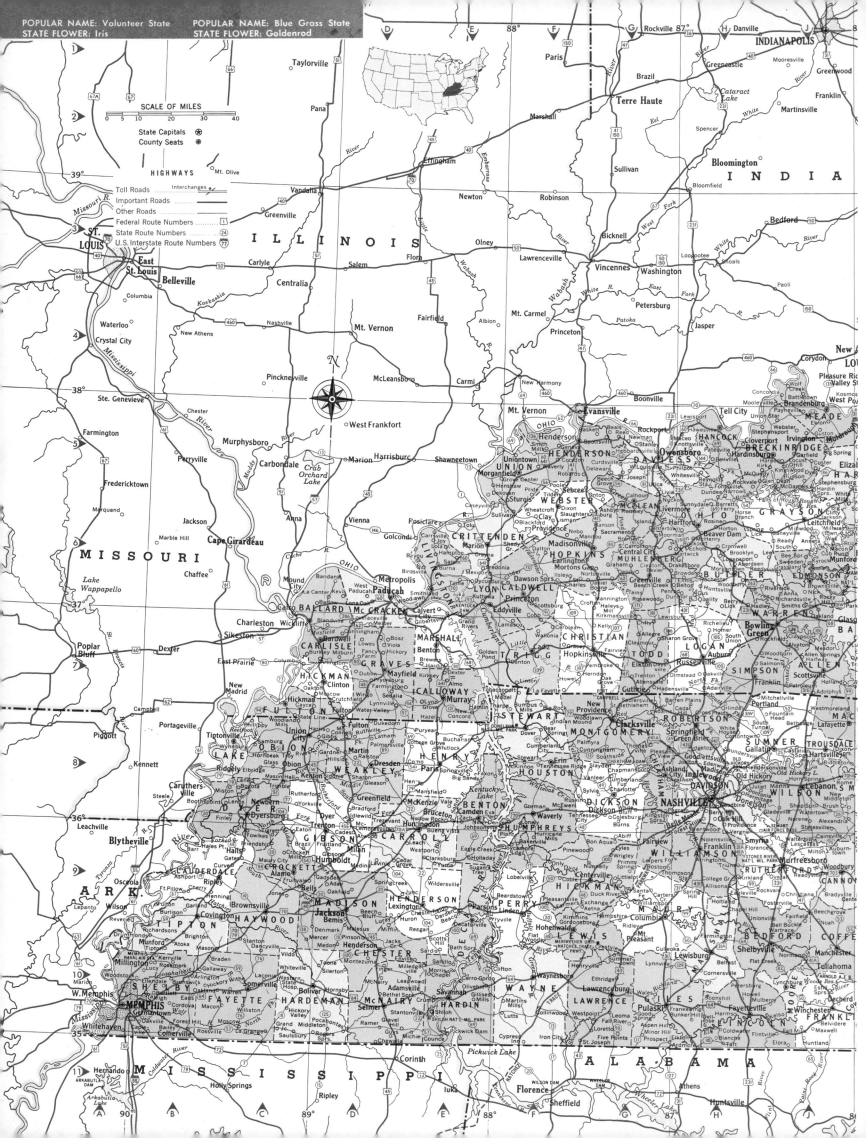

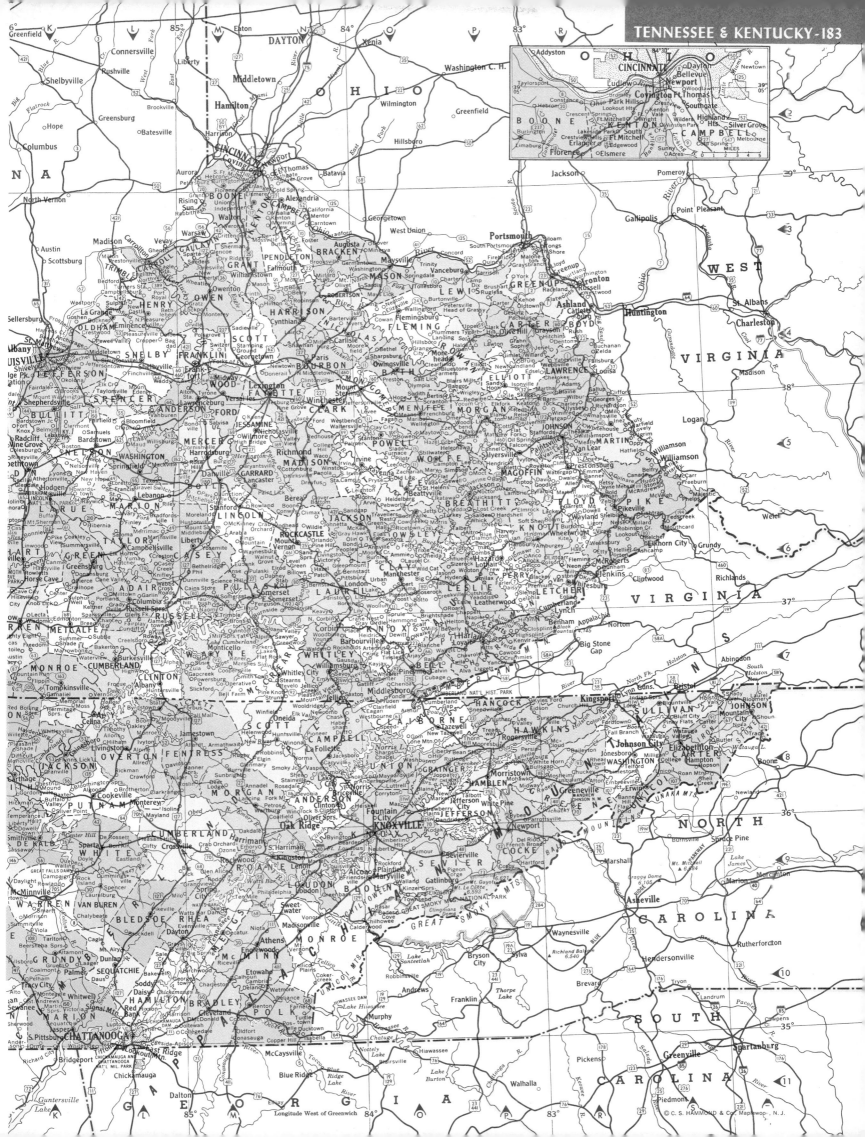

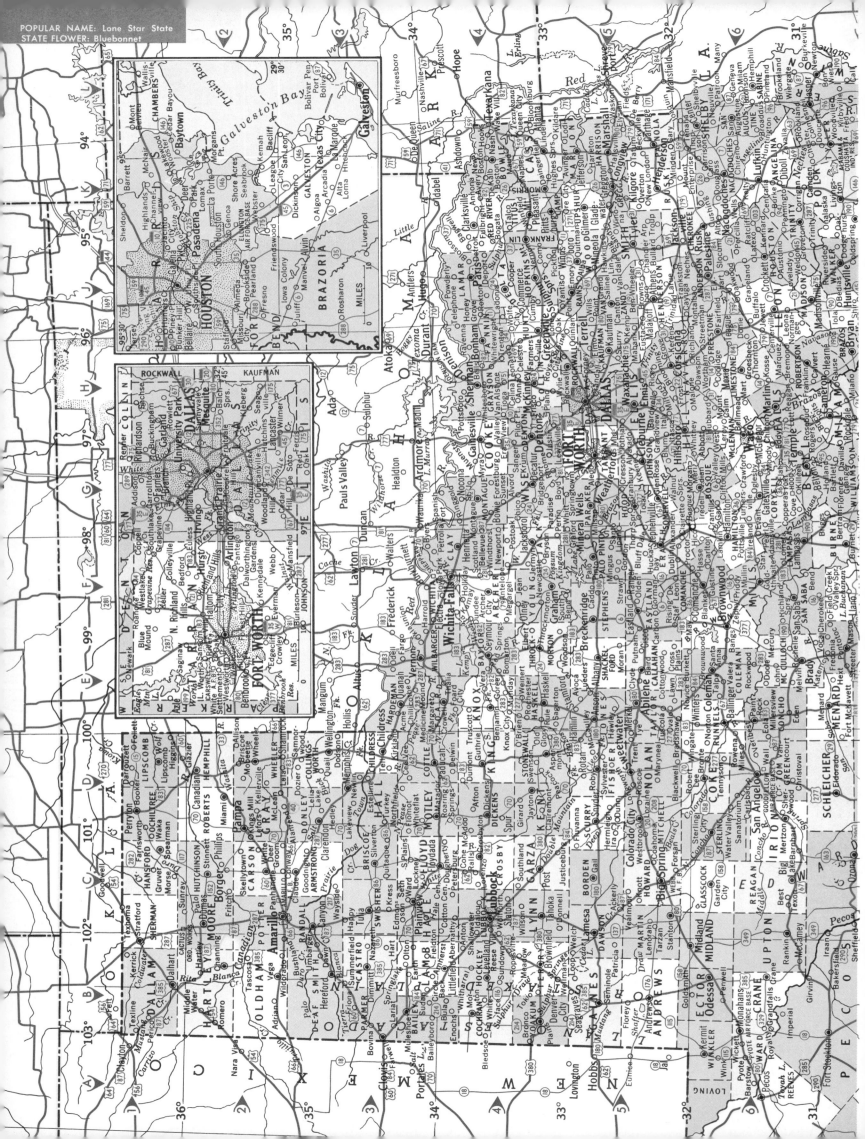

POPULAR NAME: Lone Star State
STATE FLOWER: Bluebonnet

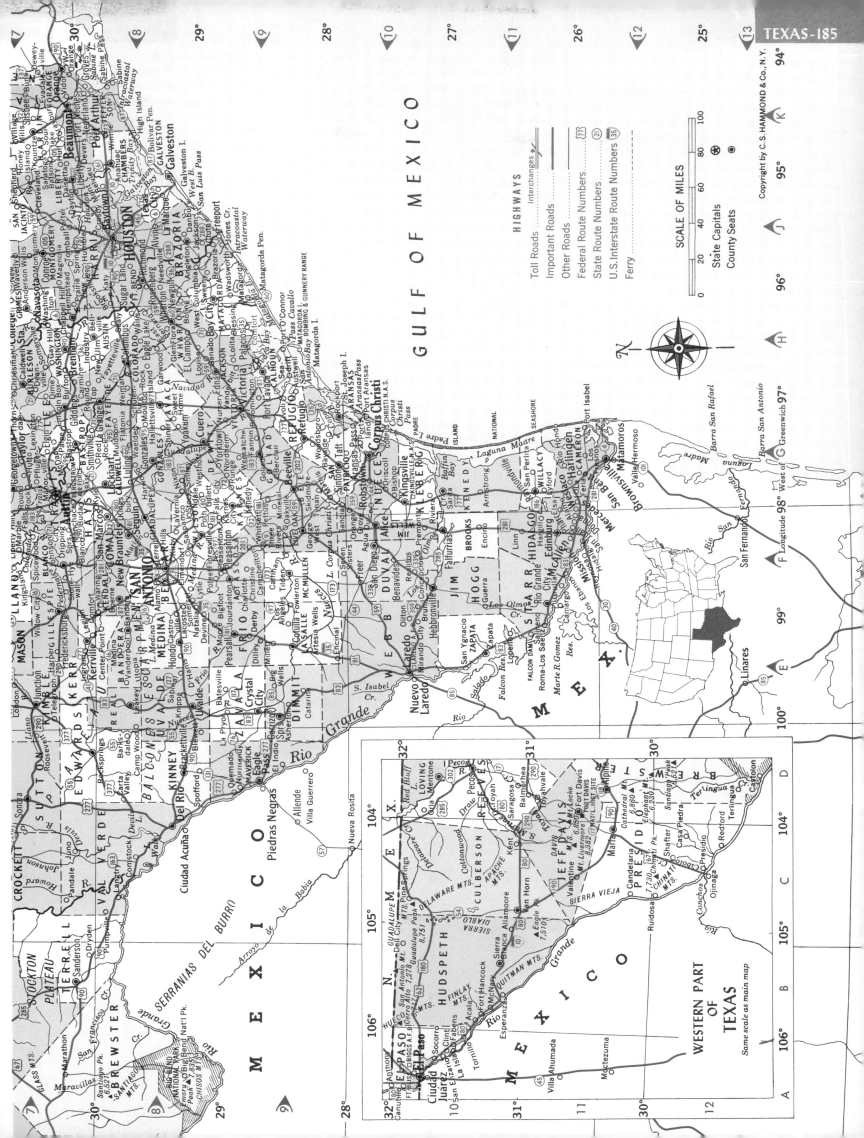

GULF OF MEXICO

## HIGHWAYS

Toll Roads .................... ✻
Interchanges .................. ✻
Important Roads ...............
Other Roads ..................
Federal Route Numbers ........ ⑦⑦
State Route Numbers .......... ㉑
U.S. Interstate Route Numbers ㉟
Ferry .........................

SCALE OF MILES

⊛ State Capitals
◉ County Seats

Copyright by C. S. HAMMOND & Co., N.Y.

MEXICO

WESTERN PART
OF
TEXAS
Same scale as main map

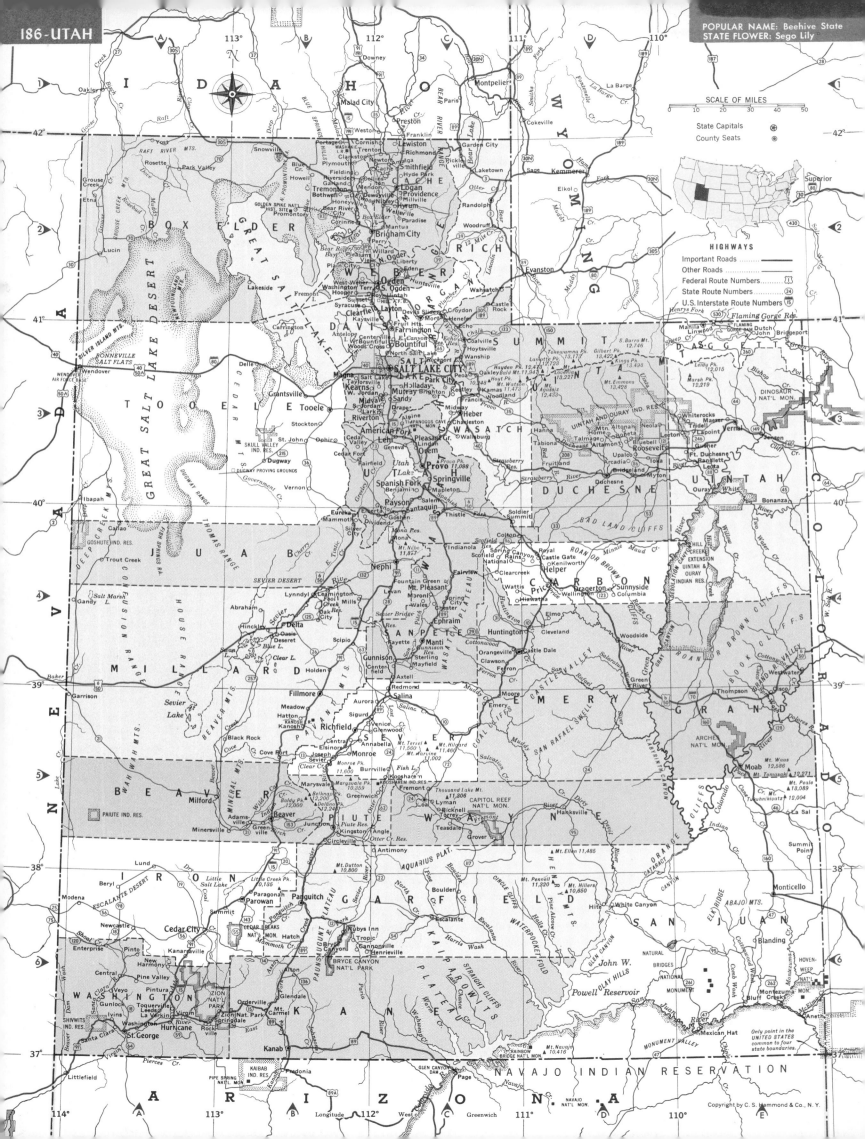

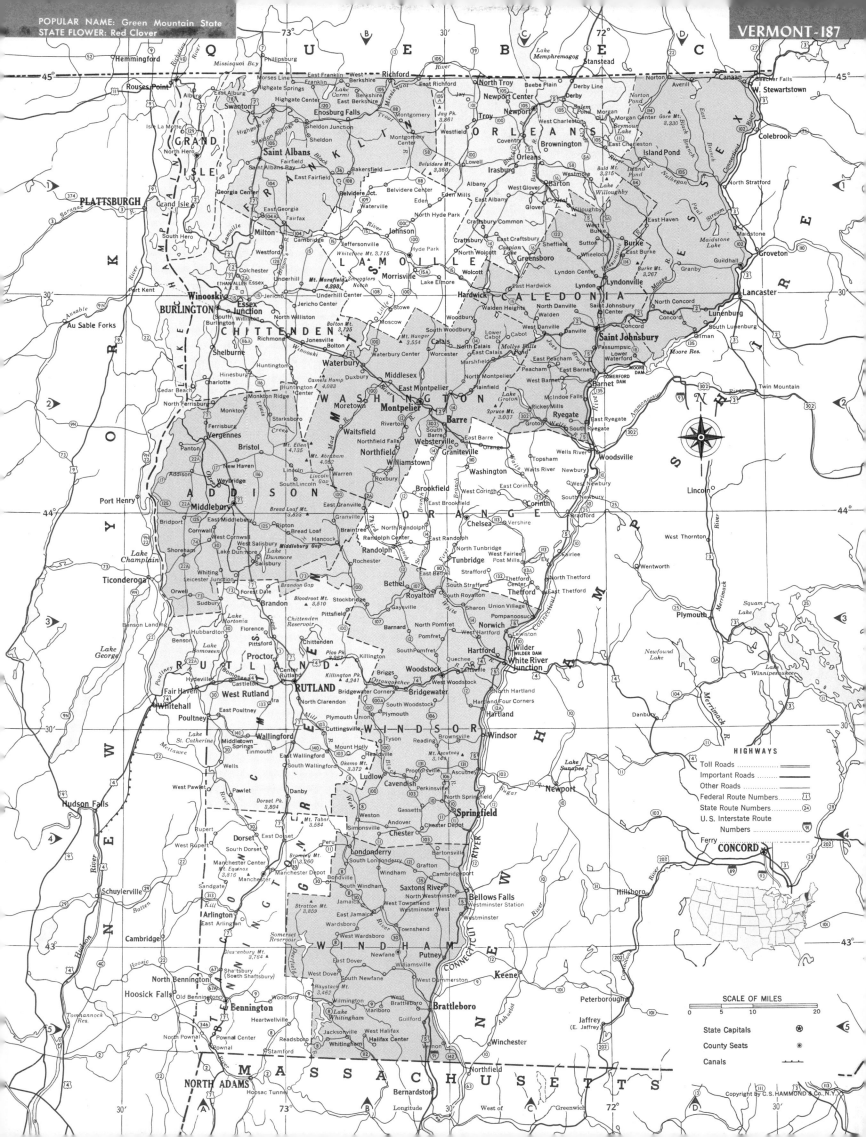

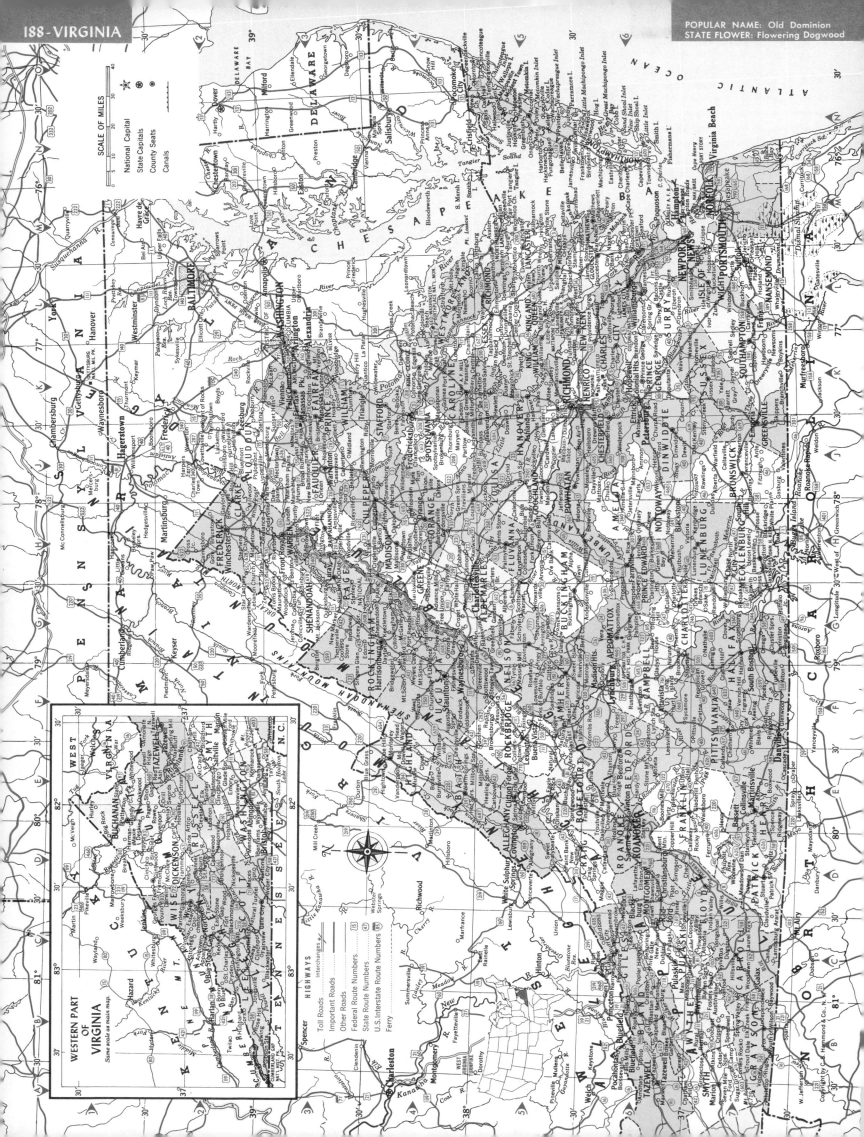

POPULAR NAME: Old Dominion
STATE FLOWER: Flowering Dogwood

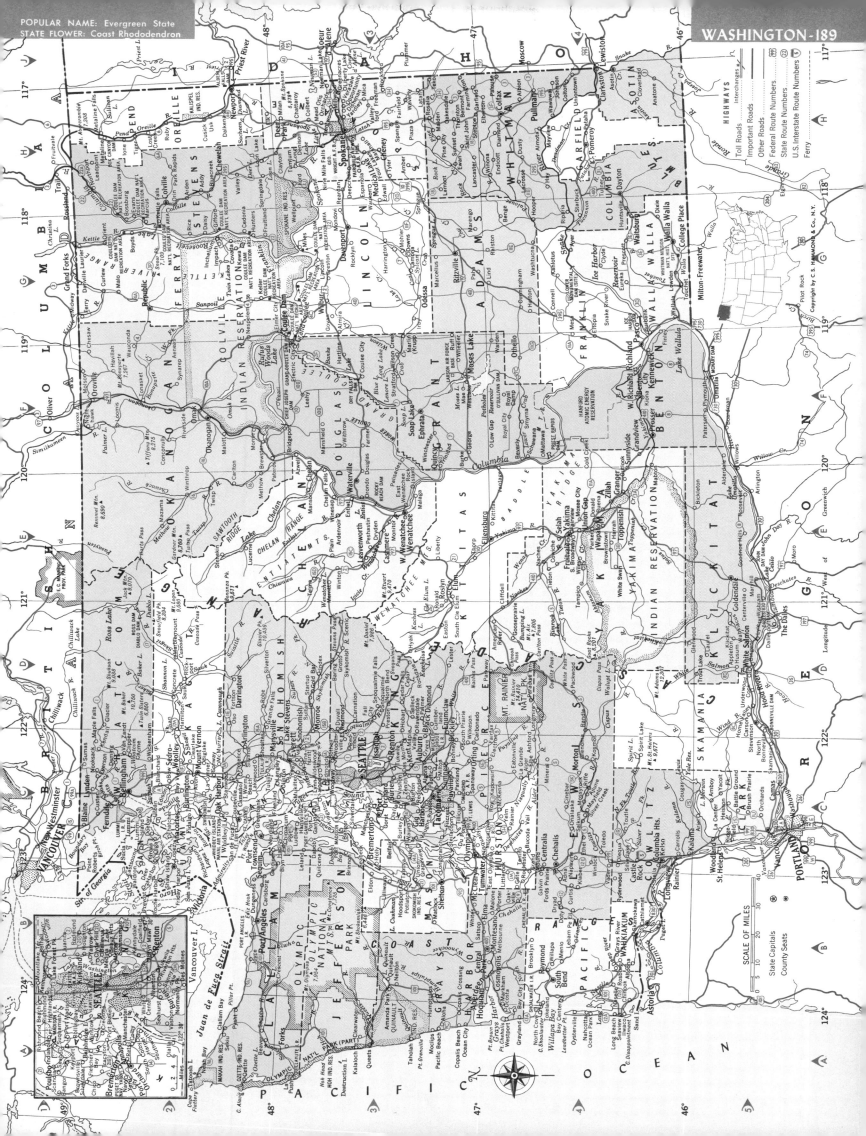

POPULAR NAME: Evergreen State
STATE FLOWER: Coast Rhododendron

POPULAR NAME: Mountain State
STATE FLOWER: Rhododendron

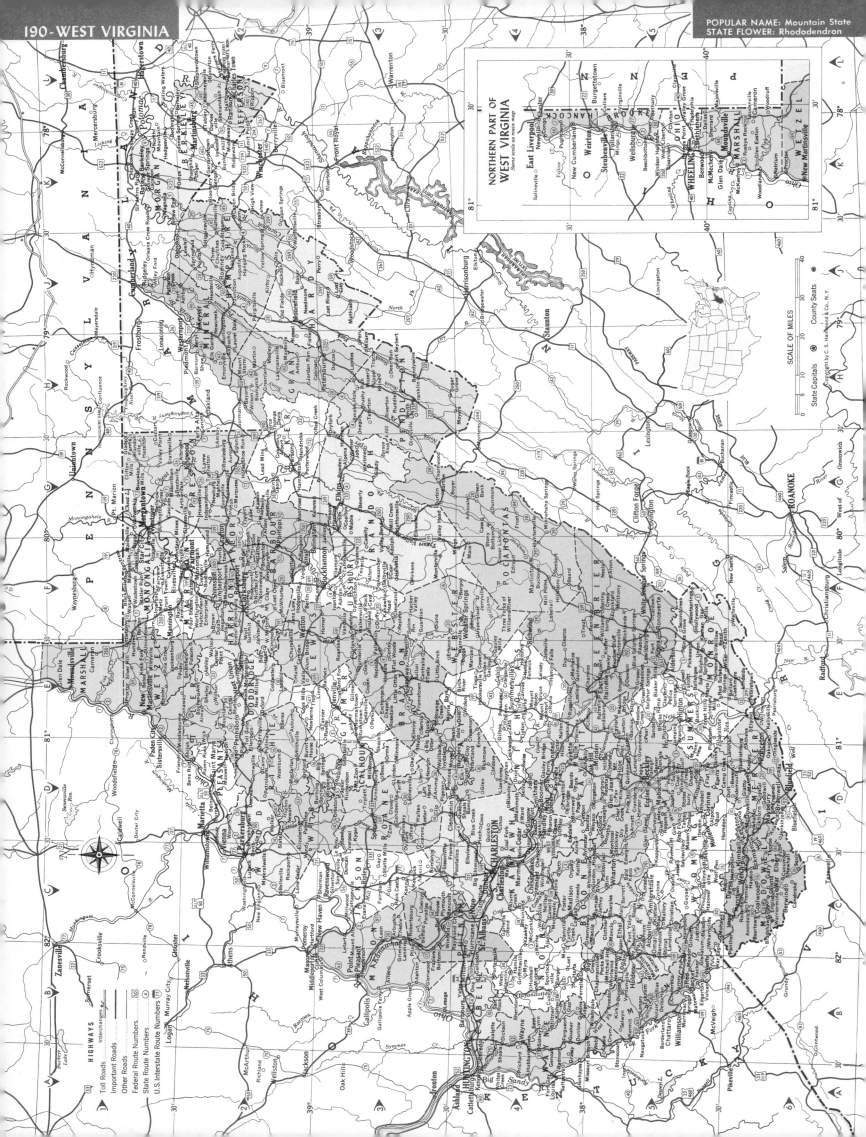

NORTHERN PART OF
WEST VIRGINIA
*Same scale as main map*

SCALE OF MILES

⊕ County Seats
● State Capitals

HIGHWAYS
Toll Roads
Important Roads
Other Roads
Interchanges
Federal Route Numbers
State Route Numbers
U.S. Interstate Route Numbers

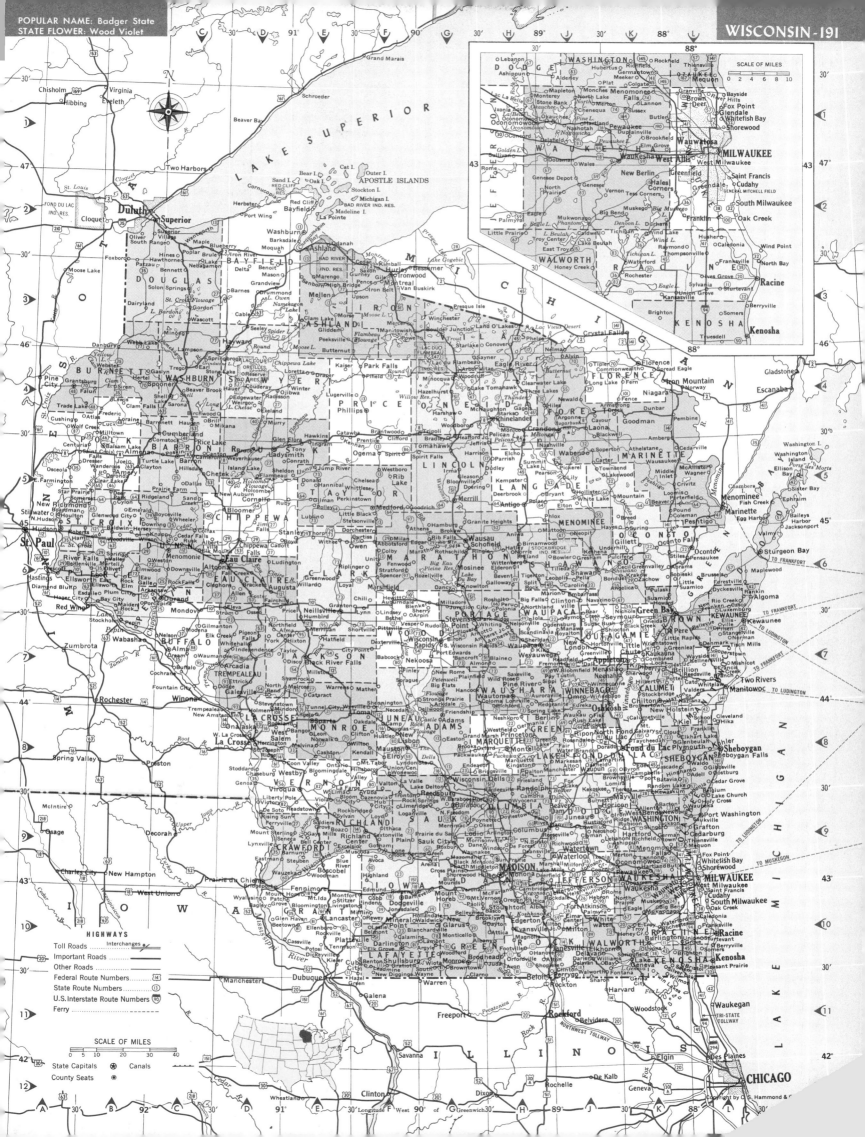

POPULAR NAME: Badger State
STATE FLOWER: Wood Violet

SCALE OF MILES

HIGHWAYS

Toll Roads ........... Interchanges
Important Roads ...........
Other Roads ...........
Federal Route Numbers ...........
State Route Numbers ...........
U.S. Interstate Route Numbers ...........
Ferry ...........

SCALE OF MILES

State Capitals
County Seats

Canals

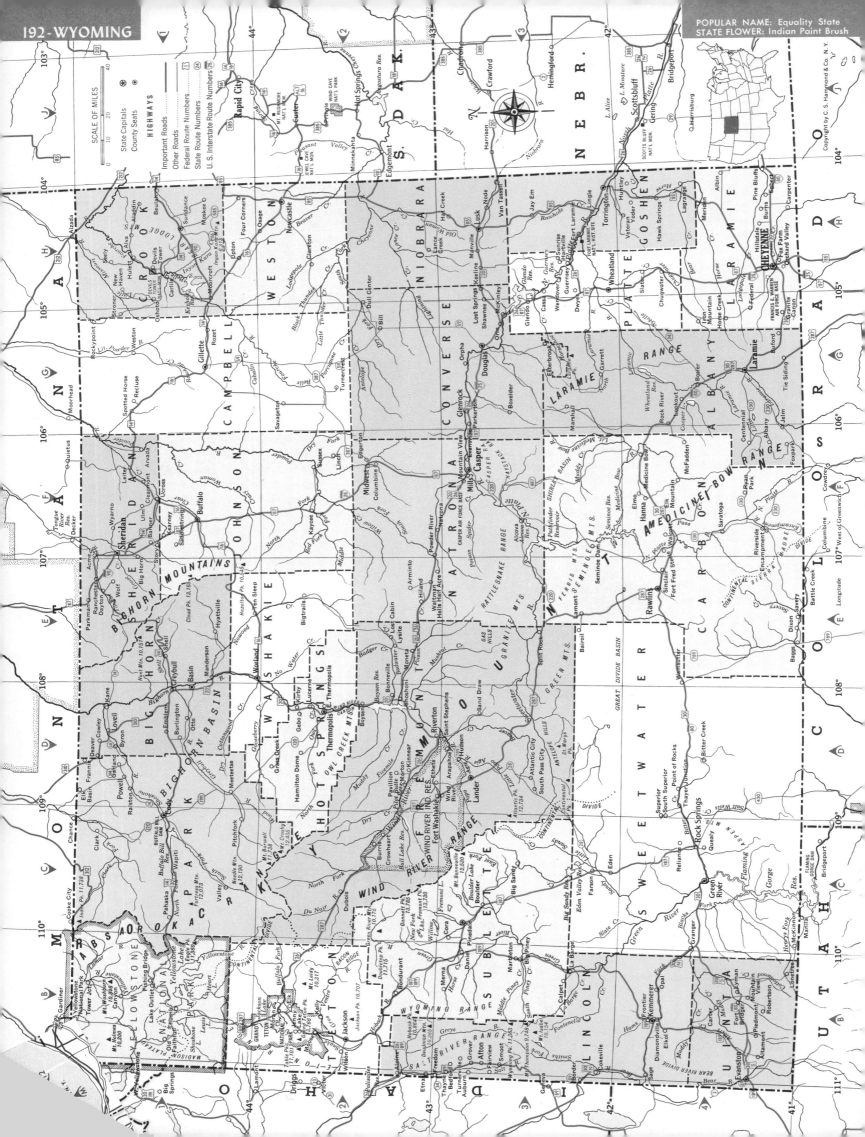

Copyright by C. S. Hammond & Co. N.Y.

SCALE OF MILES

HIGHWAYS

State Capitals
County Seats

Important Roads
Other Roads
Federal Route Numbers
State Route Numbers
U.S. Interstate Route Numbers